THE QUEST FOR LIBERATION

IDIOM   INVENTING WRITING THEORY
         Jacques Lezra and Paul North, series editors

THE QUEST FOR LIBERATION

PHILOSOPHY AND THE MAKING OF WORLD CULTURE
IN CHINA AND THE WEST

CHUNJIE ZHANG

Fordham University Press   *New York 2025*

Fordham University Press gratefully acknowledges financial assistance and support provided for the publication of this book by the University of California, Davis.

This book is freely available in an open access edition thanks to the generous support by the University of California Davis Library.

This title is licensed under the Creative Commons Attribution-NonCommercial 4.0 International License (CC BY-NC). Read the license at https://creativecommons.org/licenses/by-nc/4.0/legalcode.

DOI: https://doi.org/10.5422/TOME/2279

Copyright © 2025 Fordham University Press

All rights reserved. No part of this publication may be reproduced, stored in a retrieval system, or transmitted in any form or by any means—electronic, mechanical, photocopy, recording, or any other—except for brief quotations in printed reviews, without the prior permission of the publisher.

Fordham University Press has no responsibility for the persistence or accuracy of URLs for external or third-party Internet websites referred to in this publication and does not guarantee that any content on such websites is, or will remain, accurate or appropriate.

Fordham University Press also publishes its books in a variety of electronic formats. Some content that appears in print may not be available in electronic books.

Visit us online at www.fordhampress.com.

For EU safety / GPSR concerns: Mare Nostrum Group B.V., Mauritskade 21D, 1091 GC Amsterdam, The Netherlands, gpsr@mare-nostrum.co.uk

Library of Congress Cataloging-in-Publication Data available online at https://catalog.loc.gov.

Printed in the United States of America

27 26 25   5 4 3 2 1

First edition

献给妈妈、爸爸、佳瑜和霈琳
For Mama, Baba, Jiayu, and Peilin

CONTENTS

Introduction: Global Intellectual History, Ecology of Little Beings, and World Culture   1

1. Encounter in Beijing: Hermann Graf Keyserling, Gu Hongming, and Confucian Cosmopolitanism   25
2. Re-enchanting Confucianism: Max Weber, Care of the Self, and Charisma   46
3. Zhang Junmai as Philosopher: Rudolf Eucken, Life, and Spirituality   82
4. Liang Shuming, World Culture, and Rural Modernity   114
5. Early Feng Youlan's Negative Method: Metaphysics, World Philosophy, and Sage   144
6. Bertolt Brecht's *Me-ti* or the Aesthetics of Translation: Universal Love, Mutual Benefits, and Transience   177

Coda: Conservatism or Alternative Modernity   193

    Acknowledgments   *197*

    Notes   *201*

    Works Cited   *239*

    Index   *253*

THE QUEST FOR LIBERATION

INTRODUCTION: GLOBAL INTELLECTUAL HISTORY, ECOLOGY OF LITTLE BEINGS, AND WORLD CULTURE

In October 1912, the German economist and sociologist Max Weber (1864–1920) and his wife, Marianne Weber (1870–1954), welcomed a young philosopher into their Heidelberg home: Hermann Graf von Keyserling (1880–1946). During his four-day sojourn at the Webers, a popular destination among the educated elites, the Baltic-Prussian count vividly talked about his recent journey around the world, which he also described in his successful *Travel Diary of a Philosopher* (*Das Reisetagebuch eines Philosophen*, 1918). Keyserling's visit to China and his ideas about Confucianism as a new cosmopolitanism were fascinating to his listeners. A few years later, when Weber published his last book, *Confucianism and Taoism* (1920), he explicitly cited Keyserling's *Travel Diary* as a reference for his favorable depiction of classical Chinese philosophy. A comment in Weber's treatise, however, would raise eyebrows today: namely, the downfall of the Qing dynasty and the 1911 Chinese Revolution, for a true Confucian, only proved the correctness of the belief in the charisma of Confucian ethics.[1] This overt confidence in Confucianism was rather unusual for someone like Weber who had never set foot in China or Asia.

Indeed, contemporaneous Western thinkers with comparable intellectual stature, such as the American philosopher John Dewey (1859–1952) and the British philosopher Bertrand Russell (1872–1970), both of whom visited and lectured in China for a longer period of time, prophesized instead that Confucian China as a country and civilization needed to be reformed from the inside to become more compatible with the standard of (Western) modernity.² Dewey's propositions of science and democracy for China's future found considerable resonance in China through the New Culture Movement in the 1920s and beyond.³ Confucianism, once the dominant social ethics and political philosophy of Chinese monarchies over thousands of years, was regarded by Westerners and East Asians alike as a major obstacle to China's modernization. It was broadly under attack as the cause of the Qing dynasty's loss of wars to Western powers in the nineteenth century. Confucian ethics was associated with historical backwardness and political inefficiency. The famous Chinese writer Lu Xun (鲁迅, 1881–1936) penned the short story *Kong Yiji* (孔乙己, 1919) to illustrate the decline of Confucianism by portraying a pedantic Confucian scholar as a book stealer and a laughingstock in a local tavern. More recent studies resurrect Confucianism as a continuous social ethics and observe its renaissance since the 1980s.⁴ These thinkers and scholars firmly situate Confucianism within a Chinese and East Asian context. Weber's enigmatic comment on Confucianism, however, induces us to inquire about Confucianism's global connections. Indeed, given Weber's profound intellectual impact to date, his exceptionally favorable position toward Confucianism deserves greater scrutiny.

Keyserling, in his travelogue, described his conversations with the Chinese-Malay thinker Gu Hongming (辜鸿铭, aka Ku Hung-ming, 1857–1928) in Beijing, a staunch defender of Confucianism and a fierce critic of Western imperialism. Gu's upbringing in British Malaja, his education in Europe, and his political career in the office of the viceroy Zhang Zhidong (张之洞, 1837–1909) all provided him with a unique perspective on world history and distinguished him from his contemporaries in China and Europe alike. Gu's insistence on the triumph of Confucianism, which earned him a reputation as a recalcitrant conservative, was well known among his friends as well as his researchers. His anti-colonial position as a former colonial subject, however, was often ignored. Gu's promotion of Confucianism was rarely viewed as his anti-imperialist attempt at decolonization. I surmise Keyserling's conversations with Gu must have provided the background for Weber's belief in a "true Confucian," as embodied by Keyserling's portrayal of Gu and other mandarins. At the same time, Weber did not just fantasize about Confucianism. Rather, he diligently consulted many sources about Confucianism and Taoism and came to understand Confucianism as a balanced social ethics, promising a life with greater freedom than the Protestant ethic and capitalism.

Weber's critical perspective of Western culture and his interest in non-Western cultures, in particular China and Asia, were shared by many of his European contemporaries. George Steinmetz points out that this re-emerging Enlightenment-era Sinophilia among German intellectuals was deeply connected to a unique German colonial policy in appreciating Chinese civilization; it also reflects a culturally conservative critique of modernity.[5] Yet what motivates me to focus on the specific German thinkers in this book, including Keyserling, Weber, Rudolf Eucken (1848–1926), and Bertolt Brecht (1898–1956), is their engagement with classical Chinese philosophy for the purpose of seeking an alternative modernity not only for the West, but also for humanity as a whole. Together with their Chinese counterparts, they questioned the universal validity of Western ethical values and were envisioning a world culture based on the integration of European and non-European cultural genealogies. The philosophers discussed in this book were interested in Confucianism and rationalism in relation to the questions of international politics, national sovereignty, social justice, and morality. Their thinking coheres well with that of the Chinese New Confucians in a philosophical discourse. At the same time, in literary discourse, other thinkers and writers such as Martin Buber, Martin Heidegger, Carl Gustav Jung, Hermann Hesse, Alfred Döblin, and Franz Kafka were more attuned to Taoism and the concerns about individuality, consciousness, spiritual healing, and the cosmos. Their works form a special European literary and cultural phenomenon of modernism that should receive further attention and will not be discussed at length in this book.

Meanwhile, if World War I shattered Europe's confidence in its cultural heritage, the Shandong Question at the 1919 Paris Peace Conference enraged the Chinese people when the winning powers did not fulfill their promise of returning the Shandong peninsula to China after Germany possessed it as a colony and Japan annexed it in 1914. The May Fourth Movement erupted from this political mood and protested against the weak response of the Chinese government. The imperialist treatment destroyed many Chinese people's hope to become an equal to the West and led to the disintegration of their favorable disposition toward Western culture. While supporters of New Culture Movement still believed in Western science and democracy as a means to save China, some thinkers, known as the New Confucians, came to re-evaluate and re-appreciate Chinese tradition. Like Gu Hongming, New Confucians Zhang Junmai (张君劢, aka Carsun Chang, 1887–1969), Liang Shuming (梁漱溟, 1893–1988), and Feng Youlan (冯友兰, aka Fung Yu-lan, 1895–1990) claimed that Confucianism should not be condemned to the dustbin of history as an antiquated past. Rather, it needed to be reformed and repurposed to meet the challenges in the twentieth century. After all, Confucianism had experienced reformulation, repurposing, emulation, misunderstanding, catachresis, and appropriation across two thousand years. A new Confucianism would allow humanity to imagine a different rationalism and ethics of life other than Western modernity. Their endeavor put them either in direct contact with or in indirect engagement with European philosophers such as Rudolf Eucken, Henri Bergson, and Ludwig Wittgenstein. In a larger context, New Confucianism was one of many intellectual interactions between China and the West. Friedrich Nietzsche, Arthur Schopenhauer, Karl Marx, Charles Darwin, and Thomas Henry Huxley all inspired Chinese thinkers such as Wang Guowei (王国维), Li Dazhao (李大钊), Hu Shi (胡适), Chen Duxiu (陈独秀), and many others to search for a solution for the cultural and political impasse caused by Western imperialism and to avoid the imminent loss of sovereignty and independence.[6] The New Confucians, however, made a unique contribution to re-envision the world, which has not been thoroughly studied in a global intellectual context. Of course, not all New Confucian thinkers were concerned with the question of the global. Xiong Shili (熊十力) and his student Mou Zongsan (牟宗三), for example, represented a prominent philosophical voice of New Confucianism and intensely engaged with Kantian philosophy from the perspective of Buddhist epistemology. Yet they were less inclined to concern themselves with the sociopolitical and historical dimensions of philosophy than those discussed in this book.

Translation played an essential role in this intellectual exchange between China and the West. Lydia H. Liu's canonical study of translingual practice provides ample historical and theoretical insights in this matter.[7] I highlight two translators for the sake of this study: Richard Wilhelm (1873–1930) and Yan Fu (严复, 1854–1921). Richard Wilhelm, a German Protestant missionary in the German colony in Shandong for more than two decades (1899–1924), translated and introduced many classical Chinese philosophy and poetry works to German audiences. During his China years, Wilhelm learned to appreciate and even adopt traditional Chinese culture.[8] His translations were hugely influential during and after his lifetime. His translation of *Yi Jing* (易经, or *I Ching*) into German served as the foundation for the English translation of the book, which became impactful for religious movements in the West, such as the New Age Movement. Without Wilhelm's efforts, the German and European thinkers and writers would not have been able to engage with Confucianism, Taoism, or Mohism in such a profound and creative manner. In China, Yan Fu, a high-ranking naval official turned educator and writer, studied in the UK and translated numerous philosophical and social theoretical works, such as Thomas Henry Huxley's *Evolution and Ethics*, Adam Smith's *The Wealth of Nations*, Herbert Spencer's *The Study of*

Sociology, John Stuart Mill's *On Liberty*, and Montesquieu's *The Spirit of Law*. Yan was not only among the first intellectuals who introduced Western thoughts to China, he was also a prominent scholar and politician himself. Yan extensively used less-common words in classical Chinese to render his translations and thus connected Western thoughts with ancient Chinese language, creating a semantically familiar but astonishingly fresh realm of knowledge.[9] In his translation of the social Darwinist work *Evolution and Ethics*, Yan in fact revealed his understanding of freedom as a natural state, not as a value. This idea is based on the cosmology in *Yi Jing* and Taoism that the universe is constantly changing, witnessing the transformation of life's forces.[10] Indeed, translation is not merely an act of transmitting content from one language into another. The condition of translation is deeply associated with "discursive practices that ensue from initial interlingual contacts between languages."[11] Thus "translingual practice examines the process in which new words, meanings, discourses, and modes of representation arise, circulate, and acquire legitimacy within the host language due to, or in spite of, the latter's contact/collision with the guest language."[12] Translation is never neutral and always carries political and ideological interests of the parties across the linguistic line. From this perspective, the Chinese and Western philosophers in this study were translingual practitioners who adapted and reformed ideas in Chinese and Western philosophies. At the same time, I'd like to add, they were also transhistorical practitioners who reformulated and refunctioned Confucian, Taoist, Buddhist, and Mohist thoughts and reintroduced them from their ancient context to the global world in the early 1900s.

In sum, in this book, I delineate the philosophical discourse of visions of the world and highlight the intellectual connections between German-speaking Europe and China. Contemporary debate on cosmopolitanism routinely refers to Immanuel Kant as its intellectual origin. The Chinese and German thinkers mentioned previously, however, use classical Chinese philosophy as an alternative intellectual genealogy to imagine different cosmopolitan ethics in economics, politics, and society in the early twentieth century. Their engagement with Confucianism, Taoism, Buddhism, and Mohism broadens the scope of global intellectual history by including a non-European origin of concepts and ideas. Their intellectual programs, in rich variations, all reveal an intensive pursuit of a spiritual and ethical life for global humanity while envisioning the equality of all cultural and intellectual traditions in the world. As a result of the differences in their local crises, the Chinese and the European stories are often narrated in separate national and cultural contexts.[13] I intend to bridge the critical divide between Europe and China and examine the thinkers' shared interest in classical

Chinese philosophy and their common effort to envision a different modernity. This book breaks with the common logic of either studying the reception and adaptation of Western ideas in the East or critiquing the misrepresentation of the East in the West. Instead, I emphasize the entanglements between Chinese and European thinkers and highlight their quest for liberation in a globalizing world. The entanglements of the philosophers' visions transgress geography and history. Space and time are inextricably entwined with each other here. If the spatial turn as a methodological perspective aims to deconstruct historicism and its hierarchical logic imposed on cultures, then the effort to see the Chinese classics not only as Chinese but also as a world intellectual heritage and the endeavor to transform it for the present in both Europe and China are transhistorical.

The main title of this book, *The Quest for Liberation*, captures the quintessential aspirations of the thinkers. Echoing Weber's metaphor of an iron cage (*stahlhartes Gehäuse*) created by capitalism and the desire to be freed from the Protestant ethic, Lu Xun also used the metaphor of an iron house (*tiewuzi*, 铁屋子) to portray China's urgent situation in his short story anthology *Call to Arms: Na Han* (呐喊, 1923). Lu wanted to loudly awaken those sleeping inside the house to their imminent death. In the same mood, Chinese philosophers longed for liberating China from Western imperialism and Japanese invasion. Since either the thinkers in this book were philosophers by training or their pertinent works are philosophical in nature, the term "philosophy" naturally captures the medium and the means of their intellectual endeavors. I also took inspiration from Jonathan Israel's magnum opus, *Radical Enlightenment: Philosophy and the Making of Modernity, 1650–1750* (2002). Israel's book depicts the Europe-wide intellectual and philosophical preparation for the French Revolution, highlighting radical French thought as a seminal force ushering in democracy. My book examines the contribution of philosophy to an alternative global modernity beyond the binary of capitalism and communism. In the scholarship of global intellectual history and Bruno Latour's work, this alternative or idealist modernity finds its postmodern expression. The title phrase "The Making of World Culture" thus reflects my interpretation of the purpose of this philosophical discourse. I prioritize the Chinese words for "world" and "culture" in this case. The Chinese term for "world," *shijie* (世界), was used by Buddhist monks to translate the Sanskrit word *lokadhātu*, meaning time (*shi*) and space (*jie*). *Wenhua* (文化) is used to translate "culture" from European languages, meaning cultivation in agriculture and human education. *Wen* means "spiritual and nonviolent strength in opposition to physical forces" (*wu*, 武); *hua* means "gradual transformation," according to the classical Chinese dictionary *Ciyuan* (辞源). I thus choose the term "world culture," which reflects both the Chinese perspective of cultivating time, space, and spirituality and the European idea of *Bildung*. Haun Saussy's illuminating account of seeing translation as creation is seminal for my choice of "world culture" here.[14] I avoid using the word "cosmopolitanism" with its heavily loaded Kantian and European Enlightenment connotations (more in the fourth section in this introduction). Although the European thinkers in this book are German speaking, they did not necessarily identify themselves as German nationals: Keyserling, for example, felt himself a foreigner in Germany his entire life. Their biographies and the reception of their ideas are representative of Western thinking across a broad spectrum. More importantly, to call them "Western" reflects a Chinese perspective in the early 1900s from which the fine differences between European nations did not matter as much as their shared imperialism and cultural hegemony toward China, hence the phrase "in China and the West."

This book has emerged in dialogue with the field of global intellectual history. Its attention toward historical network breaks down the barriers between nation states, cultural spheres, and ideological camps. Global intellectual history intends to join the force of critiquing Eurocentrism, which was vehemently introduced through postcolonial studies in the late 1970s and has since powerfully informed the mode of inquiry and interpretation in the studies of literature, culture, and history. Even though global intellectual history articulates such a theoretical vision, there are few studies that have been undertaken to study an intellectual phenomenon that originates in a non-European context. And even if the theoretical perspective critiques Eurocentrism, the vocabularies that global intellectual history uses and the inquiries with which it is occupied are still very much European in origin. There are few non-European ideas that have been acknowledged as central to the theoretical repertoire of global intellectual historiography.

Committed to adjusting the Europe-centered genealogy, I consciously switch perspectives to posit Chinese philosophy as a different point of origin for the discussions about cosmopolitanism and anti-colonialism, rationalism and capitalism, irrationalism and spirituality, care of the self and the history of sexuality, and rural education and universal love. I will show how Confucianism was adapted, reformulated, repurposed, and rethought, and I will interpret these attempts as a part of a genuinely global intellectual movement whose participants shared concerns about the future of the world, faced with crises and warfare, and brought forth diverse solutions. By means of a double globality, Confucianism connects thinkers in the West and China and informs their visions of the world.

Before I delve more into the methodology of global intellectual history and into the notion of world culture in the following sections, I would like to touch on three points to clarify why I chose to focus on these philosophers and what this book is not meant to be. First, my book differs from the study of exoticism in Europe that understands non-European characters or images, in particular those from East Asia, in European literature and culture as unessential covers that are used to hide real European problems. For many, the exotic garment is merely borrowed to reduce the pungency of direct references to European social or political circumstances. Thus, Asian elements have been routinely dismissed as a lesser style in literature, art, and philosophy—from Oliver Goldsmith's *The Citizen of the World* (1762) down to Bertolt Brecht's *The Good Person of Szechwan* (*Der gute Mensch von Sezuan*, 1938–40). This book aims to show that Confucianism, Taoism, and Buddhism were not a superficial style but an essential constituent in the global intellectual discussion.

Second, my book both builds on and departs from the postcolonial perspective of Orientalism that focuses on the misrepresentations of non-European cultures in Western discourse and critiques the colonial and imperial politics of representation. Neither do I focus on how European thinkers exoticize or fantasize about China and East Asia, although I acknowledge it with due diligence if it is relevant. Nor do I dispute the possibility of projection in their appreciative writings about China. In fact, I aim to show that Chinese thinkers similarly projected their own visions through their interpretations of Confucian canons and European philosophy alike. Hence it was not so much a matter of how the West appropriated the East, but rather of how both European and Chinese thinkers referred to Chinese philosophical tradition as a common human cultural heritage that could form a shared future.

Finally, my book is not a typical study that focuses on Western influence on China in the modernist era, even though I recognize the strong trend of admiring and learning from the West in twentieth-century Chinese intellectual history. Yet I do not intend to portray Chinese thinkers as voiceless victims under the hegemony of Western master narrative. My goal is to describe the philosophical efforts of both European and Chinese thinkers on equal footing. I want to show that European and Chinese thinkers took inspiration from Chinese philosophy, used the world as method, and saw it as their shared realm of attention. The welfare of the world was in their heart, and life itself was both their starting point and the ultimate goal of their thought.

By taking the less trodden path via global intellectual history, I hope this study will unearth a new ground for discussing global historical entanglements and, more importantly, for imagining a more peaceful future. Global intellectual history is not only a theoretical approach that I use in this book. There is indeed a historical continuation or an undercurrent of world culture from the philosophers discussed in this book to the recent trend of global intellectual history in the twenty-first century, when the Chinese economy became a prominent part of the global market again. This continuity had lain dormant between the 1950s to the 1990s.

SPATIALITY, NETWORK, AND GLOBAL CONNECTIONS FROM THE OTHER SIDE

In their field-defining *Global Intellectual History* (2013), Samuel Moyn and Andrew Sartori discuss the shift from temporality to spatiality. Global intellectual history should no longer be a type of comparative or universal history in which historians use the global as a meta-analytical category to select, put together, or compare the values of intellectual phenomena from all over the world. Such historiography, often written in Hegelian historicism, at once claims European values as universalizable and thus recounts a story of their global spread and reception—which is also the Europeanization of the world. Moyn and Sartori mention Joseph Levenson's *Confucian China and Its Modern Fate* as this type of "global" intellectual history. Levenson's work implies that "Confucian China's fate would be the fate of the nonmodern non-West everywhere as institutionally or culturally contingent rationality was forced to come to terms with the better reason of the modern West. Such an approach was also implicit in much of the area studies and developmentalist work of the postwar period in the United States, and it still has adherents today."[15]

In his unfinished work *Revolution and Cosmopolitanism*, Levenson argues that "when Confucianism was vital . . . , it was cosmopolitan: it did not simply correspond to 'day-to-day life in rural China.' But when China ceased to be the world and became a nation, or struggled to become one, Confucianism was provincial in that larger world that contained the Chinese nation."[16] He thinks that "what the West has probably done to China is to change the latter's language—what China has done to the West is to enlarge the latter's vocabulary."[17] There is a clear qualitative difference between the change in the West and the change in China. While China changes its language and its identity, the West benefits from it and enriches its assets. Levenson's interpretation of Chinese history bears an air of triumph, as if Western modernity were the only option left for China and other non-Western cultures. The New Confucian thinkers in this book tried to hold on to Confucian cosmopolitanism and reinvent it for a global modernity.

Moyn criticizes the belief in auto-globalization that understands European ideas, such as human rights or freedom, as universalizable concepts that await actualization by subaltern non-European agents in different political communities around the world. He comments that "the model is a strikingly idealist one, and not least in its presentation of confused actors whose ostensible antagonism actually works to advance unintended designs, and in its considerable allocation of agency to the built-in destiny of a concept in itself."[18] For a meaningful global intellectual history, "an acknowledgment of dual and plural structures permeated with cultural meaning . . . makes obvious that it is this complexity, rather than ineffable or unconstituted agency, that must be the starting point for understanding how individual actors choose to use concepts in some specific, conjunctural, and culturally laden moment."[19] Moyn specifies that "the project of global intellectual history at its most ambitious must both describe and explain this breakthrough in modern times to global transmissibility, which only the fact that 'some fundamental structures of social practice span the real and enormous differences that separate diverse and regional lifeworlds' could explain."[20] A global intellectual history would "emphasize intermediating agents or modes of circulation, or else theories of larger structural transformations (Marxism, notably) that allow for new conceptual movement or networking practices."[21]

The concept of network has the potential to resist the Eurocentric tendency in global intellectual history and enables studies that unearth, reconstruct, and emphasize the contexts and circulations in which ideas and values travel and unfold worldwide, not only moving from the West to the rest. Network, as the French anthropologist and sociologist Bruno Latour points out, does not suffice as a stand-alone idea because it is always tied to some lasting values. While it is crucial for intellectual history to trace the emergence, transformation, and translation of ideas beyond linguistic, national, social, and cultural boundaries, a network of ideas bears its own social preferences, political ideologies, and cultural customs. Network per se could be infinite and marked by discontinuities and hiatuses, but values persist and continue.

For Latour, network is important for the understanding of any given situation: "The essence of a situation, as it were, will be for a [net], the list of the other beings through which it is necessary to pass so that this situation can endure, can be prolonged, maintained, or extended. To trace a network is thus always to reconstitute by a trial . . . the antecedents and the consequences, the precursors and the heirs, the ins and outs, as it were, of a being. Or, to put it more philosophically, the others through which one has to pass in order to become or remain the same—which presupposes . . . that no one can simply 'remain the same,' as it were, 'without doing anything.' To remain, one needs to pass—or at all events to 'pass through'—something we shall call a translation."[22] While the idea of network as context and connection is essential for the understanding and description of a situation, historical or contemporary, Latour argues that network is always attached to values. Values "too are defined by leaps, discontinuities, hiatuses. But unlike networks, they create sequences that do not simply lead to heterogeneous lists of unexpected actors, but rather to a type of continuity specific to each instance."[23] A network can extend endlessly, yet values are finite. Values are always attached to a thing or an actor and define them within certain realms, "as are the values that the Moderns have learned to defend."[24]

Indeed, the seemingly neutral category of network is inadvertently fraught with ideological and historical values and their limits. European colonialism and Western imperialism have created networks and promoted circulations but have also imposed their locally produced values onto non-European cultures. Hence the type of global history with the premise that European values are universalizable is problematic. It is indispensable to recognize that some values have been spread through colonial and imperial networks to achieve their spatial continuities. Sebastian Conrad aptly comments, "Many older world history texts locate the driving force of world history in Europe and chronicle the spread of European achievements to the rest of the world: world history as a one-way street."[25] It is thus high time to challenge "the parochialisms of Hegelian universal history" and to create an alternative language for discussions of ideas and concepts that go beyond the paradigm of European history, without necessarily excluding Europe.[26] European history should not be the only foundation but one of many sources from which intellectual history could be written.[27]

In *Provincializing Europe*, Dipesh Chakrabarty discusses the dilemma that Indian intellectuals have in relation to the European tradition that supposedly reached back to ancient Greece. Chakrabarty admits that, even though he is aware that the European intellectual tradition is a fabricated continuity of recent history, he still sees himself, a member of the modern Bengali-educated middle class, deeply rooted in this genealogy of thought. The Sanskrit, Persian, or Arabic traditions that once existed in the subcontinent were interrupted by British colonialism and thus lost their contemporaneity for theoretical inquiry. Hence "European thought has a contradictory relationship to such an instance of political modernity. It is both indispensable and inadequate in helping us to think through the various life practices that constitute the political and the historical in India."[28] Moyn and Sartori comment, "For Chakrabarty and others, the discipline of history is bound to the theoretical sovereignty of a hyperreal 'Europe.' This is not the real Europe with all its complexities but the imaginary Europe of the social sciences and humanities that has so often figured as the model and vehicle of progress, development, reason, and modernity and has thus served as the measure of the relative successes and failures of all other peoples' histories."[29] Hence even if Chakrabarty claims to provincialize Europe, his focus on the role of Marx and Heidegger in the making of South Asian political modernity remains European in origin.

Unlike in India, the intellectual continuity in China and East Asia, including Confucianism, Taoism, and Buddhism, was not disrupted by prolonged European colonialism. My book thus takes one step further in the project of provincializing Europe without encountering the dilemma described by Chakrabarty. Reorienting from the European tradition to the Chinese philosophical genealogy in global intellectual history, I offer an example of tracing ideas of non-European origins not only in their own cultural sphere but also in the West, thus revealing global connections from the other side. It is an alternative account that diverges from the common logic of tracing ideas from the West to the rest. I aim to show that ideas, whether European or Asian or otherwise, are all part of our shared human heritage and belong to the ontological common of humanity. They thus should be treated equally as ideas, neither as representatives of political positions nor as stakeholders of imagined historicism. If Chakrabarty claims that Marx and Heidegger are naturally South Asian, then European thinkers' engagement with Chinese philosophy makes Confucius or Zhuangzi inherently European. This view from the other side also requires a different causality of global intellectual history.

CAUSALITY AND ABSTRACT RELATIONS

The causality that has often been evoked to explain the shift from temporality to spatiality in global intellectual history is the theory of global capitalism. Moyn and Sartori point out, "In this Marxian global intellectual history, circulation as a general historical phenomenon must be distinguished from circulation specifically in a capitalist society, to the extent that in a capitalist society, circulation is bound to practices of generalized commodity production."[30] Transmission and mobility of intellectual concepts are understood as part of the larger global transformation of material and capital flows. Yet the parallel between the circulation of capital and the transmission of ideas might not be seamless. The abstract connections through labor, market, consumption, and capital circulation were critiqued as dehumanizing rationalization, for example, by Adorno and

Horkheimer in *Dialectic of Enlightenment* (1947). It is thus not unproblematic to use capitalist circulation as the causality for the circulation of ideas in intellectual history.

In *Bengal in Global Concept History: Culturalism in the Age of Capital*, Andrew Sartori uses the causality of global capitalism to read the concept of culture in rural Bengal not as a Western concept imported and imposed by the Europeans in Bengal, but as an idea that has adopted its Bengali roots and expression.[31] Sartori argues that, even though the notion of culture originated in the work of the German philosopher Johann Gottfried Herder in the eighteenth century, it has developed new meanings and implications in new contexts. Sartori challenges the assumption that Bengal culturalism is a reception and imitation of the original idea of culture in Europe. Sartori is critical of the Hegelian historicism that sees European history as the universal model for the entire world's development and understands non-Western history as the belated imitation or flawed reiteration of this model. Capitalism at a global scale necessarily construes the context and generates the force with which ideas and concepts circulate and transform from one place to another.

Marxian understanding of abstract human relationships defined by labor, commodity production, market economy, and capital circulation is fundamental for Sartori's culturalism. These relationships are impersonal mediations "that, as the most fundamental conditions for the reproduction of individual and collective life, saturate the practical structures of modern life and link complete strangers in mutual objective interdependence through the mediation of both exchange and production by a historically specific form of social totality that Marx called *capital*."[32] Humans are bound to each other "most fundamentally through the exchange of labor rather than by concrete institutional or sentimental bonds."[33] These abstract labor relations are translated into the reproduction and circulation of capital in the global context.

Hence Bengal is intrinsically tied to the West through global capitalism, which equally incorporates and permeates local circumstances. Bengal was a contributing part of the complex processes of global capital circulation. Sartori then criticizes the historicist labeling of Bengal as a semi-feudal society that was supposedly at a lower developmental stage than capitalist countries in Europe. Sartori intends to show that Bengal was not less developed and inferior; rather, capitalism was something that was equally owned and practiced in Bengal as well as in the West. While Sartori attempts to put Bengal and the West on an equal footing, he also inadvertently includes Bengal in the same circle of capital flow and thus forgoes the opportunity to see Bengal's potential in an alternative logic of history. Truly, Sartori disputes the romanticized binary between Western capitalism and indigenous naturalism, arguing that "the very backwardness of India's smallholding economy is grasped intrinsically as a moment of capitalist social relations. Capitalism in Bengal did not sit atop noncapitalist cultivation like a lid on a jar; it mediated social relations within agrarian society at a profound level."[34] Bengali local specificities, Sartori maintains, shall not be disregarded as unimportant or erased under the influence of Western capitalism.

As much as Bengal should be conceived as a part of global capitalism, not as a semi-feudal society, so should the notion of culture be considered as a locally grown and globally constitutive category. The culture concept is not, however, an epiphenomenon of the economy. Following Lukács, Sartori highlights the autonomy of subjectivity and the independent dissemination and circulation of concepts in the global context. The notion of culture thus should no longer be purely identified as German and Western. It has assumed a global status and should be given its local Bengali intellectual significance—"and it is this translatability and transmissibility that remains inadequately explained."[35]

Sartori's approach, however, still remains within the vocabulary of the European tradition. Even though he tries to interpret culture as a global concept, he still focuses on a European idea and extensively discusses its European origin. Aamir R. Mufti points out in his book *Forget English!* that ideas such as global society, universalism, and world literature all share "a genealogy that leads to Enlightenment-era intellectual and literary practices."[36] Mufti hence forcefully and humorously calls upon his readers to "forget English" as the language of global imperialism.

Sartori shares a similar dilemma with Chakrabarty: the move to provincialize Europe inadvertently confirms Europe's centrality as the provider of normative concepts in global intellectual history. If one intends to continue on the pluralistic path of a global intellectual history and see the European tradition only as one of many cultural heritages, one might want to move beyond the European archive and turn to non-European cultures and present their global entanglements. This is one of the fundamental aims of my book: to trace the global circulation of classical Chinese philosophy in the West and China alike. The philosophers discussed in this book, such as Max Weber and Rudolf Eucken, however, have heavily critiqued the abstract and impersonal relationships of labor, market, and consumption in a capitalist social order. It would be self-contradictory to apply the global capitalist causality to interpret the discourse of world culture. Bruno Latour's emphasis on the "beings of passionate interest" offers an alternative causality for the story in this book.

ECOLOGY OF BEINGS OF PASSIONATE INTEREST

In Bruno Latour's *An Inquiry into Modes of Existence: An Anthropology of the Moderns*, a female anthropologist conducts fieldwork in the West to understand Western modernity. "This may appear astonishing and even somewhat backward-looking, but it is in the Moderns, in 'Occidentals,' yes even in 'Europeans,' that we are going to have to take an interest, *at last*, in this inquiry."[37] Latour argues that the discipline of anthropology believes in the opposition between "the other cultures and a process of modernization that was European, or in any case Western, in origin. . . . Nevertheless, it was always in relation to that standard, defined by default, that the irrationality, or, more charitably, the alternative rationalities manifested by other cultures were judged."[38] Latour's portrayal of a female anthropologist doing fieldwork in Europe reverses the direction of anthropology commonly conducted by a male researcher of European descent in a non-European place. Western modernity is now likened as an indigenous culture under scrutiny.

Latour redefines the capitalist human actors of labor, reproduction, and distribution as "the beings of passionate interests." For Latour, the actors in the global network are no longer connected through abstract invisible relations, but rather through their innate human nature and their passion. Latour deliberately avoids using conventional vocabularies to describe the experience of modernity and thus experiments innovatively with redescribing modes of existence, including science, law, economy, religion, and fiction. He hopes that "the work of redescription may be of value in that it may allow us to give more space to other values that are very commonly encountered but that did not necessarily find a comfortable slot for themselves within the framework offered by modernity."[39] Latour refers to this new framework as a richer ecosystem capable of hosting in cohabitation a larger number of values.

Latour is skeptical of using the economy as the causal foundation for politics, society, and culture. He humorously calls economy "a utopia—or rather a dystopia, something like the opium of the people."[40] Latour proposes that we abandon the idea of economy and move into the realm of ecology, "which was sold to us as being more habitable and more sustainable but which for the moment has no more form or substance than the Economy, which we are in such a hurry to leave behind."[41] He compares the economy to "a metaphysics of inclusion and exclusion determined in the name of Reason."[42] Questioning the Enlightenment doctrine that individuals are endowed with innate rationality, succinctly expressed in the Kantian *sapere aude* in *What Is Enlightenment?*, Latour contends that the individual is not the primary actor in knowledge production and dissemination. Instead, Latour proposes "quivering little beings wandering around groping in the dark while waiting to receive something from the passage of scripts: sometimes fragments of projects, sometimes allocations of preferences, sometimes suggested roles, sometimes quittances."[43] The little beings are situated in a network and constitute it with their partial ecological and aesthetic contributions.

With a style of thick description, Latour replaces the Marxian categories of economy and individuals with ecology and little beings. He decentralizes the idea of the individual and the role of subjectivity. For Latour, human individuals are always part of a larger network and represent various values within a certain process. The fictional female anthropologist in Latour's narrative is astonished to find out that people think "as if they were individual agents calculating rationally? And they have managed to extend this implausible cosmology to billions of other beings? What ethnographic discovery can top this one? But of course she knows that this is not the fruit of a tragic illusion of the Moderns about themselves: she is beginning to see to what apparatuses, institutions, networks, schools, and arrangements one must be connected, what apps one must learn to download, in order to believe in something so contrary to all experience, so manifestly utopian."[44] Latour thus proposes to de-idealize economy and resituate it in a larger sociocultural context so that it is no longer taken for granted as the fundamental cause and foundation for cultural life. This distinguishes Latour from the approach based on the critique of capitalism in global intellectual history.

Economic difference might not be taken as the only fundamental token to define social differences. Passion as a human quality should replace labor as an impersonal factor. Latour argues:

> We could get a whole alternative philosophy, for the good reason that *avidity* (unlike *identity*) defines in reversible fashion the being that *possesses* and the being that is *possessed* . . . poor and rich are in the same boat, for what we do not possess attaches us as much as what we can easily acquire for ourselves. In this sense, we are *altered*, *alienated*. It is as though, here again, a philosophy of identity and essence—of being-as-being—had played a trick on us by concealing the avidity, the pleasure, the passion, the concupiscence, the hood, of *having* and *had*. This philosophy would have forced us never to confess our attachment to the things capable of giving us *properties* that we didn't know we had.[45]

The abstract labor relation, as a theoretical perspective, does not fully capture the essence of humanity and runs the risk of alienating humans from their innate qualities of passion. Hence, we should switch our attention from people with economic interests to beings of passionate interests. This reorientation would allow us to embrace a new mode of existence dictated by the human heart, which Latour calls "mobilization" or "attachment."

In Latour's definition, attachment represents "everything that lies between, everything through which an entity must pass to go somewhere," while passion is something that "defines the degree of *intensity* of the attachment."[46] Latour vividly imagines that "the icy calculations of The Economy melt everywhere before the wildfire of passionate attachments."[47] These attachments permeate the past, present, and future and constitute the inextricable entanglements between the order of nature and the order of society. "And what is worse: 'we' no longer know who we are, nor of course where we are, we who had believed we were modern. . . . End of modernization. End of story. Time to start over."[48] A new set of coordinates will have to replace the modernist paradigm, and Western modernity shall be redescribed with other stories in other frames.

Indeed, Latour's emphasis on passion continues the philosophical effort of the thinkers discussed in this book. The Latourian "beings of passionate interest" corresponds to the philosophers' quest for spiritual liberation in the age of rationalization. Their visions of the world also demand an alternative naming.

COSMOPOLITANISM, WORLD CULTURE, AND WORLD AS METHOD

I hesitate to use the notion of cosmopolitanism to summarize the philosophical discourse in this book because of the word's heavy Kantian connotation. Indeed, contemporary thinkers almost exclusively draw on Immanuel Kant and his treatises *Idea for a Universal History with a Cosmopolitan Purpose* (*Idee zu einer allgemeinen Geschichte in weltbürgerlicher Absicht*, 1784) and *Perpetual Peace: A Philosophical Sketch* (*Zum ewigen Frieden: Ein philosophischer Entwurf*, 1796) as the intellectual origin for their discussions of global orders of equality, justice, and ethics. Their ideas of new cosmopolitanisms correspond to the expanding transnational economic and cultural networks after the Cold War. David Harvey and Jürgen Habermas, for example, saw a realization of Kantian cosmopolitanism in the European Union as a trade-based political entity.[49] Seyla Benhabib saw the *United Nations Declaration of Human Rights* (1948) as a milestone in cosmopolitan norms of universal justice, which stands in tension with national self-determination.[50]

Kant's belief in the interdependence between nations and the realization of a perpetual peace through trade and commerce are based on a teleology necessitated by natural laws. Kant predicts a perpetual peace that would ultimately prevent wars and foster Enlightenment in all nations. Kant is first optimistic about wars in general because wars' resultant evils still have a beneficial effect because they compel societies to discover a law of equilibrium to regulate the essentially healthy hostility. For him, even though historical experience can reveal little of nature's teleological purpose, one still needs to act according to nature's a priori purpose because one's view is limited by time and space. Commerce and trade will eventually break down political borders. War would become an artificial undertaking with enhanced risk factors. Then Enlightenment would gradually come about, and, finally, a universal cosmopolitan existence could be reached. Cosmopolitanism thus signifies a moral and political maturity of the human race. Kant's vision is a European perspective from the historical moment around 1800, a time period of emerging global trade and active European colonial enterprise. Theorists of cosmopolitanism such as Jeremy Waldron, Martha Nussbaum, and Kwame Anthony Appiah evoke Kant to advance their specific arguments about economic globalization, cosmopolitan education, and identity and differences.[51]

Bruce Robbins, however, contends that cosmopolitanism today no longer means a detachment from national belonging in favor of universal principles and virtues in the Kantian fashion. Rather, there is a shift from singular cosmopolitanism to plural cosmopolitanisms that need to be further explored in their historical, cultural, and social diversity.[52] Robbins argues that discrepant visions of the world could collide with each other like nations or civilizations would, as Samuel Huntington hypothesized.[53] We need to move from the Kantian singularity to a pluralism of cosmopolitanism.

Agreeing with Robbins, I also argue that it is not necessarily always the nations or local cultures that construct incommensurable values and cause irreconcilable conflicts. Rather, their approaches to envisioning global orders and their expectations from others on an international scale give rise to disputes and disagreements. Dominic Sachsenmaier and Sebastian Conrad point out the similarities between the global situations in the early twentieth century and those during the post–Cold War. Learning from the early twentieth century could help us to envision a modern but not necessarily Western global system that is interconnected, but not monopolized.[54] Hence, this book's focus on the first half of the twentieth century wishes to contribute to the current and future discussions about cosmopolitan vision in its plurality. I propose to use the phrase "world culture" to describe the philosophical discourse in this book instead of the heavily loaded Kantian notion of cosmopolitanism. "World culture" does not subsume the philosophers' work under a trade-based international order of world citizenship (*Weltbürgertum*) dating back to the European Enlightenment.

In addition to the lexical explications of "world" and "culture" for the theoretical foundation of this book, I define "world" as the method that the philosophers use to articulate their visions. I am inspired by the Japanese sinologist Yūzō Mizogushi's argument about "China as method." Mizogushi proposes to "take China as a method" in order to "take the world as a goal" in 1989.[55] Mizogushi observes, "When we Japanese People are interested in medieval or ancient Europe, whether consciously or not, behind this interest, there lie, to some degree, our own images of European modernity. . . . In contrast to this, in the case of people's interests in ancient China . . . one's interests in these texts often have nothing to do with their knowledge or concern about Chinese modernity."[56] Mizogushi sees the reason for this disparity in the perceived superiority of Europe and the inferiority of Chinese modernity since the Meiji era. Japanese scholars have been using Europe as the universal standard to evaluate China. Europe represents the world for Japan. This world, Mizogushi contends, "was nothing but a conceptualized world, a world of fixed and pre-arranged method . . . therefore the uniqueness of the Chinese revolution was, in the end, also merely subsumed under the "world" of the Marxist model."[57] Mizogushi, however, imagines "a world in which China is a constitutive element . . . it would be a pluralistic world in which Europe is also one of the constitutive elements."[58] It is time to take China as a method and relativize Europe as the universal method. This new method also "implies relativizing China by relativizing even Japan, and then, through this China, ensuring that people recognize other worlds pluralistically."[59] Mizogushi concludes that "if one agrees about the standpoint of relativization, one could examine Europe from the perspective of China, Asia, or vice versa."[60] With China as a new methodological perspective, one could renegotiate history and create a shared space of knowledge.

Drawing on Mizogushi, the Taiwanese scholar Kuan-Hsing Chen proposes to use "Asia as method" because "using the idea of Asia as an imaginary anchoring point, societies in Asia can become each other's points of reference, so that the understanding of the self may be transformed, and subjectivity rebuilt. On this basis, the diverse historical experiences and rich social practices of Asia may be mobilized to provide alternative horizons and perspectives."[61] Seoul, Kyoto, Singapore, Bangalore, Shanghai, and Taipei could be as prominent meeting points as New York, Paris, and London. Like Mizogushi, Chen aims to decentralize the habit of using the West as the standard for observing and evaluating Asia. Asia as method would allow Asians to pluralize the references in knowledge production and shift the mapping and trajectories of knowledge dissemination. Chen believes that Asia as method would potentially transform the understanding of world history and modernity.

Building on these two theoretical moves, I propose "world as method" to mediate between the East and the West in an ontological common, a state of being fundamentally human and sharing humanity. It allows us to interpret Europe and China from each other's perspectives, as Mizoguchi imagines. It also allows us to see from a relativist position the cosmopolitan visions of the thinkers discussed in this book. "World as method" is not a theoretical gaze I impose upon them—in fact, their tremendous intellectual practice of learning from others and of adopting different perspectives already embodies this phrase in its truest meaning.

Furthermore, the thinkers in this book all repeatedly use the words "world" and "culture" in their writings. For example, Liang Shuming explicitly imagines a world culture (*shijie wenhua*, 世界文化) in his book *Eastern and Western Cultures and Their Philosophies*; Feng Youlan illustrates his idea of "world philosophy" in an essay he published in English; Zhang Junmai coauthored a manifesto about Chinese culture and world culture (*zhongguo wenhua yu shijie wenhua*, 中国文化与世界文化); Keyserling admires Confucianism as an alternative cosmopolitanism; Weber understands *The Economic Ethic of World Religions* as a universal history of culture (*eine Universalgeschichte der Kultur*). Hence the notion of "world culture" aptly captures the quintessential nature of the philosophers' shared concern and purpose.

Certainly, this book is not the first attempt at unearthing alternative world views; it builds on the pioneering and inspiring works of others. Ban Wang discusses the Confucian idea of *tianxia* (天下), "an alternative vision to the current international system."[62] Wang advances the argument that contemporary Chinese worldviews include ancient Confucian ideals of unity and equality as well as Western Enlightenment ideas of humanism and socialism. This combination expresses "China's deep yearning to be recognized as an equal part of the world."[63] Chinese thinkers are poised to transcend the narrow nation state toward a broader world community. In his monumental work *Rise of Modern Chinese Thought* (现代中国思想的兴起), Wang Hui (汪晖) also emphasizes the inheritance and transformation of Chinese traditions in the process of modernization and challenges the binary between nation and empire in the study of Chinese intellectual history. Wang recognizes a strong cosmopolitanism (世界主义), or a pursuit of universal truth (普遍的真理) or *dao* (or *tao*, 道) beyond cultural and historical differences, in Liang Qichao, Liang Shuming, and Zhang Junmai, whom I also discuss in this book.[64] Yet, Wang does not further expand on this astute observation. Rather, he remarkably captures the essence of modern Chinese intellectual history and identifies scientific knowledge as the foundational paradigm, using the phrase "a unity of scientific language" (科学话语共同体) to describe the goal that Chinese intellectuals aimed to achieve in their conversations with Western modernity. In the case of Liang Qichao, for example, Wang sees his purpose as the critique of modern scientific knowledge (科学知识问题) in a global context.[65] The New Confucian skepticism toward modernity profoundly questions the precondition of modern knowledge (现代性的知识前提).[66] Wang argues: "In the intellectual environment since late Qing in China, science symbolizes the calling of liberation and also serves as the objective evidence for various kinds of social and cultural reform."[67] The idealist efforts of New Confucianism, such as the identification of metaphysics and ethics as the foundation for a global future of humanity, were not perfectly attuned to the materialist discourse of science and knowledge. Hence Wang's study could not accommodate extensive discussions of New Confucianism. Yet Wang still dedicates several substantial chapters to the cosmopolitan and New Confucianist tendency in the fourth volume of his book and points out its importance.[68]

I thus follow Ban Wang and Wang Hui's lead and expand their observations of the cosmopolitan trend in modern Chinese and European intellectual history in a global context. My book, as the following outline reveals, demonstrates the efforts of both Chinese and European thinkers to borrow from classical philosophy and to imagine economics, politics, ethics, spirituality, and modernity with greater global justice and less imperialist hegemony.

CHAPTER OVERVIEWS

The chapters follow a more or less chronological order. Chapter 1, "Encounter in Beijing: Hermann Graf Keyserling, Gu Hongming, and Confucian Cosmopolitanism," presents the aforementioned encounter between Hermann Graf Keyserling and Gu Hongming and discusses their promotion of Confucianism as a means to counter Western imperialism in China. While Gu's support for Confucianism and the Qing dynasty has earned him the reputation of a conservative monarchist, his position also reveals his resistance to Western imperialism. Gu's background as a colonial subject in British Malaya, his European education, and the reclaim of his Chinese heritage as a new identity all led to his insistence on Confucianism as an alternative moral and political order to Western modernity. Deeply impressed with Gu, Keyserling also highly praises Confucianism as a new cosmopolitanism and the ethical foundation for a future world culture. While Keyserling's own aristocratic background could explain his admiration for Confucianism and his conservative political position in the European context, he also disapproves of Western imperialism in China and critiques the tendency of replacing the Chinese tradition with Western modernity. Keyserling's understanding of Confucian cosmopolitanism influenced Weber during his visit.

In Chapter 2, "Re-enchanting Confucianism: Max Weber, Care of the Self, and Charisma," I read Weber's treatise *Confucianism and Taoism* and discuss two major aspects in it: economic ethics and political charisma. In *The Protestant Ethic and the Spirit of Capitalism* (1904/1905), Weber identifies Protestantism as the driving force behind industrial capitalism. While Weber's thesis has often been used as a justification for Western superiority, his critique of Protestantism reveals his deep dissatisfaction with the West. Seeking alternatives, Weber claims Confucianism as a more balanced rational culture. He maintains that Confucianism does not attempt to suppress beliefs in magic and religious cults; rather, it accepts and values them as a meaningful part of an aesthetic way of life. Weber also develops one of his most influential concepts, charisma, in his description of the Chinese emperor and Confucian literati. While Weber defines the concept of charisma as an ideal type and a universal idea, in Confucian literati, Weber has found a historical example of charisma. In his speech *The Profession and Vocation of Politics* (1919), Weber calls for a charismatic political leader with responsibility in an effort to make charisma applicable to his time of crisis at the end of WWI. Weber ultimately envisions a future world culture that would ensure greater freedom for all. His emphasis on aesthetic self-cultivation in the Confucian tradition inspired French philosopher Michel Foucault's idea of the aesthetic care of the self in his *History of Sexuality* (1976–84). While Weber uses Chinese philosophy to counter Protestant rationalization, Foucault evokes ancient Greece to propose an aesthetic mode of being. They echo each other's thinking and feeling across more than half a century.

Sharing Weber's pursuit of spiritual liberation, Zhang Junmai transitioned from politics to philosophy after being deeply disappointed by the 1919 Paris Peace Conference. This construes Chapter 3, "Zhang Junmai as Philosopher: Rudolf Eucken, Life, and Spirituality." In his attempt to secure Chinese sovereignty and to achieve greater international justice, Zhang decided to study German idealism and became a New Confucianist. Zhang's transition marked a significant event in modern Chinese intellectual history. *A Manifesto for a Re-appraisal of Sinology and Reconstruction of Chinese Culture* (1958) reveals Zhang's and his fellow New Confucianists' quintessential position toward Confucianism as a world ethic. In *The Problem of Life in China and in Europe* (*Das Lebensproblem in China und in Europa*, 1922), Zhang and his German teacher, Nobel laureate

Rudolf Eucken, maintain that a synthesis of Chinese and German idealism would provide the foundation for a philosophy of the world, offsetting the damages brought by warfare and imperialist injustice. Back in China, in 1923, Zhang advanced this philosophical view in a public dispute with Ding Wenjiang on science and the philosophy of life. Zhang challenged positivist scientism and pointed out that scientism was considered bankrupt after World War I according to Western cultural pessimism. He insisted that life, spirituality, and Confucian ethics should lead China and the world toward greater freedom.

Zhang's colleague at Peking University, Liang Shuming, shared Zhang's concerns about China and the world. A devoted Buddhist, Liang adopted Confucian ethics to become more socially engaged. Chapter 4, "Liang Shuming, World Culture, and Rural Modernity," first highlights Liang's interpretation of Confucianism as a joyous, intuitive rationalism from the perspective of Buddhist epistemology in his *Eastern and Western Cultures and Their Philosophies* (1921). Liang aimed to introduce his ideas to farmers in his rural reform projects and identified the rural area as the foundation of a sustainable culture for China and the world. Summarizing his experience in *Theory of Rural Construction* (1937), Liang emphasizes the importance of education and, in his experiments in Shandong and elsewhere, reports how he transformed local government to rural schools so that learning and solving problems were placed at the center of government work. Liang envisions a utopian society founded on Confucian ethics and a rural socialism. Such a society would overcome capitalist and imperialist shortcomings and counterbalance the urbanization and industrialization brought about by Western modernity.

Liang's Confucian rural reform did not result in an innovation of Confucianism as a philosophy. A former student of Liang's, Feng Youlan, thoroughly reshaped Confucianism as New Rationalism, which is the content of Chapter 5, "Early Feng Youlan's Negative Method: Metaphysics, World Philosophy, and Sage." In exile during the Sino-Japanese War, Feng decided to continue the tradition of Song-Ming Confucianism and to connect the Chinese and European traditions through metaphysics. Feng argues that, while Kant sees no way of crossing the boundary between the known and the unknown through logical analysis, Taoism and Zen Buddhism abolish this boundary through silence and the negation of reason. This negative method, Feng argues, points toward mysticism. This is the contribution that Chinese philosophy could make to a world philosophical union beyond national, cultural, linguistic, and racial boundaries. Philosophy should not only serve to legitimize the positive accumulation of knowledge in the modern sciences; it should also move past the limits of logic and recognize experiences that cannot be expressed through language. What cannot be expressed is a mystical experience that construes a universal cosmic union of all humans. Feng refers to Wittgenstein as a companion on the path to achieving negation through poetic silence. In the ideal of a sage, Feng envisions a practitioner and a personification of world philosophy.

I contrast the aforementioned philosophical discourse of world culture to Communist internationalism because it is important to recognize their difference. In Chapter 6, "Bertolt Brecht's *Me-ti* or the Aesthetics of Translation: Universal Love, Mutual Benefits, and Transience," I turn to the German dramatist Bertolt Brecht's (1898–1956) posthumously published book *Me-ti: Book of Transformation (Me-ti: Buch der Wendungen*, 1965), a fictional "translation" of the ancient Chinese classic *Mozi*. Engaging with Mohism over more than thirty years, Brecht connects Marxism and the European socialist movement with the teaching of Mozi, an ancient philosopher known as an opponent to Confucius in his lifetime. With the decline of Confucianism in China and the surge of a worldwide communist movement, Mohism became more prominent in China and came to be called "early Chinese socialism." Brecht's fervent interest in Mohism could not be severed from the renaissance of Mohism in China, which led to the German translation of the Chinese classic *Mozi* by Alfred Forke in 1922. This all construed a global moment for Mohism. Sharing the efforts of other philosophers to integrate Chinese and Western philosophy, in this philosophical work, Brecht translates the teaching of Mohism from its ancient context into the twentieth century and uses it as a way to comment on and interpret German politics and Russian socialism, thereby emphasizing the ethical function of Mohism across time. *Me-ti* evinces an intertextuality that weaves both *Mozi*'s and Brecht's creative reflections on universal love, mutual benefit, and the transience of things. Brecht's *Me-ti* represents a form of philosophical thinking that breaks free from a linear tradition and creates a world literature that integrates China and the West through translation and transformation.

1

ENCOUNTER IN BEIJING:
HERMANN GRAF KEYSERLING, GU HONGMING, AND CONFUCIAN COSMOPOLITANISM

When the German-Estonian aristocrat Hermann Graf Keyserling traveled around the world (1911–12), he arrived in Hong Kong from India in March 1912, toward the end of China's 1911 Revolution (1911–12). About a month earlier, on February 12, the last emperor of the Qing Dynasty, Aisin-Gioro Puyi (爱新觉罗溥仪), had abdicated, putting an end to China's millennia-long tradition of monarchism. Despite the political upheavals, Keyserling spent several months in China and traveled from the southern tip of the country all the way to the north to visit Beijing. Even amidst this political turbulence and the nationalist movement against monarchy in China, Keyserling highly praised the Qing nobles whom he met in China and confidently touted Chinese Confucianism, the state philosophy of the dynasty, as a future utopian vision for life and society throughout the world, as documented in his hugely popular *Das Reisetagebuch eines Philosophen* (1918; *The Travel Diary of a Philosopher*, English translation, 1925). Keyserling's predilection for Confucianism, however, is not so much a philosophical or intellectual position as a political one. It contains a strong justification of monarchism as an ideal form of government, which corresponds to his own aristocratic background and reflects his nostalgia for the dwindling monarchism in Europe.

The source of Keyserling's Confucian enthusiasm was probably the Chinese-Malay thinker Gu Hongming (辜鸿铭, 1857–1928, also known as Ku Hungming), whom Keyserling met in Beijing. Keyserling, immediately impressed with

Gu's personality, also agreed with his political and philosophical views. While Gu shared Keyserling's anti-liberal monarchism and his conservative critique of modernity, Gu's background differed considerably from Keyserling's. Gu grew up as a colonial subject of Chinese descent in British Malaya and received his education in Europe, mostly in the United Kingdom. However, Gu later denounced British colonialism and moved to China to reclaim his cultural and national belonging. Gu's defense of Confucianism thus contains an anti-colonial impetus, even though he was dismissed by his contemporary Chinese revolutionaries as a conservative. Compared to Keyserling, Gu more sharply critiques Western imperialism in China and rejects technological modernity. His position, for example, was demonstrated in one of his books, *The Story of a Chinese Oxford Movement: An Essay in Political and Social Criticism in China* (1910), which had just been published in English when Keyserling visited China. Gu was a staunch opponent of introducing Western constitutionalism and republicanism to China and considered it a form of Western imperialist interference with Chinese tradition. Despite Gu's stronger anti-imperialist stance, Keyserling also supported Gu's position against anti-Western modernity. Most importantly, they both shared the opinion that Confucianism should become a new cosmopolitan ethics.

While Keyserling and Gu both insisted on the idiosyncrasy of Chinese Confucianism as an alternative to the dominance of Western culture, and while they were both considered politically conservative in Europe and China, respectively, their different backgrounds and different motivations for promoting Confucianism point to the complexity in the repurposing of Confucianism—not only in China but also in the West, on a global scale. It would be easy to criticize Keyserling's admiration for Confucianism as a type of Orientalism, and we could contend that it has little to do with reality but is merely created to serve his own purpose of bemoaning the decline of aristocratic rule in Europe. Edward Said once argued, along these lines, that the European representation of the Orient is never a "delivered present, but a *re-presence*.... The value, efficacy, strength, apparent veracity of a written statement about the Orient therefore relies very little, and can't instrumentally depend, on the Orient as such. On the contrary, the written statement is a presence to the reader by virtue of its having excluded, displaced, made supererogatory any such *real thing* as the 'the Orient.'"[1] But while Said's argument emphasizes the power imbalance in British and French colonies and points out the logic of the justification for colonization in European cultural products, Keyserling's case invites a different interpretation. Keyserling's representation of Confucianism is quite positive and is directly related to his experience in China and with Chinese people. Even though his praise of Confucianism reflects his own projection onto monarchism, his attitude is by no means geared toward the justification of Western imperialism. Keyserling, in particular, shared Gu's critique of imperialism and agreed with him about the idiosyncrasy of Chinese language, writing, and culture and promoted Confucianism as a world ethics.

Given the complex constellation of Keyserling and Gu, it is necessary to take a global approach to this story and consider the European and non-European sides on an equal footing. Keyserling and Gu's concentration on Confucianism also urges us to understand their thinking from the perspective of Chinese intellectual history instead of from a concept rooted in a European tradition. (Said's critique of Orientalism draws on a French poststructuralist understanding of self-referential representation.) Using Confucianism as the perspective to connect and distinguish Keyserling and Gu provides us the opportunity to rebalance the East and the West in terms of theoretical approach and historical precision and consider their cosmopolitan thinking in an alternative paradigm: Chinese Confucianism. I deem the entanglements between Keyserling and Gu a unique opportunity to highlight a story outside of mainstream Western cosmopolitan thinking that is routinely traced back to Immanuel Kant and the European Enlightenment.[2] While Keyserling and Gu both published in the European languages of German and English, their backgrounds were by no means nationally German or English. They consciously chose the Chinese Confucian genealogy as their intellectual and philosophical orientation, thus diverging from the European tradition.

In addition to the issue of how to interpret Keyserling, their case raises the question of how to refine and redefine our understanding of political conservatism. It is true that both thinkers opposed liberal democracy and fervently supported monarchy as an ideal form of government; however, a closer examination of the discourse of conservatism in both Europe and China in the early twentieth century reveals many historical nuances. In the European context, for example, the "conservative revolution" promoted and refashioned the mythical tradition of the blood-bound German *Volk* as its national origin. Consisting of elite intellectuals in German-speaking countries, this movement also spread to and emerged in other European countries and still serves as a source for conservatism in today's Germany.[3] The conservative revolutionaries believed in the superiority of German *Kultur* to socialist Marxism, liberal democracy, and capitalism. A prominent trend in this conservative movement was the combination of the fetishization of industrial technology and the refusal of a rationalist view in politics and culture, which eventually transformed into Nazi ideology.[4] However, this understanding was not universally shared; for example, the Austrian writer Hugo von Hofmannsthal, from whom the phrase "conservative revolution" was taken, supposedly meant it to be a *schöpferische Restauration* (creative restoration), and his followers included liberal thinkers such as Walter Benjamin and Max Weber.[5] Hofmannsthal's phrase was thus refashioned and turned in a sociopolitical direction. Given this background, Keyserling's nostalgic monarchism does not support democracy, nor does it favor *völkisch* reactionism. His predilection for Chinese Confucianism dilutes or even negates this prominent nationalist and blood-bound conservatism in twentieth-century Europe.

Likewise, in China, Gu differs from what is generally thought of as conservatism in the early twentieth century. While nationalism is considered the foremost feature of Chinese conservatism at that time, it carries a cultural rather than a sociopolitical connotation. Benjamin Schwartz comments that "one might, of course, use the term 'traditionalist' rather than conservative to describe all those in modern China such as Chang Ping-lin, Hsiung Shih-li, Liang Shu-ming, and others who have claimed that ideas and values of the past had present validity for them."[6] The term "conservatism" describes not these thinkers' political position, but their investment in Confucian Chinese cultural values. Gu's insistence on Confucian morality and monarchism as an alternative sociopolitical system to Western republicanism primarily entails not anti-liberalism but rather resistance to Western imperialism. Gu's position also represents an anti-colonial critique of the Chinese emulation of the West. His background as a colonial subject in British Malaya contributed to his conception of a Confucian cosmopolitanism, a position that was not shared by many of his Chinese contemporaries who were educated in the West. Since Gu was against almost all things Western, including liberal democracy and Western technology, his anti-liberal attitude should be understood in the context of his rejection of Western imperialism. Of course, he did not necessarily have to support monarchism, and this choice qualifies him as a conservative on the surface.

Yet at least in the cases of Keyserling and Gu, the received political and intellectual distinctions between colonizer and colonized, left and right, or the West and the East do not seem to be perennially valid categories, and they may not offer the most useful framework to help us explore less-trodden paths and develop a more refined understanding of history that would enable us to reframe and reshape our future perspective. It is thus sensible to move beyond the given binary and highlight less-visited sources in intellectual history. The cases of Keyserling and Gu give us an opportunity to renegotiate the well-worn paradigms of Orientalism and conservatism and recognize that their shared embrace of Confucianism creates a new global intellectual connection that reshapes and enriches the understanding of cosmopolitanism, coloniality, and modernity in both Europe and China. In the following pages, I will discuss first Keyserling's *Reisetagebuch* and then Gu's *Story of a Chinese Oxford Movement* to illustrate their Confucian cosmopolitanism and their critique of Western modernity and imperialism.

HERMANN GRAF KEYSERLING'S TRAVEL DIARY OF A PHILOSOPHER

Like the Chinese aristocrats in exile, Keyserling himself was also expropriated— in his case, by the Estonian government after the Russian Revolution—and he emigrated to Germany in 1918. Born into a Prussian noble family with a continuous lineage tracing back to the fifteenth century in the Baltic region, Keyserling belonged to the Prussian ruling class that dominated the Baltic for centuries. Having sold over 50,000 copies by 1932, when its eighth edition was released, Keyserling's *Reisetagebuch* instantaneously became a huge success upon its publication in December 1918 and was translated into many other languages. The German writer Hermann Hesse even predicted that Keyserling would become one of the most important philosophers of the twentieth century.[7] Even though Keyserling's name has sunk into oblivion today, he was considered a major philosophical voice by many of his prominent contemporaries, such as Carl Gustav Jung, Rabindranath Tagore, Thomas Mann, Richard Wilhelm, Leo Baeck, Ernst Troeltsch, Max Scheler, Henri Bergson, and Paul Valéry. Many of these writers and intellectuals supported the *Schule der Weisheit* (School of Wisdom), a circle engaging with and cultivating *Lebensphilosophie* (the philosophy of life), which Keyserling founded and directed in Darmstadt from 1920 to 1934. In the introduction to *Reisetagebuch*, Keyserling attributes its popularity to the general enthusiasm for the East after World War I. He even states that he was so obsessed with the East in 1914 that he would transform his identity and hardly portray himself as an *Abendländer* (Westerner).[8]

When Keyserling arrived in Qingdao (青岛, written as "Tsingtau" in *Reisetagebuch*), a city in northern China under German occupation from 1898 to 1914, Richard Wilhelm, as mentioned in the Introduction, the German missionary and prominent translator of Chinese classics, introduced him to Qing aristocrats who were in exile from Beijing because of the revolution.[9] Keyserling was enchanted by these nobles of high rank and praised them as the highest possible type of Chinese people.[10] He reported that his expectations were far exceeded when he met them in person, because these Chinese aristocrats represented the living Confucianism that he had read about in books. For the first time in his life,

Keyserling claims, he has seen a type of human being whose deepest depth is morality; such humans do not exist in the West. Not only do individual human beings practice Confucianism, Keyserling writes, the political state as a collective entity also follows the rules to guarantee social justice. This harmonious integration at both the individual and the state level is achieved by instilling an internal education in Confucian morality, not through the external regulation of legality. Keyserling suggests here that Confucian ethics, not the rule of law, regulates Chinese society:

> Moral force is the fundamental force of the world; as soon as it can assert itself duly everything else is regulated of its own accord. Kant spoke of two things which filled his heart with ever-new reverence: the starry sky above him and the moral law within him. For the Chinese the heavenly cosmos itself is an expression of moral law.

> Das Moralische ist die Grundkraft der Welt; sobald es zur Geltung kommt, reguliert sich das übrige von selbst. Kant sprach von zwei Dingen, die sein Herz mit immer neuer Ehrfurcht erfüllten: dem bestirnten Himmel über ihm und dem moralischen Gesetze in ihm. Dem Chinesen ist der himmlische Kosmos selbst ein Ausdruck des moralischen Gesetzes.[11]

While the Enlightenment philosopher Kant still saw cosmic order and ethical principles as two separate things, Keyserling writes, Confucians integrate both the cosmic and the moral universes into a harmonious unity in which the moral law is expressed through the cosmic order. Accordingly, humanity is understood as part of nature and the cosmos. Thus, if ethics permeates humanity and the cosmos, the government has no need of violence to control human behavior:

> Moral force as the primary force of the world manifests its influence directly; particular action is not required. Therefore, it is handed down concerning the greatest emperors of China that they—did not rule.... The Mandarins have at their disposal neither military force nor police in order to carry out their orders, which are yet obeyed most readily. The prestige of their dignity is sufficient, for it is presupposed that it corresponds to their value, and that it guarantees the reverence for what stands below them.

> Das Moralische als Urkraft der Welt übt seinen Einfluß unmittelbar aus, besonderen Handelns bedarf es nicht. Deshalb wird von den größten Kaisern Chinas berichtet, daß sie—nicht regiert hätten.... Die Mandarine verfügen weder über Militär, noch über Polizei, um ihre Befehle durchzusetzen, und doch wird ihnen bereitwilligst gehorcht. Es genügt das Prestige ihrer Würde, von welcher vorausgesetzt wird, daß sie dem Wert entspricht, daß sie das Dasein der Ehrfurcht vor dem, was unter ihnen steht, garantiert.[12]

This legendary society of peaceful harmony in Confucian vision is deeply connected to monarchism as a form of government. In this ideal moral order, the social prestige of the ruling class, based either on birth, such as the nobility, or on their education, such as the mandarin literati, should promise and ensure a perfect society, or even a perfect world, without violence. The emperor, then, has a nearly mythic function. Hence, Keyserling observes, Chinese society has been governed for thousands of years just as well as modern Europe, even though it lacks a juridical mechanism. In a Western system, Keyserling contends, anarchism, nationalism, and *Rassenfanatismus* (racism) all replace natural existence with artificiality.

Keyserling also points out that, philosophically speaking, Confucianism is a deeply rationalist pragmatism:

> Kung Fu Tse struck me, until now, as a rationalising moralist, and the high praise which falls to the lot of Mencius astonished me to some extent since I could only regard his conception of the world as no doubt exceedingly reasonable but not profound. Now I realise that Confucian philosophy must be understood in quite a different way from the Indian and from the German: as philosophy it does not represent any intrinsic and independent expression at all, but it represents the abstract formula of a reality which has either been experienced or is to be experienced; the word of Kung Fu Tse must be understood as flesh, or as a reference to existing flesh.

> Kung Fu-Tse erschien mir bisher als rationalistischer Moralist, und die hohe Wertschätzung zumal, deren sich Mencius erfreut, befremdete mich einigermaßen, da ich dessen Weltanschauung wohl als überaus vernünftig, nicht aber als *tief* beurteilen konnte. Nun erkenne ich, daß die konfuzianische Philosophie ganz anders verstanden werden muß, als die indische und auch die deutsche: sie ist als Philosophie gar kein eigentlicher, selbständiger Ausdruck, sondern das abstrahierte Schema einer gelebten oder zu lebenden Wirklichkeit; man muß Kung Fu-Tses Wort als Fleisch verstehen oder als Hinweis auf vorhandenes Fleisch.[13]

Keyserling's first observation that Confucianism differs from Western philosophy, such as the complex systems of Kant, Fichte, and Hegel, is accurate. As someone trained in European and German philosophical tradition, his usage of the word *tief* (profound, deep) to refer to the lack of theoretical depth of philosophical expression in Confucianism, as it is in the European context, is understandable. Keyserling, however, was able to shift his European perspective and learned to adopt the Chinese view and recognize the profundity of Confucianism in its practical guidance in everyday life. Keyserling's comment of Confucianism as carnal knowledge resembles the Christian metaphor of Jesus as the embodiment of divine love. At the same time, it also indicates Keyserling's imagination of a harmonious integration of body and mind, desire and thinking, and practice and theory. If Confucianism were merely a theoretical philosophical expression, it would lose its practical appeal in the complex flow of life. Confucian doctrines are not empty labels but embodied and lived morality, deeply engrained in life's reality. Keyserling comments, "They live in Confucianism (sie leben den Konfuzianismus)."[14]

In the imperial capital of Beijing, the Temple of Heaven greatly impressed Keyserling: "The gigantic marble altar towers up from the wide, desolate expanse of sand, surrounded by a few dusky pines. Every now and again one hears the cawing of a crow; the district is as if deserted by man."[15] In this serene description of the atmosphere in the Temple of Heaven, Keyserling realizes that the Chinese emperor functions as a connector between heaven and earth, just as peasants are the connector between the earth and humanity. "What a wonderful conception," he exclaims.[16] According to Confucianism, moral laws and natural laws belong together in one unified system. They represent identical norms that regulate human conduct, the vicissitude of the seasons, and the transition between day and night. In this all-encompassing context, the human and the inhuman, the organic and the inorganic, the natural and the ethical dimensions are integrated into a single harmony. Thus, morality is not something that is imposed on people from the outside; it is the natural path that everyone has a responsibility to follow: "Accordingly, nature stands in danger of sinking back from cosmos into chaos if men fail to do their natural duty."[17]

Like John Locke in *The Treatises of Government* (1689), Keyserling emphasizes the Confucian understanding of society as a state of nature. Yet it is not a natural state of perfect freedom, as Locke imagines it; rather, it is a natural state of duties, including the submission to the imperial rule of the Son of Heaven—the emperor. A Confucian official explains this to Keyserling during breakfast:

> I had [breakfast] yesterday with an old priest, who was glowing with enthusiasm for his religion, who saw in it the salvation of the whole of mankind, and who traced the downfall of China exclusively to the deterioration of Confucianism. I suggested to him that he should step forth and shake the people from their coma with inspiring words. He replied that he was not fitted for such a task; this was the business of the emperor and of the highest authorities; the condition into which he had been born confined his attention to the faithful fulfilment of his duties towards his parents and his family.

> Gestern frühstückte ich mit einem alten Priester, der durchglüht war von Begeisterung für seine Religion, der in ihr das Heil für die gesamte Menschheit sah und Chinas Niedergang ausschließlich auf den des Konfuzianismus zurückführte. Ich legte ihm nahe, er möge doch auftreten und mit begeisterndem Wort das Volk aufrütteln aus seinem komatischen Schlaf. Er erwiderte, hierzu sei er nicht berufen; das sei Sache des Kaisers und der höchsten Obrigkeit; bei der Stellung, in die er hineingeboren sei, komme nur treue Erfüllung der Pflichten gegen Eltern und Familie für ihn in Frage.[18]

It is curious that Keyserling calls Confucianism a "religion" and probably a Confucian literatus a "priest." While Confucianism cultivates rituals and upholds ethical principles, it is more a practical philosophy and less an institutionalized religion such as a Christian church in the West. Gottfried Wilhelm Leibniz has recognized this difference between Chinese spirituality and European Christianity in his *Preface to the Novissima Sinica* (1697/1699): "And so if we are their equals in the industrial arts, and ahead of them in contemplative sciences, certainly they surpass us (though it is almost shameful to confess this) in practical philosophy, that is, in the precepts of ethics and politics adapted to the present life an use of mortals."[19] Leibniz further comments in *On the Civil Cult of Confucius* (1700/1701) that "I was inclined to believe that when the Chinese literati render honor to Confucius, they consider it a civil ceremony rather than a religious cult."[20] More than two centuries later, Keyserling, however, still applied Western Christian vocabularies to describe Chinese culture. Unlike Leibniz, Keyserling couldn't properly present Confucianism and Confucian literati with their adequate and precise social and political meaning in a European language entrenched in the spiritual history of Christianity. At the same time, Keyserling probably used these terms such as "religion" and "priest" to translate his experience in China for his readership in German-speaking Europe. As discussed earlier, Keyserling did recognize Confucianism's significance as a practical philosophy. This "priest" was most likely a Confucian scholar-official, probably in charge of a particular type of civil ceremony at the royal court such as the temple of the ancestors.

The Confucian official's deference to the emperor and the highest authorities as the only ones with the power to incur any social changes is appealing to Keyserling. After the breakfast, Keyserling wonders how this type of passive obedience to the duties could rejuvenate the world. Then he positively confirms that, if all individuals diligently fulfill their duties, then a molecular (*molekuläre*) environment will emerge in the world system (*Weltsystem*) that gradually leads to the highest harmonious equilibrium. Keyserling considers Confucianism the ideal moral order for a utopian society for all humanity. He contends that there is nothing more ideal than a social order that is established on moral education instead of controlled by a mechanical legal system. If such a society could become a world society, then not only the ancient Chinese but also the Europeans would be Confucian. Keyserling's point here strongly resonates with Max Weber's thinking (see Chapter 2 in this book).

This Confucian sense of duty as a submissive acceptance of the monarch's absolute authority matches his own desire to be such a ruler because of his Junker background. Facing the dwindling of aristocratic power in his own case and in Europe more generally, Keyserling reveals his distaste for republicanism. The once rich and powerful Reich's Junker, penniless, but full of spirit, still endeavored to reestablish aristocratic rule in the Baltic with the aid of the British. Keyserling's political essay *The Baltic Problem* (1919), which he penned in English and published in the British newspaper the *Westminster Gazette*, lays out a blueprint of a great Baltic State under an aristocratic regime.[21] The British, however, were not interested in supporting his vision.

In the Chinese context, Keyserling contends, the Qing nobility must certainly be conservative, like all politically educated persons. If the Confucian moral principles upon which the state is built resonate with the cosmic order, Keyserling concludes, all the efforts to reform or improve the state are unnecessary or even ridiculous. The Chinese emperor does not interfere with local politics, and the provinces are almost autonomous in their own government. Neither an aristocratic nor a caste system prevents social mobility like in other places in the world: in China, the highest offices are available for commoners through a civic exam system. Keyserling argues that nowhere in the world is the government less oppressive than in dynastic China. The palaces, pagodas, massive walls, and giant gates in Beijing demonstrate the sublimity of imperial power in China itself. For Keyserling, China has no need for a republic, and America is not as free as the Chinese under monarchic rule once were.

When Keyserling left China and arrived in New York City during his journey around the world, he formed the impression that Americans were no freer than others: general suffrage does not guarantee a fair election, because of intrigue and bribery; people are deprived of their privileges by a dead legal system of rights and duties; and the principle of equality has degraded the human spirit to the lowest level. Keyserling argues that republicanism does not promise liberation (*Befreiung*) but rather slavery (*Knechtung*).[22] A parliament does not necessarily represent the people. In a monarchy, Keyserling contends, the level of attention toward the people has never sunk as low as in a republic. Keyserling considers China the only country that has solved its social question of inequality, the only country in which the masses lead a happy life. Unlike earlier thinkers such as Johann Gottfried Herder and G. W. F. Hegel, who interpreted China as a backward, stagnant state lacking innovation, Keyserling sees this lack of change as advantageous.[23] He argues that today's Chinese still surprisingly resemble their ancient ancestors because for thousands of years they have followed a similar beneficial life practice and social order based on Confucian morality. Of course, Keyserling's aristocratic nostalgia led to his debasement of American democracy and his peculiar and imaginative admiration of monarchic China.

Keyserling's position resembles the apotheosis of Native American warriors by French aristocratic travelers after the French Revolution that Harry Liebersohn describes in his book *Aristocratic Encounters: European Travelers and North American Indians* (1998).[24] Liebersohn argues that this transcultural sense of a blue-blood affinity with fellow noblemen in America emerged when elite Europeans felt the decline of their status after 1789. Keyserling's wishful interpretation of Confucian monarchism, although in a different cultural and historical context, follows a similar logic. Indeed, after the French Revolution, the British conservative philosopher and politician Edmund Burke argued that monarchism was a universal form of government, not confined to one country or to Europe.[25] "Rather, Burke believes that monarchic rule is one of the essential marks of all civilizations. Burke once critiqued British colonialism's intentional destruction of aristocratic regimes in India because he compared Indian civilization to European civilization and considered the damage done to India similar to the destruction of Europe incurred by the French Revolution."[26] European monarchist thinkers thus incorporate the entire world without excluding any cultures, nations, or geographical locations from the rule of a monarch. It is rather a borderless vision of government and social order: a monarchic cosmopolitanism before or alongside the rise of the nation-state. Keyserling's admiration of China clearly falls into this European conservative tradition of cosmopolitan monarchism. Keyserling's conservatism differs from reactionary modernism, as Jeffrey Herf observes that it is not a combination of irrationality and the fetishization of technology. Keyserling's admiration for Confucianism is not confined to his own nostalgia and self-pity. Rather, like Burke, Keyserling was poised to critique Western imperialism and make clear the damage caused by Western technological modernity that he saw in China and elsewhere in the world during his voyage.

He considers China's imitation of the West—including its mistakes—as a consequence of negative Western influence. For Keyserling, the coolies in the streets of Shanghai are superior to the arrogant Westerners whom they pull behind them in their rickshaws. How dare the missionaries preach Christianity to these hungry but morally superior men, Keyserling exclaims![27] Keyserling contends that, although Europeans have gone further than the Chinese in conquering nature, human life has reached its highest manifestation only in China: "And, after all, we are parts of nature; whether as rulers or as subjects—the fundamental synthesis remains the same. The Chinaman is fully conscious of this synthesis, and we are not; to this extent he stands above us."[28] He holds that this fundamental synthesis remains true and predicts that it will triumph in a future world culture in a Confucian fashion. Even though Keyserling does not lay out his future vision in detail, he critiques the historicist logic of the development of societies.[29] For Keyserling, Western modernity with its logic of development needs to be curbed because it is more harmful than beneficial to China. The internal moral quality of being human is more essential than external technological advancement. People with a high degree of inner freedom are the bearers of a culture in its most elevated form. Once such a highly cultivated interiority has been attained, effort should be put into keeping it intact (*Aufhaltenwollen*).[30]

Keyserling further argues that China cannot rejuvenate itself through Western republicanism and an imported foreign culture. It can only cure the chaotic situation caused by warfare with Western powers and internal social unrest with the resources of its own rich spiritual past. While Western machines, institutions, instruments, and methods could be imported, internal coherence and spiritual peace could only be achieved through traditional Chinese culture and Confucianism.[31] Keyserling reflects that one should not understand Chinese culture as a residue of the past, according to the logic of development; rather, it should be seen as an anticipation of the future. There is no doubt, Keyserling claims, that the most highly educated people of the future are closer to Confucians than to modern Europeans or that the social order of the future also resembles traditional Chinese society more than it does any visions of European utopian thinkers.[32] Again, Keyserling advances the idea of implementing Confucian ethics as the foundation of social order instead of maintaining a mechanistic legal system to secure it. Such an order should not remain a Chinese one but should become a universal principle.[33] In this future scenario, Keyserling imagines, human beings would all become autonomous and free from external barriers. A rich, free, and independent inner life would be the utopian ideal for humanity. Confucianism can usher in this life of spirituality that denounces the materialism associated with technological modernity and promises greater inner power of liberation.

Shortly before his departure, Keyserling gave a lecture at the International Institute of China in Shanghai: *On the Inner Relationship between the Cultural*

Problems of the Orient and the Occident (*Über die innere Beziehung zwischen den Kulturproblemen des Orients und des Okzidents*). In it, Keyserling connects the West and the East together through a universal spiritual path and once again promotes Confucianism as the general basis for an ideal cultural system. He observes that some Chinese people want to replace Chinese civilization with that of the West. He would like to tell them, out of his deepest conviction, that they had only exchanged an organic lively system (*organisch-lebendiges System*) for a burdensome and dead machine (*einen lastenden, toten Apparat*).[34] Keyserling contends that civilization must sprout from living roots to have some values and that China's reforms and changes must not happen in a foreign Western spirit (*nicht im Geiste der fremden aus dem Westen*) but only in its own.[35] He wishes for a revival and renaissance of the ancient classical spirit of Chinese culture, which would become the soul of a modern China. He also envisions that the East and the West, instead of opposing each other as is the situation now, would form a union and strive for the same ideal that Confucian wisdom offers for the future. This ideal exists beyond the boundaries defined by the East and the West and is the foundation of humanity (*Grund des Menschentums*).[36] He affirmed this point to the audience: "Gentlemen, this is not a utopia" (*Meine Herren, das ist keine Utopie*).[37]

In sum, Keyserling's Confucian cosmopolitanism consists of two major traits: monarchism and moral spirituality. The former is a social collective vision that has a clear tradition; the latter is a personal individual aspiration. While Keyserling's support for monarchism betrays his own Junker background, his pursuit of spiritual freedom and his defense of Chinese cultural specificities against Western imperialism contain a critical force that moves beyond mere aristocratic nostalgia and points to an idealist cosmopolitanism that transcends national, cultural, and linguistic borders. As I have shown, Keyserling is entangled in a European intellectual and historical context. At the same time, he is deeply interested in the Confucian idea of inner freedom and ethical cultivation of the self and has willingly adopted these Confucian ideas and moved beyond the European intellectual tradition. His highlighting of Confucianism as a future utopian vision reveals that he does not hesitate to move away from Europe to the alternative orientation of Confucianism. It is a cosmopolitanism that deliberately does not go back to the European eighteenth century and instead starts its genealogy in China. This Confucian turn, I argue, represents a break from the European tradition and points toward a more pluralistic future that is still relevant in the twenty-first century. Even though Keyserling uses Confucianism to justify his conservative monarchism, it is more important to recognize the rupture that

Keyserling's influential *Reisetagebuch* called forth. In his friend Gu Hongming's writing, this break with the Western tradition and an overt critique of Western imperialism are even more pronounced.

DECOLONIAL CONFUCIAN COSMOPOLITANISM IN GU HONGMING'S THE STORY OF A CHINESE OXFORD MOVEMENT

During his sojourn in Beijing, Keyserling met Gu, reporting in his *Reisetagebuch*: "I spend many hours each day with Ku Hung-Ming and his friends and supporters. He is a man of such wit and such a fiery temperament that I am sometimes reminded of a Latin" (*Viele Stunden jedes Tages verbringe ich mit Ku Hung-Ming und dessen Freunden und Anhängern. Der Mann ist überaus geistreich und so feurigen Temperamentes, daß ich manches Mal an einen Romanen gemahnt werde*").[38] This favorable impression of Gu goes hand in hand with Gu's critique of Western imperialism. Keyserling recounts one encounter with Gu: "To-day he was explaining at great length how wrong the Europeans, and especially the sinologists are, in considering the development of Chinese culture quite by itself, without comparison with that of the West: for both have evolved, according to him, within the frame of an identical formula" (*"Heute setzte er des Langen und Breiten auseinander, wie ungerecht die Europäer, und besonders die Sinologen täten, die chinesische Kulturentwicklung ganz für sich, ohne Vergleich mit der okzidentalischen, zu betrachten: denn tatsächlich seien beide nach einem identischen Schema abgelaufen"*).[39] Indeed, Gu contends in his English-language book *The Spirit of the Chinese People* (1915), "There is very little difference between the East of Confucius and the West of Shakespeare and Goethe, but you will find a great deal of difference between even the West of Dr. Legge . . . the scholar who can appreciate and admire zeal for literature, and the West of the Rev. Arthur Smith."[40] James Legge (1815–97) was a Scottish sinologist and missionary known for his translation of Confucian classics. Arthur Smith was an American missionary and sinologist who lived in China for decades. Legge had a more positive image of China than Smith did. Gu argues here that general cultural differences are not as insurmountable as the specific differences between individual opinions, especially those of Western sinologists such as Legge and Smith under the influence of imperialism.

The boundaries between the East and the West are more permeable than those between one Western sinologist's discrimination against and another's appreciation of China. Hence Gu intends "to show how and why men, foreigners who are looked upon as authorities on the subject, do not really understand the real Chinaman and the Chinese language."[41] Gu uses the derogatory term for Chinese as self-referential irony to point out the ignorance of Western sinology. In *The Story of a Chinese Oxford Movement* (1910), Gu tries to place China and Europe in a parallel and comparable historical process. There he compares two nineteenth-century political and intellectual reform movements in China and Great Britain and endeavors to argue for a Confucian cosmopolitanism as an effective method of undermining Western imperialism. Three aspects are essential for my analysis here: Gu's background as a colonial subject, his anti-liberalism, and his proposal to use Confucian morality to resist Western technological modernity.

Gu's unique perspective—his refusal to treat China as a separate entity developing within itself and his approach of connecting Chinese and European histories in numerous details—are attributable, at least in part, to his background as a colonial subject in Southeast Asia. Gu Hongming was born in Penang, then British Malaya, to a wealthy and prominent Chinese-Malaysian family that had originally emigrated from Fujian (福建) in southern China. His father worked for a plantation owned by the British colonist Forbes Scott Brown. After some English schooling in Penang, Gu went to Scotland for further education in his teenage years. He acquired a systematic European school education, excelling in Latin, and then moved to the University of Edinburgh to study the arts and humanities. After graduation, Gu traveled in Europe and became proficient in German, French, and Italian. He also studied German literature, immensely admiring Goethe. Gu returned to Asia in 1879 and worked in British offices in Beijing, Singapore, and Hong Kong.[42]

In Singapore, Gu met Ma Jianzhong (马建中), a Chinese government official en route from India back to China. As Wen Yuan-ning narrates, Gu and Ma sat down, "drinking wine and conversing in fluent French in one of the rooms of the Strand Hotel at Singapore."[43] They spoke French because Gu couldn't speak Mandarin Chinese at that time and Ma, a converted Roman Catholic, was educated by the Jesuits in France.[44] This conversation with Ma was so transformative for Gu that he immediately decided to study more Chinese thought and abandon the "imitation Western man" he had become.[45] Gu went to China and worked as a private secretary to Viceroy Zhang Zhidong (张之洞), one of the most powerful late-Qing viceroys and a Confucian scholar, from 1885 until Zhang's death in 1909.

Gu's writings, mostly in English, commenting on contemporary Chinese and Western affairs, articulate his unperturbed insistence on Confucianism as the ultimate body of ethical and political teachings for China and the world to solve wars and conflicts. Given Gu's colonial background and European education, his promotion of Confucianism is not merely a loyalist ultra-conservatism favoring the monarchy, a position represented by some Qing aristocrats and their followers. It is instead a consciously chosen attitude geared toward creating a cultural, not necessarily a national, identity that is neither Western nor colonial, but anti-colonial, Confucian, and cosmopolitan, as I will demonstrate. Just as Gu stated, in the passage quoted earlier, that he no longer wanted to remain "an imitation Western man," he developed from a colonial subject, who is "almost the same, but not quite," to a cultural theorist who insists on a lifestyle that is philosophically permeated with the alternative mode of Confucian thinking represented by Qing China.[46] It is Gu's conscious decision to reject Western modernity in the most resolute way. The historian Chunmei Du describes Gu's identity transformation as problematic because he projected onto China an ideal antidote to the West while, as history shows, China had become dependent on the West. Du argues that Gu needs this idealized China to construe his psychological self-image as an authentic Chinese Confucian literatus to resist the West, which turns out to be a futile attempt.[47] Du also questions the label of Gu as a "cultural conservative" and prefers to define him as a "cultural amphibian" who transcends "the dichotomous characterizations of Eastern and Western, conservative or radical, traditionalist or modernist, and nationalist or cosmopolitan."[48]

I propose instead that the intellectual value of Gu's thinking should not be easily dismissed as futile. Even though the conservatism that Gu and others represented could not have prevented the Qing Dynasty from losing wars to Britain, France, or Japan in the nineteenth and early twentieth centuries, his intellectual vigor sustains its impact in later times and offers a powerful alternative of resistance to Westernization. Gu's conscious change of identity sets an unprecedented example in detouring from the mainstream Westernization in China to experimenting with a different pathway toward liberation from the logic of imperialism and subjugation. He consciously and realistically decided to pay homage to a declining social and moral order that does not harm others but reminds them of an alternative vision of the world. Hence Gu is not merely an amphibian residing on both sides of the East and the West; rather, he has created his own idiosyncratic position as an anti-colonial Confucianist.

Indeed, Gu shows that he is well aware of the failure of Qing China in facing Western imperialism in *The Story of a Chinese Oxford Movement* (1910). There he offers a political historical commentary on the "the party of National Purification," which is historically known as the "Pure Stream Group" (qingliu dang, 清流, or qingliu pai, 清流派). This group was a circle of officials and intellectuals surrounding the viceroy Zhang Zhidong and was active in the decades around

1900.⁴⁹ Gu counted himself as a member of this group and regretted its failure to achieve "the final victory for our cause, the cause of Chinese civilisation against modern European ideas of progress and new learning." (4) As the name suggests, this circle of officials insisted on the strict observation of Confucian moral principles without compromise in domestic politics and promoted the use of force in foreign affairs toward European and Japanese imperialism.⁵⁰ Most famously, Zhang and his circle proposed the development of Western industrialization without losing the foundation of Confucian moral values.

Zhang proposes an integrated pedagogy of Western and Chinese learning in his widely read book *Exhortation to Learning (quanxue pian*, 劝学篇, 1898; translated into English as *China's Only Hope*, 1900) but stresses that, while "both are imperative, . . . we repeat that the old [Confucian learning] is to form the basis and the new [Western learning] is for practical purposes."⁵¹ By "basis," Zhang means the foundation of ethics, social structure, family relations, and the political system. The new learning should only serve the need for better technology and weaponry. The hierarchy between Confucian and Western learning is set in a clear order; Confucianism is to remain the philosophical and moral foundation. While Zhang established schools to teach Western science and European languages and developed industries of machine-driven production, he was committed to traditional monarchism and was against the Hundred Days' Reform that attempted to introduce constitutional monarchy in China. Zhang's effort, however, could not prevent Qing China from losing the Sino-Japanese War (1894–95) and the Boxer Rebellion (*Yihequan* or *Yihetuan*, 1899–1901) to Western troops.

The Welsh Christian missionary Griffith John comments on Zhang's effort:

> He [Zhang] rests his hope on two things—namely, the renaissance of Confucianism and the adoption of Western science and methods. . . . The enthusiasm of the Viceroy for Confucianism is natural and doubtless very sincere. What he needs to see is that Confucianism is effete and altogether too weak to bear the weight of a reformation such as he desires. . . . Christ alone can save China.⁵²

Gu sharply attacks this type of Christian imperialism and argues that Christianity offered moral force in Europe for "controlling human passions," but the First World War has shown that "Christianity has become ineffective as a moral force."⁵³ Confucianism will offer the moral ground for the entire world: "The study of the Chinese civilisation, of Chinese books and literature will . . . be of benefit to all the people of Europe and America."⁵⁴

Gu compares the Oxford Movement in the Church of England to the Pure

Stream Group and draws a parallel between a Christian conservative movement in the nineteenth century and a Confucian restoration movement in a China that is facing Western intrusion, warfare, and internal unrest. Gu states that, like the Oxford movement in the Anglican Church, the "Chinese Oxford movement was also directed against Liberalism, against the modern European ideas of progress and new learning."[55] Yet unlike Keyserling's, Gu's distaste for liberalism is not only associated with aristocratic status and nostalgia for lost privilege; rather, Gu is more invested in a decolonial attitude, promoting a non-Western model of society. In China, he argues, although there is no legal constitution as in the West, Confucianism is a moral constitution, and this moral constitution justifies aristocratic rule. He also completely dismisses the Hundred Days' Reform and calls it Chinese Jacobinism because it is "the wholesale Europeanization of China."[56] At the same time, Gu also promotes the reform of Chinese monarchism from within, not only for "a new China . . . but . . . for civilisation and humanity."[57] Gu's anti-liberalism is not necessarily a rejection of republicanism per se but of its Western origin in the time of imperialism. Gu argues that the reform should be done under the leadership of a "foreign-educated Chinese . . . who can combine in himself a true sense for the moral worth and beauty of the old Chinese civilisation with an aptitude for interpreting and understanding the expansive, progressive ideas of the modern European civilisation."[58] Gu clearly meant himself to be such a leader. His praise of the progressiveness of some European ideas interestingly contradicts his critique of Western modernity. Hence Gu does not dismiss all things Western. Rather he was against those elements in Western culture, such as the Christian mission, closely associated with colonialism and imperialism.

Indeed, Sun Yat-sen (孙逸仙, 1866–1925), highly regarded as the father of modern China and the leader of the Chinese Revolution that overthrew the Qing Dynasty, was strongly influenced by Christian missionaries whom he met as a teenager in Hawai'i and by whom he was baptized. His revolutionary ideas to radically change China and establish a Western-style republic can be attributed to his Christian education.[59] For Gu, however, China does not necessarily need such a republic. Rather, the world needs more diverse ways of life and social organizations. Thus, Gu's monarchism contains two forces: a negative force rejecting Western imperialism and a positive force promoting a cosmopolitanism based on Confucianism, a world without Western colonialism or militarized modernity. Gu's anti-liberalism, like his promotion of Confucianism, reflects his anti-colonial and anti-Western attitude.

Gu's support of the Qing dynasty, as the literary and cultural studies scholar Lydia Liu argues, has often been seen as his nationalism. Liu comments that Gu's attempt to trade the identity of a colonial subject for that of a Qing nationalist is ineffective because of "the conceptual limits of the sovereign state as the realm of freedom."[60] Liu takes seriously the colonial identity of Gu as the origin from which Gu has departed, but, like Du, Liu does not seem to recognize Gu's devotion to Confucianism as his opposition to Western imperialism. Liu concludes: In a poignant way, his battle was lost not so much to the British as to the nationalist revolutionaries who overthrew the Qing dynasty in 1911 to establish a new Republican state."[61] It certainly makes sense to point out Gu's practical mistake in misunderstanding the Qing dynasty as a viable regime. Nonetheless, the thrust of Gu's vision moves beyond nationalism and has a cosmopolitan and even utopian quality that imagines an alternative, non-Western path promising human dignity, reciprocal respect, equality, and social justice, not only in China but in the entire world. Hence Gu's anti-colonial turn did not necessarily transform into a narrow Chinese nationalism; rather, it turned into an anti-imperialist and anti-Western impulse. I certainly do not mean hereby to excuse Gu's anti-liberalism. Rather, I aim to explain a historical figure's intellectual position from an angle that could become productive for today's decolonial efforts.

Toward the end of *The Story of a Chinese Oxford Movement*, Gu discusses three previously used strategies for undermining Western technological modernity and their disadvantages. The first strategy is to block the tramways in Shanghai, which symbolize Western technology in China: to "stand on the streets, and challenge the tram car driver to stop running or run over his or their bodies."[62] This is the tragic example of the Boxer Rebellion, because one would then "become a mangled corpse."[63] This strategy is thus not applicable. The second way is to enter into economic competition and found one's own tram company to financially undercut the tramway run by Western powers. Zhang Zhidong tried this route but failed, Gu comments. The third way is to boycott everything European, the strategy that Leo Tolstoy had advised China to pursue in an open letter to Gu.[64] Gu declares boycotting ineffective because it is "a selfishness and an immoral tyranny" that does not forcefully engage in correcting the wrong and will never truly reform an institution.[65]

The fourth path of Confucianism, he argues, is the most effective one:

> That, I say, is Confucius' method of stopping a social or political evil and reforming the world, namely, by gaining or acquiring moral force, through a life of self respect

[*sic*] and integrity. Confucius says: "The moral man by living a life of simple truth and earnestness alone, can help to bring peace and order, help the cause of true civilisation in the world." (君子笃恭而天下平) This then, I say, is the force, the only force upon which the Chinese nation will have to depend, in order to save their ancient civilisation, from the destructive forces of the materialistic civilisation of the nations of modern Europe.[66]

Gu imagines an ethical perpetual peace that is constructive in establishing a cosmopolitan order contributing to everyone's benefit; it is neither a national order for China nor an imperialist order that is only beneficial to one part of the world or the elites of a given society. Gu criticizes the imperialism of the British statesman Joseph Chamberlain (1836–1914) because it merely serves the needs of the British Empire and does not promote the civilization of the world. A "good imperialism," according to Gu, should promote good government and world civilization. Thus, Gu considers Confucian cosmopolitanism a better option than Chamberlain's destructive British imperialism. True Confucian constitutionalism proves a superior form of world government. World peace could only come to fruition if European colonialism and imperialism stopped spreading.

The popular English novelist Somerset Maugham visited Gu Hongming as a philosopher of international repute in 1921. Gu sarcastically belittled European racism, imperialism, and mechanical technology and projected a Confucian victory in the future. Maugham took an instant dislike to Gu and described him as a "pathetic figure" in his travel writing *On a Chinese Screen*.[67] As this anecdote shows, Gu's Confucian cosmopolitanism and critique of imperialism also met with resistance in the West. Hence the friendly and fruitful encounter between Keyserling and Gu was by no means a matter of course. Even though Gu and Keyserling have very similar thoughts and share hybridity of background, their motivations are different: one is a former ruling-class aristocrat, melancholic over his loss, while the other is a former colonial subject who has turned to debunking Western imperialism. While Keyserling's Confucian cosmopolitanism has a stronger monarchist tendency, Gu's thinking contains a decidedly anticolonial impetus directed against Western imperialism. Yet Keyserling's openminded appreciation of Chinese culture and his identification with the Confucian ethic's internal strength enable him to endorse Gu's anti-imperialism. Thus, they both see the necessity of preserving the diversity of human civilization and cultivating a transcultural literacy that welcomes borrowing and mutual benefits instead of imposing monolithic imperial subjugation. More importantly, for our purposes here, their intellectual connection through Confucianism provides a fresh perspective for a global intellectual history beyond the received cultural boundary between the East and the West as well as the political divide between conservatism and progressivism; it enables us to imagine an alternative coordinate in intellectual history and to appreciate Keyserling and Gu's conscious assertion of a Confucian world order. These two thinkers represent neither the East nor the West; they both embrace a cosmopolitan and anti-imperialist vision based on Confucianism.

As mentioned in the introduction, Keyserling took Gu's influence and his own ideas about Confucian cosmopolitanism back to Europe, especially to the home of the German sociologist Max Weber. Weber's understanding of Confucianism astoundingly echoes that of Keyserling.

2

RE-ENCHANTING CONFUCIANISM:
MAX WEBER, CARE OF THE SELF,
AND CHARISMA

Max Weber's critique of rationalization in capitalist economy, parliamentary politics, law, religion, and culture in the West has become one of the most foundational theses of social and cultural theory to date. A major thinker of the twentieth century, Weber is probably better known as the source of a set of controversial Weberianisms. His name is burdened with ideological and political interpretations from different sides. To name just a few: while recognizing Weber's effort in establishing parliamentary democracy in Germany, the historian Wolfgang J. Mommsen critiques Weber for imperialism, nationalism, and an undifferentiated concept of charismatic leadership.[1] The Frankfurt School philosopher Herbert Marcuse accuses Weber of connecting rationality to the destiny of the West and Bismarck's Germany and deplores Weber's distance from the socialist movement.[2] More recently, Weber has also become a target of decolonizing scholarship and has been critiqued for his Eurocentric institutionalism as well as the cultural-racist and national-chauvinist statements that he made about Polish laborers in Germany in his 1895 Freiburg inaugural address.[3] Since the end of the global Cold War, Weber's thesis in *The Protestant Ethic and the Spirit of Capitalism*, that the Protestant rationalist work ethic and asceticism were necessary preconditions to industrial capitalism, has often been taken as justifying Western cultural and economic superiority and has accordingly been questioned and dismissed. At the same time, however, Weber's scathing criticism of Protestant rationalism and his pessimism toward Western capitalism have not been properly recognized by these scholars. Jürgen Habermas comments in his study of communicative reason that Weber is the only classical sociologist who broke with the premises of eighteenth-century historicism and nineteenth-century evolutionism and understood European modernity not as a unique phenomenon of the West but as a result of the world historical process of rationalization.[4] To place Weber in the context of global intellectual history not only reveals my attempt at highlighting interrelation and co-creation of ideas between Europe and China, but also reflects his own wish of seeking liberation from the Protestant ethic, pursuing a well-balanced rationalism through Confucianism, and imagining an aesthetic way of life as world culture.

Indeed, Weber was actively looking to other cultures such as China for an alternative rationalism to Protestant ethic that has enabled capitalism, exemplified in his treatise *Confucianism and Taoism* (*Konfuzianismus und Taoismus*, 1915/1920). There he glimpsed a social and spiritual order from the perspective of the individual, something he calls a way of life (*Lebensführung*). Weber's statement about the unique combination of Protestantism and capitalism is thus not necessarily self-congratulatory praise of the West but rather a critique. Set at the conjunction of Chinese intellectual, religious, and economic history, *Confucianism and Taoism* has been read by some as a sociological study that evidences Weber's thesis about rationalist capitalism and its absence in China. In this case, scholars either positively recognize it as another proof of Western superiority (as does Talcott Parsons), analyze it as Weber's contribution to comparative cultural theory, or critique its Eurocentrism.[5] Other scholars see *Confucianism and Taoism* as a study of Chinese civilization; they have either criticized its limit of sources, erroneous details, lack of insights, and its Eurocentrism, confirmed as a correct study, or admired its comparativism.[6] But Weber's critics as well as his defenders generally agree that his thesis about Protestantism and capitalism is meant to prove the superiority of European culture and that this work conversely shows that Confucianism prevents China from having capitalism and becoming modern.

This chapter focuses on Max Weber's book publication *Confucianism and Taoism* (1920) and explores two major aspects in this work: the economic ethic and the care of the self; and charisma and politics. These two aspects represent key areas of life and society, which Weber aimed to liberate from the radical rationalization based on Protestant ethics. In the first section, I read *Confucianism and Taoism* along with *The Protestant Ethic and the Spirit of Capitalism* (*Die protestantische Ethik und der Geist des Kapitalismus*, 1905) and argue that Weber considers Confucian rationalism a more balanced ethics because it tolerates Taoist magic and irrationalism, whereas Protestantism completely rejects magic and irrationalism, which are part and parcel of humanity. Michel Foucault's notion of the care of the self in the 1980s echoes Weber's pursuit of individual and social freedom from the constraints imposed by the Protestant ethic. In the second section, I explore Weber's definition and depiction of charisma in *Confucianism and Taoism* and read it along with his famous speech *The Profession and Vocation of Politics* (*Politik als Beruf*, 1919). I argue that Weber saw in Confucian literati a model of charismatic political leaders and developed an ethic of responsibility for contemporary politics in Germany and elsewhere. Weber did not mean to replace Protestantism with Confucianism. Rather, he was in search of a universal rationalism as the foundation for a world culture.

CONFUCIAN CARE OF THE SELF

In a rare, genuinely comparative response to Weber's thesis, Yu Ying-shih (余英时) explores the Weberian question about religion and economics in China from the sixteenth to the eighteenth centuries, a period before the onset of Western influence in the nineteenth century. In *Religious Ethics and Merchant Spirit in Early Modern China* (中国近世宗教伦理与商人精神), Yu argues that, like Protestantism, the three major spiritual orientations in China—Buddhism, Taoism, and Confucianism—also promote an ascetic work ethic, frugality, and honesty; all three have profoundly influenced Chinese merchants during the Ming and Qing periods, with reformed neo-Confucianism exerting the strongest appeal. Unlike Weber, Yu disputes the determining force of religion in economic behavior.[7] He reflects that religions, ethical systems, and social theories are not necessarily tailored to serve the needs of a social group; sometimes they could be used and directed in ways contrary to their original purposes. Yu thus grants more agency to the merchants who use neo-Confucian ethics for their own profit instead of interpreting their economic zeal as religious passion, as Weber does. Yet Yu considers that, although Weber's thesis might be one-sided and his statements about China factually erroneous, his question about the correlation between spirituality and economy is meaningful.

Yu's distance from the controversial question about Weber's Eurocentrism and capitalist superiority urges us to take a step back and explore the critical intention of Weber's thesis and its historical background. Indeed, if we look more closely at *The Protestant Ethic* and *Confucianism and Taoism*, we notice that Weber was interested in putting Western modernity in perspective, critiquing Protestant rational asceticism's restriction and control, and seeking a liberation from it. It is time to reread these works, abandoning the Cold War and nationalistic perspectives that for decades overdetermined their interpretation.

The incompleteness of the English translation of *Confucianism and Taoism* also contributes to a possible misunderstanding about Weber's sociology of religion in the English-speaking world and beyond. A brief overview of the publication and translation of Weber's treatises will establish the frame for my discussion. Around ten years after the publication of *The Protestant Ethic* (1904/1905), Weber started publishing three major studies under the title *The Economic Ethic of World Religions* (*Die Wirtschaftsethik der Weltreligionen*, 1916–20) in the journal *Archive for Social Sciences and Social Politics* (*Archiv für Sozialwissenschaft und Sozialpolitik*). The first treatise, *Confucianism* (*Konfuzianismus*, 1915–16), the title of which was later changed to *Confucianism and Taoism* (*Konfuzianismus und Taoismus*) in the book publication, was followed by *Hinduism and Buddhism* (*Hinduismus und Buddhismus*, 1916–17), and finally a treatise on *Ancient Judaism* (*Das antike Judentum*, 1917–19).[8] After some hesitations about publisher Paul Siebeck's suggestion to republish *The Protestant Ethic* as a book in the first months of the World War in 1914, Weber agreed to reprint it with the other three studies under the general title *Collected Essays in the Sociology of Religion* (*Gesammelte Aufsätze zur Religionssoziologie*, 1920). The collection's aim was to place European/Western Protestantism with other major religions comparatively in one context and on equal footing. Weber, however, could only finish, revise, and submit for publication the first volume containing *The Protestant Ethic* and *Confucianism and Taoism*. The printed book came out a week before his death on June 14, 1920. The other two volumes, *Hinduism and Buddhism* and *Ancient Judaism*, were posthumously revised and published by Marianne Weber in 1921.

Marianne Weber also edited and published *Economy and Society* (*Wirtschaft und Gesellschaft*, 1921), which is considered one of the most important sociological works of the twentieth century. Yet scholars have seen discrepancies between Marianne Weber's publication and Max Weber's original intentions.[9] Broadly speaking, Marianne Weber included almost all of Max Weber's unpublished papers and fragments and divided them, rather randomly, into three parts. She also gave the collection the general title *Economy and Society* and added many other subtitles to the fragments. Max Weber's papers, however, contain various unfinished projects that do not cohere as a single work. Many difficulties in the editing process arose because of the mistakes, inconsistencies, and arbitrary choices of Melchior Palyi, Marianne Weber's assistant. Publishers and readers, however, have believed for a long time that the major life's work of Max

Weber is indeed titled *Economy and Society*.¹⁰ The editors of the most recent and comprehensive *Collected Works* of *Max Weber* (*Max Weber Gesamtausgabe*) decided to treat *Economy and Society* as an aggregate and to signal the unfinished writings so as to reflect more precisely the history of Max Weber's papers.¹¹

It is similarly unfortunate that Weber's *Collected Essays in the Sociology of Religion* were translated into English in merely fragmentary fashion and published disjointedly without regard to their interrelations. *Confucianism and Taoism* was partially translated as *The Religion of China: Confucianism and Taoism* (1951).¹² Omitted in the translation are the *Prefatory Remarks* (*Vorbemerkung*), which Weber envisioned as a general introduction to his *Collected Essays*, the *Introduction* (*Einleitung*) to *Confucianism and Taoism*, and the *Intermediate Reflection* (*Zwischenbetrachtung*) connecting the studies on China and India. These were separately translated and placed in a collection of Weber's essays or in the appendices of different English translations of *The Protestant Ethic*.¹³ The programmatic *Prefatory Remarks* that articulate Weber's understanding of a universal history and comparative cultural theory have never been placed in the original order that Weber envisioned.¹⁴ Even in the *Collected Works* of *Max Weber* (*Max Weber Gesamtausgabe*), the editors published the *Prefatory Remarks* before *The Protestant Ethic*, as it was originally placed, but separated this volume from the other three treatises on China, India, and ancient Israel. Although the order is correct, this separation departs from Weber's original intention to place Europe and the other cultures in one global context. In the *Prefatory Remarks*, Weber explicitly writes, "Two older essays have been included at the beginning," which are *The Protestant Ethic* and *The Protestant Sects and the Spirit of Capitalism* (*Die protestantischen Sekten und der Geist des Kapitalismus*, 1920).¹⁵ Most English-speaking scholars use the fragmentary *The Religion of China*, unaware of the *Prefatory Remarks*, *Introduction*, and *Intermediate Reflection*. It is thus not surprising that scholarship about *The Religion of China* in English has been more focused on examining and debating the veracity and the completeness of Weber's descriptions of Chinese traditional culture and society and on criticizing his Eurocentrism.¹⁶ Weber's global historical vision is obscured by the complex publication and translation history of his sociology of religion. The foreword succinctly and powerfully articulates Weber's conceptual framework for his comparative cultural theory and philosophy of life. Wolfgang Schluchter rightly points out, "In *China* in particular, Weber expounded a very complex argument.... It can be fully appreciated only if one views it in terms of his overall project. It has to be historically criticized, as is shown by a host of essays. However, it is also an argument the value of which cannot be measured simply by its historical accuracy in terms of today's standards. It is much more an argument establishing a direction of investigation, a specific perspective, and even more, a research program."[17]

Indeed, Weber declares in the neglected *Prefatory Remarks* that, in his book, "scholars in Sinology, Indology, Semitic studies, and Egyptology will certainly find nothing here that is substantially new. . . . It is merely to be hoped that at least they will find nothing *essential* that they would have to judge to be *untrue* to the fact."[18] He is clearly aware that he doesn't provide novel research or even a completely accurate description of these cultures because he is only confined to translated sources, whose number is still very small, and secondary literature, which often contradicts each other. Hence, he has to remain modest about the value of his achievement, and only the expert may have the last word. Furthermore, Weber also avoids situating cultures in a hierarchical order of values (*Wertverhältnis*). Weber remarks that those who are not humble enough when facing the seas and the high mountains (*vor dem Anblick des Meeres und des Hochgebirges*) of other cultures have little respect and distance (*Distanzlosigkeit*) for the object.[19] Weber's metaphors reveal his effort to remain neutral and respectful in his interpretation and his intention to treat Christian and non-Christian cultures equally. Moreover, toward the end of *Prefatory Remarks*, Weber reveals his skepsis toward the idea of inheritance (*Erbqualität*) as a means to explain his question of why industrial capitalism emerged in the West. He argues that even if he highly regards the theories of biological inheritance (*biologisches Erbgut*), race neurology (*Rassen-Neurologie*), and race psychology (*Rassen-Psychologie*), for now, he still considers it necessary to follow the path of sociological and historical studies to explore the influences and causalities of certain reactions to human fates and social environments. Eventually in the future, Weber concludes, the race-based sciences could offer some satisfying results; but it would be an immature renunciation of meaningful insights if one shifted the problems to this still unknown terrain.[20]

The ultimate goal of Weber's sociology of world religions lies in finding another type of rationalism in other cultures, especially in classical Chinese Confucianism, as an alternative to Western Protestant rationalism. Weber frequently uses the individualistic notion of *Lebensführung* (the way of life) instead of collective concepts such as the social order or the world system as a vantage point from which to critique capitalism or imagine a better life.[21] Hence Weber's interpretation of Confucianism also betrays his individualistic philosophy of life. In the ensuing pages, I will first discuss Weber's *The Protestant Ethic* from the perspective of his critique of rationalism. Then I will show that Weber understands

Confucianism as a rational ethical system that tolerates the magical thinking of Taoism. Weber nostalgically imagines the lifestyle of classical Chinese literati in terms of holistic beauty. In allusion to Michel Foucault, I will call Weber's philosophy of life a Confucian care of the self.

CAPITALIST RATIONALISM OR PROTESTANT IRRATIONALISM

For Weber, a highly rationalized practice of life (*Lebensführung*) plays the key role in the emergence of industrial capitalism in the Occident. This rationalism is deeply embedded in Protestantism, especially Puritanism, and instills the internal control of the mind and a sense of ethical responsibility. For Weber, sciences, music, architecture, painting, officialdom, parliamentary politics, and legal systems are permeated with Protestant rationalism. All these areas construe Western capitalism, the most fatal power of our modern life (*schicksalsvollste Macht unsres modernen Lebens*).[22] Weber claims that, even though early capitalism and (proto-)capitalist enterprises have existed in such cultural spheres as China, India, Babylon, and Egypt, as well as in other historical periods such as the Middle Ages, the rational capitalist organization of formally free labor, with the essential development of the separation of household from business and rational accounting, exists in the modern West alone.[23] Hence, rational socialism, Weber contends, also only exists in the West, as do the bourgeoisie, the proletariat, and their class struggle.

Yet Weber does not claim Western superiority at this point. Instead, Weber claims that he intends to write a universal history of culture (*Universalgeschichte der Kultur*) around the central question of the emergence of bourgeois industrial capitalism and its rational organization of free labor.[24] Weber asks why capitalist interests did not lead the arts, sciences, politics, and economy toward the path of rationalization (*Rationalisierung*) in China, India, or other cultures as was the case in the Occident. The reason, Weber argues, lies in a special type of rationalism. It is neither technological rationalism nor juridical rationalism, but rather is economic rationalism practiced as a spiritual way of life (*Lebensführung*) that fundamentally defines Western industrial capitalism—it is a rationalism based on Protestant ethic.[25] Weber does not intend to claim the superiority of the Protestant ethic; rather, he plans to critique it later in his treatise and sees it as having impeded the West from having a balanced way of life. In Chinese Confucianism, Weber sees a better rationalism.

Because of the lack of coherence in the publication and translation of Weber's papers, Weber's statement about the uniqueness of Protestant asceticism in the

West has met with counterarguments. In East Asian history, as mentioned previously, Yu's study demonstrates an ascetic ethics in Confucianism and Buddhism and the mutual influence between neo-Confucian ethics and economic behavior in early modern China. Tetsuo Najita's *Visions of Virtue in Tokugawa Japan* also delineates merchants' pursuits of intellectual and ethical stature in the eighteenth century, as represented by the flourishing Osaka merchant academy Kaitokudō. Najita shows that, despite their traditionally low social status, important merchants were able to influence politics and shape the Tokugawa political economy.[26] Merchant scholars argued for a universal natural virtue "in which all human beings, regardless of class, possessed the capacity to know, albeit in relative degrees, the form and substance of external moral and political norms."[27] Najita comments that the Osaka merchant scholars used the idea of universal virtue and other doctrines from Chinese neo-Confucianism to develop Tokugawa Confucianism and the "merchant way"—*Chōnin dō* (商人道), a symbiosis between economy and ethics expressed similarly in both early modern China and Japan.[28] Yu and Najita demonstrate that the economic rationalism observed by Weber might not be a uniquely Western way of life but a phenomenon that appears in various versions at different global locations. But unlike Yu and Najita, Weber critiques Protestant ascetic restrictions and seeks liberation from them.

In *The Protestant Ethic*, Weber observes that the English, Dutch, American, and German Protestants practiced religious asceticism while diligently pursuing economic profit. The common perception that Protestants enjoy life's pleasures more than Catholics is not necessarily true, he says. He shows the inner affinity between the seeming oppositions of Protestant ascetic piety and capitalist business rationalism.[29] Weber uses a passage from the American Benjamin Franklin's *Advice to a Young Tradesman* (1748) and defines the Protestant spirit as a pure work ethic, something apparently formally dissociated from any direct relation to metaphysical religiosity.[30] The ethic holds that

> the acquisition of money, and more and more money, takes place here simultaneously with the strictest avoidance of all spontaneous enjoyment of it. The pursuit of riches is fully stripped of all pleasurable . . . , and surely all hedonistic, aspects. Accordingly, this striving becomes understood completely as an end in itself—to such an extent that it appears as fully outside the normal course of affairs and simply irrational, at least when viewed from the perspective of "happiness" or "utility" of the single individual.[31]

Weber points out that the radical exclusion of every bit of the enjoyment of life betrays a fanatic irrationalism. The seemingly rational profit-driven behavior turns out to be irrational because of its religious roots in Protestantism. Indeed, the phrase in the title "the spirit of capitalism" is an oxymoron because capitalism is deemed rational while religion, irrational. This rationally irrational work ethic, Weber avers, only exists in the modern West, while early capitalism existed in other parts of the world and in the past. Yu and Najita have shown that China and Japan might show a different set of results. Making more and more profit does not seem to be correlated with any religious purpose on the surface. Yet, for Weber, this seemingly secular ethic discloses a religious zeal that seeks salvation in work and profit. Gaining profit is understood as a divine mission, as a service to God, by the Protestants. It has become a purpose for itself (*Selbstzweck*), an enchanted disenchantment, and a hidden paradox in modern capitalism.

While Weber acknowledges that the capitalist work ethic could have been part of the process of Enlightenment rationalization and secularization that started in the eighteenth century, he still endeavors to show the religious undercurrent of this ethic, arguing:

> Thus it appears that the development of the "capitalist spirit" can be most easily understood as one component part in a larger and overarching development of rationalism as a whole. . . . However, as soon as one seriously attempts to formulate the problem of the development of the spirit of capitalism in this way, it becomes clear that such a simple approach to this theme is inadequate. The reason is that the history of rationalism *by no means* charts out a progressive unfolding, according to which all the separate realms of life follow a *parallel* developmental line.[32]

Weber presents a complex understanding of temporality. While he does not completely denounce a linear, teleological, historical development of rationalism, he insists on a more nuanced observation of different developments in various areas of social life.[33] Even if one social realm such as the economy has become extremely rationalized in Britain, other realms such as private law remain underdeveloped.[34] Hence economy does not necessarily determine other areas of life. This marks a major difference between Weber and Marxian political economy. When Weber started his teaching career in economics at the University of Freiburg in 1894, the year in which the third volume of Marx's *Capital* appeared, two major conflicts existed in the discipline: one conflict of method between history and theory and one conflict of content between subjective and objective value. Wolfgang Schluchter comments that while the Marxists were mostly followers of the theoretical and objective direction, Weber took a historical and empirical move so that he did not reduce economic value to either internal motivation of needs or external conditions.[35] Weber's *The Protestant Ethic* can be read as a critique of Marxist historical materialism and its dialectical epistemology of totality. Weber characterizes Marxist historical materialism as "naïve" because the capitalist spirit emerged before modern capitalism, at least in Franklin's birthplace, Massachusetts. Hence ideas are not merely mirroring economic circumstances, as historical materialism understands it.[36] Weber is skeptic toward the materialist theory that ideas are the superstructure of economic basis. He states that, at least in the colonies in New England, the capitalist spirit preceded capitalist materialist development. Religion played a key role in economic life there. Hence Weber concludes that neither the one-sided materialistic nor the one-sided spiritual explanation is sufficient as a cultural and historical exegesis. Weber contends that one can't reduce complex social and historical phenomena to only one working formula. Yet one has to admit the supporting as well as the impeding influence of Christianity on capitalist development.[37] The separation between church and state is for Weber illusory. Schluchter, however, argues that Weber believes in the possibility of a partial or perspectival understanding of history because partiality reflects the totality of reality. Hence, in *The Protestant Ethic*, Weber intentionally practices a one-sided and less realistic reading of the impact of religious faith on the economy in reply to Marx's historical materialism of development.[38] Schluchter comments that Weber's later works, however, are more balanced and evince both materialist and idealist approaches.

Weber's emphasis on spiritual and ethical impacts on economic behavior met with enthusiasm in China and Taiwan in the 1980s. The Chinese sociologist Su Guoxun (苏国勋) was a pioneer in introducing Weber's thinking to China in 1988.[39] Su reflects in 2011 that Weber's reception in China took off only in the 1980s because his emphasis on individualism and spiritual influence on the economy found no echo during the heyday of Marxism as state philosophy from the 1950s to the 1970s. The tremendous economic and social reforms in China and the economic successes of South Korea, Singapore, Taiwan, and Hong Kong have induced scholars to retrace Weberian logic and inquire about the relationship between Confucianism and the economy.[40] Tu Wei-ming argues that, from a Weberian perspective, Confucian ethics have contributed to the unique success of East Asian economies. Hence East Asia could economically develop capitalism while remaining culturally Asian.[41] Tu's argument drawing on Weber was welcomed in China in the 1980s and 1990s when China was in search of a path of economic development with "Chinese characteristics" and was eager to break down the Cold War dichotomy of socialism versus capitalism.[42] Weber's non-teleological multivalent understanding of historical transformation served this purpose well.

After disputing the Enlightenment secularism as the foundation for the capitalist work ethic, Weber claims that he will approach the notion of profession (*Beruf*), the most rationalized idea in modern capitalism, from a perspective of irrationalism. Weber connects the German word *Beruf*, derived from the verb *rufen* (to call), with the English noun "calling" and identifies the religious nature of the capitalist work ethic as a task given by God.[43] Weber argues that Luther and later Protestantism played a central role in coining the notion of *Beruf*: "As a divine decree, the calling is something that must be submitted to: persons must 'resign' themselves to it."[44] The reason he is invested in finding out the religious impacts on the qualitative formation and quantitative expansion of industrial capitalism lies in his interest in the development of modern culture (*moderne Kulturinhlate*) and material culture (*materielle Kultur*).[45] Weber now links the Calvinist Puritan asceticism to the endless capitalist hunt for profit and, at the same time, its denunciation of pleasure. Weber makes clear that Puritanism in fact plants the ascetic practice deep into the heart of social and economic life, not outside of society in a monastery or religious community. The ascetic practice of life thus is no longer treated as a religious cult but is celebrated as an achievement within society. Unwilling to work or unwilling to become rich is not merely a personal choice but rather a sin and a sign of not searching for salvation. Puritan asceticism renounces the world in that it controls the world as a monastery.[46] Weber further observes that, unlike Catholicism, Protestantism entirely renounces magic as a healing method. It is a further disenchantment of the world (*Entzauberung der Welt*), which, in its extremity, proves its irrationality and its nature as an enchanted disenchantment.[47]

In this paradox, Weber comments, work, ordained by God, has become the most important purpose for life after all.[48] Religious irrationality has transformed into a worldly enterprise infused with rational control. More specifically, this ascetic way of life forbids orgiastic enjoyment. Emotion and eroticism rarely exist in Puritan art and literature. Everything needs to have a cold purposiveness and is strictly rationed. Hence, capitalism is characterized by an excessive drive for profit paired up with an extreme frugality. Consumption and luxury are prohibited, whereas the acquisition of capital knows no limit. The accumulation of capital through ascetic compulsive saving (*Kapitalbildung durch asketischen Sparzwang*) is, however, not materialistic greed (*Habgier*); rather, it is a religious service done for divine purposes in a worldly context and defines the capitalist *homo economicus*.[49]

Even though Weber stresses that his observations are intended neither sociopolitically nor religiously to evaluate (*werten*) Protestantism, his description discloses a negative view of it.[50] He sees a "passionate inhumanity" (*pathetische*

Unmenschlichkeit) in Calvinism that drives persons toward an unprecedented inner isolation (*eine unerhörte innere Vereinsammung*).[51] Weber calls the capitalist economic order a monstrous cosmos (*ungeheurer Kosmos*), into which individuals are born and live like in a given and unchangeable cage (*Gehäuse*).[52] Like Marx, Weber uses Robinson Crusoe, the literary figure in Daniel Defoe's *The Life and Adventures of Robinson Crusoe* (1719), to illustrate his understanding of life in capitalism. Weber calls Crusoe an isolated *homo economicus* who also does missionary work alongside his insular existence.[53] He represents a predecessor of an ascetic, industrious, and frugal Protestant businessman, someone Weber calls *stahlhart*, as hard as steel.[54] Weber combines this adjective and the noun *Gehäuse* to describe ascetic capitalism as a *stahlhartes Gehäuse*, an iron cage.[55] Weber's metaphor, indeed, is not an inspiring one. The German word *Gehäuse* means "casing" or "housing," as well as a "shell for snails." It conveys a strong sense of constraint and limit, like a snail in a narrow shell. Life is not an expanding experience. Rather, life is already confined before one's birth. This shell, Weber continues, forces (*aufzwingen*) individuals to accept business standards in the context of market economy. The verb *aufzwingen*, again, betrays Weber's pessimistic view of the pursuit of freedom. Weber concludes that if one does not follow or accept capitalist standards, one is doomed to poverty and ruin. Continuing in this cultural development, the last *homo economicus* of this type would be "narrow specialists without minds, pleasure-seekers without heart; in its conceit this nothingness imagines it has climbed to a level of humanity never before attained."[56]

Weber regrets that the Faustian type of holistic humanity (*die faustische Allseitigkeit des Menschentums*), as in Johann Wolfgang Goethe's vision, is being abandoned and replaced by modern capitalist asceticism.[57] Weber's contemporary Oswald Spengler echoed Weber's sentiment of cultural pessimism and idealized Faustian humanity and called for a renewed vitality in his popular yet controversial book *The Decline of the West* (*Der Untergang des Abendlandes*, 1918–22). Spengler also expanded Weber's Goethe cult to the extent that Goethe is affirmed as the national literary icon of German culture. Like Spengler, Weber was pessimistic about Western culture and sought to find a balance between rationalism and irrationalism in other cultures.

In his treatise *Science as a Vocation* (*Wissenschaft als Beruf*, 1919), Weber discloses his skepticism about the rationalism of science. Even though Weber positively confirms to his audience science's function in clarifying thoughts, he insinuates that science does not solve or even attempt to answer the fundamental problems about the meaning (*Sinn*) and purpose of life. Weber was indirect or even innocuous with his critique of rationalism in his essay. Yet his view toward the inability of scientists or university professors to create a real community (*eine echte Gemeinschaft schaffen*) and his sarcastic conclusion, that to fulfill the duty of the day is to find and follow the devil (*Dämon*) who holds one's life's threads, both evince his pessimistic judgment of Western rationalism that gives rise to science and capitalism.[58]

This pessimism was not unique to Weber but prevalent in the world. The Chinese scholar and politician Liang Qichao (梁启超) recorded in his travel memoir *Records of the Shadow of My Heart during a European Journey* (欧游心影录, 1919) that, after World War I, European and American thinkers were deeply disappointed by Western modernity and, instead, keenly interested in looking for an alternative way of life in other cultural traditions, especially in Asian cultures. Facing the challenges posed by Western imperialism, military violence, industrial capitalism, and the downfall of the dynastic tradition in China, Liang came to share the pessimism in science and rationalism. He transformed from a courageous reformer advocating Western education and social values in China to a scholar interested in the study and dissemination of Chinese philosophical tradition, especially Confucianism, as an inspiration for the global crisis of rationalism. Liang contends that it is crucial for China to become a "cosmopolitan country for the world" (shi jie zhu yi de guo jia, 世界主义的国家).[59] (I will discuss Liang's work more in Chapter 3.) Weber's *Confucianism and Taoism*, published right after the war in 1920, not only contradicts a triumphant Eurocentric reading but also reveals that his question probably intends to seek a way out of the restricting and chaotic capitalism, which he dismissively calls an "iron cage" in the *Protestant Ethic*, and pursues a cosmopolitan and holistic vision that is still relevant for us today.[60] In Chinese Confucianism, Weber believes that he has found something exceptional.

CONFUCIAN AESTHETIC AND TAOIST MAGIC

After showing the irrationality of capitalist rationality, Weber imagines that Chinese Confucianism and Taoism offer a balanced way of life and the ideal combination for a rational practice of life. Weber does not debate the validity of calling Confucianism a religion, but he clearly understands Confucianism as a rational system of ethics that consciously tolerates the existence of magic, whereas Protestantism completely suppresses irrationality. Weber first extensively describes four sociological foundations of Chinese society: the city, the state, the administration and agriculture, and law and capitalism. Then he focuses on interpreting the charisma of Confucian literati and the role of magic in their aesthetic cultivation of life in dynastic China. Weber depicts the literati's charisma and considers it a key feature of political leadership. Weber describes that ancient documents are considered magical and the scholars of these documents the carriers of magical charisma.[61] The literati's life is filled with literature, art, and classical documents. The internal administrative order and the monarch's charismatic practice of political life depend on the expertise of the literati and their knowledge of ancient wisdom.[62] Weber is very idealistic in his description of Confucian literati that, according to his sources, the rulers in China do not win a battle because they are great warriors, but rather because they are bestowed with moral charisma by heaven.[63] I will discuss this more in the section on charisma.

Weber reports that the Chinese people see a double quality in the successful candidates in the mandarin exams in dynastic China: a learned scholar and a carrier of charisma, bestowed by heavenly grace.[64] High officials are considered to possess magical qualities.[65] Of course, the literati do not rule with pure poetry, Weber avers, and they are not well trained in mathematics. Yet the Chinese officials evince their status through their usage of canonical literary forms in the communication of government affairs.[66] Even though dynastic China did not develop a comprehensive trade policy (*Handelspolitik*) and only implemented a simple laissez-faire kind of economic policy, and even though the political power persecuted the literati several times in Chinese history, Weber concludes that the literati are always successful.[67]

Despite his euphoric description of the literati and their inherent magical quality, Weber turns to state that Confucianism is a system of rationalist ethics.[68] Confucianism promotes a moderate interpersonal relationship.[69] Weber uses the word "coolheaded" (*kühl*) to describe Confucianism, whereas he uses stronger words such as "cold" or "steel-hard" to describe Protestantism and capitalism. Weber stresses the strong rationalist characteristics of the literati's cultivation of the self and their pacifist education of the society and politics. Weber observes that Confucianism does not openly promote magic as a healing method, precisely as the Jews, the Christians, and the Puritans do not. Magic is never considered as powerful as Confucian ethical teachings, which include lifelong literary training.[70] Yet Confucianism never intends to rationalize such existing religious beliefs as Taoism, merely tolerating their existence in political, social, and cultural spheres.[71] Weber makes clear that Confucianism is always the major teaching that Chinese literati have received and accepted.[72]

In Taoism, Weber sees a crucial power of religious salvation that focuses on the practice of life.[73] Weber highlights the word *lebensorientierend* here and, once again, shows that life or the care of the self is central to his concern.[74] In Weber's view, Taoism follows two goals in its method of healing: a long life through macrobiotic diet and a positive cultivation of magic and animistic imagination (*eine positive Pflege der Magie und animistischen Vorstellungen*).[75] Life is like the possession of a spirit and macrobiotics is the care of that spirit. Weber comments that the pursuit of a long life is shared by both Taoism and Confucianism, even though they use different methods to reach this goal. Yet Taoist practice of magic is not accepted by the Confucians:

> Confucianism had erased all ecstatic and orgiastic remains from the cult and rejected them as undignified, as the Roman nobility officials did. But the practice of magic had known ecstasy and orgy here and everywhere. Wu (men or women) and Hih (men), old medicine men and rain makers have existed until the present time and are mentioned in literary works in all times.[76]

Weber connects Roman and Chinese antiquity and establishes a universal historical connection. He also asserts the existence of magic and thus connects the past to the present. Rationalism and magic are not unique in China, also existing elsewhere in the world. Weber reconciles the particular with the universal without subsuming one under another. He observes that Taoism has become deeply rooted among businesspeople in China. He comments that this connection demonstrates that economic conditions can never determine the religious orientations of a social group in any society.[77] At the same time, since magic interprets the world through geomantic divination, it prevents the development of technology, machinery, and industrialization.[78]

Observing Confucianism and Taoism together, Weber concludes that magic has never lost its effects on Confucian rationalism. Confucian literati tolerate and accept the existence of Taoism and its practice of magic. Neither Confucianism nor Taoism has any trace of the satanic power of the evil in their teachings, against which Puritanism instructs its believers to struggle for the sake of salvation.[79] To a certain extent, Weber's analysis of Taoism may be seen as a means to advance his opposition to Puritan rationalism. The attitude toward magic fundamentally contrasts Confucianism with Puritanism. Weber claims that Puritanism is the least tolerant religion, whereas Confucianism is the most tolerant one. While Weber uses the metaphor of an iron cage to describe capitalist rationalism, he uses the metaphor of a magic garden (*Zaubergarten*) to refer to Taoism.[80] He states that the most intimate tendency in Confucian ethics is to keep and maintain this magic garden.[81] Weber notes that, while Confucianism leaves the positive (*positiv*) healing power of magic unperturbed, Puritanism condemns magic as devilish (*teuflisch*) and merely considers the rational ethic as religiously valuable.[82] He states that Confucianism is the only rational ethics that least reduces the impact of irrationalism.[83] The enchantment of the world is essential to a healthy economic ethic in a society.

Weber states that, in their practice of life, typical Confucians use their earnings and savings to pursue literary education for themselves and their families. Their goal is to achieve and sustain a distinguished social status for their existence (*eine ständisch vornehme Existenz*) through an aesthetic training or *Bildung*.[84] A Puritan, however, earns much, spends little, and invests the money as capital to achieve more earnings according to the principle of ascetic compulsory saving. Confucian rationalism means rational adaptation to the world; Puritan rationalism is rational control of the world.[85] Weber understands the Puritan control of the world as a radical religious rejection of the world to serve God's will. Yet the Confucian adaptation to the world contains an aesthetic value (*ästhetischer Wert*) and a noble ideal (*Vornehmheitsideal*). Confucians aspire to become human beings of nobility and dignity (*fürstlicher Mann*), whereas the ascetic Puritans only see themselves as the instruments of God on earth.[86]

Toward the end of this comparison, Weber contends that the Chinese are able to adapt to the technologies and economy of modern capitalism. It is not a question of natural talent. In China, as in the Occident, in India, and in the Near East, similar political and economic circumstances or warfare promoted or hindered the development of modern capitalism. Hence these structural and historical conditions do not reveal the essential elements for the rise of modern capitalism in Europe and America. The spiritual undercurrent of an ethos, articulated in the practice of life, is the essential factor.[87]

THE CARE OF THE SELF

Obviously, in Weber's understanding, life should be a balanced combination of practical rationalism and the recognition of magical and supernatural healing power. Life is a perpetual cultivation of the self through learning and the acceptance of the self and the world. Weber's critique of Puritan ethic articulates his desire for more freedom and tolerance toward oneself and others at the same time. Yet Weber does not promote a radical rejection of a rational way of life as in, for example, the Nietzschean-Dionysian spirit. The care of the self, as Weber finds it in Confucianism and Taoism, is an aesthetic way of life through literature and art. Economic institutions, in the end, play a lesser role in the Weberian ideal of life.

Weber's concept of self-cultivation through the Confucian way of life points to substantial connection to the French philosopher Michel Foucault through their shared intellectual debt to Friedrich Nietzsche. Scholars who have noticed this connection have stressed analogies in their concepts of power, sovereignty, rationality, and the control of discipline and social practice.[88] Weber's study of bureaucracy and Foucault's work on prisons have often been compared to each other, as both are concerned with power's control over the individual's body and soul. However, the impact of Weber's concept of self-cultivation on Foucault's idea of the care of the self has not been much discussed. In particular, Weber's philosophy of life from the perspective of the individual, not from the perspective of collectivity, has been underemphasized. Arpád Szakolczai delineates Weber's and Foucault's similar life experiences and their relations to their works.[89] He briefly connects Weber's interest in spirituality in China, India, and ancient Israel with Foucault's explorations in ancient Greece and Rome. I take this suggestion and stress that Weber's pursuit of an alternative way of life and cultivation of the self seems to foreshadow Foucault's concept of the care of the self. Both Weber and Foucault, toward the end of their lives, turn to work on self-cultivation as liberation.

Foucault takes recourse to the ancient Greek philosophy and uses "the Socratic injunction 'Take care of yourself,' in other words, 'Make freedom your foundation, through the mastery of yourself'" to make clear his understanding of freedom within the game of power.[90] Unlike Weber, who pessimistically critiques Puritan asceticism and capitalism, Foucault takes asceticism in a more general sense. Foucault also shares Weber's distaste for the Puritan renunciation of life and the pursuit of salvation after life and sees the meaning of life in its current existence. Foucault argues that the care of the self, "a practice of self-formation of the subject," has been a neglected area of study but an important component of life in the West since the Greco-Roman period.[91] Foucault sees this practice as an ascetic one, yet "not in the sense of a morality of renunciation but as an exercise of the self on the self by which one attempts to develop and transform oneself, and to attain to a certain mode of being."[92] Foucault does not see asceticism as a constraint of something like a desire that needs to be liberated from repression and prohibition. His critique of Freud makes this point clear. Foucault suggests that the practice of freedom is a practice of ethical principles that leads to well-balanced and satisfying relationships. "Freedom is the ontological condition of ethics. But ethics is the considered form that freedom takes when it is informed by reflection."[93] In ancient Greece, Foucault contends, the care of the self was articulated through the conscious and reflected practice of freedom and ethical conduct. Only those who practice freedom ascetically take good care of themselves and enjoy freedom in good relationships. The ethos for the practice of freedom should be "good, beautiful, honorable, estimable, memorable, and exemplary."[94]

According to this understanding of freedom, Foucault contends that "power is not evil. Power is games of strategy."[95] Foucault explains that "we must distinguish between power relations understood as strategic games between liberties—in which some try to control the conduct of others, who in turn try to avoid allowing their conduct to be controlled or try to control the conduct of the others—and the states of domination that people ordinarily call 'power.' And between the two, between games of power and states of domination, you have technologies of government—understood, of course, in a very broad sense that includes not only the way one governs one's wife and children."[96] Foucault claims that it is important to study the techniques of control in these three forms. From this perspective, Weber's study of the economic ethic of world religions is a study of the form of control in Puritanism and Confucianism. Foucault writes that, if, in a society, "the control of the conduct of others is so well regulated in advance," then, "in a sense, the game is already over."[97] This statement resembles Weber's "iron cage." Foucault continues, "However, the freer people are with respect to each other, the more they want to control each other's conduct. The more open the game, the more appealing and fascinating it becomes."[98] Then in Weber's case, Confucian openness to Taoist magic promises such an open and fascinating game as an ideal practice of the care of the self in a Foucauldian sense. Foucault takes up Weber's focus on self-cultivation and develops it into his concept of the care of the self.

Foucault paraphrases that "Max Weber posed the question: If one wants to behave rationally and regulate one's action according to true principles, what part of one's self should one renounce? What is the ascetic price of reason? To what kind of asceticism should one submit?" Yet he poses "the opposite question: How have certain kinds of interdictions required the price of certain kinds of knowledge about oneself? What must one know about oneself in order to be willing to renounce anything?"[99] Obviously, Foucault places more emphasis on the knowledge of the self that regulates the choices in life as "one of the main rules for social and personal conduct and for the art of life" in ancient Greece.[100]

In Weber, the alternative to the "iron cage" is a hybrid pursuit of literary education and erudition in classical teaching with accommodation of Taoist magic and macrobiotics in an aesthetic "conduct of life."

If we place Weber in historical context, his wishful image of Chinese Confucianism and Taoism betrays a pursuit of freedom that leads away from the Protestant cultural milieu and the pessimism that followed World War I. Weber uses Chinese culture, in particular Confucianism, as methodological coordinates to navigate difference and promote a this-worldly life and the cultivation of the self in its fullest beauty and freedom. Besides his critiques of capitalism and asceticism, Weber's comparativism involves dual temporalities (in both historical development and cultural typology) and demonstrates a non-deterministic relation between economy and culture. Weber's comparative philosophy of life imagines a Confucian care of the self for the future. Finally, when we connect Weber and Foucault over six decades, we see a transition from Weber's focus on the critique of rationalism to Foucault's choice and self-knowledge in the care of the self, from capitalist asceticism to an open game of power, from Wilhelminian imperialism to neoliberal global capitalism. My reading of Weber in conjunction with Foucault intends to highlight a cosmopolitan theme in the pursuit of the freedom in self-cultivation—a vision that germinated in the early twentieth century and has remained powerful, though little discussed, until now. The cosmopolitanism of self-cultivation points beyond economic, cultural, historical, and political differences and takes the form of an aesthetically and ethically heterogeneous practice of freedom.

In the discussion about Confucian literati, I mentioned that Weber considered them as carriers of magical charisma. Even though Weber has extensively used the concept of charisma in describing the Chinese literati and the Confucian tolerance toward Taoist irrational believes and practices, the current discussion over this influential notion has not paid sufficient attention to this work. As a matter of fact, Weber's understanding of charisma based on Confucianism and Taoism offers an alternative and, probably, more productive way to use this term toward a more positive vision of politics in his famous speech *Politics as a Vocation*.

CONFUCIAN ETHIC AND THE RE-ENCHANTMENT OF CHARISMA

Weber's endeavor to diverge from further rationalization toward a more balanced direction in all these pertinent areas of life, which he calls *Lebensführung* (the conduct of life or the way of life), led him to highlight things that are intangible for rationalization such as magic, myth, ritual, and charisma. In particular, the notion of charisma not only remains a key idea in Weber's sociology of domination (*Herrschaftssoziologie*) but has also been widely used in the study of twentieth-century power and politics in mass movements, including fascism and communism, without being theoretically and systematically further developed.[101]

American social scientists and German *émigré* intellectuals often invoked charisma in a negative manner to describe the irrational or demonic leadership of Hitler, Mussolini, and Stalin.[102] These scholars interpreted fascist and communist movements as modern political "religions," sometimes without explicitly referring to Weber's work.[103] The sociologist Theodore Abel used charisma to explain the strong and almost mythical and enigmatic attraction that National Socialism exerted over its followers, and he interpreted Hitler as a charismatic prophet to the Germans. The *émigré* sociologist Hans Gerth considered the Nazi party an organization with inherent charismatic elements and Hitler a paradigmatic charismatic leader based on his dismissal of experts and his administrative favoritism. During the 1930s and 1940s the notion of charisma had been exclusively applied to European politics; starting in the mid-1950s, American scholars began to use charisma to characterize political leaders in Africa, Asia, and Latin America during the anticolonial, anti-imperialist, and nationalist movements. Kwame Nkrumah in Ghana, Fidel Castro in Cuba, Mao Zedong in China, and Kemal Atatürk in Turkey were all dubbed as being charismatic to explain their popular support.[104]

This seemingly positive turn in the application of charisma, however, is not unproblematic. After the end of World War II, the stronger tendency toward rationalization made charisma something more primitive and irrational. The *émigré* political scientist Karl Loewenstein argued that charisma could merely be applied to the pre-Cartesian West and to Asia and Africa in the twentieth century, which were still in the stage of a prehistoric mythical and religious state.[105] By the mid-1960s, charisma was almost exclusively used to describe the political leadership in Asia and Africa among American social scientists. Joshua Derman comments, "This kind of Orientalism, however, was never part of the concept of charisma as Weber originally intended it."[106] The concept of charisma has been detached from its Weberian context and taken to fulfill other ideological undercurrents. In addition to its academic usage, the notion of charisma entered the American popular discourse in the 1960s. In 1969, *Time* magazine sardonically claimed charisma as one of "the dominant clichés of the '60s."[107] American politicians were increasingly expected to possess charismatic media presence as a political tool to attract voters and execute policies. In the twenty-first century, the British historian Ian Kershaw invoked charisma yet again to describe Adolf Hitler in his famous biography of the Nazi politician.[108]

Tracing the multiplicity of the notion of charisma in its usage and connotation, I have explored how this term was originally defined and for what purpose it was developed in Weber's writings. I have found that Weber extensively used charisma to describe the Chinese emperor and Confucian literati in his treatise *Confucianism and Taoism* (*Konfuzianismus* und *Taoismus*, 1915/1920). He not only theoretically defined the key features of charisma but depicted its historical transformation with concrete examples from Chinese history. Moreover, in his famous speech *Politics as a Vocation* (*Politik als Beruf*, 1919), Weber intended to apply charisma, based on the Chinese model, to German politics at the end of World War I.[109] He called for a charismatic political leader to guide the German society out of the time of global crisis. For me, Weber's theoretical and historical exploration of charisma in *Confucianism and Taoism* serves as the foundation for his attempt to re-enchant charisma as an applicable idea in German politics in *Politics as a Vocation*. The connection between these two texts not only offers a new and important pathway to understand and interpret Weber's notion of charisma; it also breaks through the boundary between Western and East Asian intellectual traditions and makes global entanglements visible.

Regrettably, very few scholars working on charisma have paid attention to *Confucianism and Taoism* and *Politics as a Vocation*. Similarly, few scholars working on Weber's engagement with China have discussed charisma at length.[110] I thus place these texts in context and argue that Weber's engagement with Chinese classical philosophy is decisive for his conceptualization of the influential idea of charisma. Charisma is an alloy containing both Chinese and European ores. Charisma embodies and memorializes the inextricable entanglement between European and Chinese histories of ideas, as I discussed earlier about Weber's awareness that the translated sources available to him were translated and filtered information. In the ensuing pages, I will first discuss why I foreground these two texts of Weber. Then I will sketch the intellectual historical background against which Weber conceived of charisma. Weber's interlocutors include Rudolf Sohm, Friedrich Nietzsche, and neo-Kantian thinkers. In the third and fourth sections, I will interpret charisma in *Confucianism and Taoism* as well as *Politics as a Vocation* and highlight the Chinese aspect. In conclusion, I am committed to discovering global intellectual entanglements between seemingly disparate cultures such as East Asia and Europe. Key ideas such as charisma are fruits of open-minded transcultural inquiries. They are not necessarily and exclusively confined to the national and cultural background of the thinker.

PUBLISHED VERSUS UNPUBLISHED WORKS

Scholarship on Weber routinely refers to his posthumously published work *Economy and Society* (*Wirtschaft und Gesellschaft*, 1921–22) as the main source for the definition of charisma as an ideal type and its relationship to political leadership and domination (*Herrschaft*).[111] As discussed previously, *Economy and Society* rather proves to be a collection of fragmentary and unfinished work of Weber's. Among the contingent subtitles that Marianne Weber added in *Economy and Society*, "charisma" is in fact one of them. Recent research on charisma has also extensively dealt with Weber's other treatises on world religions, including *Hinduism and Buddhism* (*Hinduismus und Buddhismus*, 1921) and *Ancient Judaism* (*Das antike Judentum*, 1921), both of which were published posthumously as books.[112]

Among the works that Weber authorized for publication, *Confucianism and Taoism* and *Politics as a Vocation* were the only two texts containing extensive discussions of charisma. I am prone to prioritizing the published work as the more primary source for the discussion of charisma, given the rather random conglomeration of Weber's papers. Hugo Drochon also debates the issue of published versus unpublished texts in his study on Friedrich Nietzsche, writing, "Bernd Magnus has separated Nietzsche interpreters into two blocs: 'lumpers' and 'splitters.' Lumpers are those who take Nietzsche's writings *en bloc*, making no distinction between his published and unpublished work, whereas the splitters prioritize the published work."[113] Drochon tends to side with the splitters because Nietzsche's thoughts in the unpublished notebooks have more or less made their way into the published documents. Hence, the published work should retain a central place. In the case of Weber, I would take a similar stance and highlight Weber's two published works to discuss charisma, particularly because they have been somehow neglected in scholarship on charisma. Moreover, in my effort to enhance the visibility of global intellectual entanglement, I emphasize Weber's engagement with Chinese philosophy and, indeed, consider it indispensable for us to approach and appreciate charisma more comprehensively.

Before delving into the Chinese sources of charisma, I'd like to turn to the German intellectual sources of Weber's charisma in the works of Rudolf Sohm and Friedrich Nietzsche and to the influence of neo-Kantianism on Weber. This background is crucial to understanding Weber's interpretation of charisma in Chinese culture and his call for a charismatic leader in German politics.

CHARISMA BETWEEN UNIVERSALITY AND PARTICULARITY: SOHM, NIETZSCHE, AND NEO-KANTIANISM

It is common knowledge in charisma scholarship that Weber explicitly cited the Lutheran jurist Rudolf Sohm's book *Kirchenrecht* (*Church Law*, 1892) in *Economy and Society*. While Weber considered Sohm's thesis of the "charismatic organization" of the ecclesiastic authority of the early church meaningful, he disagreed with Sohm's claim that the relation between charisma and domination is unique and distinctive in Christianity. Weber maintained that this relation can be universally observed in many other spiritual orientations such as Judaism, Melanesian religions, and Confucianism. Not only an authority figure of a Christian church but also other leadership roles, including magicians, abbots, and political leaders, are considered charismatic.[114] Peter Ghosh comments that Sohm coined and extensively used the term "charisma" to critique the stiffening church organization. For Sohm, a Christian church should be a charismatic organization to allow creativity. Weber took inspiration from Sohm and developed "charisma" into a remarkable sociological category.[115] David Norman Smith points out that the way in which charisma has been widely but uncritically used to explain dictatorship rather reflects Sohm's understanding of charisma as a bestowed quality of divine grace. Smith argues that Weber, however, saw charisma as the result of public projection on political leaders.[116] Yet, as I will show in the next section, Weber's charisma is not only an irrational public belief in a politician but a personal quality, a creative energy, and a confidence in ethics.[117]

Weber, however, did not refer to Sohm in *Confucianism and Taoism* and *Politics as a Vocation*, the two published works. I assume that the reason lies in the political opposition between Weber and Sohm. The Social Democratic Party was legalized in 1889 and started to gain broad popularity and influence. In April 1890, the Protestant High Consistory called upon the clergy in Germany to curb the development of social democracy. The Evangelical-Social Congress was founded in May. Weber and Sohm were both elected Congress members, "Weber among the liberals and Sohm on the right."[118] Sohm published *Kirchenrecht* in 1892 to elaborate his political position on moral evangelism. Hence Weber might not be willing to explicitly refer to Sohm in his published works because of his political rivalries, even if he recognizes Sohm's insight in his unpublished notes.

The affinity between Weber and Friedrich Nietzsche is also well recognized because of their interest in great individuals, either as an *Übermensch* (superman) or a charismatic leader.[119] According to Wolfgang Mommsen, Weber's vision of a charismatic leader is a liberalist committed to the greater good, whereas Nietzsche's domineering superman purely seeks to achieve his own glory to fulfill his will to power. Weber's sociology of domination focuses on such a charismatic "aristocratic liberal" because his fear of bureaucratization overshadows the downside of creative charisma. "The attitude was one of heroic pessimism," Mommsen sighed, concluding that Weber, in line with Nietzsche, "did not want to see the dynamism of 'will to power' eliminated entirely from human evolution, for the concept of freedom would thereby also largely lose its meaning."[120] More recent studies on Nietzsche, however, point out that the idea of a superman is not necessarily an individual who is hungry for power. Nietzsche's superman essentially means a self-overcoming either at the individual level or at the species level in order to reach a harmony of philosophy and culture, as the Greeks exemplified.[121] From this perspective, Weber's call for a charismatic leader who could direct German society away from the one-sidedness of rational bureaucratization does not contradict Nietzsche's vision of a more optimized human individual and society. Rather, Weber continues Nietzsche's legacy. Indeed, Nietzsche's critique of abstract rationalization and his endorsement of myth, as he makes clear in *The Birth of Tragedy* (1872), unambiguously resonates with Weber's work. Similarly, neither Weber nor Nietzsche advocate a revolutionary overthrow of state authority. Instead, their ideals of a superman and a charismatic leader are reformative.[122]

Unlike in Sohm's case, Weber explicitly refers to Nietzsche's *Will to Power*, *Beyond Good and Evil*, and *On the Genealogy of Morals* in *Confucianism and Taoism*. Yet Weber disagrees with Nietzsche's psychological analysis of *ressentiment* as the cause for the slave revolt of disadvantaged people against the ruling class—"then it would obviously result in a very easy solution for the most important problems in the typology of religious ethics."[123] Instead, Weber uses a historical approach and sees the cause in the gradual rationalization of religion that leads to the suppression of charisma and human desire in the West.

Weber's difference to Sohm in terms of generalization and to Nietzsche in terms of historical approach reveals the influence of the Southwest German School of neo-Kantianism. The philosophers Heinrich Rickert, Weber's friend from his Freiburg period, and Rickert's student Emil Lask both impacted Weber's understanding of value, culture, and knowledge. The Southwest School maintained the Kantian divisions of concept and reality, theory and history, generalization and individualization, and the rational and the irrational. They attempted, however, to overcome the gap between rational and irrational forces through the establishment of cultural science and the idea of internal value.[124] Weber, inspired by the neo-Kantian method, developed his own methodology—shaping a general ideal type and searching for its historical embodiment at the same time. Charisma is a prime example based on this epistemology, which connects an ideal type and a historical individual.[125]

Furthermore, Beatrice Centi points out that neo-Kantian thinkers aimed to grasp the universal, while, at the same time, they wanted neo-Kantianism to be a philosophy of culture and dealt intensively with the particular. "Ethics thus becomes a privileged field of inquiry, in that it displays in a particularly conspicuous manner the overarching problem of mediating between the universal and the particular, i.e., between a priori lawfulness and determinate individual reality."[126] Centi argues that, for Rickert, logic and ethics are one and the same thing: "Knowledge is an act through which the subject grasps the object and, so to speak, takes possession of it. This practical component underlies the sphere of ethics, too. The tight connection between knowing and willing consists in their being fundamental kinds of position-taking with respect to a value, that is, acknowledgments of the ought and its validity manifested in the value."[127] Weber's charisma is thus a cultural historical concept, mediating between bureaucratization and absolutism, between the rule of law and the will of an arbitrary ruler. Charisma reflects both the Kantian universal metaphysics of morals and the neo-Kantian individual embodiment of ethical practice.

Weber's separation of value (*Wert*) from purpose (*Zweck*) reflects Kant's definition of autonomy and heteronomy.[128] While value reflects an intrinsic quality, purpose proves only superficial and ephemeral. Thus, morality resides in the internal value; external purposeful actions, however, may or may not reflect moral values. Charisma, as an inner quality and moral value, should induce political leaders to act with responsibility from the inside. An action in favor of justice should reflect the politicians' moral position; it should not stem from their practical considerations about income or hierarchy. Against this backdrop, Weber interprets Chinese emperors and Confucian literati as historical examples of the ideal type of charisma.

CHARISMA, RATIONALIZATION, AND ETHICS

Truly, Weber has already used the word "charisma" in *The Protestant Ethic and the Spirit of Capitalism* (1904/1905), yet merely twice. Peter Ghosh observes that "the PE [Protestant Ethic] marks the first time Weber uses the words charisma and *rational*; but, whereas rational and its adjuncts make up a major and explicit theme, charisma is apparently negligible, and this has justified scholars in setting it aside. There are just two usages, both of which relate to the Pietists' interest in doctrines emanating from Christ's Apostles that are touched by their 'charisma.'"[129] Despite the scarcity of the term itself, Ghosh still argues for the importance of charisma in *The Protestant Ethic* because many crucial ideas are already present that will be associated with charisma in its later development, such as "personal proof" and "grace." Nonetheless, chronologically speaking, the concept of charisma receives its first intense discussion in *Confucianism and Taoism* (1915/1920).

In the introduction to *Confucianism and Taoism*, Weber claims that he aims to understand in an objective manner (*in ganz wertfreier Art*) the systems of life regulation (*Lebensreglementierung*) in six world religions—namely, the Confucian, Hinduist, Buddhist, Christian, Islamic, and Judaic ethics.[130] For Weber, historical forms of ruling do not stop in the past; they reach down to the present in their rudiments. Charismatic ruling and traditionalist ruling are the two most fundamental forms of authority. Weber defines charisma as "an . . . *extraordinary* (*außeralltäglich*) human quality." A charismatic authority is a rule "under which the ruled people submit themselves because of their belief in the quality of this certain *person*."[131] "A magician (*magischer Zauberer*), a prophet, a master of the hunt (*Führer auf Jagd- und Beutezügen*), a warrior (*Kriegshäuptling*), a so-called 'Caesarian' ruler, or a party leader" are examples of charismatic rulers in ancient times. The legitimacy of charismatic rule lies in the belief in and the devotion to the extraordinary quality of the leader.

Weber maintains that, while charisma is considered supernatural in antiquity, as registered in tales of divine revelation or heroic sagas, charisma should not be considered a permanent quality because it constantly needs to be proven true. Such a proof (*Bewährung*) is demonstrated through wonder, victory, and other successes and, most importantly, through the well-being of the ruled people. Once the effects of wonder and magic disappear and the ruler seems to be abandoned by his gods, his charisma ceases and the authority it conferred vanishes. Weber argues that rule under such charismatic leaders does not follow traditional or rational principles but depends on concrete revelations (*Offenbarung*) and divine inspirations (*Eingebung*)—a charismatic rule is thus irrational.[132] Ghosh aptly comments, "It was, above all personal, not impersonal."[133]

In addition, charismatic rule is also "revolutionary" because of "its independence from all previously existing norms (*die Ungebundenheit an alles Bestehende*)."[134] In this sense, charismatic rule is universal. It starkly differs from traditionalist rule, which Weber defines as the familiar, quotidian, and constant norm of action. Patriarchalism, Weber contends, is a typical form of traditionalist ruling because it is founded on the authority of father, husband, the oldest man in a household or in a community, the master, or the prince over their children, women, slaves, servants, and their subjects. Yet traditionalism is as irrational as charismatism because patriarchy is contingent upon the arbitrary will and mercy of the ruler as well as upon the acceptance of a set of seemingly unchanging or even divine principles, "whose violation would entail magical or religious evil."[135] In principle, traditionalism follows personal relations instead of objective rules and is thus irrational (*nur nach persönlichen, nicht nach sachlichen Beziehungen wertet und in diesem Sinne irrational ist*).[136] While traditionalism manifests a belief in the divinity of the quotidian (*Heiligkeit des Alltäglichen*), charismatic rule expresses a trust in the extraordinary (*Außeralltäglichem*).[137] These two types of rule, because of their shared irrationality, are not mutually exclusive; rather, Weber understands them as being in a historical succession. When charisma loses its divinity and gradually becomes quotidian, a set of rules is established that becomes tradition.

In Weber's analysis of the West, the disciples, apostles, and followers of a charismatic ruler transform into priests, vassals, and, most importantly, bureaucrats. In the economic sphere, a charismatically ruled community with gifts, alms, and war booty becomes a social group of people with salaried positions and granted rights who help legitimate the power of the ruler to different administrative degrees. Thus, traditionalist rule develops into a modern state with a rationalized bureaucratic structure. Jurists, Weber points out, emerged as the representative of rationalized rule of law in Europe. According to Weber, this rationalization grew out of irrational roots in charismatism and traditionalism. The movement from irrational charismatic rule to the modern bureaucratic state discloses a historical process of rationalization in the West. For Weber, charisma is first and foremost a historical phenomenon.[138] Weber's endeavor to reveal the irrational roots of the rule of law draws his readers' attention to the inherent irrationality in the routine banality of politics in Western capitalism. In China, however, Weber sees a different path for the development of charisma that leads to Confucian ethics.

Weber claims that in ancient China charisma was intimately tied to magic. Charismatic leaders were those who were endowed with a supernatural capability of expelling evil spirits and thus of protecting and healing their followers with their extraordinary spirit. Their charismatic power came from heaven: "Since the power of heaven was also the highest benign leader of the social cosmos, the *shen*-spirit in humans and in the world must be supported in their function."[139]

The earliest emperors in ancient China were such charismatic leaders. Weber comments that the emperors were fully aware of the charismatic quality of their rule, and they also knew that they needed to behave in a certain way to prove their extraordinary ability granted by heaven. Weber identifies a historical caesura in Chinese history at the moment when personal charisma became ethics—namely, when Confucianism was established as a pacifistic state philosophy and peace was restored after the warring states period in Chinese history.[140] Charisma became represented by a tradition of classical moral values that legitimized the wars waged by the kings and justified the subjugation of their enemies who had lost their charisma and had violated the ancient convention.

In Confucian China, Weber argues, "the Chinese emperor is primarily a pontifex: transformed from the ancient 'rain maker' with magical religiosity to the realm of ethics. Since the ethically rationalized heaven protected a permanent order, the monarch's charisma depended on his ethical virtues."[141] Like the Catholic pope, Weber portrays the Chinese monarch as a bridge of communication between heaven and the people—thus a pontifex. The Confucian vision of heaven, at first glance a metaphysical category, is explicated as rational by Weber, whereas he calls the rain maker magical and irrational. The charismatic Chinese emperor transformed from a shaman to an authority of ethics. While Confucianism is rational, it recognizes and accepts its inherent charismatic roots, the irrational roots in its historical genealogy. Weber's neo-Kantian epistemology induces him to present the relationship between charisma and ethics in a historical development. The rationalization of ethics is derived from something deeply irrational in origin. At the same time, Weber does not intend to synthesize charisma and rationalism into a third category. The emperor is thus both rational and irrational. Charisma connects the rain maker to the monarch. It has become less explicit, as in magic, but it is still evident in ethics. Despite historical changes, charisma remains a constant force. In addition to the emperor, Weber observes, charisma is also attached to a family or a clan in China: "The positions of minister and even certain diplomat[s], as we find out, are held firmly in the hands of some families in the Chinese Middle Ages. Confucius was also noble because he was descended from a ruling class family."[142] According to Weber, the administration from the smallest size *xian* (县) to the larger provinces in China was also organized through the recognized and dominating charisma of the local officers and their advisory boards.

More importantly, in Confucian literati, the scholar-officials, Weber has found his ideal type of the political administrator. The literati represent charismatic ethics among the commoners. Weber argues that charisma cannot be taught but may only be awakened and tested (*wecken und erproben*) through education and personal cultivation because it is an innate quality of a person. Hence the Chinese people endeavor to transmit culture, not only knowledge, to their younger generations with the hope of awakening their charisma. Their ideal is a cultivated human (*Kulturmensch*): a well-educated person consciously following internal and external principles of life (*einen Menschen von bestimmter innerer und äußerer Lebensführung*).[143] In the West, Weber contrasts, the rational bureaucratic structure of a regime is based on specialized training and disciplining and thus can be taught.

Weber euphorically describes the charisma of mandarins and praises their erudition in Confucian ethics, the essential learning that qualify them as the carriers of supernatural charisma (*Träger magischen Charismas*).[144] The literati's extraordinary ability is manifested through their success in civil exams, their writing skills in poetry, and their expertise in canonical textual genres (*kanonische Richtigkeit seiner literaturgerechten Formen*), which are indispensable for the documentation and communication of governmental affairs. After they have proven their charisma through their success in civil exams on Confucian classics, the mandarins are able to influence the life of the masses, from which they stem. Hence the literati embody charisma in their person, scholarship, and moral conduct of life:

> Despite the aforementioned strong apoliticism of the masses, the influence of the views and opinions of the officials on the way in which one conducts one's life is very important among the middle class, first and foremost, because the popular magical-charismatic understanding of the office qualification is being tested through examination. The candidate has proven with his achievement on the exam that he is the carrier of the *shen*-spirit to an eminent degree. High mandarins are considered to have magical quality. They themselves could always become the object of a cult after their death or already during their lifetime, given that their charisma is being proven and preserved.[145]

The verified charisma of the literati essentially constitutes the spirituality of Chinese society. Their charisma influences the economy and other areas of social life. The spiritual well-being of society depends on the existence of the charismatic and extraordinary ability performed and maintained by the literati. After the civil exam, the literati's charisma is expressed through their harmonious style of administration, which does not disturb nature or humanity (*ohne Störungen durch unruhige Geister der Natur oder der Menschen*).[146] Their knowledge of classical literature, their ability to write creatively, and their style of harmonious rule are the proof (*Bewährung*) of their charisma.

Weber points out that Confucius and Laozi were both officials before they became teachers and writers without office. The intimate relationship between the Confucian scholar and state power, Weber comments, is essential to Confucianism, in which political power becomes more and more centralized and embodied in the literati and their special *métier* of Confucian classics. The body politic is immediately related to Confucian ethics and scholarship. The emperor functions like an overseer of the literati's administration in the public sphere. Charisma is thus both individual and collective. While this duality of charisma remains a constant throughout history and across cultural spheres, Weber observes that it has a more harmonious and lengthy existence in Confucian China. Weber's favorable analysis of charisma and Confucian ethics in *Confucianism and Taoism* leads to his attempt to re-enchant charisma in German politics after World War I.

CHARISMA AS VOCATION

In *Politics as a Vocation* (*Politik als Beruf*) in 1919, Weber vehemently calls for a charismatic leader with an acute moral consciousness of responsibility (*Verantwortungsethik*). Weber's vision of a charismatic politician is closely associated with his description of Confucian literati. The recognition and cultivation of charisma in a modern political persona promises a better integration of the rational and the irrational forces of humanity and a more balanced social harmony.[147] German politics was in dire need of charismatic mandarins.

As the English translation of the German title reveals, Weber aims to make clear the double meaning of the word *Beruf*, meaning "profession" and "vocation" simultaneously. According to Weber, while "vocation" reflects a religious or irrational belief, "profession" reflects a product of modern rationalization. In the beginning pages of *Politics as a Vocation*, Weber briefly mentions three types of political rule: traditional rule, charismatic rule, and legal rule. Weber claims that he is particularly interested in charismatic rule: "rule by virtue of devotion to the purely personal 'charisma' of the leader on the part of those who obey him."[148] Only those who have the inner strength to lead and the external characteristics to attract followers qualify as charismatic politicians. Their leadership is not instated and guaranteed by customs, as in traditional rule, or by law, as in legal rule. They carry out politics as a vocation (*Beruf*) because they know that they are meant to be leaders based on personal qualities. Weber mentions magicians and prophets as examples of charismatic leaders whom supporters, disciples, and party members willingly follow. In the West, especially in Mediterranean culture, Weber sees in demagogues the figure of a charismatic leader. Weber's description of Confucian literati also unambiguously fits the characterization of an ideal politician by vocation in this new context.

In the West, however, professional politicians (*Berufspolitiker*) gradually took center stage as a result of the process of rationalization, the second meaning of *Beruf*. According to Weber, this type of politician didn't want to be a leader. Rather, these politicians pursued financial security for their political service, mostly at court. And they emerged in the city state (*Stadtstaat*) as a political community in the Mediterranean and lived off the politics (*von der Politik*). The nobility, however, lived for and in politics, either because they enjoyed political power as such or because they wanted to serve a cause and to give life meaning. The aristocracy thus established a plutocracy in which only wealth equaled power. Professional politicians were not necessarily wealthy and thus needed to pursue financial security through politics as a profession and to serve the aristocracy.

Weber lists five types of professional politicians. The first type is the clergy or religious personnel (*Kleriker*) in the Christian Middle Ages as well as in India, China, Japan, Tibet, and Mongolia. The second type includes scholars with a humanistic education (*humanistisch gebildete Literaten*) during the European Renaissance. The court nobility (*Hofadel*), the English gentry, and the jurists are the third, fourth, and fifth types of professional politicians, respectively. Weber highly admires the humanist scholars because they were scholars and politicians at the same time and closely resembled the Confucian literati. Hence, Weber laments the short-livedness of the Renaissance scholars in the West, in contrast to the long tradition in China:

> There was a time when one learned how to write speeches in Latin and verses in Greek in order to become the political adviser and above all the writer of political memoranda for a prince. That was the time when the first flowering of humanist schools and princely foundations of chairs of "poetics" took place. In the case of Germany this epoch passed quickly, yet it had a lasting influence on our system of education, although it was without any more profound political consequences. Things were different in Eastern Asia. The Chinese Mandarin is, or rather was in his origins, approximately the same thing as the humanist during the Renaissance period here—a man of letters trained and examined along humanist lines in the linguistic monuments of the distant past. If you read the diaries of Li Hung Chang you will find that he was most proud of the fact that he wrote poems and was a good calligrapher. This stratum,

with the conventions it developed on the model of the ancient Chinese past, has determined the entire fate of China. Our own fate would perhaps have been similar if, at the time, the humanists had had the slightest chance of establishing their influence with the same degree of success.[149]

Weber's use of the subjunctive in the last sentence reveals his nostalgic wish that the Renaissance could have led European history in a different direction like that of Confucian China. Praising the royal endowments in the study of ancient literature in Renaissance Europe, Weber highly admires the parallel East Asian phenomenon of Confucian literati and mentions as an example the Chinese viceroy and diplomat Li Hongzhang (1823–1901, 李鴻章, Li Hung-Tschang in Weber's transliteration). Li, almost a contemporary of Weber, negotiated with European powers to end warfare, directed the Chinese military during the first Sino-Japanese war, but fell out of favor after China's loss to Japan (1894–95). Li toured Europe as a Chinese diplomat and was received with the highest honor at the British court. Weber highlighted Li's wish to become a distinguished poet and calligrapher, thus emphasizing his charisma and his ability to be a scholar and a politician simultaneously. Even though Weber's source *Memoiren des Vizekönigs Li Hung Tschang* was translated from the popular but fabricated account *Memoirs of Li Hung Chang* (1913), the ambition of being an exalted literary writer and calligrapher is very common among Chinese intellectuals.[150]

While the tradition of Confucian literati has a lengthy existence in China, Weber makes clear that the jurist is a unique type of rationalized professional politician in Europe:

> A fifth stratum, that of jurists with a university training, was peculiar to the West, particularly the mainland of Europe, and was of decisive importance for its entire political structure. There is no clearer evidence of the powerful long-term effects of Roman law, as transformed by the late Roman bureaucratic state, than the fact that trained jurists were the main bearers everywhere of the revolutionary transformation of the conduct and organisation (*Betrieb*) of politics, in the sense of developing it in the direction of the rational state.[151]

Weber identifies jurists as the central force in the rationalization of state politics in the West. He traces this development back to the Roman Empire and identifies the legal tradition as the backbone of European politics. Weber observes that the rationalizing juridical spirit (*Juristengeist*) dominated the major political upheavals in Europe such as the French Revolution. In the French Convent, Weber stresses, there was only one person from the proletariat, very few (*sehr wenige*) from the bourgeoisie, but a great mass (*massenhaft*) of jurists of all kinds because, without them, it would not be possible to cultivate the specific spirit that nurtured the radical intellectuals and their social visions.[152]

Weber's critique of the jurist as the outcome of the process leading from charisma to rationalization points us in the other direction of charisma's development toward ethics. He asks, "What then is the real relationship between *ethics* and *politics*? Have they nothing at all to do with one another, as has sometimes been said? Or is the opposite true, namely that political action is subject to 'the same' ethic as every other form of activity?"[153] Weber intends to introduce the ethic of responsibility as the essence of a politician by vocation. He claims that the question of an ideal political leader "takes us into the area of ethical questions, for to ask what kind of a human being one must be in order to have the right to seize the spokes of the wheel of history is to post an ethical question. One can say that three qualities are pre-eminently decisive for a politician: passion, a sense of responsibility, judgement."[154] Weber sees judgment (*Augenmaß*) as "the decisive psychological quality of a politician" because it is "the ability to maintain one's inner composure and calm while being receptive to realities, in other words to keep distance from things and people."[155] Both heated passion (*heiße Leidenschaft*) and cool distance (*kühles Augenmaß*), yet not cold rationality, should be reconciled within a person who is to become a political personality. Weber explains that, even though politics must result from the mind, one still needs inner warmth and passion to approach politics as a mission.

While the ideal politician needs to integrate both passion and judgment within himself, the ethos of politics also requires the coexistence of rational and irrational forces in human nature. This dualistic moral economy resembles Weber's understanding of Confucian ethics that accepts the supernatural quality of charisma and the irrationality of Taoism in its belief in magic and wonder. Even though Weber is not explicitly citing Confucianism here, his line of argument reveals that he is promoting a type of politician with the quality of a Confucian literatus, someone who reconciles both charisma and ethical responsibility, irrationality and rationality, and heart and head. Such a person performs politics as a vocation: fearing no ethical paradox between conviction and responsibility and knowingly getting involved with the diabolic power of violence:

> [It] is immensely moving when a mature person (whether old or young) who feels with his entire soul the responsibility he bears for the real consequences of his actions, and who acts on the basis of an ethics of responsibility, says at some point, "Here I stand, I can do no other." That is something genuinely human and profoundly moving. For it must be *possible* for *each* of us to find ourselves in such a situation at some point if we are not inwardly dead. In this respect, the ethics of conviction and the ethics of

responsibility are not absolute opposites. They are complementary to one another, and only in combination do they produce the true human being who is *capable* of having a "vocation for politics."[156]

A politician by vocation has the integrity that guarantees the responsible use of violence and the brave acceptance of its consequences. It is the politician's charisma that is inextricably connected to the ethics of responsibility.

Weber, however, is not optimistic about the emergence of such a politician by vocation in the near future. Citing a Shakespeare sonnet (in Stefan George's translation) that praises the maturity of love in its quiet vicissitude, Weber contrasts it to German politics after World War I, which was by no means in such a euphoric phase of a flowering summer:

> Damals war der Lenz und unsere Liebe grün,
> Da grüßt' ich täglich sie mit meinem Sang,
> So schlägt die Nachtigall in Sommers Blühn,
> Und schweigt den Ton in reifrer Tage Gang.
>
> Our love was new, and then but in the spring,
> When I was wont to greet it with my lays;
> As Philomel in summer's front doth sing,
> And stops her pipe in growth of riper days.[157]

Integrating poetry into his writing, Weber imitates the style of Confucian literati, or a humanist scholar, and intentionally breaks with the rational style of academic writing. Weber changes the warm atmosphere that the poem creates by comparing the current political situation to a polar night (*Polarnacht*) and darkness (*Finsternis*).[158] He thus envisions a politician who is a hero (*Held*) in the simplest meaning of the word (*in einem sehr schlichten Wortsinn*).[159] Only such a heroic person, who braves all the difficulties with a strong heart and doesn't shatter to pieces when facing the failures of hopes, can practice politics as a vocation.

Historically speaking, Weber's discussion of charisma and ethics was deeply related to the 1917 conflict between the nationalistic and the pacifistic student groups in Munich over war and peace. When Weber accepted the invitation from the Bavarian branch of the Free Student Union (*der freistudentische Bund*) to deliver a lecture, it was clear that he needed to take a position. In *Politics as a Vocation*, Weber again identifies the problem in Protestant ethics, as he does in *The Protestant Ethic and the Spirit of Capitalism*. He calls it an absolute ethics and harshly critiques its inadequacy in solving the problem of violence. He explicitly refers to the Sermon on the Mount (*Bergpredigt*) in the Gospel of Matthew in the New Testament as an example of the absolute ethics of evangelism (*die absolute Ethik des Evangeliums*). Such an ethics would not encourage people to inquire about the cause of things and protect them against the exploitation and taxation of the state. While Protestantism absolutely refuses violence in social behavior, it unconditionally accepts violence in politics.[160]

Weber saw the paradox in the contemporary acceptance of World War I and the support for its continuation by radical socialist groups. Showing his dislike of radical socialism and social revolution as phenomena based on Protestant ethics, he was disappointed that the socialists did not strive for an economic system different from capitalism and that they instead insisted on war and violence as a means to achieve greater social justice.[161] Weber condemned the use of war because violence was deeply unethical and destructive. He was dissatisfied to see that the Bolsheviks and the members the Spartacus League, the Russian and German revolutionary socialist groups, critiqued the ancien régime and called the aristocrats "politicians of violence" (*Gewaltpolitiker*), whereas they themselves followed the same path of violence to solve social problems.

For Weber in *Politics as a Vocation*, Protestant ethics legitimizes the political state as a tool of violence (*Mittel der Gewaltsamkeit*), an absolute divine institution (*göttliche Einrichtung absolut*), and a hierarchical authority (*Obrigkeitsstaat insbesondere*).[162] He points out that Martin Luther, probably the most prominent figure in Protestantism, denied the individual right of war but legitimized that of the state. Indeed, the German writer Heinrich von Kleist's novella *Michael Kohlhaas* depicts precisely this injustice in the use of violence and portrays Luther as a questionable figure. Imitating the Confucian and humanist style again, Weber cites literary characters in novels by Tolstoy and Dostoevsky to illustrate the inner psychological conflicts between the god of love and political violence caused by the Protestant ethics of conviction.[163] Weber comments that this paradox discloses an irrationality that a believer in the ethics of conviction (*Gesinnungsethik*) cannot tolerate. The ethics of conviction, based on Protestant ethics, is an absolute ethics that presents a unidirectional result of action: good produces good and evil produces evil. Yet it fails to address inherent paradoxes concerning value and means, love and violence, and irrationality and rationality.

Weber thus prefers the ethics of responsibility, embodied by a politician by vocation, who has the ability to accept and bear unconditionally naked reality with sufficient inner strength and to ease the tension between love and violence. Charisma, inextricably associated with Weber's interpretation of Confucianism, summarizes the overall quality of a politician by vocation for future German politics.

Fritz Ringer calls Weber's ideal types "simplifications or 'one-sidedly' exaggerated characterizations of complex phenomena that can be hypothetically posited and then 'compared' with the realities they are meant to elucidate."[164] This observation accurately applies to charisma, a well-known ideal type of Weber's. Charisma is theoretically posited and historically interpreted in Chinese history. If we had not paid attention to *Confucianism and Taoism*, we would not be able to unearth Weber's rich historical explanation of charisma as a universal idea in multiple cultures and as a historical reality in Confucian China. If we had not connected Confucian charisma to Weber's vision of politics as a vocation, we would not be able to understand and appreciate Weber's attempt to re-enchant charisma to counter bureaucratization in German politics after World War I; more importantly, we would not be able to see in Weber's work the inextricable connections between China and Europe in a global context. These counterfactual statements do not mean to undermine the focus on the Western context in scholarship on charisma. Rather, by highlighting Weber's engagement with Confucian ethics, I shed light on his open-minded reception of non-Western cultures and his relentless effort to imagine and create a more balanced rationalism. The entanglement of Chinese and European thought in charisma is not a coincidence; rather, it is Weber's purposeful creation. His holistic and integrative approach to charisma sets an example for a pluralistic method and practice in social and cultural sciences.

Both Confucian care of the self and charisma in Weber's description and application provide a window through which we gain a view of transcultural entanglements in the genesis of ideas in global modernity. This view provides a complex image of history that urges us to diverge from focusing on the Western tradition as the only universalizable norm and to become open-minded, like Weber, and ready to embrace the pluriversality of the world. Weber's representation of Chinese Confucianism and Taoism is an emblem of connection and communication across cultures, languages, and histories.

In the same year that Weber delivered the speech *Politics as Vocation*, the Chinese politician and political theorist Zhang Junmai was in Paris observing the Peace Conference (1919).

3

ZHANG JUNMAI AS PHILOSOPHER: RUDOLF EUCKEN, LIFE, AND SPIRITUALITY

In 1918, I went to Europe with Liang Rengong [Liang Qichao] to observe the Paris Peace Conference. Liang wanted to unofficially observe and inspect the war sites in Europe and also hoped to regain some rights for China. We lived for about a year in Paris, during which we gave the five official representatives of China some suggestions as private persons. At the same time, we had some communications and contacts with the French government. When the question of Qingdao was solved, Liang left Paris and toured several countries. *En route* from the famous south German city Munich to Berlin, Liang suddenly recalled two European thinkers well-known in the Far East. One was the French philosopher [Henri] Bergson, and the other was the German philosopher [Rudolf] Eucken. Liang then suggested that we visit Eucken. The first time we met Eucken, his sincere attitude deeply touched me and immensely inspired my interest to study his philosophy.... When Liang returned home in 1920, I decided to move to Jena and study philosophy with Eucken, reading the history of philosophy and other related philosophical books. This encounter was the decisive moment in my turn from social sciences toward philosophy.[1]

This change of the Chinese philosopher and political theorist Zhang Junmai (张君劢, aka Carsun Chang, 1887–1969), however, did not just happen because of the visit to Eucken. More importantly, at the Peace Conference, Zhang learned that, even though China was on the side of the victorious countries of World War I, it could not regain Qingdao (青岛), a former German colony, as it was promised to China during the war. The Western powers had acquiesced in

Japan's occupation of Qingdao since 1914. Zhang then claimed to burn all his international law books because he had lost faith in justice. For Zhang, the outcome about Qingdao had made clear to him that international politics was only about power games; justice and equality were merely empty ideas of political theorists. He came to see that the weak military power of China could not produce effective diplomacy: a nation thus has to build its independence on its own strength to gain respect from other countries. Zhang used the German words *Völkerrecht* (international law) and *Völkerunrecht* (international injustice) to contrast political ideals with political practice in 1919: "I felt that the statements about justice and humanity by the politicians of the negotiating countries were all deceit. Hence thinking of the so-called international law, I now see it as international injustice."[2]

Zhang came to realize that philosophy contains the fundamental observations and analyses of movements, trends, and theories in social sciences. Philosophers are closer to the fundamental truth of the universe; they move beyond the divisions of academic disciplines and can achieve a more holistic view of life. In peaceful times, Zhang argues, people could just focus on their own work and do not need to care much about philosophy. In troubled times like his own, however, philosophy provides deeper and more comprehensive insights to understand and solve major social and political problems.[3] Thus Zhang, a political scientist by training, decided to become a philosopher after 1919. Like other thinkers discussed in this book, Zhang held philosophy, especially Confucian ethics, as a special path toward social and individual liberation for China and for the world.

Zhang clearly shows his predilection for philosophical idealism (唯心论). He is not convinced that the history of humanity is primarily based on matter; for him, material interaction and modification are not the determining foundation for subjective thinking and feeling. Zhang maintains that materialists "deny the existence of morality in the world and do not recognize that nation is a community with consciousness. They see nation as a machine oppressing the poor. Hence there is no political improvement other than seizing the ruling power by force."[4] For an idealist, however, human spirituality is the foundation for government, society, politics, law, religion, and arts and sciences. Zhang claims that, if a human being lacks spirituality and merely resembles lifeless things such as wood and stone, then there would be no individual sacrifice for the sake of community, no selfless altruism, and no universal love and religion. Idealism is more essential and constant because it does not merely disappear as a historical phenomenon and change with time like materialism does. Zhang's transition from political science to philosophy was a decisive intellectual transformation and allowed him to move from a national to a global context, placing China in the world and envisioning a world culture for all. Although it is not incorrect to situate Zhang primarily as a politician in the context of Chinese nationalism, given Zhang's lifelong political activities across continents, I propose that we read Zhang as a philosopher, even though his political activities have been more prominently recognized in scholarship.[5] Doing so will highlight his idealist vision of Song-Ming Confucianism as a world ethics, which could be meaningful today as well.

In this chapter, I first offer a brief biographical sketch of Zhang's legendary life. Then I discuss *A Manifesto for a Re-appraisal of Sinology and Reconstruction of Chinese Culture* (1958) and Zhang's emphasis of Confucianism as a world ethic. Further, I read *The Problem of Life in China and in Europe* (*Das Lebensproblem in China und in Europa*, 1922), which Zhang cowrote with the German philosopher Rudolf Eucken, to show their shared idea that a synthesis of Chinese and German idealism could serve as the foundation for future world ethics. Finally, I describe the public dispute between Zhang and his friend Ding Wenjiang on science and the view of life in 1923, in which New Confucianism challenges positivist scientism. Zhang's position echoes Weber's critique of scientism in *Science as a Vocation* (1917) and his promotion of Confucianism as a liberating rational world culture.

A TURBULENT LIFE

Zhang's understanding of philosophy was always embedded in his sociopolitical activities. A fervent lifetime constitutionalist, Zhang drafted the first Chinese constitution in 1948, thus he is known as the Father of the Constitution of the Republic of China (中国民国宪法之父). Born in 1887 during the Qing Dynasty, Zhang's early education was still defined by traditional Confucian classics and the system of Imperial Examination (*ke ju*, 科举). Zhang achieved the status of *xiucai* (秀才) in 1902, the first step toward higher degrees. Yet he aspired to the novel Western-style education and went on to learn English, mathematics, physics, chemistry, and geography in Shanghai. He then studied abroad in Japan and concentrated on political science at Waseda University (1906–10), where he earned a bachelor's degree. In Japan, Zhang met Liang Qichao (梁启超, 1873–1929) and became his lifelong follower. Liang was a prominent statesman and a leader of the Hundred Days' Reform in 1898, a movement promoting constitutional monarchy in China. Zhang recalled that, as a boy, he "saw pictures of Kang Yu-wei and Liang Chi-chao posted upon the school gates, with the notice that they were 'wanted' as a result of the *coup d'état* of 1898."[6] Zhang joined Liang's new party, the Political Information Society (Zhengwen She, 政闻社), in 1907 to promote constitutional reform of the Qing monarchy. At Waseda, Zhang was deeply impressed by a course on political philosophy and read John Locke's *Two Treatises of Government* (1689/90). Zhang's draft of the Chinese constitution in 1948 still retained the influence of Locke's liberalism from his early years.

Zhang recounted that Japanese universities primarily used English textbooks for teaching. Professors admired German scholars as experts in the fields.[7] Hence, Zhang decided to continue his study in Germany and went to Berlin in 1913. With the goal of earning a doctorate in political science, Zhang avidly attended lectures by the German scholars whose names he had learned about in Japan. Yet the less-organized style at German universities, which lacked a formal curriculum, posed a challenge to Zhang as a foreign student. He commented that, "during the time of the last years of the Qing Dynasty and the beginning years of the Republican era, there was a common trend among Chinese students and academics: the pursuit of knowledge should aim for the improvement of politics and for saving China. Therefore, higher education was not considered an academic career for life in its own right; rather it should be useful to save China. My own education in Japan and Germany could not escape this trend."[8] Since his academic experience in Germany could not satisfy his expectations to save China from Western imperialism, when World War I started in 1914, he abandoned his study and was completely absorbed by the development of the war and by China's role in it. He went to the United Kingdom in 1915 to experience the British Parliament's debates and hearings; he also visited battlefields in Belgium. When he learned that Yuan Shikai had commenced the coronation to become the emperor of China, Zhang decided to go home to protest Yuan's coronation. He then actively participated in various political campaigns. After the death of Yuan, as a protégé of Liang Qichao, who became the finance minister in the new government led by Duan Qirui's (段祺瑞), Zhang also held prominent offices until the end of 1917. Fierce political feuds among the warlords victimized the Liang group and forced them to resign. Shortly thereafter, World War I came to an end and Zhang accompanied Liang Qichao on his European journey (1918–21), as mentioned before. Zhang was impressed with Eucken and remained in Jena for months to study with him. When Zhang returned to China, he took on a professorship at Peking University and gave a lecture in 1923 at Tsinghua University. He critiqued the dominance of science and positivism in China and promoted a New Confucian and idealist position. This led to a public debate on science and the view of life between 1923 and 1927, which established Zhang as a public intellectual and a leading philosophical voice in China.

Combining New Confucianism and politics, with his friends and allies, Zhang secretly founded the Chinese National Socialist Party (NSP, Zhongguo Guojia Shehui Dang, 中国国家社会党) in 1932 as a third force, in addition to Guomin Dang (GMD, 国民党) and the Chinese Communist Party (CCP, 共产党). Zhang was elected the secretary general of the NSP in 1934 and continued publishing New Confucian–inspired essays and op-eds to promote his vision of constitutionalism and New Confucian world culture. As a member of the Chinese Delegation to the first United Nations conference in San Francisco in 1945, Zhang represented the China Democratic League alongside the ruling party GMD and CCP. After the end of World War II, upon the invitation from the GMD, Zhang was called upon to lead the drafting of the first constitution of the Republic of China in 1946, which was later adopted by the National Assembly in 1947. Yet the outbreak of the Civil War in China dashed Zhang's hopes and eliminated any opportunity to put into effect his draft of the constitution. When the war ended in 1949, Zhang was declared a war criminal by the CCP and had to flee China to the United States. He was also committed to writing and publishing books in English to promote his New Confucian idealism until his passing in 1969 in Berkeley, California.

Brian Tsui comments that Zhang "was consistent in believing that spiritual and moral might, rather than an economic and political system, determined a nation's health."[9] Yet Tsui, like other critics, does not further discuss Zhang's New Confucianism as the spiritual moral foundation of his political thinking.[10] Indeed, Zhang himself also forwent his staunch devotion to philosophy in his political autobiography, *The Third Force in China*, in 1952. His coauthored 1958 *Manifesto*, however, marked his return to the philosophical New Confucianism that served as the intellectual foundation for his political activism.

NEW CONFUCIANIST MANIFESTO (1958)

In 1958, Zhang, along with three other prominent philosophers, Tang Junyi (唐君毅, aka Tang Chun-i), Mou Zongsan (牟宗三, aka Mou Tsung-san), and Xu Fuguan (徐复观, aka Hsu Fo-kuan), published *A Manifesto for a Re-appraisal of Sinology and Reconstruction of Chinese Culture* (为中国文化敬告世界人士宣言—我们对中国学术研究及中国文化与世界文化前途之共同认识). Zhang initiated the project and was joined by the others in the writing of the manifesto. The brevity of the English translation of the lengthy Chinese title, however, reflects neither the target audience, whom the authors aimed to reach, nor their aim of connecting the future of China to the world. The title, which literally means "a manifesto for Chinese culture to all the people in the world: our shared opinions on the study of China and the future of Chinese culture and world culture," articulates the authors' intention to promote traditional Chinese culture, particularly Confucianism, to the world because they believe in the inextricable connection between China's and the world's future.[11] As the foreword of the manifesto makes clear, the authors were not content with the "shortcomings in the methods which some Westerners used to tackle the study of [China] . . . and the various deficiencies of their basic understanding of the Chinese cultural and political outlook."[12] The philosophers discuss the major problems in Western academic approaches toward China, present their understanding and appreciation of Chinese culture and what the world could learn from China, and articulate their expectations for a world citizen and a world ethic. Given China's long unbroken cultural history, its contribution to humanity, and its huge population, comprising one-fourth of the people in the world, the authors believe that "China's problem has long since become a world problem."[13] Hence, it is crucial for the world community to have a genuine understanding of Chinese culture in its past, present, and future. In essence, as the foundation of a world ethic, Zhang and his co-authors promote the Confucian notion of *xin xing* (心性), which literally means the "nature of heart," the token of a rational ethic in its social practice and self-discipline.

Despite its aim of targeting Western scholars of China, this text has been considered a watershed in the intellectual movement of New Confucianism in the twentieth century. It was published by a group of eminent New Confucian scholars and thus bore the identity of their shared intellectual agenda.[14] While the manifesto has been often read as a statement of Chinese conservativism because of its emphasis on Confucianism, from a philosophical perspective, this document articulates a New Confucian vision of world culture. While the cosmopolitan quality of the manifesto has not been adequately addressed by scholars, it is an important point for the purpose of this book.[15]

The authors of the manifesto first lament that the West's interest in China focuses either on its antiquity, as research of Sinology has shown, or on its contemporary politics and institutions, as reporting on current affairs and scholarship in the social sciences have both evinced. The former trend of studying Chinese antiquity treats China as an extinct civilization such as the ancient Egyptian and Mesopotamian civilizations without connecting this past to contemporary China as a living country. Sinologists rarely show interest in China's current situation or in its future development from the perspective of historical sources. The second trend of studying modern China, undertaken mostly by former government advisors, diplomats, or journalists, pays little attention to Chinese history. Rather than taking a historical perspective, their studies reflect their subjective strategies and personal views on dealing with China in the present moment. Zhang and his colleagues, however, stress the continuity and vibrancy of the long Chinese cultural tradition and its spiritual significance for the present and future of both China and the entire world.

The philosophers claim: "Chinese culture arose out of the extension of primordial religious passion to ethico-moral principles and to daily living."[16] Confucianism consists foremost in ethical principles and contains less religious quality than Christianity.[17] The quintessential idea of Confucian ethics, which has been neglected in the study of China in the West, is *xin xing* (心性), defined as the "concentration of mind on an exhaustive study of the nature of the universe."[18] *Xin* could be translated as "heart" and *xing* as "nature" or "temperament." *Xin xing* was developed in Song-Ming neo-Confucianism and represents the highest intellectual achievement of Chinese rationalism. Yet, in contrast to rationalism in the European tradition, the authors argue, Confucian rationalism is concerned neither with the question of the immortality of a rational soul nor with an epistemology that explains how the rational mind acquires knowledge. Rather, it is committed to being the moral foundation of life and its daily practice in society. The philosophers recognize that "this doctrine does implicitly contain a metaphysics, but this metaphysics is more like Kant's 'ethical' metaphysics. It serves as the basis for moral conduct, and in turn is testified to by this conduct."[19] They also claim that, in general, Song-Ming neo-Confucianism "is more in line with Kantianism."[20] Thus they want to rectify the misunderstanding that "Chinese culture limits itself to external relations between people, with neither inner spiritual life nor religious or metaphysical sentiment."[21]

Thus, moral behaviors in various social contexts count as the most important manifestations of *xin xing* and its cosmological validity. They argue that "practice arises out of understanding, and understanding is realized by practice. In this mutual dependence, the moral acts are oriented towards the outward while understanding is purely within oneself. If therefore the acts are extended to one's family, one's understanding correspondingly comprises the family; and if the acts are extended to the nation, to the entire universe, so too the understanding comes to comprise the nation and the entire universe. The two do and must progress in conjunction."[22] *Xin xing* is thus not an abstract idea but is reflected in the practices of individuals, societies, and the universe. It contains a cosmological appeal beyond the boundaries of cultures, nations, languages, and religions. It promises a rational social order through concrete individual self-discipline. "In that sense, whoever acts conscientiously and knows nature also knows heaven; whoever regulates his emotions serves also heaven. Human nature reflects the nature of heaven; the morality of man is also that of heaven. What man does to perfect his own nature is also what gives praise to the manifold manifestations of the universe. . . . All these express once more the idea of the oneness of heaven and man."[23] Zhang and his co-authors thus intend to demonstrate that Confucianism was a most tolerant doctrine and that Confucian China was tolerant toward all kinds of religions.

The philosophers also claim that Confucianism is not merely a set of dry and dull moral rules; rather, it teaches people to control and preserve life's forces and vitality: "With moral strength, one can accumulate all the vital energy of life. . . . This kind of virtuousness is able not only to preserve man's vitality within himself but also to manifest itself by penetrating through his body. That is, this virtuousness has also the function of keeping one in good health; as the saying goes, 'Virtue nurtures the body.' In Western ethical studies, discussion of morality is usually devoted to consideration of the regulations of human behavior, or the social or religious values of moral codes. Few writers have particularly stressed this thorough transformation of man's natural life by moral practices so that his attitudes and manners manifest his inner virtues and enrich and illuminate this life."[24] The spiritual entanglement among ethics, bodily vitality, virtuous practice, and heavenly reason produces a causal coherence between Confucian ethics and cosmology, which is summarized by the idea of *xin xing*.

The ambition of the philosophers moves beyond explaining the central doctrine of *xin xing* and expecting more appreciation of the vibrant continuity between China's past and present from Western scholars. They recommend that the West learn from Confucian ethics according to five points, the first four of which are: the ability to recognize what is at stake in the moment and to give up things if necessary; the wisdom of comprehending things with intuition and spirit; a feeling of compassion and mildness; the preservation of culture. The fifth point is the idea, derived from *xin xing*, that "the whole world is like one family. Though there are many nations now, mankind will eventually become one and undivided. Chinese thought has emphasized this attitude."[25] They argue that Confucianism is more capable of fostering a world union than Christianity because it does not include the idea of original sin, believing instead in the good of human nature. Unlike Christianity, Confucianism is not an organized religion. It neither makes acceptance of a doctrine or membership in a church the precondition for salvation nor requires worshipping Confucius as a deity. Hence, everyone could potentially become a sage, like Confucius. Confucianism thus has little conflict with other religions and emphasizes the harmony between nature and humanity, between heaven and earth, without the punishing vision of a hell for those who disagree. Zhang and his co-authors are confident: "If indeed the world is to be united, the Confucian spirit certainly deserves emulation."[26]

In their conclusion, the New Confucianists observe that the expansion of the West has brought cultures and peoples closer to each other, but also that it has caused conflict and friction. Everyone should urgently see and understand the future of humanity as a whole and treat other cultures with respect and compassion. Not surprisingly, the philosophers promote yet again *xin xing* as the guiding principle for such a world culture, in which everyone will conduct a moral life and then attain spiritual enlightenment in harmony with heaven and earth. They see this type of universal ethics, however, not as something unique to Confucianism. They claim that similar ideas also exist in India and Europe—only they haven't been developed as mainstream thinking. In this vein, they claim, "The time has come for the world to co-operate in bearing the burden of human suffering, and to open a new road for humanity."[27] They envision this to become the new direction of the world community after two world wars. At the same time, the authors do not intend to replace Western or any other culture with Confucianism. They preach Confucian tolerance and acceptance of others and consider such an attitude the best way to avoid further conflict and division.

Of course, with its emphasis on Confucianism, the manifesto did not match any existing political programs in that specific historical period around 1958. It was somewhat naïve politically, yet not necessarily conservative, because it didn't decidedly oppose any established political agenda.[28] The authors didn't mean to restore monarchy; rather, they intended to reform and repurpose Confucian philosophy for a global future. Philosophically and culturally speaking, the New Confucianists presented a world ethics as the foundation of a less radical rationalism. Their vision of world ethics expanded the debate on cosmopolitanism and introduced new ideas such as spirituality, moral practice, and bodily embodiment.

The manifesto was by no means only a product of Chinese tradition. Indeed, it reflected Zhang and his cowriters' prolonged engagement with Western, especially German, philosophy. Their experience of global injustice and prevalent violence in the first half of the twentieth century led them to revive the Confucian doctrine of *xin xing* after they gained knowledge in Western tradition. The decision not to restore Qingdao directly to China at the 1919 Paris Peace Conference pushed Zhang to search for a path to save China from Western imperialism that was different from the European model of constitutionalism. He found philosophy in Jena, Germany, and his discussion with German philosopher Rudolf Eucken served as the intellectual origin for the New Confucian manifesto and for Zhang's future political activities.

JENA, RUDOLF EUCKEN, AND *THE PROBLEM OF LIFE IN CHINA AND IN EUROPE*

The Problem of Life in China and in Europe (*Das Lebensproblem in China und in Europa*, 1922) is a booklet co-authored by Zhang and the German philosopher Rudolf Eucken during Zhang's sojourn in Jena. The reason Zhang cowrote this book with Eucken lies in Zhang's understanding of Eucken's new idealist philosophy as the most meaningful idea for him after his loss of faith in political justice at the Paris Peace Conference. In a letter to Lin Zaipin (林宰平) from Jena, Zhang yet again described the agonizing process in which he was deciding to abandon his political activities, which had not yielded successful results. He recounted how he had instead firmly turned to the study of philosophy as his new life goal. Zhang surmised that his friends would be greatly dismayed by this news, but he did not waver in his decision: his academic ambitions replaced his political aspirations (去了一政治国, 又来了一学问国).[29] He felt that his mental state had been liberated from bondage and that a heavy burden had been suddenly removed from his chest. He terminated his engagement in politics (断念政治), which had served as the subsistence and staple of his life (饮食水火) in the years prior.[30] He thus bid farewell to the writings of politicians such as Camillo Benso di Cavour, Otto von Bismarck, and William Ewart Gladstone and sought intellectual company with Kant and Hegel, avidly planning how to develop his intellectual growth every day. Zhang also described to his friend the charming and inviting natural environment of Jena and its premier cultural tradition, which counted Goethe and Schiller as prominent former residents. Yet it was clear to Zhang that his purpose in Jena was to be found neither in the alluring natural landscape nor in the rich cultural history. Rudolf Eucken, Zhang stated vehemently, was the only reason he was there. Zhang recognized in Eucken someone whose new idealism defied the world-wide influential materialist orientation, which for Zhang also included the positivism of Auguste Comte (1798–1857) and Charles Darwin's theory of evolution.[31]

Having faded into oblivion today, Rudolf Eucken (1846–1926) was broadly known as a leading voice of *Lebensphilosophie* and achieved international fame during his lifetime. Eucken's works had been translated into multiple languages. Having received awards and honorable doctorates from Glasgow University, Syracuse University, and New York University, Eucken's achievements culminated with the Nobel Prize for literature in 1908. Having taught as a professor of philosophy at the University of Jena for more than fifty years, when he passed away, *The Times Educational Supplement* published an obituary merely four days later, on Saturday, September 18, 1926, to commemorate him as "the most popular of philosophers in his own country."[32] The obituary continues that "his readers in Germany were counted by thousands, and they included multitudes of persons who never before he wrote opened a book upon philosophy. His popularity had been scarcely less here. Some of his books or pamphlets, such as 'Can we still be Christians?' have circulated very widely, especially, or not least, among the clergy. It is said that in Scotland, even among ministers who would fain keep to the old ways, his influence was greater than that of any other contemporary teacher. His most important work, on the life philosophies of the great thinkers, which is remarkable for a certain geniality and sympathy no less than for learning, passed through many editions."[33]

Eucken reflected in his autobiography that, even though he was a loyal subject of the German Empire, his main philosophical and social problem was "above national differences. It concerned all nations and civilisations. It was to deliver contemporary life from a pronounced insincerity from which it suffered, and to bring about an inner elevation of, in fact revolution in, the human condition."[34] Eucken saw this transnational trend in his thinking the major reason for his wide reception outside of Germany in Finland, Holland, England, Scotland, and France, as well as for his Nobel Prize for literature (1908) and his membership in the Swedish Academy of Sciences. Eucken, however, did first support imperial Germany in World War I.[35] But he changed his position shortly later.

Indeed, Eucken's popularity was not limited to Europe but extended also to East Asia.[36] As noted previously, Zhang and Liang Qichao came to know of Eucken through the Japanese. Eucken, along with the biologist Ernst Haeckel, attracted Japanese students, some of whom had later become prominent figures in Japan, to study in Jena.[37] For example, the liberal philosopher and educator Yoshishige Abe (1883–1966) studied with Eucken and became Japan's first minister of education after World War II in 1946, overseeing major reforms of the Japanese educational system. Abe corresponded with Eucken and informed him of his broad influence among Japanese scholars.

In Zhang's essay *An Outline of Eucken's Philosophy of Spiritual Life* (倭伊铿精神生活哲学大概), published just three months after his letter to Lin had been published in the same journal, *Reform* (改造), he explicates his understanding of Eucken's philosophy. In Zhang's understanding, Eucken's central idea is first and foremost "spiritual life" (*Geistesleben*, 精神生活), similar to Bergson's concept of *élan vital*.[38] When Zhang asked Eucken one day where the origin of life was, if life provided the foundation for all other things, Eucken acknowledged that he could not explain the origin of life in his thinking because life is a given thing. Zhang thus took Eucken's explanation as the worldliness of his idea of life. As evidence, Zhang refers to Eucken's book *Die Lebensanschauungen der großen Denker* (1890, translated into English as *The Problem of Human Life: As Viewed by the Great Thinkers from Plato to the Present Time*), which claims that a spiritual life is a personal life, which also means a life in the world (世界生活).[39] Zhang further explains that a personal life belongs to the realm of humanity (自我生活, 人也), while life in the world belongs to the domain of gods (世界生活, 神也).[40] For Zhang, then, divinity is the origin of the universe (宇宙之真源). He points out that Eucken places this origin in humanity and unites humanity and divinity in the notion of a spiritual life.

Eucken introduces his definition of life with three questions at the beginning of *The Problem of Human Life*: "What does our life mean when viewed as a whole? What are the purposes it seeks to realise? What prospect of happiness does it hold out to us? To ask these questions is to set ourselves the Problem of Life, nor need we stay to justify our right to ask them. They force themselves on us today with resistless insistence."[41] Eucken takes the "problem of life" as the most essential question of his own philosophical inquiry. In this book, he traces the European history of philosophy from Plato to the end of the nineteenth century from the perspective of "life." Eucken defines life as the inner life, the soul. He argues that "if our powers are wholly concentrated on outward things and there is an ever-diminishing interest in the inner life, the soul inevitably suffers. Inflated with success, we yet find ourselves empty and poor. We have become the mere tools and instruments of an impersonal civilisation which first uses and then forsakes us, the victims of a power as pitiless as it is inhuman, which rides rough-shod over nations and individuals alike, ruthless of life or death, knowing neither plan nor reason, void of all love or care for man."[42] Interiority, spirit, and emotion are the focus and the essence of life in Eucken's philosophy. For him, material possessions and outward activities are less important than the cultivation of the inner dimensions of human nature. In his reading of the history of philosophy, the discussion of life is not something random or occasional. It is meant to reveal the fundamental quality of a philosopher's thinking. Philosophy is thus the product of a philosopher's inner life across centuries. Eucken points out that art and religion will help people find their inner souls and spiritual belongings in a time of utilitarianism. Philosophy, Eucken laments, has either become a service discipline to the sciences, justifying positivist reasoning, or it has been devoted to unoriginal epistemology and critical analysis of knowledge. For Eucken, however, philosophy needs to delve into spiritual creation and discover strength in metaphysics so that it could provide guidance to individual and social activities in the present and future. Eucken still remains optimistic about the future: "Thus, despite all the complexities of the present situation, we may conclude our historical survey without any gloomy forebodings. So long as belief can rise from the contemplation of that which is merely human to the recognition of a spiritual world, we can look on our perplexities as purely transitional, and, while striving to mould life afresh, can still draw much that is of value from the spiritual treasure-house of the past. For the past, rightly understood, is no mere past."[43]

As abstract and vague as it seems to be, Eucken's philosophical thinking was deeply entangled with German and European history in the late nineteenth century. After Eucken's return from Switzerland in 1874, when Bismarck successfully won battles against France and Denmark and established the second German Empire, Eucken commented on German political life as something peculiar: "A great military victory had been won, and the strength and ability of a great statesman seemed to have delivered the country from every peril. But within itself there were menacing developments, though they were slow to enter into the public mind. One could, at least, recognise a pronounced narrowness: a political development, on the one hand, which made the Government the centre of gravity of all action and gave little play to the independence of the people, and, on the other hand, a rapid evolution of economic interests, which assumed an ever-increasing importance. Great things were done on both sides, but life was wholly taken up with these enterprises. There was no common goal for the whole of human nature, no inner exaltation, no clear understanding of the problems and conflicts of modern life. The main feature of the times was an unrestricted affirmation of life. Material existence increasingly absorbed all the available energy, and there was an unmistakable insincerity in the general profession of a belief in a spiritual world and a religion of a Christian complexion."[44] Eucken was worried that this materialist focus would lead to the ignorance of the human soul and its spiritual needs.

The *Times* obituary also commented that Eucken critiqued his own time as "a soulless civilization. He deplored the ruthless destruction of the older without substituting for it something better, and he put himself in many forms the question: How are we to make men spiritually minded in times when the material world is so much with us, and all else is dim and elusive? . . . How to make life worth living, how to fill life with gladness, to free it from impurity, to make us masters, not slaves, of the powers which science has put in our hands, was his concern."[45] Eucken belonged to the generation of philosophers who distrusted reason and favored instinct and intuition as an approach to truth and soul, which they thought science failed to explain with positivist and instrumentalist reason.

Similarly, Zhang observes that there is a clear distinction between life and thinking/reason in Eucken's philosophy: Life should be the foundation of thinking, not the other way around. Zhang argues that, while previous idealist philosophers such as Georg Wilhelm Friedrich Hegel held thinking (思) as the origin of the truth (真理) and as the energy for all things in the world, Eucken considers thinking merely a fraction of spiritual life. Thinking alone does not lead to the truth. Only experience of spiritual life does.[46] Zhang points out that the focus on thinking disregards emotion at the deepest level of the soul and leads human civilization toward an intellectualist mechanization. For Zhang, spiritual life should be the basis for thinking.[47] Zhang opines that Eucken's idea of life resembles the idealist nature of the American psychologist and philosopher William James and the French philosopher Henri Bergson, even though Eucken himself often cites Kant and intends to remain in his tradition. While James's idealism is based on psychology and Bergson's on biology and psychology, Eucken's notion of spiritual life is founded on religion and ethics.[48]

In his later work *The Struggle for a Spiritual Content of Life* (1896), Eucken also criticizes the inadequacy of previous iterations of German idealism and aims to establish a new spiritual orientation by himself. He claims: "Quite apart from religion, I felt strongly the insincerity of contemporary life, professing spirituality, as it did, yet wholly taken up with material things. My remarks in that work were sharply opposed to the conventional and official Idealism, since they too obviously treated the problems as in a state of suspense, and they demanded changes far too radical to please those who thought that everything was settled and fixed. . . . Throughout the work I demanded that we should clearly work out what was necessary to the maintenance of the spiritual process of life."[49] Eucken thus concludes that "nothing but the attainment of a spiritual content of life will save mankind from an inner collapse. It must either rise or fall. It is impossible to remain stationary in the present condition."[50]

In his letter to Lin, Zhang argues that Eucken considers spiritual life capable of curbing the negative impact of the external world and of providing the internal mind with greater clarity and brighter light. Zhang compares Eucken's concept of spirituality to the Confucian idea of sincerity (诚), citing the Confucian classic *Doctrine of the Mean* (Zhongyong, 中庸): "Only the sincerest person can thoroughly develop one's individual nature and use their talent; through the full development of one's individual nature and talent, one can help thoroughly develop the human nature; the full development of human nature leads to the thorough development of the nature of everything, thus aiding the transformation and procreation in the world."[51] Zhang comments that, in essence, Confucianism and Eucken's philosophy agree with each other in a significant way.

Zhang observes that, for Eucken, moral values about justice, truth, good and evil cannot originate purely inside an individual human; they exist in the world of spirit beyond human power. Yet once an individual believes in divinity, the spiritual world will reveal itself immediately with moral values, guiding the individual on the path toward a spiritual life. Thus, spiritual life is a living reality (*lebendige Wirklichkeit*, 活实在). Truth and divinity exist within everyday life. It takes, however, a great deal of effort to strive for a moral and spiritual life. The conflict between the material world and spirituality is an ongoing and never-ending battle in life (*Lebenskampf*). Zhang comments that Eucken's idea of constant pursuit of a better moral and spiritual life resembles a classical Chinese teaching in *Yi Jing* (aka I Ging, 易经): the universe relentlessly moves and changes, a well-educated and morally good person should never cease to better oneself (天行健, 君子以自强不息). Even though Eucken sees in religion the ultimate solution of the struggle for a spiritual life, his emphasis still centers on human life and human effort in this world. Literature, philosophy, music, and art all reflect the struggle for spiritual life. This struggle is not only confined to an individual's betterment of the self, it also is the driving force behind social historical movements. Zhang summarizes that divinity, truth, life, and struggle belong to the same category in Eucken's thinking.[52]

Zhang claimed that, while East Asians started to believe firmly in the omnipotence of materialism like the Westerners did before World War I, Westerners were losing their faith in materialism after the catastrophic warfare. He thus aimed to introduce Eucken to China to awaken his fellow citizens. Zhang announced to Lin his plans to write books about Eucken in Chinese. At the same time, he asked his friend to be quiet about this idea because, if he couldn't deliver the result, it would be unnecessary to publicize his tentative plan. Indeed, Zhang did not deliver. He never even wrote the second part of his essay *An Outline of Eucken's Philosophy of Spiritual Life*, which he had promised to do. The reason was probably that he ended up cowriting the book *Problem of Life in China and in Europe* in German with Eucken and imagined a world culture based on Confucianism and German idealism.[53]

In his part of the preface to the book, Eucken called it a unique piece of writing (*eine eigentümliche Schrift*) because he and Zhang compose it as a "guidance of life for the Chinese" (*eine Lebenslehre für Chinesen*).⁵⁴ The book was meant to be neither a special system of ethics nor a contribution to Sinology; rather, this book came into being as the result of inspirations brought to him by Chinese state officials and scholars. Eucken reported, "These men considered it important to connect their lives, which were held in strong inner motions, to German philosophical idealism and, at the same time, with my activism."⁵⁵ Eucken regretted that he could not follow the invitation to a lecture tour in China. He thus wished that this book would become a token of spiritual and intellectual connection between China and Germany, which has been done with the best possible effort (*eine geistige Verbindung von China und Deutschland nach bestem Vermögen*). Reflecting this connection, the organization of the chapters in the book demonstrates a dialogue (*Zwiesprache*) between Chinese and European cultures, which allows each culture to speak for its distinctiveness and idiosyncrasy. Eucken added that this book be first and foremost geared toward the readership of Chinese intellectuals (*chinesische Intelligenz*), but he hoped that it also would find readers in Germany, especially among those readers who respected and recognized the immeasurable significance of a closer interrelation between the East and the West (*die unermeßliche Bedeutung einer engeren Verbindung von Osten und Westen*) and who would like to contribute seriously to this collaborative project. Eucken stated that the leading philosophical idea in this book is the design and conception of life as a holistic entity (*die Gestaltung des Lebens als eines Ganzen*), an idea that he also discussed in his other writings.⁵⁶ While Zhang, in his part of the preface, confirmed Eucken's attempt at a synthesis of European and Chinese philosophies, his concerns were more urgent. He wrote, "The foundations for morality and ethics were shaken in China as well. To what extent could we preserve the old, to what extent must we accept European culture? This is the most important question for the Chinese intellectuals."⁵⁷

With a "dialogic style," as Eucken calls it, the chapters in the book alternate discussions of the ethical and spiritual dimensions of life in European and Confucian philosophy. In the first chapter, "Description of European Characteristics" (*Darstellung der europäischen Art*), Eucken offers a brief summary of the historical trajectory of European philosophy from Greek antiquity to the present. Then Zhang describes the genealogy of Confucian ethics from the ancient time of Confucius, across the Han and Tang Dynasties, the Song-Ming neo-Confucianism, and to the Qing dynasty in the second chapter, titled "The Historical Development of Ethics in China" (*Die geschichtliche Entwicklung der Ethik in China*). In the third and fourth chapters, Eucken comments on the idiosyncrasy of Chinese life, or spirituality, and points toward the possibilities of its further development. In the fifth chapter, both authors offer their observations on life and its philosophical foundation in their present time. At the end, they return to the question of China and discuss its tasks in the present and in the future.

As in his book *The Problem of Human Life*, Eucken presents in the first chapter a concise overview of the history of European philosophy and interprets it from the vantage point of the philosophy of life. Eucken discusses three major stages: the antique teaching of life (*die antike Lebenslehre*); the turn to religion (*die Wendung zur Religion*); and the modern time (*die Neuzeit*), paying great attention to the contributions of philosophers of the inner life. Eucken ranks Kant as the high point of German spiritual life (*des deutschen geistigen Lebens*) and sees in him an advocate of life, which is defined through the dutiful fulfillment of ethical principles by both the individual and the entire world. "The leading thought of this life is duty or the free-willed submission to a self-generated law."[58] Through the acceptance of moral duties, freedom emerges as human beings' independence from themselves. According to Eucken, with the notion of spiritual life (*geistiges Leben*), Kant makes an unprecedented contribution to the philosophy of life in the German tradition, which differs from the English tradition's focus on psychological (*seelisch*) life. Kant deepens the idea of humanity and distinguishes it from psychology. Then Eucken only briefly mentions Fichte, Schelling, and Hegel and concludes that Germany has reached the peak of idealism, according to which one cultivates life from the inside and does not focus on the useful (*das Nützliche*), but on the good and the beautiful (*das Gute und Schöne*).[59] Eucken comments that, in the decades around 1900, Darwinism and socialism, as two life forms (*Lebensgestaltung*), have emerged as major forces. Since they are based on sensory experience and material evidence, they don't conform with idealism, which seeks to give meaning and value to life from an invisible realm. Eucken claims that life in the present and the near future oscillates between two poles: religion, representing spirituality, and economics, representing the foundation for individual and social survival. These two poles threaten to tear human life asunder. It is thus the most important task of the time to overcome the conflict between the religious and economic poles. Eucken argues that only idealism can synthesize them and solve the conflict through a spiritual reform (*geistige Reformation*).[60]

In Zhang's outline of Chinese philosophy, he foregrounds Confucian ethics in the last four thousand years, from the time before Confucius to the Qing dynasty. Zhang explains that the spirit of Confucianism lies in its practical focus on the betterment of the self, according to moral principles, so that the family, the state, and the world could remain in peace and order.[61] This spirit of self-cultivation has been further developed toward a set of social and universal morality by Mencius, often referred to as the "Second Sage" after Confucius. Mencius maintains that human virtues do not depend on the external world but are determined by internal conviction. For Mencius, pure humanity is not far off; one only needs to willingly own it. The will is thus the essential motivator for humans to become virtuous and to live judiciously in the world. Zhang points out that Mencius's teaching places great value on the principles of humanity and justice. Its highest political goal is world union and fraternity (*Welteinheit und Weltverbrüderung*).[62]

Comparing Confucianism to Taoism and Mohism, Zhang argues that only Confucianism is suited for dynastic government based on its legitimization of monarchy and its practical attention to everyday life. Taoist emphasis on nonaction is profound for metaphysics but unpractical in sociopolitical realms. Laozi and Zhuangzi mocked emperors and dismissed their rule as the origin of chaos. Mohism's theory of universal love prescribes equality among all human beings—it is thus incompatible with the long tradition of dynastic absolutism and its strict hierarchy in China. Zhang observes:

> The Confucianist was different. He stresses order, hierarchical difference, and the rights of the ruler. Their representatives have had personal contact to various kings in their lifetimes, with the hope that their teachings could be realized. Confucianism means a pillar of the monarchy. This is the main reason why the emperors of different dynasties always preferred Confucianism. The dominance of Confucianism thus lies in its character as a philosophy of life and a philosophy of the state, and in the advantage that was granted to it by the monarchy based on its character in the vicissitudes of history.[63]

Zhang calls Confucianism primarily a philosophy of life and clearly demonstrates his affinity with Eucken's thinking. His explanation that Confucianism is a dominant doctrine in dynastic China based on its character as a philosophy of life also resembles Eucken's interpretation of European philosophy from the perspective of life. Hence Zhang's further description of the development of neo-Confucianism in the Song and Ming Dynasties, roughly between the 1050s and 1700s, foregrounds its idealist and spiritual dimensions, yet not so much its political impact.

Zhang argues that, even though the neo-Confucian thinkers maintain that their teaching is based on Confucianism, Buddhism is a major driving force behind the formation of neo-Confucianism. Ancient Confucianism does not discuss much the cosmic dimension and the inner conscience, while neo-Confucianism takes these elements from Buddhism and integrates them with Confucianism. Zhang considers Zhu Xi (朱熹) the most important representative of neo-Confucianism and probably the most influential thinker in Chinese history of all times. *Li* (reason, 理, *Vernunft* in Zhang's translation) and *qi* (energy, 气) are the two fundamental concepts in Zhu's philosophy. The primordial state of the world is called *taiji* (太极). While *li* is metaphysical and eternal, *qi* is physical and temporal, evolving into the manifold of different creatures and beings. *Li* is always inherent in *qi* and in every being. *Qi* emerges from the foundation of *li* and can give rise to good and evil, wisdom and stupidity.[64] The human heart is the locus of *li*, which is the ultimate principle of morality in attunement with the universe. At the same time, the heart also expresses *qi* in the forms of sensory drives, emotions, and sentiments. Zhang states that, according to Zhu Xi, "the right path of life should be in the exploration of reason and in the taming of the heart."[65] Zhang reports that neo-Confucianists of later generations such as Lu Xiangshan (陆象山) and Wang Yangming (王阳明) do not acknowledge the two sides or the two functions of the heart and only argue that heart is reason (*Herz ist Vernunft*).[66]

Zhang does not randomly choose the translation of *li* as reason, nor does he emphasize by chance the neo-Confucian doctrine of the heart as reason. In fact, he aims to compare Confucianism with Kantian philosophy as his contribution to a deeper exchange between China and Europe. Of course, Eucken's praise of Kant as the apex of German idealism also serves as inspiration for Zhang's comparison. He explicates:

> After the school of Confucius, morality is founded on human nature, which means that the standard for our action lies in the latter. For Kant, morality also stems from our interiority, namely in the awareness of what should be done—this awareness prescribes certain actions to the will. The main question for Confucius is how to develop human nature toward the good and curb passions. Kant also has the opinion that, through sensuality, the constant possibility of deviating from the determination of pure reason is given; therefore a moral standpoint must be first achieved through the overcoming of sensual drives. Confucius says: "It does not depend on others, but it depends on ourselves whether we reach humanity." Just as much as Kant says that the practical reason is subject to its own law; it is autonomous.[67]

Zhang closely connects Confucianism to Kant's critique of practical reason through human nature, *xin xing* (discussed previously), as the foundation of morality. Chinese and European traditions are thus intertwined with each other through Zhang's idealist reading. Despite these philosophical affinities, for Zhang, Confucianism differs from Kantian philosophy in practical matters. For example, Zhang points out, Confucianism understands law only as an aid for morality so that ethics could reach its fullest potential. Ethics, however, has a more prominent position in practical life than legal order: "Much is expected from self-discipline and material enjoyment is despised."[68] Only the encounter with Europe became the catalyst for change in the nineteenth century: it brought with it the ideas of constitution, socialism, individualism. Then people started to doubt the older ideas and traditions in China.

One major change can be seen in the Confucian definitions of the five basic relationships between rulers and subjects, parents and children, men and women, younger and older brothers, and friends. They no longer remained the foundation of the Chinese society and have changed forever. This Confucian social structure, Zhang comments, has advantages that are simultaneously its disadvantages: "The social foundation is rooted in morality; therefore it lacks an awareness of following the laws. The traditional duties of this ethic limit the freedom of movement and thought in practical life. Then the creative power will be inhibited."[69] Zhang criticizes the Confucian ethic's neglect of the rule of law in comparison to the European tradition and considers the perfection of jurisdiction a necessity for China's future.

Zhang noted, not unbegrudgingly, that since the opening of international trade in China in the 1840s, Confucianism had yielded to European sciences and that, since World War I, new philosophical ideas, including socialism, had become influential in China. At first, however, the Chinese held the opinion that European culture had merely technical and material advantages. Yet the Russo-Japanese War proved the advantage of the European style of constitutional monarchy, which Japan adopted from Europe, over the absolutist monarchy, which was the political system in imperial Russia. "Hence we came to the insight that European culture also has its inner values that become visible in its constitution and legal life among others. Because of this insight, in the last fifty years, the belief in old Chinese culture was shaken to extremes."[70] Zhang, however, differed from his fellow Chinese intellectuals and disagreed with a total imitation of European culture or a complete negation of Chinese culture. Rather, he preached for mutual learning and the creation of a new culture, writing, "One goes a step further since the World War and tries to penetrate into the spiritual depth of Europe, which means into its philosophy. The bridge between both cultures has been built. In the course of time, a new culture will grow out of the ever-deeper exchange of ideas in both cultures."[71] The connection that Zhang makes between Confucianism and Kantian philosophy is clearly his attempt at such an integration. For him, a philosophical exchange is not merely paving the path toward greater liberation for himself and for China, but also for the entire world. Zhang's ambition echoes the teaching of Mencius about world union and world fraternity. It is a Confucian view expanded to include the entire world after China has become involved in the global capitalist network of trade and exploitation.

In the subsequent chapters, Eucken confirms Zhang's comparison of Confucianism with Kant and their foundation in reason. Like Weber, Eucken considers Confucianism the rational side of Chinese thinking and Taoism the irrational side. Yet he considers Confucianism the major philosophy of China because it exerts the greatest impact on Chinese society. Eucken draws on Zhang's explanation of Chinese philosophy and understands the core of Confucianism as a world reason (*Weltvernunft*), writing, "All the weight of life is being carried by a world reason (*tao*). Humanity is under this reason and they must create out of it."[72] It is thus no surprise that Confucianism shares many affinities with the European Enlightenment. For Eucken, the Sinophilia in the European eighteenth century was a matter of course: "Leading thinkers of that time could appreciate the Chinese way of organizing life as a magnificent realization of their own convictions, for example, Leibniz, also Christian Wolff. Later this favor moved to India in European life."[73] At the same time, Eucken observes that, notwithstanding its rational side, Chinese life is more empirical, more positive, and warmer than the European Enlightenment. "One can say that rationality and naivety complement as well as contradict each other in this country. It is the rule to keep in mind the effects of these two trends together and, from there, to illuminate the actual treatment of individual problems of life. Each great civilization holds a major paradox in itself and primarily proves its greatness in conquering the paradox. This also holds true for the Chinese."[74] Here Eucken describes Chinese society before the encounter with the West in the nineteenth century as a coherent entity. With the onset of Western imperialism and capitalism in the nineteenth century, however, the problems in the West also affected China. Eucken comments that "life has entered more and more from a naïve state to a critical and active terrain. Humanity has gained more self-ascribed actions; at the same time, the entire picture of reality has changed."[75] The superiority of European technology, trade, and industry overshadows the Confucian life of rationality and naivety. Chinese social hierarchy, individual souls, and their relation to cosmos and truth, ultimately, has lost their balance and sunk in a crisis. Eucken, however, is highly skeptical toward the position that European life is superior to that of China and should be taken as the ultimate model of truth and education for China's future. European life, he contends, is full of difficult problems that need solutions. It is thus indispensable for the Europeans to investigate and understand these problems to gain insights and find solutions. This would help China, as well.

Eucken emphasizes the importance of metaphysics as the articulation of spiritual life. For him, metaphysics also serves as the foundation for ethics, not only in the form of social ethical conduct but also in the sense of an inner truthful selfhood. Through metaphysics, life will receive its full meaning and value; humanity will appear as world creature (*Weltwesen*) and become an independent energy of life; humans will reach a comprehensive goal, an inner confidence, and joy; they can now be convinced to be part of a great world movement (*Weltbewegung*).[76] Eucken introduces here the term "world creature" (*Weltwesen*) to describe humanity as inherently connected to each other, to other lives, and to the universe through spirituality. Humanity is thus part of a world movement (*Weltbewegung*) of life energy that includes everyone and everything on earth. Life, committed to growth and duty, is the driving force behind human activities—while religion and art provide easier access for spiritual life than natural sciences, life is the axiom of science and all things in the world process (*Weltprozeß*). In Eucken's terminology, life and world are closely related to each other. They are each other's expression and foundation. In Europe, Eucken observes, the new turn to modern work (*die Wendung zu der modernen Arbeit*) has ushered in a complication in the world movement of human life:

> Selfishness, lies, and injustice have reached such a height that all meanings and values of life are in danger. We obviously stand in a great spiritual and moral crisis; the great progress of working culture can cover this crisis, but it can't overcome it. It is urgently necessary that we strive more powerfully to the grounds of life and reveal its original entanglements. We must deal with the darkness and sorrow of life much more and then grow in our interiority. We are yearning for a spiritual Reformation, an inner renewal, which heartily attacks and drives out all the rotten and crumbling things in our culture.[77]

Eucken's spiritual reform is meant to disentangle humanity from modern economics and return it to the original truthful simplicity of life and spiritual commitment. In the last chapter of the book, "Prospects and Tasks of Chinese Life" (*Aussichten und Aufgaben des chinesischen Lebens*), both Eucken and Zhang argue that precisely because of the decline of spiritual life, China should by no means simply imitate Europe.[78] Facing similar problems of modernity, China also needed a transformation of its traditional way of life to meet the new challenges. The authors point out that Confucianism also offers metaphysics and ethics.

Confirming Zhang's comparison between Confucianism and Kant, Eucken emphasizes that humanity and justice are the two most distinct features of Confucian ethics, similar to ancient Greek stoicism.

They dismiss the Anglo-American imperialism that considers itself the single most superior form of life. They recommend that "China . . . be very careful about this attitude so that no foreign and superficial ideas are imposed on it against its wish and will."[79] Instead, Eucken and Zhang promote German idealism, or Eucken's own idealist philosophy, as a better option because of its concern with all the greatness and values of humanity (*alle Größen und Werte des menschlichen Bereiches*) and with the totality of life (*Gesamtleben*). In their view, German idealism moves beyond individuals and nations and addresses the problems of modernity in Europe, in China, and globally.[80] They envision that Chinese Confucianism and German idealism could join forces (*Hand in Hand geben*) to solve the problems of modernity with an enhanced potency, even though they are not clear about how this joined force could concretely solve problems. For them, both philosophical traditions share the essential qualities of truthfulness, objectivity, diligence, and humanitarianism, and a decided rejection of utilitarianism and hedonism.[81] The authors claim toward the end of the book:

> It would be to the highest degree desirable that the most possibly close relation between Germany and China would emerge and that a shared belief in life would connect both countries in a fruitful exchange. Nothing holds our peoples more firmly than a community of great tasks, worries, and sorrows, which our peoples have experienced. We hope that such a community would connect them in friendship and their collaboration would give human life more meaning and value than the present time contains![82]

Both Confucianism and German idealism would promote more ethical reflections and create greater distance toward utilitarianism. They would create greater spiritual strength for people to live a simple and true life. Their synergy would unleash a stronger force to tackle the exigencies of modernity. Indeed, a synthesis of Chinese and German idealist philosophies would provide the foundation for a philosophy of the world. Even though the authors speak about German and Chinese philosophies, their intention is to design a world philosophy offsetting the damages brought by warfare, imperialism, and international political injustice, all of which continue to be global problems. In this world philosophy, spirituality connects personal life with the universe to create "a system of the universal personal life."[83] The ultimate goal of this philosophy of life lies in freedom.

THE CONTROVERSY OVER SCIENCE AND VIEW OF LIFE (1923)

Lebensanschauung (view of life), a key word in Eucken's philosophy of life, was probably first translated into Japanese and then into Chinese. Yoshishige Abe, once Eucken's student in Jena, whom I mentioned a few pages prior, translated Eucken's book *Die Lebensanschauungen der großen Denker* (1890) into Japanese as 大思想家の人生観 (*Dai shisoka no jinseikan*) in 1914.[84] *Jinseikan* in its kanji form, 人生観, was directly taken into Chinese as 人生观 (renshengguan) by Zhang and his fellow Chinese thinkers. Most notably, this term became one of the most contentious ideas in modern Chinese intellectual history. In February 1923, Zhang gave a lecture at Tsinghua University titled "View of Life" (Renshengguan).[85] Zhang's lecture soon provoked a heated debate over "science and the view of life" (科学与人生观) that is also referred to as the debate over "science and metaphysics" (科学与玄学).

Of course, science has been an influential idea for modern society since the nineteenth century. In 1911, Peter H. Eijkman's manifesto *L'internationalisme scientifique* called for the establishment of more international organizations of scientific collaborations and envisaged a supranational society of international organizations. Followers of this scientific internationalism, including prominent figures such as Marie Curie, Max Planck, and Albert Einstein, believed that scientific collaborations and institutions across nations could foster peace and growth. Liang Qichao translated the French writer Jules Verne's novels to enhance the awareness of science among Chinese people and to accommodate Western standards. Science also became one of the most important slogans in China's New Culture Movement. Literary writers in Europe and China, such as Anna Seghers, Erwin Piscator, Bertolt Brecht, Lu Xun, Tian Han, and Ding Ling, saw international communist movement as the way to achieve global equality.[86] Critics, however, also pointed out that internationalism inadvertently led to nationalist conflicts in the twentieth century. Science, thus, was not necessarily the path toward peace. Zhang, while not opposing science per se, was skeptical toward scientism, the claim of the omnipotence of scientific positivism, especially after his conversion to a New Confucian-German idealism.

Upon his return from Germany, Zhang was invited by Tsinghua University to address a class of students getting ready to study in the United States. Zhang critiqued scientism and stressed the importance of subjectivity, intuition, and spirituality. The published article based on his lecture immediately generated almost thirty responses in various newspapers and journals. This debate reflected the disagreement between the prominent New Culture Movement, promoting

Western science and democracy as the two pillars of Chinese modernity, and New Confucianism, insisting on reforming and repurposing Confucianism for spiritual and moral values. An important episode during the New Culture Movement, this controversy was also a global intellectual event revealing connections between discussions in Europe and East Asia about spiritual life, rational ethics, and freedom. Eucken's idealist notion of *Lebensanschauung* became further rooted in East Asian intellectual history. The controversy was also a prelude to the 1958 *Manifesto* and a consequence of Zhang's disillusionment after the Paris Peace Conference. Indeed, both the representatives of the New Culture Movement and Zhang were deeply disappointed by the Paris Peace Conference and Western imperialism. They placed, however, different emphases on Confucianism and developed different strategies to address China's role in global modernity. The New Culture Movement and New Confucianism shared the same goal of debunking imperialism in China, but they differed in means. The former aimed to use Western modernity to replace the Confucian foundation and create a new culture, while the latter intended to revive Chinese tradition and reclaim Confucian wisdoms for the entire world. It was New Confucianism that placed the Chinese cultural tradition at a global level. From today's perspective, New Confucianism contributed significantly to reimagine global intellectual history.

In his lecture *View of Life* (Renshengguan, 人生观), Zhang posits five statements on the differences between science and life. First, Zhang declares that science is objective and life subjective. He contends that formulas in sciences are universally valid and not confined to one nation or culture. The conduct of life, however, could be very different and depends on one's own decision and opinion. For example, he points out, Mencius considers human nature inherently good, but Xunzi (荀子) considers it evil; Confucius emphasizes social activism, whereas Laozi praises non-action for a perfect society. Hence, he sees views of life as subjective and unable to be proven by scientific evidence. Second, he declares that science is based on logical analysis (论理), whereas life follows intuition (直觉). In his view, Schopenhauer's pessimism, Confucian social and family hierarchy, and Mozi's universal love defy logical investigation and are based on belief and experience. Propositions about the conduct of life do not require definition or methodology. Thus, for Zhang, life is intuitive. Zhang's third point is that science uses the method of breaking down and dismantling a complex problem into pieces, while life is comprehensive and cannot be separated and dissected. Fourth, science follows the principle of causality, but life depends on free will. If a person is to feel remorse and intend to change herself/himself, this behavioral change cannot be explained by an objective principle of causality such as gravity, but rather by personal decisions. Fifth, Zhang thinks that science has emerged from the commonality of natural phenomena, while a human life is always unique, individual, and not comparable to that of others.

Zhang contends that "no matter how much science has developed, it does not have the power to solve all the problems of the view on life. It can only be solved by humanity itself."[87] Two elements in Zhang's agenda develop further in his thinking: the emphasis on spiritual life according to Song-Ming Confucianism and the stressing of world culture. This was already a rehearsal of the 1958 *Manifesto*. Zhang observes that Song-Ming Confucianism has paid great attention to the cultivation of human inner life, while European culture in the last three centuries focused on controlling nature. The former results in a spiritual culture and the latter in a material culture. Zhang comments that, while Chinese people have come to admire Western industrialization and commerce and regarded Chinese culture as backward, Westerners started to detest their material culture after World War I and began to value the spiritual dimension of life. In the West, Zhang names some philosophers, such as Karl Marx, Adam Smith, Plato, and Hegel, as having contributed their idiosyncratic ideas to the philosophy of life in the long history of humanity and, even if he doesn't judge them as right or false, as being able to light up the path for later generations. Zhang also contends that the Chinese Confucian tradition prefers peace (和), balance (平), and integration of the entire world (大同), and it does not support narrow nationalism. Zhang warns that the preference for national products and the insistence on national rights will run the risk of becoming narrow nationalism and breaking peace and balance. Zhang concludes that, while promoting a new culture (新文化) in China, one should understand that Chinese culture and Western culture both have positive and negative elements for a meaningful life in the future. To recognize what is beneficial and what is not, one needs to have a sound view of life.

However, the geologist Ding Wenjiang (丁文江), once Zhang's roommate in Paris, took issue with Zhang's piece and published a polemic rejoinder, ridiculing Zhang's postulation on life. In his piece *Metaphysics and Science* (Xuanxue yu Kexue, 玄学与科学), Ding defines Zhang's promotion of life as groundless metaphysics that has been proven wrong by science in Europe. Ding contends that the view of life cannot be separated from scientific objectivism. If something cannot be positively proven, then it is not true knowledge. Ding uses the example of Galileo Galilei to show how science has defeated the theological understanding of the world and revealed the objective truth of the earth and the universe. "Since then, the universe that had always belonged to metaphysics was raided by science."[88] Ding further refers to Charles Darwin's *On the Origin of Species* (1859), which has infuriated theologians and metaphysicians and has made biology a science; he finally points to psychology, which also became a science around 1900. Ding disagrees with Zhang's judgment that European culture is bankrupt after World War I. He argues that, even if the West is at its end, science does not assume responsibility for that because politicians and religious educators are mostly responsible for the war and these people are not scientists. As for Confucian spirituality, Ding strongly devalues the representative thinkers of Song-Ming Confucianism and disapproves of the way that Zhang connects the Chinese intellectual tradition to metaphysics in the European tradition. Ding concludes that one has to "apply scientific methods to guide life's problems" (把科学的方法应用到人生问题上去) and that Zhang's ideas are merely "built on extremely loose and unstable mud and sand" (建筑在很松散的泥沙之上).[89]

Ding's reprimand was published in Beijing's weekly *Effort* (努力周报) on April 12, 1923, roughly two months after Zhang's initial publication of his lecture at Tsinghua University on February 14, 1923. Zhang swiftly published a lengthy rebuke of Ding's piece. He reports that Ding is enraged by his lecture and that he has argued with him for over two hours about the usage of science for life in private. Zhang complains that Ding has gone public with their dispute, even using harsh words—for example, Ding writes that "Zhang was being occupied by the evil ghost of metaphysics" (玄学的鬼附在张君劢身上).[90] Zhang shows understanding and notes that it does not surprise him that even his friends disagree with him because science has become such a powerful ideology and because the omnipotence of science has never been questioned. Science, for Zhang, spreads its influence and veracity through school education and social engineering. He cites many European and American philosophers and thinkers such as Henri Bergson, Rudolf Eucken, and the American philosopher H. G. Wells in support for his argument that, even in the West, prominent voices are expressing the idea that life cannot be guided only by external positivist scientism and that it needs internal spirituality. His view of life rests on a higher level than scientific experimental method and factual knowledge. Hence life and science, he argues, should not be placed in opposition to each other because they address different areas of the world. Zhang points out that famous Western scientists admit that there are many areas that science cannot yet explain. After the scientific revelation of one small problem, greater mysteries loom ahead—he writes, "Wonders of the cosmos definitely cannot be fully explained by science."[91] Zhang reiterates that World War I is the tragic outcome of the excessive belief in the material culture of industry and commerce as well as in the omnipotence of science.

Zhang further compares China to the West: "The primary principles of building our country are stability but not mobility, spiritual satisfaction but not joy at material possession, agricultural self-sufficiency but not interest-driven commerce, and unity through ethics and education but not separation based on race and ethnicity.... Aided by its colonialism, European economic policy could maintain Europe's peace and prosperity for several decades. Yet our country was not able to have colonialism like Europe. What we can attract was only foreign investment, and those whom we can exploit are our lower-class laborers. If we build our country on the foundation of industry and commerce, would it last longer than Europe? This can't be true."[92] Zhang's critique of Western industry and commerce based on colonialism reveals his opinion that European prosperity is something that cannot be imitated by China to achieve similar social affluence. Industry and commerce, however, are important to him. Zhang suggests that two things are indispensable to introduce industry and commerce into China: first, socialism appears to be a reasonable way to ensure relatively equal distribution; second, education is effective in maintaining social justice. For Zhang, all activities in the world should emanate from the motivation of promoting the happiness of humanity (人类幸福): "Yet since the nineteenth century, people sacrificed human lives for the sake of wealth and power. When we reflect on it today, then we should rather sacrifice wealth and power and would not allow humanity to become slaves and cattle in a factory."[93] He claims that this is something that China needs, by all means, to avoid.

Zhang thus more explicitly and extensively discusses his position toward Song-Ming Confucian spiritual cultivation as his solution for China and the world. As discussed in the *Manifesto*, Zhang sees a profound commitment to cosmopolitan unity in Confucianism through ethics. Race, ethnicity, and nationality should not be applied to divide people from each other. Commerce and industry cause greed, competition, and irresponsibility among people. Yet Confucian ethics unite people with each other in a more peaceful and harmonious manner. Zhang thus vehemently promotes the renaissance of Song-Ming Confucianism, whose teaching, like a healing medicine, he sees as so effective that even the deaf would be able to hear its sound (发聋振聩之药).[94] Zhang again compares Song-Ming Confucianism to Bergson's and Eucken's philosophy and intends to make meaningful connections to contribute to world ethics.

The debate on science and metaphysics raised interest among many Chinese intellectuals of the time. Since Zhang and Ding were both Liang Qichao's students, Liang joined the debate and commented, "This question [about science and life] is the greatest one in the universe. This type of dispute has never taken place in our country. It is extremely delightful to have such a magnificent phenomenon in academia."⁹⁵ Liang hopes that both parties will exhaust their arguments and lead a complete discussion of this fundamental question on science and life. He also thinks that this dispute should last as long as possible and extend as far as possible. Yet Liang criticizes Ding's impolite wording and warns that future polemics need to follow appropriate rules of respectful communication. Ideologically speaking, however, Liang clearly sides with Zhang.

Indeed, Zhang's skepticism toward science has developed over time, especially during his journey with Liang Qichao to the Paris Peace Conference in 1919. Liang penned a well-known travel report, *The Impressions of My European Journey* (Ouyou Xinying Lu, 欧游心影录), to describe and reflect his travel experience as a private person at the conference (Liang's journey was privately funded, and he had no office at that time). Yet Liang's prominent status as a former high-profile politician and his international reputation as a prominent leader of the Hundred Days Reform gave him access to insider information from the conference. Liang's travelogue already articulates a deep skepticism toward science and materialism, as detailed in Zhang's open polemic. Indeed, after the European journey, Liang also transformed from being a constitutionalist reformer of monarchy to becoming an advocate of Confucian culture. Liang recognizes the potential contribution of traditional Chinese culture to a world organization and a world culture. He reflects on warfare in Europe and observes that both the winning countries, including France and Britain, as well as the losing countries, such as Germany and Austria, were suffering severe consequences of the war. The major reason for the war in Europe, Liang argues, is the belief in the omnipotence of science (过信科学万能).⁹⁶ Liang comments that the development of science and the industrial revolution have resulted in the fundamental uprooting of traditional economic production and social structure in Europe. The inner spiritual life and the outer material change cannot catch up with each other. The most conspicuous phenomenon is the stark contrast between modern urban life and rural community.⁹⁷ Liang observes that the rapid change in the materiality of life causes anxiety and confusion in one's inner spiritual life. Philosophy and Christianity, which have functioned as a moral compass for common people and intellectuals, now succumb to the logic of scientific materialism. He thus complains, "Fundamental cosmic principles now should be testified by science with evidence but should no longer be obtained through philosophical meditation. These materialist philosophers have established a purely materialist and mechanical view of life and subsumed all inner and outer life under the law of necessity of material movement."[98] In this, Liang sees a risk of losing social morality to scientific necessity and considers it the greatest crisis of the mind in the world. He contends that not everything can be proven by scientific experiment and that each experiment will undermine the results of former ones. Science, for him, is not interested in perpetual moral principles as guidance in social and spiritual life. Liang predicts that warlords and fierce social and financial competitions will emerge without any concern for morality or honor. Life would become meaningless if it were only a fight for food and resources: "Those who then [are] praised for the omnipotence of science expected the success of science, which promised the emergence of a golden world anytime. Now science is finally successful; the material improvement of the last century surpassed that of the last three millennia manifoldly. Yet humanity has not acquired happiness; rather we have suffered many disasters. We are like those lost travelers in a desert, seeing a big black shadow in the distance and rushing forward with all our energies to reach the shadow as a reliable guide. But after we have caught up with it after a few miles, the shadow disappeared. We are thus infinitely saddened and disappointed. Who is the shadow? It is the Mister Science. Europeans have dreamt a huge dream of science's omnipotence, but now they are talking about the bankruptcy of science. This is a crucial point in the recent transformation of the mind."[99] Given the strong advocacy for science by the New Culture Movement, Liang hastens to add that he is not debasing science and does not consider science bankrupt. He only intends to point out that science is not omnipotent in every aspect.

Liang narrates that *fin-de-siècle* pessimism is prevalent in Europe during his European tour. He reports that, once when he was conversing with an American journalist named Simon, the journalist asked him what he would do after returning to China and whether he would take some Western culture back to China. Of course, Liang responded. Simon sighed, saying that Western civilization was bankrupt. Liang inquired, "What are you going to do after returning to America?" Simon responded, "I will close the door and wait until your imported Chinese civilization to rescue us." Liang comments:

> When I first heard this, I thought he was intentionally ridiculing me. After I heard this type of statement often everywhere else, I realized that those who had the premonition of danger were extremely distressed about the situation, considering their material civilization as the seeds of dangerous social phenomena. Instead, utopian otherworldly China still has some solutions. This was one aspect of the psychology of the majority of Europeans.[100]

Upon acknowledging the pessimism about science in the West, Liang surmises that there would be a revival of philosophy and religion after the great trauma of war. The view of life must undergo a dramatic change (人生观自然要起一大变化).[101]

After having similar conversations with Westerners about Chinese culture, Liang decides to promote more Chinese tradition and arrives at the conclusion that China should become a cosmopolitan country to contribute to world culture. China, indeed, has a lot of things to offer to the world, Liang confirms. He discusses the best attitude for the Chinese tradition:

> The old generations in China, being complacent and conservative, claimed that China already had all the Western learning. This is truly laughable. Yet those, who are indulged in the wind from the West, dismissed everything in China as worthless, as if we had nothing for thousands of years, like a savage tribe. Is this even more ridiculous? We need to know that, when we observe one school of thought, we should see it against its historical time as its background. We should learn the fundamental spirit in that thought, not the conditions that gave rise to it. If we come down to the conditions, then they are always confined to history. For example, Confucius said a lot about aristocratic ethics which is not applicable anymore. But we can't despise him based on this ground. Plato also said that slavery should be conserved. Should we execrate Plato because of this? Once we have understood this point, we will be able to pass fair judgment in our study of Chinese traditional culture without making mistakes during the process of acquiring knowledge.[102]

Liang is carefully navigating a new path in connecting Chinese tradition with Western modernity, separating his program from both the conservative camp and the radical Westernization group. Liang, however, still considers the Western method of research (研究学问的方法) superior because it will help find historical truth. He is transforming from a constitutional monarchist to a scholar of Confucianism in the interest of a world culture. He detests narrow nationalism and patriotism, contending that one's love of one's country should not prevent a person from seeing individuals and the world beyond the nation. "The primary purpose of life," Liang claims, "lies in contributing to all of humanity. Why? Humanity as an entirety is the ultimate amount of one human being. Then if one person aims to develop oneself, one must follow the path of the world with great effort."[103] In a cosmopolitan country (世界主义的国家), Liang imagines, everyone can fully unfold their potentials and talents to contribute to the entire world civilization (世界人类全体文明).[104] Not only China but also all countries in the world should become such a cosmopolitan country to construe a meaningful world culture.

Liang's travelogue, in a sense, predated the controversy over science and the view of life. Even though Ding was also part of Liang's retinue and shared a room with Zhang during their stay in Paris, Liang clearly shared a position more like Zhang's toward scientism. Zhang's 1958 Manifesto recapitulated the essence of Liang's travelogue and gave it a more theoretical and philosophical expression. Both Zhang and Liang came to the insight that Confucian ethics could serve as the basis of a world culture. Despite his avowed turn to philosophy, Zhang remained a politician. While he did not further develop the Song-Ming Confucian notion of *xin xing*, Zhang introduced the idea to politics and saw its validity in a global context. Similarly, Liang Shuming, Zhang's colleague at Peking University, reinterpreted Confucianism and applied it to rural reform as a basis for world culture.

4

LIANG SHUMING, WORLD CULTURE, AND RURAL MODERNITY

Last year shortly before the summer vacation [1920], colleagues held a party to bid farewell to Professor Cai Jiemin (蔡子民, aka Cai Yuanpei蔡元培) of Peking University and other professors who were about to travel to Europe and the United States. I remember that some colleagues gave speeches and they all more or less had the idea that these professors should bring Chinese culture to the West and then import Western culture back home. After I heard this repeatedly, I asked: "What you proposed to Professor Cai and others is also what we all think, but I want to know what exactly of Chinese culture you want to export to the West? If we could first leave Western culture aside—what on earth is Chinese culture?" No one responded to me. Afterward, Professor Tao Menghe (陶孟和) and Professor Hu Shizhi (胡适之, aka Hu Shi 胡适) smilingly said to me: "Your questions were really good, but it was too hot, people didn't want to use their mind too much."[1]

Liang Shuming (1893–1988, 梁漱溟), a self-taught philosopher and later a rural reformer, wanted to show the imprecision in the understanding and definition of Western and Eastern (Chinese) cultures among the leading intellectuals of his time through this anecdote. In his book *Eastern and Western Cultures and Their Philosophies* (*Dongxi wenhua ji qi zhexue*, 东西文化及其哲学, 1921; hereafter *Eastern and Western Cultures*), Liang insists that Confucian idealism is the essence and foundation of Eastern culture. Unlike other thinkers, like Cai and Hu, who were more interested in introducing Western culture to China, Liang had other thoughts. He asks: "Should Eastern culture be entirely uprooted or could it still be liberated and emancipated (翻身)? What I mean by liberation does not imply whether Chinese people should still use Eastern culture; rather what I mean is the hypothesis, whether Eastern culture could, like Western culture, become a world culture (世界的文化). In this moment, Western science and democracy are prevalent everywhere in the world. Hence, the most straightforward question is whether Eastern culture could become a world culture. If it could not become a world culture, then it would not exist; if it could still exist, then it should not only be confined to China but become available for the entire world."[2] Clearly, the silence at the party might not be the result of the sweltering summer weather in Beijing. Rather, it indicated an embarrassing moment in which the participants felt the deep disappointment and humiliation caused by China's lost wars against Britain, France, Russia, Japan, and other Western powers. While Liang shared his colleagues' despair about the inability of the Chinese government to retain its sovereignty and dignity, he disagreed with their hope to revive China with Western modernity. Liang's insistence on the revival of the Chinese tradition, a position that was known among his colleagues, was unpopular at the moment.

Teaching at Peking University until 1924, Liang was a prominent social activist, politician, and scholar throughout his ninety-three-year life. The communist leader Mao Zedong counted Liang as an old friend.[3] Liang shared Zhang Junmai and many others' concerns about the future of China in a time of Western imperialism and identified philosophy as a medium for his contribution to overcome the crisis. Unlike many other Chinese thinkers, such as Lu Xun, Feng Youlan, Hu Shi, and Liang Qichao, Liang Shuming did not study or live abroad but remained in China his entire life. Liang's effort to establish schools and promote education in rural areas reveals his idea of practical Confucianism. No other New Confucian thinkers discussed in this book embarked on this path. Liang's philosophy of a world culture and his rural reform as its social foundation integrate thinking with practice. Zhang Junmai saw in New Confucianism political and philosophical meanings; and Feng Youlan (see Chapter 5) developed a New Rationalism in the academic discipline of philosophy. In comparison to Zhang and Feng's rather elitist approaches to Confucianism, Liang's rural reform, with the prominent example in Zouping (邹平), Shandong (山东), was down to earth and became extremely influential in China.[4]

Liang has been commonly referred to as a conservative and a nationalist. Guy Alitto surmises that "the reasons for such designations vary from Liang's fervent Confucianism to his insistence on wearing a long scholar's gown even in sweltering heat."[5] Depicting major steps in Liang's intellectual and political life, Alitto calls Liang "the last Confucian." The nostalgic tone in this phrase captures the transformation of Confucianism from a dominant state philosophy and social ethics to a teaching condemned as backward, useless, and damaging in China's path toward modernity. Alitto characterizes Liang as "the century's foremost Confucian traditionalist," who legendarily braved the tirade from the communist leader Mao Zedong in a public meeting of the Central People's Government Council in 1953 and, after his criticism of the government was mercilessly rejected, asked to speak yet again.[6] Alitto contrasts the clash between the chief Marxist in China and his long-term friend Liang as the clash between modernization and its conservative critique. Mao's disagreement with Liang seems to render him a conservative thinker in perpetuity. Alitto situates Liang's position in a worldwide conservative movement that seems "to take, and then idealize, a traditional form of society as the touchstone for social excellence."[7] Conservatives share a common hostility toward political and economic liberalism, individual material pursuit, the efforts and results of industrialization, and urbanization. They search for common values or a common truth and are suspicious of things Western or "foreign." Alitto explains that the conservative antagonism toward urbanization results in the conservatives' agrarianism, an idea that insists on the rural foundation of a society. Liang's lifelong dedication to Confucianism and rural reform are thus regarded as the benchmarks for his conservatism. Further, Liang's position that China could only achieve political independence by reviving the traditional Confucianist heritage brought him the label of being a nationalist.[8] Alitto argues that, for Liang, "heritage possessed not just historical but trans-historical significance. It must not be a museum piece which would serve the interests of national identity and pride, but the basis for present action. Like premodern Chinese, Liang believed that China was not just a culture among cultures but the only truly human one."[9] Given Liang's recognition of the advantage of Western democracy and science, however, I would not see him as such a narrow-minded nationalist who simply honors the Chinese tradition as the only human culture on Earth. Liang indeed tried to rescue valuable elements in Confucianism in the crisis of Western imperialism and global warfare, but it would be difficult to say that he only considered the Chinese tradition the only viable form of culture in the world.

Despite the labels of Liang as a conservatist and a nationalist, I argue that Liang endeavors to resist a total Westernization of China and its colonizing and auto-colonizing effects. Like other New Confucianists, Liang has reservations toward China's total imitation of Western modernity and still considers the Chinese cultural tradition precious and useful, not only for China but also for the entire world. He does acknowledge the advantage of technological modernization as well as the New Culture Movement's tenets of science and democracy. Simultaneously, he highlights Confucianism's significance as a practical rationalism for individual and social life, especially in a time of crisis. Liang puts his understanding of Confucianism into practice in his rural reform projects, which are characterized by his utopian socialism. Liang's critique of capitalism and the destruction of Chinese rural economy by Western-style industrialization is a major reason for his endeavor to revive rural economic life and establish a rural socialism. From this perspective, Liang is an idealist or a utopian experimentalist who does not rigidly insist on a backward-looking social order, which is what a conservatist would do. Rather, he envisions possibilities to innovate and reform the Chinese tradition to produce an alternative future to Western modernity. In fact, Liang's activity of founding experimental rural schools paralleled several projects worldwide: John Dewey's Laboratory School in Chicago, Bertrand and Dora Russell's Beacon Hill School in Sussex, Rudolf Steiner's Waldorf Schule, and Hermann Graf Keyserling's School of Wisdom in Darmstadt. Finally, Liang is deeply concerned with the quality of leading a good life. Life is for him a universal category beyond national and cultural boundaries, which is similar to the ideas of other thinkers discussed in this book.

Liang's New Confucianism and his rural reform remarkably strike a third path beyond the left and right, progressive and conservative, revolutionist and traditionalist divide in Chinese and global politics in the early twentieth century. To provide a more precise description of Liang's philosophical spirit, I refrain from portraying him according to the powerful political binary between leftism and conservatism. Rather, I emphasize his contribution as a philosopher from the perspective of world culture and his role as a reformer in terms of his pedagogical governmentality and rural modernity. While Liang's horizon of the "world" is limited to Europe, India, and East Asia, he always strives to place Chinese culture in a global context. Hence, focusing on Liang as both a philosopher and a reformer in this chapter, I will first discuss his *Eastern and Western Cultures* and then turn to his *Theory of Rural Construction (Xiangcun Jianshe Lilun,* 乡村建设理论, 1937), which he gave Mao Zedong as a gift and touchstone for their nightly conversations.

Before delving into Liang's writings, I will briefly introduce his biographical background to help illuminate his thinking.[10] Liang was born in Beijing in 1893, the same year as Mao, to an impoverished family with a lineage that included high officials and Mongolian royalty dating back to the fourteenth century. His father was a minor official at the imperial court of the Qing dynasty.

Disappointed by the downfall of the monarchy, the republican revolution, and the encroachment of Western imperialism, Liang's father committed suicide on his sixtieth birthday in 1918. He intended to use his death to awaken the Chinese people to follow the ethically right path to save China, as documented in his will. The father's suicide became a public event, broadly discussed in newspapers and magazines such as *Xin Qingnian (New Youth or La Jeunesse,* 新青年). Liang was decisively influenced by this incident in his family. He inherited his father's devout Confucian spirit of serving the country with moral rectitude and selfless commitment. After graduating from high school in 1911, the year of the Chinese Revolution, Liang became a politically active journalist. While he was for a time a radical socialist, Liang soon lost his idealism because of the political intrigues and unscrupulousness and was attracted by Buddhism as a healing method for his frustration.

In 1916, Liang published an essay, *Treatise on Finding the Foundation and Resolving the Doubt (Jiu Yuan Jue Yi Lun,* 究元决疑论) in the journal *Eastern Miscellanies (Dongfang Zazhi,* 东方杂志), in which he used Western philosophy to interpret Buddhism. The then president of Peking University, Cai Yuanpei, was impressed with Liang's essay and invited him to teach Indian philosophy in 1917, despite his lack of formal academic training. Liang asked Cai whether he could teach Buddhism and Confucianism together. Cai generously agreed, telling him that, as a subject matter, Confucianism deserves scholarly scrutiny. In fact, at Peking University, prominent scholars and politicians such as Chen Duxiu (陈独秀), Hu Shi, and Cai himself led the New Culture Movement to downplay Confucianism and promote Westernization in China. At the same time, Gu Hongming (see Chapter 1 in this book) was also on the faculty and was at odds with the thinkers of the New Culture Movement. Liang deeply appreciated Cai's open-mindedness and his cultivation of a receptive intellectual atmosphere and academic freedom between 1917 and 1923. When Liang recalled this teaching experience, he humbly called himself a student rather than a professor.[11]

After leaving Peking University, Liang was actively engaged in journalism, rural education, and politics. He came to realize that rural villages were the foundation of Chinese society and that China needed rural reform at the grassroots level to form effective governments. He founded the Shandong Rural Reconstruction Institute (山东乡村建设研究院) in 1931 to promote his rural education project, teaching the Chinese language, science, technology, arts, history, and geography to eradicate illiteracy among farmers. Starting with Zouping as the first county, Liang's social experiment became extremely successful and expanded to other counties until the Sino-Japanese war broke out in 1937. Liang also rose to fame as a social activist. Upon the invitation of Chiang Kai-shek, Liang effectively negotiated between the Nationalist Party and the Communist Party so that they formed a united front against the Japanese invasion. Disappointed by Chiang's gradual change from resisting the Japanese to eliminating the communists, Liang, representing the party of rural constructionists (乡村建设派), cofounded the political party China Democratic League (中国民主政团同盟) in 1941. The aim was to integrate more forces against the Japanese invasion and to promote political constitutionalism. As mentioned in Chapter 3, Zhang Junmai was one of the cofounders of this political party. After World War II, Liang failed to mediate between the Communist Party and the Nationalist Party. When the Civil War broke out, he resigned from his post as the secretary general of the China Democratic League and went to live in Chongqing, Sichuan Province. After the founding of the People's Republic of China, Liang acted again as the secretary of the China Democratic League and became a representative in the People's Congress. This party remains one of the eight legally recognized political parties in the People's Republic of China until today. Liang had an enduring friendship with Mao Zedong and participated in many prominent political discussions. Despite being repeatedly critiqued in public and experiencing political persecutions during the Cultural Revolution, he always raised the issue of constitutionalism. After the Cultural Revolution, Liang was elected to the Standing Committee of Chinese People's Political Consultative Conference as well as to the committee for the amendment of the Chinese constitution in 1980. He stayed a diligent writer until his death in 1988.

JOYOUS INTUITIVE RATIONALISM AS WORLD CULTURE IN EASTERN AND WESTERN CULTURES AND THEIR PHILOSOPHIES

Liang's book *Eastern and Western Cultures and Their Philosophies* (东西文化及其哲学, 1921) was a distinctive voice during the May Fourth Movement and hit a nerve of the time. Liang's contemporary Jiang Baili (蒋百里) called it an unprecedented book that shakes history and illuminates the present (震古烁今).[12] Many prominent scholars discussed or critiqued this book, including Liu Boming (刘伯明), Zhang Donxun (张东荪), Hu Shi, and Chen Duxiu (陈独秀). Hu and Chen later ascribed Liang to the camp of Zhang Junmai during the debate on science and life (see Chapter 3 on Zhang). Liang felt misunderstood and claimed that he was by no means against science.[13] At any rate, this book "made him perhaps the most popular single neo-traditional thinker of the May Fourth period."[14] Reprinted eight times between 1921 and 1929, this book has been considered one of the seminal documents of New Confucianism.[15]

Liang argues in this book for the necessity of Confucian idealism as a practice of life and emphasizes joy, intuition, and rationalism, in addition to the New Culture Movement's advocation of Western science and democracy. Liang, however, is not a pure Confucianist thinker. Indeed, his New Confucianism is marked by his Buddhist faith. In the forward to *Eastern and Western Cultures*, Liang recounts that, when he was twenty years old, he became a firm believer in Buddhist teaching because he shared the Buddhist view that life is suffering. Liang adopted a vegetarian diet, detested luxury and material possessions, and rejected his parents' proposal to get married. Yet when Liang realized Confucianism's optimistic attitude of life and the joyousness to transcend anxiety (乐以忘忧), he decided to abandon the Buddhist monastic style of life and dedicated himself to social engagement.[16]

War and crisis also urged Liang's transition from Buddhism to Confucianism. Like Zhang Junmai's radical shift from politics to philosophy in 1919, Liang experienced a similar transformation. In a trip to southern China in 1917, Liang personally experienced the violence of unruled soldiers inflicted on the civil population during the conflicts between warlords. He thus reflects: "I could no longer ignore the circumstances around me. Everything in the society now would not allow me to follow the Buddhist path of life. When I went out, saw things in the streets, met friends, and heard various situations, all of them echoed the conclusions of my study of cultural issues. I had to vehemently reject the prevalence of the Buddhist practice of life."[17] He penned an essay, *The Duty of Good People to the Society* (*Wucao Bu Chu Ru Cangsheng He*, 吾曹不出如苍生何, 1917) and printed 3,000 copies with his own funds to distribute among friends and colleagues. Like his father, Liang wanted to wake up intellectuals and people with a good conscience to rescue China out of this turmoil. Liang observed that Westerners were sick of their materialism and yearned for spiritual rehabilitation; yet Easterners still wished to emulate the West. He intended to bring them both onto the path of Confucianism: "If Westerners could not find Confucius, then it is a matter of course. In today's China, however, some people are promoting Western learning while others are promoting Buddhism. But everyone is shy and hesitating to mention Confucianism. Then it is the same here like in the West. If I did not endorse the truth of Confucianism, who else would do so? This reason urges me to practice a Confucian life."[18]

Despite Liang's claimed transition from a Buddhist to a Confucianist, his interpretation of Confucianism reveals his deeply Buddhist perspective. Recent studies have revealed the inextricable connections between Buddhism and Confucianism in Liang's thinking.[19] John Hanafin points out that Liang's epistemology is based on Yogācāra, the theory of consciousness in the Mahāyāna branch of Buddhism.[20] Liang once reflects that Buddhism is too elitist to be popularized, whereas Confucianism has always been a teaching of social and life practice for a large population for thousands of years. Then his transition from a Buddhist to a Confucianist, I argue, is in fact a transition in the practice of life, from following the Buddhist Five Precepts and retreat to monastic life toward a life dedicated to social engagement, as Confucianism requires one to do. In fact, since he was twenty years old, Liang remained a vegetarian until the end of his life, despite his transition to Confucianism. Mao and other high-rank officials always accommodated Liang and had vegetarian food with him. This aspect discloses the multifaceted composition of New Confucianism as an intellectual movement.

In *Eastern and Western Cultures*, Liang first comprehensively defines Eastern and Western cultures. Then he compares European, Chinese, and Indian philosophical traditions as three major ones. Finally, he presents his hypothesis about Confucianism as a future world culture. He refers to multiple positions toward cultural comparisons between the East and the West, including Li Dazhao's (李大钊) *The Fundamental Difference between Eastern and Western Civilizations* (东西文明之根本异点), Chen Duxiu's (陈独秀) *Our Final Enlightenment* (吾人之最后觉悟), George William Knox's *The Spirit of the Orient*, the Japanese philosopher Kaneko Chikusui's (金子筑水) lecture on Eastern and Western civilizations, and John Dewey's lecture at Peking University on the integration of Eastern and Western cultures. Liang also mentions many popular opinions about the difference between the West and the East; for example, that the West aims to control nature while the East harmonizes with nature; that the West is dominated by movement (动) while the East by stillness (静). He disagrees with the attempt to completely discard Confucianism and its ethics and replace them with Western culture. For Liang, the ideas of science and democracy, which were prominent during the New Culture Movement, proved their advantage and usefulness everywhere—he was not against them. He points out, however, that the connection between science and democracy has not been clearly explained or thoroughly understood. They should not be used carelessly to represent the essence of Western culture. At the same time, Liang strongly opposes those who conservatively have attacked and resisted the introduction of Western culture to China. He comments that these "old-school gentlemen" (旧派先生) have neither made any constructive suggestions to improve the current situation in

China nor understood the true spirit of Confucianism, nor provided any pertinent reasons why it should not be abandoned vis-à-vis Western culture.[21]

Liang thus introduces his own philosophy of life to prepare his argument about rehabilitating the true spirit of Confucianism as a future world culture. For him, life is continuation (相续).[22] Life and the universe are one and the same thing. The universe is not outside of life because the eternity of universe is based on the continuation of life. Life is a practice, not an abstract idea. Life comprises prior selves and a present self. The continuation of life is the struggle of the present selfhood to overcome the prior selves. Life's struggle exists everywhere and all the time—it is not only confined to human beings but also extends to all living creatures. While the resistance to overcome the challenge of life is a biological intuition, conscious decisions about how to deal with life's difficulties and whether to follow through the struggles differ. Different attitudes toward how to live one's life, how to deal with life's struggles, construe different cultures. Liang defines that a culture is the way of life or an abstract spirit of life.[23] Liang also differentiates culture from civilization: while civilization represents the achievements in life (生活中的成绩品) such as pottery or political systems, culture embodies an abstract method, style, or spirit of life. Sometimes these two are interchangeable. Liang's view of life and culture reveals the influence of the Buddhist *yogācāra* tradition (the doctrine of consciousness, Chinese translation as *weishi*, 唯识). In fact, Liang published *Outline of Yogācāra* (*Weishi Shuyi*, 唯识述义) shortly before *Eastern and Western Cultures* and recognized this Buddhist idealist theory of knowledge as the most convincing one.[24] Charlotte Furth comments: "Like T'an Ssu-t'ung [Tan Sitong, 谭嗣同] Liang found in Wei-shih Buddhism and in Neo-Confucian cosmology based on the *I ching* the inspiration for a view of the total cosmos as a mind-created ceaseless flux of existence, taking shifting phenomenal form through the mediation of *yin* and *yang* forces."[25]

Liang further discusses three attitudes of life and assigns each of them to three major representative cultural spheres: the West (Europe), India, and China. The West represents the decision to positively solve problems and reform difficult situations to meet society's needs. The Chinese do not want to solve external problems. They aim to change themselves to live with the difficulties, and they try to find their own satisfaction and happiness amid unhappy situations. The Indians exemplify the most passive attitude: they want neither to solve the problems nor change themselves. They want to cancel the problems through asceticism and the denial of life. Liang comments that the first one is a movement forward, the second one is the middle ground, and the third one is a look backward. He personally supports the first attitude of positive movement forward as the most natural path of life (生活本来的路向) and discourages the third path of asceticism.²⁶ Based on his definition of culture as an abstract spirit of life, Liang claims that, in the West, the emergence of science and democracy should not be explained with the logic of historical materialism and political economy. Rather, the Western spirit of moving forward should be seen as the force that has given rise to democracy and science. This spirit is more fundamentally suited to capture the essence of Western culture. He argues: "Isn't this desire for material life derived from spirit? . . . I have the courage to say: if the transportation between Europe and Asia were not opened up, the spirit of the Chinese people would still remain the same as it had been for thousands of years. China's society and economy would definitely not have changed. [Without the spirit,] the so-called Industrial Revolution in Europe would definitely not have happened."²⁷ Here Liang echoes Weber's emphasis on the spirit of capitalism and the critique of asceticism in *The Protestant Ethic* and his other studies of world religions.

Even though Liang applauds the Western spirit of moving forward, he is also critical of capitalist competition and warfare. Echoing Weber again, Liang sees the cause for this problem in the European philosophical tradition: a strong rationalization, arguing that "using one word to summarize it, [the major trait of Western philosophy] is the admiration of reason."²⁸ Hence the West has developed science to control nature and has strived for materialism. "Their spiritual life, however, has been damaged and their life has suffered, which has been exposed as an unhidden fact since the nineteenth century!"²⁹ Liang admits that European technology and industrial revolution were truly impressive and more superior to the Chinese achievements in these areas. China, if left alone without Western intrusion, would never develop such things because the Chinese spirit of life is a different one. It is important to note that Liang does not have an inferiority complex about the West here, as many of his contemporaries have shown. Instead, Liang argues that Confucian idealism would balance the lopsided rationalism of the West and lead the world to a more moderate and harmonious world culture.

Liang claims that Confucianism is first and foremost a philosophy of life because Confucius praised and admired life. This life is not only human life but life in all forms. Confucian philosophy of life is a metaphysics of cosmic life. Liang considers life or liveliness (*sheng*, 生) the most essential concept in Confucianism. "Confucian doctrine is nothing else than telling us to follow nature's path and to live and thrive in the most lively and smoothest manner. Confucius thinks that the universe is always moving forward. Everything desires growth and should be allowed to grow. If it does not have any unnaturalness, it can definitely integrate and harmonize with the universe. Then the entire universe will have spring-like lively energy."[30] In addition, Liang emphasizes Confucianism's non-confirmative attitude. It neither insists on any firm values of good and evil nor has fixed moral principles and externalized standards. Rather, Confucian values such as respect and love should be understood with flexible applications in concrete situations. They should not be used as a fundamental principle in a causal relationship. Liang calls this attitude non-confirmatory (不认定) or non-judgmental: "Common people demand moral principles, but Confucius does not. Common people want to have logical causality, but Confucius does not. The result is that common people's causality does not make sense, but Confucius's non-causality makes sense."[31] Liang explains that Confucius depends on his intuition (*zhijue*, 直觉) while common people depend on their logical reason to argue about what is right or wrong. Yet to compromise in the middle ground is the law of the universe (调和折衷是宇宙的法则), which one must follow even without knowing it.[32] The best solution to a problem must be found via intuition.

Using Buddhist logico-epistemology (*yinming xue*, 因明学), the method of Yogācāra, Liang compares the Confucian intuition to *feiliang* (非量, translated from apramāṇa in Sanskrit). Two other terms are also important for Liang's discussion. *Xianliang* (现量, translated from *pratyakṣa-pramāṇas* in Sanskrit) describes external perceptions through sensual organs such as eyes, nose, ears, mouth, or skin. *Biliang* (比量 translated from *anumāna-pramāṇa* in Sanskrit) means knowledge gained through reasoning, logical processing, and causal relation. The Sanskrit word *Pramāṇa* refers to quality or quantity, like the Chinese word *liang*. As we see in the Sanskrit terms, both perception and reason are linguistically construed as two parts: a descriptive part and the base of *pramāṇa*. Intuition, however, is simply a negation of *pramāṇa*: *apramāṇa*. In Chinese, it was also translated as non-quality, *fei* (非), meaning non-existing or negative. While *xianliang* and *biliang* both have an outcome either through sensation or through reason, *feiliang* is abstract and can't be quantified.[33]

Liang argues that, while knowledge is based on sensation and reason, intuition is the mediation between these two human faculties. Sensation does not have any difference or meaning unless reason analyzes it and gives it meaning. Between receiving (*shou*, 受) and thinking (*xiang*, 想), Liang adds, there is something that cannot be rendered clearly in language but is immediately related to sensation and reason. This third space is intuition, which mediates experience and abstraction. Intuition gives us an inclination or a feeling, something spiritual. Our aesthetic taste for works of art is more directly related to intuition. Sensation and reason are not enough to perceive the atmosphere or the aura of the works. For example, sensation recognizes the colors or the strokes; reason compares the length, the thickness, or the color differences. Yet only intuition perceives the aesthetic mood in the ambiance. It is something lively, something moving, something not as rigid as a concept. It is something subjective and psychological that is derived from an objective quantity. Intuition is sometimes closer to sensation, for example, when we enjoy listening to music; but sometimes it is closer to reason when we enjoy reading and understanding poetry or literature in a very broad sense. While knowledge formation must be based on sensation, reason, and intuition, Liang disputes reason's status as the fundamental capacity for decision making. He believes that intuition is more essential and more flexible than reason.

From Liang's perspective, only Buddhism and Confucianism have this nonconfirmatory flexibility that mediates extreme polarities. This flexibility of mind stems from the ability of intuition in all kinds of different situations. Human life is fluid in nature and only follows the most right, convenient, and appropriate path. In Confucianism, intuition is intrinsically related to human nature and leads humans on the right path. It is an inborn ability to choose and do good things and to recognize beauty without thinking and learning. Only bad habits could cloud our sharp intuition and make us insensitive.

If one cultivates this intuition and keeps it intact and sensible, then one has the ability of *ren* (仁), another key Confucian concept, literally meaning kindheartedness, mercifulness, or benevolence. In Liang's explication, "Confucianism depends entirely on intuition. Hence the single most important thing is a sensitive, sharp, and enlightened intuition; the single most fearful thing is a slow, blunt, and numb intuition. All evils are derived from a dumb intuition. There are no other reasons. Therefore, Confucius taught us to pursue *ren* by all means."[34] *Ren* provides the foundation for all moral laws, not only because *ren* regulates human behaviors but also because *ren* recognizes and accepts all human intuitive feelings and desires, including the basic needs for food and sexuality. The Confucian idea of *ren* acknowledges the entirety of natural and emotional inclinations of humanity, whereas rationalism numbs intuition and splits the holistic selfhood between objectivity and subjectivity (物我). Therefore, Liang thinks that Confucianism does not overtly promote rationalism (理智) because it would encourage selfishness and subdue sensations and emotions, even though Confucianism is a type of rationalism, as other thinkers have recognized. *Ren* is not merely an intuitive quality, Liang further specifies; it is a lively, stable, and balanced mental state. In the state of being *ren*, one forgets oneself and follows heaven's path (无私心, 合天理).[35] One is sincerely in touch with one's emotions and desires and happily accepts their existence just as it is; one is then connected to the cosmos (通天下之感).[36] *Ren* is thus the essence of the ideal inner life envisioned by Confucianism. It regulates people's behavior from their most natural interior humanity, and it does not stick to any unbendable and external moral rules. *Ren* is never extreme or polarizing; it is always moderate (调和) and incessantly flowing forward (流行不息).[37] Since *ren* is the highest ideal in Confucianism, it is extremely difficult to reach. It is the ultimate goal of the constant cultivation of one's interiority (内心修养) and self-reflection (内观).[38] This point reminds us of the Kantian vision of the Enlightenment of a person and a society, a goal that is worth continued striving but could never be fully reached. While Kant's Enlightenment is concerned with the concept of a priori reason, Liang's understanding of Confucian *ren* is immediately connected to intuition.

Liang further explains that, based on *ren* and intuition, Confucianism has developed its most important attitude (唯一重要的态度): tolerance and generosity (不计较厉害).[39] Liang compares Confucius to Mo Zi (墨子), a contemporary of Confucius, and interprets Mo Zi as a rationalist thinker. Liang argues that Mo Zi (Mohism) requests that every behavior must have a meaning and reasoning, and he calculates the rights and wrongs of things. This attitude suffocates intuition and pleasure and supports resentment and violence. (More on the renaissance of Mo Zi in the early twentieth century in Chapter 6 of this book.) Confucianism, however, recognizes the irrational or intuitive nature of humanity and promotes the enjoyment of life's pleasures. Liang's view here resounds Weber's interpretation of Confucianism. It does not mean that Confucianism fails to acknowledge evil; but Confucianism rather emphasizes the good human nature. Confucianism does not consider external behaviors essential but rather sees them as ephemeral phenomena. The heart in the inside is more fundamental. If *ren* as an intuitive psychological quality builds the foundation of Confucianism, then calculative and mechanical reason would damage this balanced state of *ren* and harm life's opportunity (伤害生机).[40] Generosity cultivates *ren*, maintains the balance of the internal mental state, and promotes life and energy flow. Hence, Liang contends that Confucianism does not support punishment because it damages *ren*, numbs intuition, fosters calculation, and causes fear. Liang comments that Western rational profit-driven culture is more attuned to Mo Zi's thinking. The passion for art in the West, however, keeps its culture in a better balance.

A life with *ren* is a life full of absolute joy (绝对乐), not relative joy (相对的乐).[41] Confucianism neither focuses on personal profit or loss nor calculates right or wrong. A Confucian life only follows good intuitions. Thus, a Confucian life promises absolute joy. A Confucian always moves forward with positive energy and does not indulge in moments of unhappiness. It is not a relative happiness but a self-sufficient contentment, an unconditional pleasure. Being *ren* is being free of worry. Being *ren* is being happy. Of course, negative emotions also exist and should be acknowledged. One intuitively reacts to different situations and accepts the emotions as they emerge. Yet one does not force anything or retain any fixed emotions or ideas. One always resides in the balanced state of *ren*.

After reviewing the various aspects and manifestations of intuition in Confucianism, Liang claims that Confucianism also uses rationalism to reflect on immediate intuitions to reach a conscious decision about action. In other words, the faculty of intuition alone is not enough to hold the middle path (中庸). Rational reflection (回省) is the key to connecting the wealth of intuition to benign deeds. This rational reflection leads to Confucian ethics. Liang explains that Confucius did not directly follow one movement of intuition but saw two movements: one goes out and the other returns. The returning movement of intuition is attached to rationality and is a reflection on an immediate intuitive reaction (回省时附于理智的直觉).[42] For example, our likes and dislikes are based on intuition. If we only follow this intuition, then we easily go astray; sometimes it could be even dangerous. Hence it is best that we reflect on what we have already felt to decide what we do next. This reflectivity is crucial in Confucianism. It enables us to make sound selections after recognizing our intuitive feelings. Liang observes that, in this respect, Confucianism is different from Buddhism and Taoism because it has this dual movement of intuition and reflection between the interiority and the external world. It is, however, extremely difficult to skillfully practice this duality.

In his later essay *Outline of Eastern Thinking* (*Dongfang Xueshu Gaiguan*, 东方学术概观, 1960/1975), Liang argues that the ability to reflect on one's own behaviors and words, either as an individual or as a society, is the foundation for world peace. While Western culture uses reason to control sensation and intuition, Confucianism uses intuition to mediate reason and sensation. In this sense, Confucianism is a more "rational" teaching because it consciously recognizes the power of intuition in human nature. In Liang's vision, a reformed Confucianism, integrated with Western tradition, would offer a profound philosophical reflexivity for humanity and its future.

In sum, I call Liang's interpretation of Confucianism a joyous intuitive rationalism. Based on this interpretation, Liang proposes that a future world culture should move toward this direction. Liang predicts that transformations would take place in the following three areas: economic life, culture, and philosophy. Transformation in the material or economic life would entail changes in culture; changes in culture would induce transformation in the sciences, psychology, and ultimately the philosophy of life. Echoing his early radical socialism, Liang critiques the economic misery that capitalism has created by producing only for profits but not for needs. Liang contends that economic life should serve the need of a society based on equal distribution, not the need of an individual hunt for money. He predicts that economic misery would lead to socialist movements and tremendous changes. Then the quest for change in Western culture would lead Westerners to appreciate and adopt the way of Confucian culture.

Since Western culture focuses on competition between human beings in economic life, they change the outside world to achieve self-satisfaction. This culture subjugates people, nature, and society to accomplish technological advancement and political reform. Liang recognizes that it is necessary to have this competitive attitude in the game of survival. Yet, after material life has entered a more affluent period, to achieve harmonious relationships between human beings, this competitive attitude is no longer appropriate. At this stage, it is more important for a society to develop spiritual harmony, for which Confucianism could offer a solution. The Western way of life should adopt more of the Confucian joyous intuitive rationalism. Liang refers to the development of Western psychology and points out that Western culture has started to realize that the calculative and instrumental reason only touches the surface of life. The peace of deeper unconscious dimensions could only be achieved through the recognition of emotion, desire, and intuition. Liang points out that Western philosophers have also noticed that reason cannot completely control emotional impulse if one's interiority is not sustained in a content, balanced, and happy state of mind (和乐恬静的心理).[43] Such an inner life is the life of *ren*, the life of Confucius. Liang maintains that evolutionists have found out the fact of competition for survival in the biological world; but they have not recognized the importance of mutual help for survival (互助图存) in addition to competition. It is a human social instinct (社会的本能) to help each other and the intuition for morality and ethics. Therefore, reason can't serve as the foundation for a viable culture and society. The nearer future should be rooted in Confucian joyous intuitive rationalism.[44] These are the two changes in economic life and culture.

According to Liang's theory, the third change in philosophy is manifested in the move from knowledge to life and intuition. Liang mentions Nietzsche, Dewey, Bergson, Eucken, and Tagore as examples and claims that the one-sided pursuit of external knowledge causes humans to lose themselves and their spirituality. Only a philosophy of life can offer a solution to the crisis of rationalism and integrate the segregated areas of life into a holistic one. Liang predicts that a universal intuition would replace rationalization and thrive (世界直觉将代理智而兴).[45] A world culture based on Liang's New Confucianism would emerge out of these three changes. Again, Liang's observation is akin to Max Weber's critique of rationalization and his admiration for Confucianism and Taoism.

To achieve his vision of a world culture, Liang promotes the Confucian idea of *gang* (刚), literally meaning strength or firmness, as the central principle of a new life and a new culture for China and the world. Liang understands *gang* as an activity or a movement that is full of energy and power (里面气力极充实的一种活动).[46] *Gang*, however, is a quality that is extremely difficult to achieve. Confucius himself even admitted, "I have never seen a person with *gang*."[47] Yet Liang encourages his readers toward this goal because *gang* is a path that leads people from easy to difficult steps, culminating in a deeper dimension of ethics. Liang maintains that *gang* is based on sincere sentiment, not on false and selfish desires. *Gang* is the spirit of life and excludes depressive negativity and desire-driven ego. Movement itself is not absolute, Liang reflects, but it is crucial to know how and where to move. Only a life infused with *gang* could avoid the blindness of rationalization and move forward with positive energy and joyous creation. Only such a Confucian spirit of life could save China from warfare and poverty. Only in this understanding and practice of life could China benefit from Western science and democracy.

Liang argues that the New Culture Movement is not a Chinese renaissance, as some people claim it to be; rather, it is a Westernization of China. If China would want to usher in a cultural renaissance comparable to European renaissance, it should be the renaissance of an attitude of life (人生态度的复兴), the renaissance of the Confucian joyous intuitive rationalism.[48] Such a Confucian philosophy of life with intuition, joy, rational reflection, and energy should serve as the foundation of a future world culture. This future world culture transcends egoistic desire and creates a state of bliss for all. Happiness (乐天) would become the fundamental attitude in world culture while one still pursues knowledge and reforms the natural environment to meet society's needs.[49]

Liang, however, is not a Chinese cultural chauvinist. While he envisions the next stage of world culture as a renaissance of Confucianism, he foresees that Indian culture would come to the fore as the new world culture after Confucianism. He comments that Chinese and Indian cultures are not wrong vis-à-vis Western culture, but they are overripe (成熟太早) and thus inappropriate for the time being (不合时宜).[50] Charlotte Furth points out: "However, this 'evolutionary' scheme was presented more as a set of autonomous ideal alternatives than as a literal temporal sequence. Basically, he presented China's as the only kind of civilization which could be seen as in harmony with the true nature of the cosmos, as 'life' itself."[51] Given Liang's inclusion of India in his developmentalist vision, he doesn't seem to privilege Chinese culture from a "sinocentric" position. Rather, I argue, Liang tries to rescue and highlight valuables in Chinese philosophy in a time of political crisis, the loss of wars and territories, and a large-scale Westernization in China. His vision of a world culture implies that a Confucian is not necessarily Chinese but could well be a Westerner if this person thinks and acts according to Confucian principles; vice versa, a Chinese person could be Western if one adopts a Western practice of life. And Liang regrets that many Chinese people have not been able to follow the Confucian path of life. From this perspective, Liang's thinking bears the potential of breaking down national, cultural, and ethnic boundaries. His ideas of cultural spheres only characterize different styles of philosophical thinking as guidance of the practice of life, but do not attach them to fixed identities such as nationality, race, and ethnicity. Liang's vision of a world culture thus does not divide people according to their origins but rather focuses on their ways of thinking and practice. This marks Liang's cosmopolitanism.

On the last page of *Eastern and Western Cultures*, Liang reflects, "Confucianism is not a type of thinking, but a kind of practice of life. I am still outside of this life. Let me try it a bit, and then come back and speak."[52] Liang went to practice this life in his rural reform. After the publication of *Eastern and Western Cultures*, Liang had reached the climax of his academic career at Peking University. Yet he didn't continue on this path but resigned from his teaching post at the Peking University in 1924. Instead, he dedicated himself to rural education projects in various parts of China. The most successful project was in Zouping (邹平), Shandong (山东).

RURAL MODERNITY AND THEORY OF RURAL CONSTRUCTION (1937)

In dark winter nights in January 1938, in a warm cave in Yan'an (延安) in northwestern China, Liang had long conversations with one of his most famous friends and contemporaries, Mao Zedong (毛泽东, 1893–1976). When Chinese society sank further into turmoil after the Japanese invasion, Liang, as a nonpartisan scholar and influential social activist, was invited by Chiang Kai-shek to join the newly formed Advisory Committee (参议会) of the central government. The task of the committee was to discuss the best strategies to fight against the Japanese after Chiang agreed to collaborate with the Communist Party. Liang was interested in learning the communist perspective and volunteered to travel to Yan'an, the base of the communists. Liang's initiative was welcomed on both sides of the political fault line. When Liang met Mao, they realized that they had met many years ago in Beijing in the residence of Yang Huaizhong (杨怀中), Liang's colleague at Peking University. At the end of the first conversation, Liang gave Mao a new book of his and suggested that they use this book to carry on their discussion the next day. It is Liang's *Theory of Rural Construction* (乡村建设理论, 1937).[53] Indeed, Mao and Liang both shared the insight that the foundation of Chinese society was not in urban areas but in the countryside. To change China, one needed to start from the countryside. Rurality is the basis of Chinese culture. Mao's 1927 *Report on an Investigation of the Peasant Movement in Hunan* (湖南农民运动考察报告) made this point clear. Liang's book registered a unique combination of philosophical thinking and social activism. Liang brought his New Confucian thinking of world culture to the commoners in China and successfully achieved rural education projects.

In *Theory of Rural Construction*, nonetheless, Liang refers to the Soviet Union several times as a point of comparison for his own project—this might be the reason Mao remained largely friendly to Liang despite their differences. The book comprises two major parts: first, identifying the problem of China; second, solving it. The problem of China is "severe cultural imbalance" (极严重的文化失调).[54] The solution for this problem lies in reformulating and reapplying Confucian ethics in China's rural area. The logic of promoting or rebalancing culture through the reform of the countryside and revitalizing an "old" culture was rather unpopular in the era of worldwide industrialization and was at odds with the influential New Culture Movement (新文化运动). On the surface, this idea may sound like the transcendental naturalism expressed in Henry David Thoreau's *Walden*. Yet, upon closer look, Liang indeed proposes a utopian blueprint of social experiment, comparable to socialist experiments by Henri de Saint-Simon, Charles Fourier, and Robert Owen in the European tradition. As mentioned previously, Liang fervently believes in socialism and the elimination of private property in his formative years.[55] Furthermore, the notion of culture, while it still contains the basic philosophical traits as it is defined in *Eastern and Western Cultures*, now encompasses politics, economy, the military, and ethics. Here, culture is not a singular stand-alone entity; rather, it is only meaningful if it is compared to others in the age of imperialism. Chinese culture is thus always situated in reference to Western culture. Liang's ambition was not merely confined to the local reform for a better life. He envisions a new and unprecedented model of global society based on a rural socialism.[56]

Liang mentions several factors that have contributed to the problem of "severe cultural imbalance." The first factor is the destruction of China's rural area, both politically and economically. Liang argues that the rural area serves as the foundation of Chinese society because "almost all culture comes from the countryside and serves the countryside: such as jurisdiction, customs, industry and commerce."[57] Liang blames Western imperial encroachment since the mid-nineteenth century as well as Chinese attempts at modernization, reforms, and revolutions for the destruction of the countryside. Almost the past century could be understood as a history of rural destruction. Liang divides modern Chinese history into two periods: from the 1860s to World War I, then from World War I to the 1930s. In the first period, China has aspired to emulate the West and its urban culture, which emerged along with industrialization. Japan was successful in its imitation. China, however, failed to establish a successful urban culture and to transform itself into an industrial nation. At the same time, the rural foundation of Chinese culture gradually declined. The imported ideas of education, industry, and jurisprudence from the West are derived from an urban culture, and they don't fit the undisciplined (散漫) Chinese peasants. Liang is thus pessimistic: even though Japan also has had problems in its countryside, it could rescue its rurality with successful industrialization. China, however, has failed on both sides.

Liang observes that Japan's success in becoming an industrialized country should be attributed to its effective politics. Yet in China, the lack of a powerful central government and internal political conflicts has inflicted damage on the countryside and caused its demolition. Generally, there are two sides under one regime: the governing side and the governed side. These two sides sometimes depend on each other, sometimes oppose each other, and thus construct a dualistic structure that stabilizes society. Liang comments that, in the current state of China, however, there are three sides: while one political force fights against another, the countryside is being left out as the third party, of which no government takes care. The countryside is rendered to the status of an absolute victim (纯被牺牲地位) during the political chaos.[58] Liang refers here to the armed conflicts between different political powers and warlords in China in the 1930s.

In addition to the damage caused by politics, serious economic devastation happened in the rural area. Liang contends that, before the introduction of foreign goods on the Chinese market, Chinese peasants were cultivating a natural and self-sufficient autarkic economy: "Growing the crops themselves and weaving the textiles themselves."⁵⁹ After international trade was allowed in China, China's agricultural products, which were not geared toward the international market, could not successfully sell for profit, while a huge amount of foreign products were imported into China. Chinese peasants could not make money with their own products but had to use money to buy things they needed. This caused a huge imbalance and inequality.⁶⁰ Liang also mentions other crisis factors such as finances, silver prices, and industrialization in China. He insists that it is absolutely crucial to rebuild and maintain a viable rural production, not industrialization, as the foundation of China.⁶¹

The second factor regarding the severe cultural imbalance in China is the decline of its cultural tradition. Although Western imperialism has caused immense damage in China, the internal crisis is the most determining reason for the decline of China. Culture plays a decisive role in this matter because culture, as a specific practice of life, connects various sectors in society and manages interpersonal relationships. Culture is the knot of complex political and economic issues and can solve these problems as a comprehensive program. While Liang highlights the value of traditional Chinese culture in maintaining stable and harmonious social relationships for centuries, he laments that Chinese culture has deteriorated to its lowest depth. The intrusion of Western culture in China has introduced substantial changes and transformations in China because the West differs considerably from Chinese culture. Chinese culture has also revealed its disadvantages and shortcomings in the encounter with Western culture. Before a new culture could be successfully construed and conjointly integrated, Liang predicts, China was facing a severe cultural imbalance, which would result in the dissolution of social structure, the disharmony of social relations, and the chaos of social order.⁶² The most important task for China is to reconstruct its culture in order to resist Western imperialism, reach peaceful agreements among different political and military powers, and achieve economic independence and political sovereignty. Yet it is imprudent for the Chinese to entirely imitate Western culture for several reasons.

First, Liang points out the differences between the Confucian tradition and Western culture. The major difference between China and Europe lies in religion and nation. Liang thinks that Western societies have turned from religious communities to nation-states. Liberalist individualism emerged to resist the collective religious bondage. In China, however, no such religious communities existed, and therefore no liberal individualism was necessary to challenge the religious authority and collectivity. The most essential element in Chinese culture, Liang argues, is ethical relations (伦理关系) that mediate among individuals, families, and communities. Family relations are especially important. A person is born into a network of family relationships and always lives within this network. One develops emotional relationships with others such as friendship and marriage, which also translate into duties and responsibilities. They are not like the technical, judicial, and unbendable (硬性的) relationships in a Western community, Liang observes; rather, they are soft, humane, and undisciplined (自由的). In such a society, "people are more inclined to consider the feelings of others (while they are more self-centered in terms of their own desires). Therefore, in ethical relationships, people mutually think for each other as if individuals do not exist just for themselves but rather in a network with others. This kind of society can be called an ethic-based society."[63]

Liang further sees a difference between the West and China as that between individuality and relation. The Leibnizian atomism is contrasted to the Confucian network. Liang clearly prefers the network and idealizes Chinese family. He argues that a family shares property, which is a type of communism (共产) based on kinship relation. It is thus fundamentally different from the Western judicial system that protects individual rights.[64] Liang also maintains that, in the Chinese tradition, religion is not as important as it has been in the West. Confucianism is not religion as Europeans understand it to be, but it is a philosophy of life, an ethical system. Here Liang seems to promote the Confucian ethical code of three cardinal relationships and five constant virtues (*sangang wuchang*, 三纲五常). While the three relationships regulate the hierarchical structure between the emperor and his subjects, husband and wife, and father and children, the five constant virtues are known as *ren* (benevolence, 仁), *yi* (righteousness, 义), *li* (propriety, 礼), *zhi* (wisdom, 智), and *xin* (trustworthiness, 信). These ethical principles appeared in interpretations of Confucian texts as early as the Han dynasty (汉, 202 BC–220 AD) and were broadly practiced through the popularization of Song Ming neo-Confucianism starting in the twelfth century. Liang, however, does not further specify whether he means the three specific relationships, in which the one between husband and wife is especially problematic. Indeed, family ethics was critiqued for its cruelty and inhumanity during the New Culture Movement. The famous writer Ba Jin (巴金) depicts the suffocating family structure and the suppression of true love by parental will in his novel *Family* (*Jia*, 家, 1933).

Probably being aware of this problem, Liang swiftly turns away from this issue and discusses the difference of class in China and the West. He maintains that class as an economic and social hierarchical category does not exist in China the way in which it has existed in the West. In China, since land often changes its owner and businesses usually have small-scale production, no monopolies can exist long enough to form a class of capitalists with secured status. Liang argues that, in imperial China, extreme imbalance of wealth distribution rarely occurred. There was a separation between profession and business (职业分立).⁶⁵ The change from poverty to wealth and vice versa can happen rapidly. This social mobility sustains a good balance. The lack of class in China is caused not only by the economic circumstances but also by social mobility. The longstanding imperial civil service exams allowed commoners in China to become officials through education, whereas, in Europe, traditionally, politics was almost always royal affairs. The social group of educated people, called *shi* (士), existed alongside the other three major social groups of peasants (*nong,* 农), workers (*gong,* 工), and merchants (*shang,* 商), which construed the social hierarchy in China and in Japan.⁶⁶ Everyone could become *shi*, the highest social status, with education and successful examination. The fact that *shi* could become officials shows the openness of the political power in imperial China. The flexibility in both economy and social status created greater equality and prevented enduring oppositions and resentment in imperial China. Liang refers to the German sociologist and political economist Franz Oppenheimer's book *The State* (*Der Staat*, 1928), which understands bureaucracy as an impartial guardian of equality and justice in a society. Since bureaucrats receive a salary from the state and are thus separated from economic exploitation, they are not part of class opposition and could be more unbiased in executing governmental affairs. A new state without class could emerge based on such a bureaucracy. Liang comments that traditional Chinese society might well serve as a role model for Oppenheimer's vision of social equality.

Liang further claims that, despite the change of dynasties and social unrest, ethics and family relations always retain their validity and vitality. Ethics proves more fundamental to Chinese society than laws. Liang writes: "That's why I have always claimed that China has a government, a ruler, but no ruling class."⁶⁷ The emperor did not possess absolutist power through law and violence; rather, the emperor heavily relied on Confucian ethical education to maintain social order. This ethical education aims to instill *li* (rationalism, 理) and self-discipline within family and society.⁶⁸ This is also the reason religion does not flourish in China, because Confucianism is deeply rational. Liang refers to the Japanese scholar Kinzo Garai (ごらい きんぞう, 五来欣造, 1875–1944), who argues that "Confucianism worships neither the heaven, the deity, the emperor, or state power; nor does it obey the majority of the people (in the modern West, one has to obey the majority). Only when one puts all these elements (heaven, deity, majority) together and uses it as a surrogate for rationalism, then Confucianism would honor it."[69] Liang deeply appreciates this insight of Garai.

As discussed in the section on *Eastern and Western Cultures*, Liang is aware of rationalism in Western culture and argues that the Confucian *li* is different from Western rationalism. He argues that the Confucian *li* (理) is concerned with subjective empathy and understanding for others (主观情理), while Western rationalism is concerned with objective or scientific principles of things (客观事理).[70] *Li* promotes and encourages people toward taking actions, while Western rationalism is about knowledge and epistemology, which is not necessarily related to action. *Li* gives people directions for life, while Western rationalism explains things and proposes options and choices.

After arguing why China should not completely imitate the West, Liang does not insist on returning to Chinese tradition. Rather, he proposes to integrate and apply certain Western ideas in the reform of the Chinese countryside and then establish a new world culture. He claims:

> What we call new construction is the construction of new customs. Then, what are the new customs? It is the integration of inherent Chinese spirit and the advantages of Western culture. Both should be connected and merged together in the application of concrete things . . . not merely at a theoretical level; it is most important for them to fundamentally merge into one thing. If there is such a point of integration, then the problem of China could be solved. The reason why the current problem in China is difficult to solve is because the problem has reached a subtle state—the conflict between Chinese and Western spirit can't find a shared point of integration. Everyone merely makes effort on the surface, which does not pertain to the essence. . . . When the integration of Chinese spirit and Western advantages could become a fact, a new society would emerge, a new life of humanity would be realized. New society, new life, new customs, or new organizational structure are all the same, only the name is different.[71]

Liang proposes that China first adopt the Western structure of organization (团体组织) and border protection. He observes that the Chinese government was traditionally not very interested in defining national borders and territories and thus did not differentiate much between self and other. While Liang considers the Western nationalist border protectionism too extreme, he suggests deducing the two extremities and creating a new direction that "the future organization in China would be a community instead of a nation."[72] The idea of nation (国家) would not benefit China because it might develop into a very narrow direction, such as nationalism or militarism. In China, the undisciplined (散漫) peasants would not appreciate the political organization of a national state. He compares four different categories between the West and China, the world or universe (*tianxia*, 天下), organization (religion or nation), family, and individual, and concludes that the Chinese people value the world and family higher than organization and individual. Liang maintains that Chinese people always have the spirit of "seeing the four oceans as one family" (四海一家) and "doing justice to everyone under the heaven" (天下为公), while referring to Liang Qichao's elaboration of the Chinese cosmopolitanism (世界主义) in his book *History of Political Thinking Before Qin* (Xianqin Zhengzhi Sixiangshi,先秦政治思想史).[73] Liang Shuming thus proposes that Chinese people learn to respect more individual wishes and desires and appreciate and participate more actively in social organizations. All this should be based on ethical sentiments (伦理情谊).[74]

Based on the new customs, the most appropriate form of social organization is not a nation-state, Liang contends, it is a rural community. The countryside should serve as the foundation for China's rebuilding of its economy, politics, and culture. The Confucian rationalism *li* should be the guiding principle. Liang believes that peasants are the best carriers for this reform. First, peasants primarily deal with the natural environment and have a peaceful and quiet mind, whereas workers and businesspeople (工商业者) work in densely populated cities, face huge walls and buildings every day, and more easily develop an unnatural myopic mind. The peaceful characteristics of the peasants are prone to adopt and practice Confucian rationalism (*li*). Second, peasants work with living plants and animals in a holistic and lively manner; but workers and businesspeople handle lifeless matter in a compartmentalized and manipulated way. Third, workers and businesspeople are always hectic and busy, while peasants calmly follow the pace of nature. Peasants can't force nature to produce faster than it does, unlike the greedy industrial production that only targets more and more profits. Peasants live a life of art because their composure enables them to savor the impressions they have received from nature. Fourth, agriculture is the best form of labor to integrate the entire family. Yet business separates men, women, and children into different factories and branches. Agriculture solidifies the family structure, whereas industrialization destroys the harmony of family. Liang points out that family is the most important place for the cultivation and development of one's emotion and life. Fifth, since peasants are closely tied to their lands and their village communities, they are capable of developing and practicing a local democratic spirit (地方公共观念).[75] Liang is highly confident about the ability of local self-government in China's rural area. Yet it would be impossible to establish any self-government in an urban area because city dwellers don't have close ties to a city such as Shanghai and only have loose relationships with each other as a result of high population density and high business mobility. The countryside fares much better than the cities in developing and establishing healthy social ethics, functioning community institutions, and political habits (政治习惯). It is best to start from smaller communities to cultivate good political habits, Liang argues.[76] Hence the root of Chinese culture is twofold: spiritually speaking, it is Confucian rationalism, and, materially speaking, it is the countryside.[77] Any new political organization needs to rely on these two essential factors instead of completely abandoning them and adopting Western ideas.

Based on Confucian rationalism, the "rural school" (乡农学校) should function as a new social organization and governmental unit. Liang contends that education is the new path toward rural reconstruction as well as the creation of a new world civilization (世界文明).[78] The common village contract (乡约) in China's countryside, which, like a code of conduct, regulates the basic moral conventions and social justice in a village, could be supplemented with a rural school as a social organization and local government. In such a school, all villagers should convene and dedicate themselves to the learning of new knowledge. While a village contract controls the village community, the rural school aims to improve it. Liang's school has four major components: school board (校董会), school principal (校长), teaching faculty (教员), and villagers as students (乡民学生).[79] These four elements construe a rural organization (乡村组织). In Liang's vision, such a school is not just a conventional one in which the teachers are the active part and the students are the passive part. Liang's school is envisioned to function as a local government. A rural school should be confined to a village of the size between one hundred and fifty and three- or four hundred households. The school board consists of leading figures among all the households. One person should come forward as the school principal. The students are all residents in the village, regardless of age and gender. It is especially important to include adult villagers. Only the teaching faculty could be from outside the village. They should be educated people with new knowledge and insights. Liang points out that other forms of rural organization, such as a local self-defense society or peasant's association, did not seem to fit in current China. Only this form of school is the most suitable one because it stresses improvement (进步/改进) and learning (学).[80] A school offers the platform for peasant students to raise their concerns and for the teachers and the school board to learn about peasants' needs to find and provide solutions to problems. A school can bring all sides together to learn to approach problems and solve them together. It is not enough to have an organization that convenes people;

it is also crucial to introduce people to new ideas, new knowledge, new methods, and new solutions. If the school board and school principal can't solve problems, teachers from outside of the village can offer help and introduce new knowledge to enrich the peasants' practical experience and improve their lives.

Liang is pragmatic enough to understand that rural schools don't need to have the same curriculum. Coursework should be determined by the local situation in a village. Liang gives his readers an example that, if a village is often raided by robbers, then they should have courses on organizing self-defense and using armament. Or, in another scenario: in a village in the southwest part of Zouping, which lies in a mountainous area, when villagers were asked why they didn't plant trees to use the land, they answered that it was difficult for them to keep the trees alive until they became fully established. After discussions, the villagers decided to have courses on how to plant and protect trees more systematically to ensure the outcome of forestation. In an area of cotton plantation, the task of a rural school is to help peasant students find good seeds, use effective planting methods, and organize the sale and transportation of cotton. These examples have shown Liang's skillful implementation of the idea of education in the organization, improvement, and government of rural economic life and labor. In his vision, a school principal functions as a village chief, but the emphasis should be placed on learning and reforming village life, not on building power and maintaining hierarchy. Liang had big ambitions and intended to use his project to fulfill the goals of the Hundred Days' Reform—namely to "place everything that has not been done well or has not been finished in the Wuxu Reform Movement and other revolutions into the rural school project. That this organization could exert such a huge impact is because it is situated in a large system. It can use knowledge and technologies from all over China and even from all over the world."[81]

With the rural school, Liang argues that three crucial problems in China can be curbed. The first problem was that of opium and drug abuse, which was prevalent in the rural area in China, especially among poor people. Governmental ban and punishment as an external force had not been effective in remote rural areas. Liang comments that, in China, it is rather the villages that control the government instead of the other way around. Therefore, it is of utmost importance for the villagers to create a firm will to uproot the excruciating drug addiction through educational efforts. Liang sees the rural school as the best path to bridle this severe problem.

The second problem was banditry. Outlaws became a troubling issue in the late imperial period but grew to a major problem in the 1920s after the import of firearms. A rural school would be able to organize the villagers and teach them how to train a self-defense team to protect families and lands against robbery. Ideally, Liang imagines, after the establishment of rural schools, violence would recede and a community committed to love, peace, and mutual help would emerge. A rural school also fosters democratic spirit among peasants and encourages them to voluntarily participate in the self-defense efforts of the village.

Third, Liang focuses on communism. He expresses great sympathy for the communist movement and disputes a common opinion that equalizes communist revolts with banditry. Liang argues that communism is indeed a rural movement, which is necessary in the current condition in China. Indeed, Liang's ideas of rural construction evince similarities with Chinese communism in that they both underscore the organization of peasants and their education. Yet Liang also points out his difference to the communist movement. Liang comments that communists have first tried to transplant strategies that were successfully used in urban settings in Europe to Chinese circumstances, but they need to acknowledge the Chinese cultural specificities, especially Confucian family ethics and the lack of social classes in the Chinese countryside. From his perspective, the communists should recognize more the undisciplined nature of Chinese peasants and thus understand why class struggle might not work as the best method. He wishes that the communists could see rural construction through education as an unavoidable step to fulfill the task of revolution and achieve greater social equality in China, in which the longstanding dynastic order was destroyed, and where a new order was in dire need of being established.

Echoing socialist and communist movements, Liang also envisions a utopian society (理想的社会) or a kind of socialism (社会主义) through his rural school government.[82] This new society should correct the flaws of Western modernity and serve as a model of normal human civilization (正常形态的人类文明).[83] He summarizes six features of this new society. First, the new society emphasizes agriculture more than industry (先农而后工).[84] Liang criticizes industry's separation from agriculture, its exploitation of agriculture, and its concentration on a few urban centers. A healthy society should have a balanced and integrated agriculture and industry. Second, the countryside and the city should be better connected and integrated. They should not be pulled apart from each other. If a government appreciates the well-being of its citizens more than financial profit, then the political emphasis should be placed more on agriculture and less on the capitalist mode of production. Liang imagines a "flat" (平铺安放) political system based on the countryside instead of a hierarchical, towering, and dominating (偏起而耸立) system centralized in a few big cities.[85] Third, in the new society, humans should control things and should not let things control them (人支配物而非物支配人).⁸⁶ Liang reminds his readers that the interpersonal competitions in the West have led to the dominance of materialism and the deterioration of personal relationships. This situation should be changed in the new society through a set of new ethics—this is Liang's fourth point. The new ethics stresses mutuality, respect, and the contextuality of an individual within a community. A community (团体) mediates between individuals and society and should become the foundation for both.⁸⁷ Fifth, in the new society, politics, economy, and education form an inseparable unity. Liang mentions that he is aware of the separation of powers in Western democracy. While he sees the merits in limiting the state's power to interfere with individual affairs such as religious beliefs, he thinks that, when society enters a new phase, the state should not passively remain silent but rather positively encourage its citizens to develop their interests and address their needs. Thus, education gains unprecedented significance while laws and prohibitions become less effective. Then politics and education should serve the same purpose. Politics and economy should also be considered together, Liang contends. Because of the problem of banditry and security, an economy can't develop without political and military protection. In the new society, the emphasis on the idea of community will foster the social spirit of collaboration and help economic growth. Politics, Liang concludes, is anything but organizing economy and education on a community basis. In his sixth and final point, Liang comes back to Confucianism: "To keep the new social order intact, one has to replace military with rationalism."⁸⁸ Western societies rely on military violence to guarantee security. In the new society, military power would gradually withdraw from the public sphere, whereas rationalism assumes greater prominence. Yet Liang admits that, at least for now, the last resort to keep order and security still lies in force (武力), not rationalism.⁸⁹ Violent social revolution is a technical way of solving crises because it comes from the technical construction of violent governance of the society (从社会之机械的构造(武力统治)而来).⁹⁰ After a society has experienced several revolutionary changes, it will reach the stage of using rationalism instead of violence for social organization. Then education would become the first and foremost important political task. Liang uses the examples of ancient Chinese education of rites and music (礼乐教化) to illustrate this point.⁹¹ Academic research would become the leading force of society. Reform would replace revolution. Human society would also transform from a technical society to a rational society.

In Liang's utopian society, profound self-love and benevolence for others (自爱爱人) form its essence.⁹² A calculative rationalism is not enough to keep communities alive and make them thrive. The Confucian virtue of benevolence beyond calculation is necessary to achieve such a goal. Liang is dissatisfied that nationalism and class conflicts have been used as tools to achieve solidarity and bipartisanship in China. One day, he predicts, the unanimity based on negativity and opposition should disappear. Confucian joyous intuitive rationalism, as a long-lasting will toward greater social good, would permeate the world and endorse a human-centered, education-based communal society. Liang believes that this is the necessary movement of universal life energy.

In response to the critics of his rural construction theory, Liang argues that his rural reform has followed the global trend because the current world is no longer alone-standing and self-contained. His education project is thus a project in a global context for local good. His reform is done for China as well as for the world. Liang's argument about Chinese cultural specificities also echoes postcolonial critique of the imposition of Western modernity onto colonized and indigenous societies. Liang's Confucian rural construction project transgresses Western modernity and its universal eligibility.

It is true that Liang's thought is at times unclear and not free of contradictions, thus interfering with a consistent interpretation of a clear logic in his writing. While Liang is in favor of Western modernity in terms of technological innovations, he is critical of dismissing Chinese traditional values. While he uncritically follows the logic of cultural development and defines Chinese and Indian cultures as "overripe," he considers Confucianism a most promising ethical system for a future world culture. "We might further add that the constituent elements of Liang's thought are not all that easy to unravel into identifiable strands if our principal purpose is to label them as specifically Yogācārin (Weishi 唯识) Buddhist, Bergsonian, Schopenhauerian, Confucian (either Wang Yangming 王阳明 [1472–1529] or Wang Gen 王艮 [1483–1540]), or Liang's own idiosyncratic innovations."[93]

This conglomeration could be attributed to Liang's lack of university training, for which Hu Shi and other educated elites once derided him. Yet if we change our perspective and read his books as a social activist's response to the challenges of imperialism, Western modernity, and the decline of Confucian social order, then his thinking contains valuable information that exemplifies the aporias, paradoxes, and irresolvable internal conflicts in global modernity from a Chinese perspective in the early twentieth century. Calling Liang a conservative and nationalist, based on his proclivity toward Confucianism, seems somehow too simple to capture the multiplicity of his thinking and the complexity of Chinese modernity. It is time to highlight Liang's contribution to the resistance against political, economic, and cultural imperialism as well as his discontent with the trend of total Westernization, which would imply an auto-colonization in China.

It is highly debatable whether Liang's vision of a world culture is still a viable idea today. We could call Liang's ideas naïve or unpractical, given the failure of his mediation between the Communists and the Nationalists and given the warfare in China in the first half of the twentieth century. Yet almost a century later, in today's situation of globalization and the resurgence of nationalistic xenophobia and environmental crises, Liang's Confucianism world culture still rings true. At least his emphasis on generosity, tolerance, and mutual help for survival offers insights in the discussions about cultural and racial diversity, economic globalization, technological competition, and political populism.

Confirming Liang's combination of Confucianism and rurality, his student Feng Youlan wrote in his *A Short History of Chinese Philosophy* that Confucian scholars and their thinking are deeply embedded in agriculture and the life of peasants. "Although the 'scholars' did not actually cultivate the land themselves, yet since they were usually landlords, their fortunes were tied up with agriculture. A good or bad harvest meant their good or bad fortune, and therefore their reaction to the universe and their outlook on life were essentially those of the farmer. In addition, their education gave them the power to express what an actual farmer felt but was incapable of expressing himself. This expression took the form of Chinese philosophy, literature, and art."[94] Referring to the ancient historiography *Lüshi Chunqiu (Master Lü's Spring and Autumn Annals,* 吕氏春秋, 239 BCE), Feng stresses that farmers are inclined to be morally noble and easy to be governed; they stay with the country when it is in trouble. Yet merchants, the lowest class in traditional Chinese society, tend to abandon their country under duress and are selfish and treacherous. Agriculture is thus more highly regarded than commerce. Feng comments that this observation shows "the root and source of the two main trends of Chinese thought, Taoism and Confucianism. They are poles apart from one another, yet they are also two poles of one and the same axis. They both express, in one way or another, the aspirations and inspirations of the farmer."[95] Following Liang's lead, Feng embarked on his own path of interpreting Chinese philosophy as world philosophy, which I discuss in Chapter 5.

5

EARLY FENG YOULAN'S NEGATIVE METHOD: METAPHYSICS, WORLD PHILOSOPHY, AND SAGE

In his classical *A Source Book in Chinese Philosophy* (1963), the Chinese-American scholar Wing-Tsit Chan (陈荣捷, 1901–94) enthusiastically lauds the Chinese philosopher Feng Youlan: "There is no doubt that Fung Yu-lan has been the most outstanding philosopher in China in the last thirty years. He was already on the way to sure prominence when he published his two-volume *History of Chinese Philosophy* in 1930 and 1934. With the publication of his *Hsin li-hsüeh* (*The New Rational Philosophy*) in 1939, his position as the leading Chinese philosopher was firmly established."[1] In Chan's view, Feng Youlan has developed the most original and comprehensive philosophical system in twentieth-century China—a reconstruction of rationalistic neo-Confucianism, while Xiong Shili has achieved a reconstruction of idealistic neo-Confucianism. Chan interprets Feng's work in light of nationalism and understands it as an attempt to renovate Chinese philosophy, claiming, "Fung frankly calls his own system a new 'tradition,' which to him not only represents a revival of Chinese philosophy but is also the symbol of a revival of the Chinese nation."[2]

Feng's ambition, however, reaches even beyond the national framework. While Feng saw in philosophy a means to counter Western imperialism in China, he did not see himself purely as a national hero who sought to give new strength to a Confucianism, Taoism, or Buddhism that should remain exclusively Chinese.[3] Rather, with his intellectual endeavor during the hardship of warfare and exile between 1937 and 1949, Feng aimed to present Chinese philosophy in relation to European philosophy to form the foundation of a world philosophy. Feng was not interested in "modernizing" Chinese philosophy with the aid of European tradition in the sense of making it less outdated, less backward, and more aligned to Western standards. Neither did he agree with those intellectuals such as Hu Shi (胡适), who strongly proposed to transform China with Western values and interpret Chinese history from the perspective of historicist developmentalism. Nor was he strictly separating Chinese and Western philosophies as two mutually exclusive systems based on distinct cultural or national identities, let alone placing them on a hierarchy.

In *"Chinese Philosophy and a Future World Philosophy,"* an essay that Feng published in English during the Chinese Civil War in 1948, he claims that he intends to review and revalue all ideas of the past, and "none of them can claim to have more authority than the others."[4] His contemporary Chinese philosophers are especially fortunate because they have the opportunity to review not only the ideas of the Chinese past but also those of the past and present of the West. "Systems proposed by the great minds of both Europe and Asia are seen and understood from new angles and in a new light. Old interests in philosophy are revived as new ones are arising. Under such circumstances it would be very surprising if there were not great changes in contemporary Chinese thought."[5] In the chaotic situation of Chinese society and its political crises, Feng saw an unprecedented opportunity for philosophers to make great progress in their thinking. It was a necessary growth out of the anguish of warfare, Western imperialism, and tremendous social and political transformation of the Chinese society "from a medieval to a modern character."[6] The vacuum that has been created between the two poles of the archaic and the modern ways of life should provide a fertile ground for meaningful philosophical thinking. Even though Feng understands the difference between China and the West as that between medieval time and modernity, he neither further develops this historicist idea nor integrates it into other more pertinent elements of his thinking. This rather underdeveloped and less reflected historicism in Feng's thinking, however, does not result in an argument about China's backwardness and its necessary need for Western modernity, as many other people, Chinese and Westerners alike, have claimed even until today. The emphasis of Feng's work was always on synthesizing Chinese and Western philosophies because they "can be complementary and . . . , in this give-and take, Chinese thought may contribute to a future world philosophy."[7] Feng's unclaimed or undercurrent historicism of understanding China progressing from ancient to modern times does not prevent him from promoting Chinese philosophical tradition as an indispensable contribution to world philosophical future, or even as the philosophical foundation of a world culture.

Aside from the interpretation of Feng from the perspectives of nationalism and modernization theory, I argue in this chapter that Feng endeavors to achieve a synthesis of Chinese and European philosophical traditions through metaphysics, toward a metaphysical common for everyone in the world. It is an ideal state of being characterized by universal spiritual and moral equality. With his philosophical work, Feng strives to make sense of the tremendous changes in the decades before and after 1900 not only in China, but also in the world. He is interested in showing the commonalities between Chinese and Western traditions and making clear that traditional Chinese thought makes an indispensable contribution to world peace and justice. Feng believes in a fundamental affinity between Chinese and European philosophical traditions and envisions a new innovative world philosophy emanating from the inextricable correlations between the two genealogies. Feng identifies metaphysics as the terrain that allows the best comparison between Chinese and Western philosophies.[8]

In *Xin Zhi Yan* (*New Understanding of Knowledge of Language*, 新知言), Feng's major work expounding his philosophical method of metaphysics, he claims metaphysics to be the most important part in philosophy because it represents humanity's ultimate experience and understanding of life (对于人生的最后觉解). It is a necessary step for humans to achieve the highest transcendental enlightenment (最高境界). Feng defines metaphysics as a conceptual realm beyond experience (超越于经验), which he calls "the realm of integration with the heaven and the earth" (天地境界). The function of metaphysics does not lie in enlarging or deepening practical knowledge in one area or another. Its function lies in enhancing the level of consciousness toward transcendental enlightenment.[9] Feng maintains that metaphysics is the most philosophical philosophy (最哲学的哲学).[10] He illustrates his philosophical system as a metaphysics of negative mysticism that articulates itself through silence, through claiming what it is not to express the idea of metaphysics beyond logical analysis. As an application of his metaphysics in the social realm, Feng defines humans in the realm of transcendence (天地境界中的人) as "sage" (圣人), the highest form of being in the universe or in the divine dimension. Confucius is often referred to as a sage. Feng argues, "Since the character of the sage is, according to Chinese tradition, one of sageliness within and kingliness without, the task of philosophy is to enable man to develop this kind of character."[11] A sage is Feng's vision of a world citizen.

As gravely concerned with China's fate during the Sino-Japanese War (1937–45) as everyone else, Feng took pride in the Chinese cultural tradition and decided to present it as a valuable world heritage. Even though the political sovereignty and independence of the Chinese nation were of great importance to Feng, he did not confine himself within a narrow nationalist rhetoric. Rather, he embarked on an intellectually unique path, stressing the values of Chinese philosophy as an integral part of world cultural heritage. In the ensuing pages, I will first recount key moments in Feng's intellectual biography: his attempt to break down the boundaries between the East and the West, his argument about the emergence of the class of Confucian scholars in Chinese history, and his conception of New Rationalism, as the continuation of Song-Ming neo-Confucianism, after the Japanese invasion in 1937. Then I will focus on Feng's negative metaphysics as his major contribution to world culture, which he also related to early Ludwig Wittgenstein. His ideal of a sage embodies the practice of negative mysticism. Like the other thinkers discussed in this book, Feng is invested in connecting philosophy to sociopolitical realities in China and the world. His two key concepts, the negative method and the sage, always have inherent social dimensions. Hence, in the final section of this chapter, I will detail his thinking about social reform, including the question of women and childcare.

BREAKING DOWN THE BOUNDARIES BETWEEN THE EAST AND THE WEST AND CONFUCIUS AS A TEACHER

In his autobiography, *Narration about Myself at Three-Pines Residence* (三松堂自序), Feng recounts his life as a philosophy student at Columbia University (1919–23) and his attempt to break down the boundaries between the East and the West (打破东、西的界限) in his doctoral dissertation.[12] When he first arrived in New York City in 1919, Feng noticed a stark contrast between Western wealth and China's poverty. He wondered why China lost wars to Western powers and failed to stand the competition with the West since the mid-nineteenth century. He wanted to understand in which areas the West was fundamentally superior to China. He came to a preliminary conclusion that it is because the West had natural sciences:

> In order to answer to these questions, I wrote an essay titled *Why China Has No Science?—An Interpretation of the History of Chinese Philosophy and Its Consequence*, which I presented at a colloquium in the Columbia philosophy department and later published in *International Journal of Ethics* (32, no. 2 [April 1922]). The basic argument of this essay is: The reason why China had no modern sciences is because

> Chinese philosophy emphasizes that one should pursue happiness through one's spiritual interiority, not through external materialism. The function of modern sciences has two major aspects: on the one hand, one seeks the knowledge of nature; on the other hand, one seeks the power to control nature. . . . If people only pursue happiness inside themselves, neither do they need the power to control nature nor the precise knowledge to understand it. That was a popular opinion of the time, characterizing the East as an idealist civilization (精神文明) and the West as a materialist civilization (物质文明). After the West entered the era of capitalism, the global constellation became that "the West controlled the East and the urban area controlled the rural area" (see Marx's *The Communist Manifesto*).[13]

After writing this essay, however, Feng changed his opinion about the differences between the West and the East. Natural sciences are no longer the essential benchmark for him—rather, Feng came to realize that similarities and entanglements between China and the West are more pertinent. He thus aimed to break down the boundaries between the East and the West, arguing

> that the opposition between idealist introversion and materialist extroversion is not the opposition between the East and the West. Human thinking is all the same and does not differentiate whether it is Eastern or Western. The opposition mentioned above exists in both Eastern and Western traditions. To illustrate my point here, I connected the histories of Chinese and Western philosophies and chose some representative philosophers.[14]

This work became Feng's dissertation, an extended version of which was published in English as *A Comparative Study of Life Ideals; The Way of Decrease and Increase with Interpretations and Illustrations from the Philosophies of the East and the West* (1924) and later in Chinese as *A Philosophy of Life* (人生哲学) in 1926.

In his erudite thesis, Feng discusses ten philosophical schools that have extensively engaged with the question of life, starting with Taoism, Plato, Buddhism, and Schopenhauer, continuing with Yang Zhu (杨朱), Mozi, Descartes, Bacon, Fichte, Confucianism, Aristotle, and Song-Ming neo-Confucianism, and ending with Hegel. During his thesis defense, John Dewey, one of Feng's advisors, inquired whether there was any historical coherence among these thinkers and schools and whether one school developed into another school. Feng admitted that he could not properly answer that question because he did not trace the historical genealogies of their thinking; rather, he took their thinking out of their historical context and placed them next to each other to illustrate his own philosophy of life. Hegel's dialectics of seeing positive changes in a negative situation were inspiring for Feng because they gave him courage to see meanings in a lost war. In the anachronistic order in his dissertation, Feng placed his emphasis on Confucianism's doctrine of the mean (*Zhongyong,* 中庸). He intended to show that "human thoughts cannot be separated by national boundaries; philosophy cannot be divided between the East and the West."[15] In Feng's later works, he followed a similar style of placing Chinese and Western thinkers next to each other, discussing the specificities of their thoughts and comparing their similarities and differences as equal human beings, without labeling them with national identities.

In the work of his mature years, *A Short History of Chinese Philosophy* (1947), Feng agrees with his editor and translator Derk Bodde's observation: "They [the Chinese] are not a people for whom religious ideas and activities constitute an all-important and absorbing part of life.... It is ethics (especially Confucian ethics), and not religion (at least not religion of a formal, organized type), that provided the spiritual basis in Chinese civilization.... All of which, of course, marks a difference of fundamental importance between China and most other major civilizations, in that a church and a priesthood have played a dominant role."[16] Feng, however, also argues that, at the fundamental spiritual level, the Chinese and the Westerners are alike, while the social organization for addressing spiritual matters differs.

Dewey's inquiry about historical coherence and transformation between philosophical thinkings, however, did not fail to induce Feng to change. After returning from the US, Feng started his teaching career at various Chinese universities and devoted his time to writing *A History of Chinese Philosophy* (中国哲学史). Feng admits the impact of Dewey's question on this work, and he comments that Dewey's influential pragmatism is an epistemology that stresses the importance of experience in search of truth. Applying this pragmatist epistemology in social and historical situations, Dewey looks for historical causes for the emergence of certain type of thinking. Feng follows suit and embeds philosophy within the genealogy of Chinese history so that dominant philosophical schools such as Confucianism are no longer presented as universal moral codes and official social norms, as it had been the case during the dynastic time. Rather, philosophical thinking has become historical phenomenon. Indeed, this book of Feng, along with Hu Shi's *Outline of the History of Chinese Philosophy* (中国哲学史大纲, 1918), became a seminal historiography of Chinese philosophy in the twentieth century. Yet Feng differs from Hu in that he does not start with Laozi (老子) but with Confucius (孔子).

Feng considers Confucius the first philosopher in Chinese history because he was the first private teacher in Chinese history who opened a school to teach Chinese classics to everybody in society. "In this respect, Confucius was no longer a conservative. In this respect his work was revolutionary. . . . In China, Confucius was the first man to popularize learning, the first professional educationist. . . . Confucius was much like the Greek sophists."[17] Feng further points out that Confucius was also a politician, which was also revolutionary, because Confucius, as a commoner, constantly discussed politics and lived on the support of his disciples and political rulers. His profession was thus teaching and discussing politics. "After Confucius, most Confucianists and others lived in this way. And soon the class of scholars emerged. Those who belonged to this class could do only two things: to be a politician or to be a school teacher."[18] Clearly, Feng intends to explain the emergence and the centuries-long influence of Confucianism as a historical phenomenon. In Feng's portrayal, Confucius is no longer a saint but a historical figure who opened a new era in Chinese history. Feng's magnum opus was translated into English by Derk Bodde and published in two volumes in 1952 by Princeton University Press, of which Feng was not aware until 1972 because of the difficult circumstances in the decades after the Chinese Civil War (1945–49). Both Feng's interest in breaking down the boundaries between the East and the West and his interest in portraying Confucius as the historical founding father of the scholarly class, the forunner of Confucian literati, led to his own philosophical system of New Rationalism and his negative method of metaphysics. His method of typology in his dissertation as well as the pragmatist historical method that Feng has adopted from Dewey remains important for his New Rationalism. Indeed, this combination of typology and pragmatist historicism also resembles neo-Kantianism and Max Weber's methlodgy in his discussion of charisma.

NEW RATIONALISM AND THE SINO-JAPANESE WAR

The outbreak of the Sino-Japanese war in 1937 marked a decisive turning point in Feng's philosophical work. He writes in his autobiography that he was no longer interested in writing about other people's philosophy—he felt compelled to write his own philosophy and develop his own thinking in the time of crisis. During the years-long exile from Beijing to Kunming (1937–46), Feng finished six books, which he also saw as six chapters of one long book containing his system of New Rationalism. He calls them "Zhen Yuan Liu Shu" (Zhen Yuan Six Books, 贞元六书), which he describes in English as a "series written at a time of national rebirth."[19] In Chinese, according to *Yi Jing*, *zhen yuan* (贞元) means the time between winter and spring, a cold and barren season that, however, bears the potential of nature's revival. Feng compares the period of *zhen yuan* to the time of the Japanese invasion, which should be an opportunity toward the renaissance of *Zhonghua minzu* (中华民族, Chinese nation). Feng recounts that the six books are in essence "a reflection on the traditional spiritual life (传统精神生活) of the Chinese civilization. Reflections only emerge when one encounters difficulties, has hindrance in life, or is in distress."[20] In the preface to the first book, *Xin Lixue* (新理学, *New Rationalism or New Principles*), which has the same name as his philosophical system, Feng writes with a heavy heart: "Thinking of the high spirit of the ancient scholars and facing the tremendous change of the present time, I can't help to write down what I feel inside."[21]

While Feng was writing, Japanese troops occupied large areas in China. The central government and relevant institutions were forced to recede to the southwest of China. Feng compared this situation to the historical periods of the Jin (晋), Song (宋), and Ming (明) dynasties, in which war-induced migrants moved from the north to the south. While most historical migrants lost their lives and could not return home, Feng was confident that, this time, *Zhonghua minzu* would return home, achieve victory, and revive again. Feng calls this time period *zhen xia qi yuan* (贞下起元), meaning that after the period of *zhen* or winter, the period of *yuan* or spring will ensue.[22] Here Feng repeatedly uses the neologism *Zhonghua mingzu*, which Liang Qichao has introduced to create a political identity of the Chinese people in the Western fashion of nations. This term should encompass all ethnic groups, including the major ones of Han (汉), Man (Manchus, 满), Meng (Mongolians, 蒙), Hui (Chinese Muslims, 回), and Zang (Tibetans, 藏). Before that, people in all ethnic groups were primarily understood as subjects of the Qing Manchu emperor. There wasn't an idea of a Chinese people or nation, but rather Qing subjects. The coinage of this term marks the political transition from empire to nation in Wang Hui's observation, which I mentioned in the introduction to this book.

The reason for Feng's confidence comes from his belief in the strength of Confucianism. He holds that, from the perspective of class analysis, his background naturally makes him sympathetic to Confucian teaching. Feng was born in a large landowner family in a village in Henan (河南) and grew up with a traditional Confucian upbringing. His father was a strict Confucian official who suddenly died during his appointment as mayor of a small town. The Japanese military invasion evoked Feng's dormant sense of solidarity with China as a political entity and a cultural community based on a long and shared tradition. While Feng vehemently argues about moving beyond the boundaries between the East and the West, he is now dedicated to the survival of China against the invasion by a neighboring East Asian country. These two aspects, however, do not necessarily contradict each other. Intellectually, Feng tries to integrate the teaching of his upbring with Western knowledge, which is becoming dominant in China and other parts of the world, to envision a more peaceful and inclusive world. Personally and politically, Feng supports the protection of his homeland against imperialist invasion and military violence, which is in line with his intellectual program of a more harmonious world unlike aggressive and predatory capitalist imperialism. The war strengthened Feng's belief and confidence in the Chinese tradition as an ideological foundation to unite the front against the intruder. He writes:

> I thought, if the orthodox ideas [Confucianism] in China's past could unite the Chinese people and make it a great nation and elevate it to a great country and a leader in the world, then this thought must be able to help *Zhonghua minzu* sail through this disastrous challenge, restore its inherited order, and engender a renaissance. My philosophical thinking at that time was very close to Cheng-Zhu rationalist doctrine. Everyone who hoped to contribute to the anti-Japanese war could only use the weapon that they had mastered. The weapon that I had mastered was the Cheng-Zhu system of thought. Hence, I took it up as weapon and continued on their path.[23]

Now, after his years in New York, Feng started to use Song-Ming neo-Confucianism to create a new path in the Zhen Yuan Six Books.

The first book is called *Xin Lixue* (*New Rationalism*, 新理学). *Lixue* was the Chinese word for "neo-Confucianism" in the Song and Ming dynasties. *Li* could be translated as moral principles or reasonable rules. *Xue* means a doctrine, teaching, or a school of thought in this context. That Feng calls his system a new teaching of *li* shows his intention to reach back to the tradition of neo-Confucianism and replenish it with a new interpretation in the twentieth century. The fifth book, *Xin Yuandao* (*New Original Path*, 新原道), translated into English as *The Spirit of the Chinese Philosophy*, offers a brief history of Chinese philosophy. In it, immediately after the chapter describing Song-Ming neo-Confucianism (*Song-Ming lixue*), Feng places a chapter on his own New Rationalism (*xin lixue*) as the newest development of Chinese philosophy, which is also the last chapter in the book. Feng titles this chapter *xin tong* (新统), a new tradition. Clearly, Feng portrays himself as the direct inheritor and innovator of the neo-Confucian tradition. He characterizes his own philosophical efforts as the continuation of neo-Confucian teaching (接着讲, *jie zhe jiang*).

To recapitulate, Feng intends to break down the boundaries between Chinese and European philosophical traditions from the beginning of his academic career. He uses a typological method in his dissertation and then adopts Dewey's pragmatist historical inquiry about the emergence of philosophical thinking in *A History of Chinese Philosophy*. Building on this foundation, now in his New Rationalism, he furthers his method from logical analysis to a negative metaphysics, which I see as the hallmark and the unique contribution of Feng's philosophy. The negative method serves Feng to reach his ultimate goal of bridging European and Chinese philosophies toward a world philosophy.

THE NEGATIVE METHOD

Chan argues that Feng's "greatest innovation is of course his conversion of neo-Confucian ideas into logical concepts. In so doing he has transformed Neo-Confucianism fundamentally."[24] Feng, however, recounts a different shift in his method—namely, that from logical analysis to a negative method:

> The method I used in the Hsin Li-hsüeh [Xin Lixue] is wholly analytic. After writing that book, however, I began to realize the importance of the negative method. . . . At present, if someone were to ask me for a definition of philosophy, I would reply paradoxically that philosophy, especially metaphysics, is that branch of knowledge which, in its development, will ultimately become "the knowledge that is not knowledge." If this be so, then the negative method needs to be used. Philosophy, especially metaphysics, is useless for the increase of our knowledge regarding matters of fact, but is indispensable for the elevation of our mind. These few points are not merely my own opinion, but, as we have previously seen, represent certain aspects of the Chinese philosophical tradition. It is these aspects that I think can contribute something to future world philosophy.[25]

Feng uses a metaphor in his autobiography to illustrate what he means by a negative method. In traditional Chinese painting, the artists do not draw a circle to illustrate the moon; rather, they paint a huge area of clouds and leave an empty space inside the clouds to insinuate the moon for the viewer. The moon is not being positively painted but negatively revealed. In philosophy, this is the negative method of metaphysics.[26] The moon here is the unspeakable truth of metaphysics.

In his essay *Chinese Philosophy and a Future World Philosophy*, Feng compares the Kantian and the Platonic metaphysics to that of the Confucianist and the Taoist traditions. "The Platonic and Confucianist traditions represent what may be called the ontological approach of metaphysics, while the Kantian and Taoist traditions, so far as their metaphysics or the metaphysical implications of their philosophies are concerned, represent what may be called the epistemological approach."[27] Even though the ontological and epistemological approaches both use a logical, rationalizing method to make sense of experience, the results at which they arrive lie beyond logical efficacy. Their thorough analysis yields "something," which defies further logical rationalization and analysis. "This is not because reason is weak, but because the 'something' is such that a rational analysis of it involves a logical contradiction."[28] This reversely confirms the existence of a transcendental metaphysics and betrays the ultimate inability of logical analysis. Feng argues that Taoism and Zen Buddhism have both developed a method to solve this logical contradiction—through the negation of reason.

Feng further develops this negative method as his own in *Xin Zhi Yan* (*New Understanding of Knowledge and Language*, 新知言), the last of the *Six Books*. Like in his essay, he defines two methods of metaphysics: the positive method, or the ontological approach, striving to use logical analysis to expound on the nature and content of metaphysics; and the negative method, or the epistemological approach, gesturing toward metaphysics without any words because metaphysics cannot be explained with words (不能讲).[29] "As the ontological approach begins with the distinction between the form and matter of things, the epistemological approach distinguishes the form and matter of knowledge."[30] Feng emphasizes that the negative method is an attempt to reconcile rationalism and mysticism.[31] He thinks that most Western philosophies have used the positive method of metaphysics. The latest example is the Vienna Circle [Wiener Kreis] in the early twentieth century, which advocates to abolish metaphysics all together and fervently promote scientific positivism.

For Feng, Plato establishes the positive method in the Western tradition. Metaphysics, or the "something" beyond logical analysis, is called "matter" in Platonism and has no form; in Confucianism, metaphysics is called *ming* (name, 名). "In Chinese philosophy the Confucianist school, from its very beginning, had a respect for the *ming* or 'name' which was thought to represent the principles of human conduct or the essences of virtue."[32] Feng refers to Zhu Xi (朱熹, 1130–1200) as a like-minded Chinese philosopher who used the positive method to maintain that metaphysics is neo-Confucian morality. Zhu's doctrine became and remained the orthodox state philosophy through the dynasties of Song, Yuan, Ming, and Qing, roughly from the thirteenth century until the abdication of the last Qing emperor in 1912. In Platonism, metaphysics also represents the vision of ultimate morality. Feng points to a story in Plato's *The Republic* that illustrates metaphysics—namely, when people just emerge out of a dark cave, their eyes cannot immediately see animals, stars, and the sun. They can only depend on their inner eyes, which is rationality, to "see" the world. Then, in the same vein, using their reason, people can recognize the absolute moral good without the aid of sensual perception and experience. Rationality is a force that elevates the human soul to the highest level for it to see and meditate on the best and purest form of existence.

Plato discusses the state of intelligence and ignorance of human condition as follows: "Imagine an underground chamber like a cave, with a long entrance open to the daylight and as wide as the cave. In this chamber are men who have been prisoners there since they were children, their legs and necks being so fastened that they can only look straight ahead of them and cannot turn their heads."[33] One day, if these men ascend to the upper world, they see the world in real sunshine. This ascent from darkness to sunlight resembles that of the mind from ignorance to knowledge, from the tutelage of immaturity to the freedom of morality. Yet the ascent only happens when the entire person is elevated, not only part of the person: "The organ by which he learns is like an eye which cannot be turned from darkness to light unless the whole body is turned; in the same way the mind as a whole must be turned away from the world of change until its eye can bear to look straight at reality, and at the brightest of all realities which is what we call the good."[34] The eye of the mind symbolizes reason, and the perception of the eye is likened to the process of knowing. The reality here is not transient but rather eternal, like the neo-Confucian principle—*li* (理) or *ming* as moral standard. The brightest reality is the most fundamental truth of ethics.

Plato writes:

> The truth of the matter is, after all, known only to god. But in my opinion, for what it is worth, the final thing to be perceived in the intelligible region, and perceived only with difficulty, is the form of the good; once seen, it is inferred to be responsible for whatever is right and valuable in anything, producing in the visible region light and the source of light, and being in the intelligible region itself controlling source of truth and intelligence. And anyone who is going to act rationally either in public or private life must have sight of it.[35]

Here, according to Feng's explanation, the term "matter" in the first sentence is metaphysics. Although Plato initially admits that the matter is unknown to humanity and thus divine, he continues to maintain that it actually should be the moral essence of goodness and gives the matter a more concrete material explication. This ultimate quality permeates everything in the world and reveals itself as light, only perceivable to people with rationality. Ethics and rationality are deeply connected to each other in Plato's metaphysics of truth. Feng comments, "Such knowledge of the good bestows our heart a transcendent dimension."[36]

Feng also points out that Plato, however, does not further define the content of the good. Plato merely gestures toward such a metaphysical dimension but does not elaborate it more in social, historical, or psychological terms. It was Aristotle who endeavored to fill Plato's void space of metaphysics with tangible and concrete things. Feng observes that this materialization of metaphysics, however, does not leave much more room for imagination and has become the foundation of modern natural sciences in the West. Like Confucianism, the pedigree of Plato's metaphysics keeps a positive method and is fundamentally based on logical analysis, or an ontological approach in Feng's nomenclature.

Unlike Platonism's attention to things, the epistemological approach of Kant and Taoism focuses on knowledge and comes closer to the unknown truth of metaphysics. Kant differentiates the various forms of knowledge from its matter. Feng comments, "What is ideally distinct from these forms may be called the matter of knowledge, but what that really is, is something that we can never know. That is what Kant called the 'thing-in-itself,' or 'noumenon,' instead of which man knows only the phenomenon."[37] The thing-in-itself is unknown, or more precisely, unknowable to human reason. Taoism also distinguishes the knowable from the unknowable. Hence in terms of metaphysics, Taoism is Kantian or Kant is a Taoist. Feng argues:

> While Confucianism considered *ming* or "name" as representing principles or essences which are the standards of things in the actual world, Taoism considered *ming* as representing subjective distinctions made by the human intellect. The term *ming-yen* was often used by the Taoists. *Yen* means language; and by the term *ming-yen* the Taoists reduced *ming* to an affair of language, which is the necessary accompaniment of knowledge. Man knows only *ming-yen*. But what is behind and beyond *ming-yen*? That is something which, in principle and by definition, cannot be known.[38]

This unknowable, the noumenon, is beyond language and knowledge, which is also the well-known Taoist idea of *wu* (无), meaning void or nothingness, leading to the related idea of *wuwei* (无为), meaning non-action. As Feng points out, while Confucianism refers to *ming* as moral principles, Taoism adds *yan* (言, yen in Feng's transliteration) to *ming* and uses *mingyan* together to refer to knowledge and its linguistic exposition. *Mingyan* is thus comparable to Kant's notion of phenomenon.[39] According to this explanation, the title of Feng's book *Xin Zhi Yan* (新知言) should be understood literally as "new understanding of knowledge and language." It is clearly a book discussing Feng's epistemology and metaphysics.

Moving forward, Feng argues that, despite their affinities, Kantian and Taoist epistemologies also differ from each other. While the boundary between the Kantian noumenon and phenomenon is permanent and firm, in Taoism, this boundary is fluid and permeable. The Taoist way of

> crossing is . . . the negation of reason. The negation of reason is itself an act of reason. . . . By the negation of reason, one gets to what the Taoists called a "realm of nondistinction and undifferentiableness." It is meaningless to ask whether by the negation of reason one really crosses the boundary, because, according to the Kantian and the Taoist, this boundary is reason's own creation. With the negation of reason, there is no longer a boundary to cross. As a matter of fact, to cross the boundary is to abolish it. It is also meaningless to ask what one can find after crossing the boundary or abolishing it; because, according to the Kantian and the Taoist, to distinguish or identify anything is just the function of reason. With the negation of reason there is nothing to distinguish.[40]

Indeed, the negation itself must be negatable, as well. Silence and non-action are the ultimate outcome of the negation of reason. Feng writes: "And in silence one also crosses the 'boundary' to the other side. This is what I call the negative method of the metaphysics."[41] The negative method leads one to the insight that one could only state what is not but never positively confirms what it is. The next step of this negative epistemology is mysticism. "If it is an idea at all, it is only a negative one. But in crossing the boundary, one has to give up even this idea. When one has crossed the boundary, one not only has no negative idea but no idea of negativity. Here we have real mysticism."[42]

Feng contends that Western philosophy does not offer as much as mystic reflections as Taoism and Zen Buddhism provide. While Chinese philosophy has not developed the positive method of logical analysis as elaborately as Western philosophy has done with arguments, examples, demonstrations, and exegesis, Western philosophers could learn more about the negative method in Taoism and Zen Buddhism. Together, they can create a world philosophy. This future world philosophy, Feng claims, shall be more rationalistic than traditional Chinese philosophy and more mystical than European philosophical tradition. "Only a union of rationalism and mysticism will make a philosophy worthy of the one world of the future."[43] According to Feng, this is the contribution of Chinese philosophy to the world.

Even though Feng tries to diverge from the positive method that uses logical analysis to define metaphysics as morality, as it has become clear in the previous quote, his negative method does not entirely leave the realm of rationalism. He is explicit that "the negation of reason is an act of reason." The fact that he calls his philosophy New Rationalism also reveals that he does not intend to leave the premise of Confucian rationalism. As I have mentioned, Feng aims to continue and reformulate Song-Ming neo-Confucianism for the new era. He is fully aware that Confucianism does not provide the negative method and rather follows the positive route. Even though he highlights the metaphysics of Taoism as the idiosyncratic distinction of Chinese thinking, he insists on the Confucian foundation as a more practical conduct of life. This pursuit of a new rationalism is similar to Weber's aspiration. If Song-Ming neo-Confucianism combines Confucianism, Taoism, and Buddhism, in Feng's New Rationalism, we see the new element of European philosophy.[44]

While Feng explains his theory of negative method by referring to Taoism, he uses stories in Zen Buddhism as concrete examples to illustrate how the negative method is being practiced. Feng argues that Zen Buddhism, a prominent branch of Buddhist teaching, was in fact very much influenced by Taoism. Feng also mentions that, although Ludwig Wittgenstein, a member of the Vienna Circle, shares the circle's intention to revoke metaphysics, he in fact demonstrates how one can explain metaphysics negatively, by chance. In addition to Feng's vision of Chinese philosophy's contribution to a world philosophy, I argue that this connection to Wittgenstein is another of Feng's contributions to the making of world culture and to global intellectual history.

ZEN BUDDHISM, LUDWIG WITTGENSTEIN, AND THE VIENNA CIRCLE

In his autobiography, Feng recounts that he met Wittgenstein while visiting Cambridge in 1933. Wittgenstein invited Feng over for tea at his place. They both realized that they had many similar ideas—especially that they were both interested in the issue of the ineffable truth in philosophy.[45] In *Xin Zhi Yan*, Feng cites several paragraphs in Wittgenstein's *Tractatus logico-philosophicus* (1921) and compares them to Zen Buddhist stories. Before I discuss Zen Buddhism and Wittgenstein, I will first provide the background of the Vienna Circle.

The Vienna Circle, a group of Austrian philosophers in the early twentieth century, seek to render metaphysics meaningless and invalid based on their logical empiricism (*logischer Empirismus*). They endeavor to affirm the positivistic method and the achievement of natural sciences. Philosophy thus should become a service to the sciences, or philosophy should become scientific after all, "a project that was itself a prelude to enlightened social reform."[46] Gottlob Frege, Ernst Mach, and Bertrand Russell were important figures for the Vienna Circle. The philosopher of science Moritz Schlick chaired the regular meetings of the group in Vienna from 1924 to 1936. Hans Hahn, Otto Neurath, Rudolf Carnap, Friedrich Waismann, and Victor Kraft were among the well-known members of Schlick's circle. The famous postwar Austrian writer Ingeborg Bachmann wrote her doctoral dissertation on Martin Heidegger under the supervision of Kraft. Wittgenstein maintained a loose relationship with the Vienna Circle. The circle's battle against metaphysics as superstition was not successful in its time. Its impact after World War II, however, was immeasurable. Feng rightly identifies the Vienna Circle's logical empiricism as a major force of positivism and thus uses its thinking to contrast to his own negative metaphysics.

Feng states that the Vienna Circle uses logical analysis to confirm the meaningfulness of evidence-based science and claims that metaphysics is meaningless. The Vienna Circle will only accept a theory, an argument, or a thesis as valid if it can be proved by empirical evidence and experiment. Otherwise, it is not an argument or a thesis at all.[47] If one says that there is life on Mars, it could be wrong, but it is a meaningful statement, because it might be verified one day in the future. Yet if one says that three angels could stand on the tip of a needle, then this statement is not meaningful because it can't be verified by experience or experiment. Hence, all statements in metaphysics are considered meaningless by the philosophers in Vienna if they cannot be empirically proved—metaphysics should thus be completely abolished. Feng observes that metaphysical statements in the West have been primarily concerned with the existence of God, the eternity of the soul (灵魂不灭), and the free will (意志自由). These statements could be either confirmed or denied, depending on one's choice and belief. In this case, Feng agrees with the Vienna Circle that these metaphysical statements don't make much sense and can be abolished. Yet, the Vienna Circle makes an extraordinary contribution to creating room for a different or, for Feng, the true metaphysics to emerge more easily. Feng argues that the Vienna Circle in fact does not deny the existence of metaphysics as meaningful in and for itself. Rather, it points out the fault line that leads to discern the meaningful and real metaphysics from the senseless and wrong metaphysics. Referring to Kant, who has tried to re-establish metaphysics after the challenge of David Hume's skeptical empiricism, Feng claims that he also intends to re-establish metaphysics after the Vienna Circle's logical empiricism in the twentieth century. He ambitiously sees his negative method as a synthesis of Taoist, Zen Buddhist, and Kantian genealogies.

Feng then uses Buddhist Sutras to illustrate his negative method, which he also terms as the method of New Rationalism (新理学的方法). He refers to the beginning two words in the *Jin Gang Jing* (金刚经, The Vajracchedika-prajna-paramita Sutra), *ru shi* (如是, meaning "as it is"), as the most succinct expression of metaphysics. *Ru shi* refers to things as they really are, *per se*. It is comparable to the word "to be" with its philosophical connotation. Feng contends: "The two words of *ru shi* should be the beginning and the ending of true metaphysics. In Zen Buddhism, what *ru shi* means is like mountain is mountain, water is water. A mountain is like how a mountain is, water is like how water is. This mountain is like how this mountain is, this water is like how this water is. Everything is like how it is, thus it means *ru shi*. That all things are like they are is reality. Metaphysics is based on the idea that reality is like how it is and explains the meaning of reality in its being."[48] The first affirmation of metaphysics confirms the existence of things (事物存在) in reality. But it does not confirm reality itself.

Zen Buddhism, a Buddhist school strongly influenced by Taoist thinking after Buddhism came to China in the first century, extensively uses a negative method to illustrate its understanding of Buddhist enlightenment. Zen Buddhism calls this method *chao fo yue zu* (超佛越祖), meaning "surpassing or transcending the Buddha."[49] Feng explains that Zen Buddhists see themselves as outsiders of the orthodox schools of Buddhism and pursue a negative position that differs from other Buddhist schools that more positively confirm Buddhist doctrines. The method of *chao fo yue zu* is characterized by silence or non-confirming response. If one tries to explain and analyze it, then it immediately loses its validity and beauty.

Feng shows several examples to illustrate this principle of silence. Once a monk asked Mazu Daoyi (马祖道一, 709–88), a famous Zen master during the Tang Dynasty, why he was saying that heart is Buddha. Mazu responded that he only wanted to calm down children's crying. The monk pestered him: What then, after the crying stops? Mazu rejoined that there is no heart as there is no Buddha.[50] Feng comments that the confirmation of the heart being Buddha is a dead statement (死语) because it does not lead the thinking anywhere, whereas the negative statement that "no heart no Buddha" (非心非佛) is a live statement (生语) because it does not determine what a thing is and thus creates a realm for imagination and experimentation.[51] The statement "there is no heart as there is no Buddha" does not mean there is really no heart as a physical organ and no Buddha as a historical figure. Rather, philosophically, this statement reveals a non-confirmative way of insinuating what is heart, what is Buddha, and what is enlightenment. Feng explains that materialism (唯物论) or idealism (唯心论) positively determines that the origin of all things or the ontology of the cosmos is either matter or mind. These statements are dead and meaningless from the perspective of Zen Buddhism. Even though the negative method does not allow explanation with words, it depends on metaphors, symbols, and stories to suggest its meanings and reach its pedagogical purpose with silent illumination.

Feng uses a story to illustrate his point. The school of Cao-dong (曹洞宗, known as Sōtō Zen in Japan), one of the five major Zen Buddhist sects starting in the twelfth century in China, which became the largest Zen school in Japan and is still active San Francisco today, has five methods in an order of primary and secondary statuses (五位君臣旨诀) to negatively explain the essence of Buddhist enlightenment. One method is to reveal the meaning of enlightenment not through words but through silent gesture (无语中有语). A popular story that radically and brutally illustrates this principle is about a boy's enlightenment after he loses a finger. When the Zen master Juzhi (俱胝) was asked about anything concerning the essence of Buddhist teaching, he always did nothing but raise one finger. One boy monk imitated Juzhi and showed a finger of his everywhere. When Juzhi saw that, he cut off the boy's finger. The boy exclaimed in pain and turned to run away. Juzhi called his name; when the boy looked back, Juzhi raised one finger. The boy suddenly reached enlightenment.[52] In this cruel and disturbing story, there is no word, no analysis, no explanation but a sudden radical action as the manifestation of the highest wisdom. The master teaches the boy the negative method after the boy has been using the positive method. No finger is a finger. No answer is the answer. No Buddha is the Buddha. It is a common Zen method to use an unexpected sudden and violent action to help one reach enlightenment. This method has entered the Chinese language and become a famous dictum: beating one's head with a stick while loudly screaming (当头棒喝). It is not through lengthy meditation and gradual progress toward fruition. Rather, it is a radical transformation to reach the highest level of Buddhist metaphysics. The one finger of the Zen master Juzhi denotes the metaphysical realm of the noumenon. The boy copies the master's external behavior and only takes it as a phenomenon, one possibility of many external manifestations of noumenon. The master cuts off the boy's finger to show that it does not matter whether one shows a finger or not as a phenomenon. It is more essential to see through the phenomenon in order to perceive the noumenon. It is one and the same thing to show or not show a finger. Hence, when the boy is not able to raise the one finger and is thus bereft of the phenomenon, the master raises his finger to reveal the truth at the end of the story. It is fundamental to perceive the void and emptiness as the most exalted manifestation of metaphysics. In a similar story, when the monk Baizhang (百丈) was asked about Buddhist law, he raised his fly-whisk; when he was asked whether he had other things to show, he put down his fly-whisk. This simpler story contains the same meaning as the story of the finger.

Another method that Feng highlights is that, despite using words, one does not directly address the question about Buddhism's essence. Rather, one responds in a nonsensical way to intentionally create a logical fallacy and negatively illustrate the Buddhist idea of emptiness. This method renders the question invalid. One uses but also does not use words at the same time, as Feng explains it. In one story, mister Pang asked Mazu Daoyi, "Who does not abide by the millions of the laws of the universe?" Mazu Daoyi replied, "When you could draw into your mouth the entire water of the West River, I would answer your question." In another story, the Zen master Yaoshan Weiyan (药山惟俨, 737–834), one of the founders of the Cao-dong School, once told a monk that he had a sentence, but he would only say it once a calf gave birth.[53] Feng comments that it is impossible for a person to suck in all the water of a river or for a calf to have a baby. Since the precondition for answering the question does not exist, then the answer will never be spoken. The Zen masters have said something in these two stories, but their statements are not positive replies to the questions. Rather, their statements refer to the indelibly ineffable. The highest state of being according to Zen Buddhism is seeing like not seeing, hearing like not hearing (无见无闻). For Feng, this does not mean that one should not see and listen anymore; rather, it means that, even though one sees and hears things, one remains calm and detached from them as if one had not seen or heard them. It is all the same. To be or not to be is no longer a question, but the same integration of humanity with the universe.

Feng argues that common knowledge requires that a human subject learns to acquire it. There is thus an opposite relation between the subject and the object through the action of knowing (*zhi*, 知). With its negative method, Zen Buddhism discloses a metaphysical area that lies beyond the realm of knowledge and does not require the act of knowing, but the intuition of *wu* (悟), which could be translated as instinctive understanding, perceiving, grasping. In this state of *wu*, there is no opposition between a subject and an object; rather, the human and the universe merge and integrate and can't be separated. In Zen Buddhism, the state of *wu* is called "entering the realm of law (*ru fa jie*, 入法界)." Feng calls it "the union with the heaven (*tong tian*, 同天)."[54] Feng skillfully uses the Confucian vocabulary of heaven to redescribe a Zen Buddhist idea. Even though Feng admires Buddhist and Taoist negative metaphysics, he always returns to Confucian rationalism as the foundation of his thinking.

Indeed, the aphoristic style in Wittgenstein's *Tractatus* startlingly echoes the succinct Zen stories. Feng comments that Wittgenstein considerably differs from other members of the Vienna Circle. Even though Wittgenstein shares the goal of other Viennese philosophers to abolish metaphysics, he in fact negatively displays metaphysics. "Wittgenstein was, in fact, always opposed to the Vienna Circle in the style and substance of his thinking. . . . while the Vienna Circle agreed with his *Tractatus logico-philosophicus* what can be said can be said clearly, it must vehemently reject the idea that there was something about which we must remain silent."[55] This silence is Wittgenstein's acquiescence to metaphysics. Feng shows that the last few paragraphs in Wittgenstein's *Tractatus* strongly resemble Zen Buddhist teaching. In 6.53, the third-to-last paragraph, Wittgenstein writes:

> The correct method in philosophy would really be the following: to say nothing except what can be said, i.e. propositions of natural science—i.e. something that has nothing to do with philosophy—and then, whenever someone else wanted to say something metaphysical, to demonstrate to him that he had failed to give a meaning to certain signs in his propositions. Although it would not be satisfying to the other person—he would not have the feeling that we were teaching him philosophy—this method would be the only strictly correct one.[56]

Wittgenstein clearly differentiates philosophy from natural sciences through the usage of language. While sciences can use language to issue statements and express their meanings, philosophy retains its myth through silence. Wittgenstein also argues here that metaphysics is something that cannot be articulated through language. This negative statement echoes Feng's position. Wittgenstein also uses the word "feeling" (*Gefühl*) to ironically describe a logical empiricist's understanding about philosophy as positivist. Hence the human faculty of logical thinking, as opposed to feeling, is not suitable for approaching philosophy, which equals metaphysics in Wittgenstein's sense. Then the "only strictly correct" method to approach metaphysics is the negative method.

In 6.54 in *Tractatus*, Wittgenstein argues, "My propositions serve as elucidations in the following way: anyone who understands me eventually recognizes them as nonsensical, when he has used them—as steps—to climb up beyond them. (He must, so to speak, throw away the ladder after he has climbed up it.) He must transcend these propositions, and then he will see the world aright."[57]

The meaning of this paragraph echoes the Zen Buddhist method of transcending the Buddha (*chao fo yue zu*), as I discussed before. The metaphor of a ladder here, symbolizing a disposable medium, also appears in other forms in Zen Buddhist stories. For example, one needs to forget the fishing trap after one has caught the fish (以筌得鱼, 既已得鱼, 则需忘筌); or one must forget the finger after pointing to the moon (以指指月, 既已见月, 则需忘指).[58] The fishing trap and the finger are both the media through which one gains access to fish and moon. The fish and the moon are the truth, not the fishing trap or the finger. Wittgenstein's ladder thus could be replaced with a fishing trap or a finger. In the last paragraph of *Tractatus*, 7, Wittgenstein, probably unintentionally, agrees with the Zen Buddhist negative method: "What we cannot speak about we must pass over in silence."[59] Wittgenstein and Feng are in full agreement with each other here.

Feng does not mention other statements of Wittgenstein in *Xin Zhi Yan*. Paragraph 6.522 in Tractatus, however, evinces yet another connection between Feng and Wittgenstein: "There are, indeed, things that cannot be put into words. They make themselves manifest. They are what is mystical."[60] This paragraph astoundingly reveals Feng and Wittgenstein's shared understanding of mysticism. As I clarified, Feng explicitly highlights the mysticism of Taoism and Buddhism as the final stage of the negative method in his essay "*Chinese Philosophy and Future World Philosophy*." I argue that the reason Wittgenstein is interested in pointing out mysticism after solving the problems of scientific facticity with logical analysis probably lies in his interest in life. Like the philosophers of life discussed in this book, including Eucken, Zhang Junmai, and Weber, Wittgenstein was also keen to solve the problem of life: "We feel that even when all possible scientific questions have been answered, the problems of life remain completely untouched. Of course, there are then no questions left, and this itself is the answer."[61] Then life is something that cannot be solved with scientific positivism. If Wittgenstein were in Beijing in 1923, he would have agreed with Zhang Junmai and Liang Qichao in the debate over science and life. Indeed, *Tractatus* was first published in 1921 and then translated into English in 1922, the same year that Zhang and Eucken published their booklet *The Problem of Life in China and in Europe* (1922). (See more in Chapter 3 in this book.) The problem of life was indeed a global intellectual issue in the 1920s.

Michael Morris and Julian Dodd realize Wittgenstein's self-contradiction in this negative aspect in *Tractatus*, commenting, "Wittgenstein, whilst occupying the philosophical perspective outlined in *Tractatus*, is simultaneously aware of its incoherence and, as such, believes (albeit self-underminingly) that it should be abandoned. He cannot but hope that there is available a space within which these problems do not arise."[62] Hans-Georg Möller also thinks that Feng Youlan misunderstood Wittgenstein because he was in fact closer to the Vienna Circle and insisted on a positive way of describing and saying the fact as truth.[63] Given the context that I have laid out, I argue that Wittgenstein does not necessarily wish to suppress the issues of silence, metaphysics, and life. Rather, he is acutely aware of the limits of logical analysis and its linguistic expression; he is aware that life cannot be fully captured by science and positivism. Wittgenstein hints at the limits of knowledge and language, or *zhi* and *yan*, because he is acutely interested in exploring the forms of life that lie beyond science.

While Wittgenstein subtly makes clear the question of life, Feng is invested in imagining the ethical actualization in life or a practice of life that reflects his New Rationalism. Feng's unspeakable metaphysical truth does not remain only as a philosophical concept. In the second part of his essay "Chinese Philosophy and a Future World Philosophy," Feng moves on to discuss "an ideal life to be achieved by philosophy."[64] Both Wittgenstein and Feng echo Weber's critique of rationalization and his pursuit of an aesthetic way of life.

THE IDEAL OF SAGE AS A COSMOPOLITAN

Feng claims in *The Spirit of Chinese Philosophy* (1947) that "philosophy of its very nature can do nothing more than exalt man's sphere of living, that philosophy is not qualified to give men positive knowledge in regard to the actual. Because this is so, it is also not qualified to give men the ability of controlling practical affairs. Philosophy has the power to enable men, in the midst of answering to the claims of humdrum affairs, to make the most of their inherent nature and achieve their highest destiny."[65] Then the negative method of crossing the boundary between the phenomenon and the noumenon is also meant for the improvement of life. In Feng's view, the highest dimension of being human in the practice life is the Confucian ideal of a sage (*shengren*, 圣人), an honorable designation that is usually only reserved for Confucius and Mencius. In *A Short History of Chinese Philosophy*, the lecture script that Feng used to teach Chinese philosophy at the University of Pennsylvania, he explains:

> The spiritual achievement of the Chinese sage corresponds to the saint's achievement in Buddhism, and in Western religion. But the Chinese sage is not one who does not

> concern himself with the business of the world. His character is described as one of "sageliness within and kingliness without." That is to say, in his inner sageliness, he accomplishes spiritual cultivation; in his kingliness without, he functions in society. It is not necessary that the sage should be the actual head of the government in his society.... The saying "sageliness within and kingliness without" means only that he who has the noblest spirit should, theoretically, be king. As to whether he actually has or has not the chance of being king, that is immaterial.[66]

The ideal of a sage has an inner and an outer dimension, called *nei sheng wai wang* (内圣外王), which Feng and his editor Derk Bodde translated as "sageliness within and kingliness without." Feng argues that the path, the *dao*, or the method of becoming a sage is the fundamental issue in Chinese philosophy. Principally, everyone could become a sage. The highest ideal is to become someone who can unite this-worldliness and other-worldliness, or realism and idealism, in both theory and practice. Philosophy should set its goal to facilitate people to become such a sage or develop sage-like characters. "Philosophy is not simply something to be known, but is also something to be *experienced*. It is not simply a sort of intellectual game, but something far more serious."[67] Therein lies philosophy's usefulness. Moreover, a sage is not confined to a nation or a culture but is an ideal cosmopolitan, a person integrated with the world and the cosmos.

In *Xin Yuan Ren (New Prime Human*, 新原人), the fourth book of the *Zhen Yuan Six Books*, Feng defines four different spheres of living: the innocent, the utilitarian, the moral, and the transcendent sphere. The first three spheres are almost self-explanatory as the developmental stages of a human from childhood to adulthood. The first two spheres are more or less in a so-called natural state, while the third and fourth spheres are more strongly directed by rational choices based on moral principles. In particular, in the transcendent sphere, Feng's metaphysics as world philosophy finds its universal application in a life that is not confined to a nation, a society, or a community. "And finally, a man may come to understand that over and above society as a whole there is the great whole which is the universe. He is not only a member of society but at the same time a member of the universe. He understands the significance of what he does and is self-conscious of the fact that he is doing what he does. This understanding and self-consciousness constitute for him a higher sphere of living, which I call the 'transcendent' sphere."[68] The transcendent sphere is deeply embedded within the society and in the most common life practice. "The perfect man is not limited to any particular profession. Any man whose avocation is of use to society can become a perfect man. But nobody can devote himself to the profession of being a perfect man. Should he attempt to do that, he would at once become like a monk devoting himself to the profession of becoming a Buddha. Immediately he would fall between the two stools of the sublime and the common."[69] The sphere of being a sage could only be achieved within social life and through social interactions. Sageness cannot be reached through designated effort outside of society, such as by a hermit. Here Feng critiques the Taoist and Buddhist retreat from society to purely devote to religious practice in pursuit of personal enlightenment. Following the Confucian spirit of social engagement, Feng situates the idea of a sage firmly in society.

Feng's sage integrates the highest understanding of the mystic unknown with the common practice of life in social affairs. The sage differs from Kant's ideal of Enlightenment or pure reason, which can be incessantly pursued but hardly reached. In fact, like Plato, Kant also connects morality to metaphysics as the noumenal imperative in his critique of practical reason. The classical Confucian idea of a sage is someone who has the highest moral standards and follows moral laws as wisdom. Feng, however, deviates from such a concrete idea and avoids filling the metaphysical emptiness with ethics, which has become clear in his discussion of Plato's metaphysics. Representing the negative method and the metaphysics of unspeakable truth, Feng's sage follows the pathway to the transcendent sphere as well as remaining keen in contributing to social affairs and maintaining an order of peace and justice. It is a delicate balance between social engagement and the awareness of cosmic order. Feng argues:

> A sage man cannot merely by virtue of being a sage become a competent man of affairs. But he can by virtue alone of being a sage become a king. What is more, and speaking strictly, it is only a sage who is supremely suited to be a king. When I say "king," I am thinking of the man who has the highest quality of leadership in a society. There is no need for such a leader to do anything very much himself. Indeed, he ought not to do anything much himself, in other words he should be *wu wei* (inactive), as Taoists maintained.... This does not mean that the supreme leader in his *wu wei* just does nothing, but that he gets all the talents in the country to do their best.... Let him do that, and he will do nothing, but everything will get done.[70]

Feng imagines that if a sage could lead a society, they would profess it in the best possible way as a confident leader with the ability to see others and recognize themselves with precision at the same time. Furthermore, this sage king should have an open mind and is impartial, selfless, and all-embracive. "He identifies himself with the Great Whole and can see things from the standpoint of the Great

Whole."⁷¹ Such a sage lets things take their turns in their natural developments, while his mind is attuned with the universe. A sage understands the *dao* and the laws of things because they have achieved full comprehension of the cosmos.

While the idea of the sage is classically Confucian, Feng fuses it to the Taoist idea of *wuwei* and transforms it into the image of a leader and philosopher. Feng claims that his New Rationalism probes into "the essential elements in this Tao."⁷² At the same time, the New Confucian thinker Feng promotes Confucianism as a guiding principle toward a moral and spiritual life. "In Chinese philosophy, the Taoists emphasized the delight and happiness which one can have in the highest sphere of living. But to the Confucianists, the elevation of one's sphere of living to the highest is not merely a matter of pleasure and enjoyment, but a realization of man as a man. A man may be perfect as some particular kind of man, an engineer or a statesman for instance, but may not be perfect as a man."⁷³ Feng's statement here echoes Weber's critique of profession and the promotion of vocation. They both realize the insufficiency of being a professional based on instrumental reason and insist on the spiritual dimension of being human in alignment with the cosmos. For Feng, the cosmos means the totality of all things together. This totality "cannot be spoken or thought. When we say 'One,' there are already two, the One which is spoken and the speaking of it."⁷⁴ Like the mystic metaphysics, this totality, in which the sage resides, is also ineffable and can only be comprehended through negation and silence. "So the totality which we think is not the totality of all that is. The totality of all that is, strictly speaking, is an idea of thought, but such that we must get rid of it in order to have it. And we must first have it in order to get rid of it."⁷⁵

Spinoza's idea of God serves as a point of reference for Feng to further elucidate his idea of the totality and the creation of spirit. Since Spinoza's God is not the object of reason but the object of love, the identification with God is a love gained through the negation of reason. Feng, however, does not only intend to negate reason, as I pointed out. Rather, he aims to reach a higher level of rationalization to mediate between noumenon and phenomenon, between *ming*, name, and *yan*, language, toward the void, *wu*. "By 'crossing the boundary' one is absorbed in the 'realm of non-distinction and undifferentiableness,' but this absorption must be made by the negation of reason through reason, otherwise the resulting sphere of living is not the fourth, but the first—not the highest, but the lowest."⁷⁶ The transcendent sphere of a sage's spiritual life is the highest achievement of rationalism in Feng's vision. "One must have the full use of reason in order to get rid of it. That is why a true mysticism must be preceded by a true rationalism, and why the negative method of metaphysics must be combined with the positive."⁷⁷ Unlike Weber, Feng does not separate the rational from the irrational and does not interpret Taoism as irrational. Rather he considers the Taoist and Zen Buddhist negative method a prelude toward a higher rationalization, a New Rationalism, a *Xin Lixue*. "It may seem that a philosophy advocating the negation of reason must be other-worldly. This is not necessarily the case, although a true philosophy cannot be merely this-worldly. It is other-worldly in attempting to get rid of man's selfishness and meanness, but this need not mean the exclusion of interest in the ordinary affairs of this world. A true philosophy is both other-worldly and this-worldly, in stressing the realization of the highest sphere of living in the daily tasks of human life."⁷⁸ A sage thus lives both this-worldly and other-worldly. Feng tries to reconcile the Confucian social engagement and the Taoist and Buddhist retreat from society and promotes a practice of life in and out of the social affairs at the same time.

A sage influences society with one's very being, not with supernatural abilities, and demonstrates the best possible conduct of life in quotidian tasks of human life. "Here is an age-old attempt to transform the meaning and value of daily life to make it most [worthwhile] in the best sense. This is why, throughout Chinese history, philosophy could guide spiritual life without any supernaturalism, and also guide practical life without being vulgar or mundane. If China can make a contribution toward a future world philosophy, it will be this open secret of realizing the highest values in daily life itself, in addition to the method of 'crossing the boundary' through the negation of reason."⁷⁹ The sage is the practitioner of this world philosophy, a synthesis of Chinese and European philosophies through metaphysics. The sage is not confined to any cultural, national, ideological, or linguistic boundaries. The sage is the embodiment of Feng's cosmopolitanism, a synthesis of Confucianism, Taoism, and Zen Buddhism in conjunction with Plato, Kant, and Wittgenstein. A world culture in Feng's vision oscillates between logical analysis and mystic metaphysics.

WESTERNIZATION, LITERATURE, AND WOMEN'S QUESTION

Neither Feng's negative method nor his ideal of a sage remains merely empty words. As discussed before, the Sino-Japanese War was the driving force for him to conceive of his New Rationalism in the Six Books.⁸⁰ In *Xin Shi Lun* (新事论, *Treatise on New Things*, 1939), the second book, he extensively discusses the political and social situations in China and the world. He claims that, to make his purpose clear with this book, he also gives it the title *China's Path toward Freedom*.

The most pertinent issue for Feng is whether China should become entirely Westernized. He tackles this question with a cultural typology. For Feng, the notion of nation or ethnicity should not be used to divide cultures. Instead, the multiplicity of cultural types and elements provides greater opportunities to broaden one's knowledge and deepen one's insights. Some cultural elements in China belong to a particular type of culture, whereas other elements in the West belong to another type of culture. Hence different types of culture and certain elements in a culture are being shared in various countries. Consequently, Chinese culture and Western culture are not mutually exclusive because they cannot be seen as stand-alone entities for themselves. Feng argues: "If one sees Western culture as an idiosyncratic entity, then it is problematic to learn from the West. If an entity is idiosyncratic, it cannot be imitated. Those who want to learn from an entity are not learning from the entirety of the entity; rather they are learning some elements from this entity, learning the quality of some aspects in the entity. For example, Mencius said that he wanted to learn from Confucius. He meant that he wanted to learn the sageness of Confucius. The other sides of Confucius, such as the facts that he was from Lu, worked as an official in Lu, and lived to his seventies, cannot be imitated at all."[81] From the perspective of cultural idiosyncrasy, different elements construe Western cultural identity. It is impossible for China to entirely take over Western culture (全盘西化) and entirely become the West with all its distinct features. It is, however, possible for China to adopt some general cultural elements that have developed well in the West. In sum, if Western culture is modern, then it is not because it is Western but because some elements in the West have gone through technological modernization; if Chinese culture is backward, it is not because it is Chinese but because some parts of Chinese society need to be modernized. Thus, China's modernization does not necessarily equal Westernization. Instead, China should continue to cultivate its own cultural tradition while modernizing some parts of its society.

Feng further insists that Chinese art and literature can't be Westernized. "We often hear that there is British industry, British science, or British literature. British industry and science are those that are in Britain, but they don't only belong to Britain; or they are the industry and science that the British people have. It does not make much sense to say that British industry and science are completely different from those in other places. But British literature is something authentically British because it is written in the English language. Many wonderful details in it come from the English language and these things are indeed untranslatable. All national literature is like that. For example, in Chinese literature, the style *duizhang* (对仗) is very important. *Duilian* (对联), *lüshi*

(律诗), *pianwen* (骈文) all depend on *duizhang* to become a particular genre of its own. *Duizhang* is inherent in the Chinese language. Other languages do not have exactly the same linguistic feature."[82] Hence, it is not necessary and is actually impossible to Westernize everything in Chinese culture in order to modernize China. Literature and art do not need to be modernized because they are idiosyncratic for those people who share the same language and history.

Feng compares the social reform in China to the reconstruction of a house and mentions two different opinions in China toward modernization. Some think that, if one uses Western materials such as concrete and steel to build a house and equip it with electric lamps and radiators, then the house must be in Western style. But some others think that a house in the traditional Chinese style embodies an ambience of beauty, dignity, peace, and solemnity. This is China's spiritual civilization. The solid and comfortable housing in the Western style belongs only to material culture. One should not sacrifice spirit in favor of materialism. Feng comments that the opposition between these two opinions is not necessary, because it is not necessarily Western but is actually modern to build a house with concrete and steel and use electric lamps and radiators in the house. Hence, one can use these materials to build a Chinese-styled house and make it comfortable and beautiful at the same time. Such a house will be new China, in which one can have railroads and factories; in which one can wear Chinese clothing, enjoy Chinese cuisine, speak Chinese, sing Chinese songs, and paint Chinese art. In culture, art, and literature, one will recognize what is Chinese, Feng concludes. The deep appreciation of cultural idiosyncrasy through literature and art generates profound happiness. Feng is thus skeptical about the imitation of Western style and the adoption of foreign words in modern Chinese literature. His reason is that this new style is detached from the common people and can't be easily appreciated and understood. "Only the art and literature that grow out of Chinese history and the lives of Chinese people is Chinese. Only this type of art and literature is vivid for Chinese people. When China becomes modernized, then Chinese culture also needs to become modernized. But modernization is not Westernization. Modernization works, but not Westernization."[83] Feng's reservation toward Westernizing Chinese literature contains a certain cultural conservatism. At the same time, his insistence on the uniqueness of Chinese language and its literary manifestations predates today's postcolonial argument against cultural imperialism.[84]

In the chapter "Explaining Inheritance and Continuity" (释继开), Feng discusses his opinion on revolution and social change, in general, and the 1911 Chinese Revolution and China's literary revolution (文学革命) around 1900, in particular. Feng contends that the 1911 Revolution was a purely political event of regime change, but it did not change Chinese society in a more fundamental way, despite the establishment of a Chinese congress and constitution.[85] Similarly, the literary revolution did not change Chinese literature completely to serve the commoners, either. Rather, Feng observes, the trend of vernacular literature has existed since the Song dynasty in the ninth century. Literature at the end of the Qing dynasty has also adopted a lot of elements from European languages and their narrative styles. Thus, the literary revolution could be successful only because it carried forward the tradition of vernacular literature. Even though the new literature enhanced its quantity and improved quality, it was not a new origin for such a movement (虽扬其波, 而不是开其源).[86] Feng emphasizes that all new things are based on and derived from old things. One could continue the tradition without innovation; but all innovations are entangled with tradition (有继往而不开来者, 但没有开来者不在一方面是继往).[87] Here Feng obviously takes inspiration from Dewey's question about the connection and coherence between philosophical schools, even though such an argument might be reminiscent of cultural conservatism. Yet Feng is not such a conservatist that he purely insists on the tradition. Rather, he calls attention to the importance of recognizing the continuation and transformation of the past in the present, even if one declines to do so.

Feng further reflects that all revolution causes anguish and suffering; thus, it is understandable that conservatives are against reform and innovation, especially against revolution. If a country or a nation must obtain something new and, for the sake of survival, go through revolution, then the pain can't be avoided. At the same time, there is no formula that promises to work for all countries—just like there is no remedy for all diseases with the symptom of fever. One needs to observe the situation and find a solution that suits the situation. The October Revolution that gave rise to the Soviet Union did not happen according to what was described and imagined by Karl Marx. It arose out of the concrete situations in Russia at that time.[88] Similarly, Feng disagrees with the opinion that the supporters of Westernization denigrate Confucian ethics as anthropophagy (吃人的礼教). He argues that one needs to situate the ethics within its sociohistorical context to properly assess its values. Women's rights were of particular importance to Feng.

Feng agrees with the advocates of women's rights who argue that, in a modern society, women should be freed from their traditional duties of rearing children and taking care of their households. Yet this should not merely remain as lip service. Concrete social and institutional reforms need to take place to turn this idea into social reality. For Feng, there are two types of society: a society whose mode of production is based on family (生产家庭化的社会) and a society whose mode of production is based on social organization (生产社会化的社会). In the former one, the economic mode of production is based on the closely tied units of extended family. The latter one has transformed out of family production through industrialization and machine production. The individuals are freed from the need of their families and work outside their family enterprises. These two types of societies also have different moral values and social practices, especially in terms of women's rights.[89] Feng reminds his readers that, before the time of the Wei (魏) and Jin (晋) Dynasties (220–589 AD), it was not a rare case for widows to remarry. It was not considered unethical. Yet during and after the Song (宋) Dynasty, women's chastity was held as the highest value by neo-Confucianists. Death became comparably a smaller matter. Women's suicide was even recommended and applauded as a practice to avoid the loss of loyalty to their men. Neo-Confucian ethics served the patriarchal social order and victimized women's lives. Gayatri Spivak's famous argument about the subalternity of women and their lack of agency in a patriarchal society, as shown in the ritual of widow burning in India, echoes Feng's point here.[90]

In dynastic China, love was not a criterion for marriage. Rather, marriage was a family affair and should be decided by the parents of the marrying parties. Feng comments that this practice is understandable in a society that depends on family as its economic foundation. This type of society functions around the core family structure and its extended network of relations. Under such circumstances, before the introduction of machines and industrialization, when peasant parents looked for wives for their sons, they would focus on whether the new women could be an effective additional work force in the family. For families of the officials at court, the choice was made according to the symbolic value of the wife's background—also not based on love and mutual attraction. Feng explains that, in such a family-based mode of production, almost everyone has to practice and think according to these rules to survive. He also makes clear that he is not interested in finding an excuse for such a behavior, in any case, but only does a contextualization of the particular ethics concerning the women question and its historicity in a mode of production based on family.

In a society based on social production, industrialization, and machine production, Feng further differs two types: in one type, social production still controls the function of family; in the other, social production is purely supported by socially independent members of society. In the first type, while men are relatively free, women can't be freed from the family because they can't work properly during their pregnancy, nursing, and the time of caring for young children. Women thus not only depend on their husbands but are also confined and controlled by men. In such a social structure, the best time of a woman's life, alas, must be spent at home performing their duties of bearing and rearing children. It is very common for women to choose between career and family in a society in which social production controls family life. But men don't have to deal with similar issues faced by women. In Feng's time, some people who were critical of Confucian ethics, claimed equality between men and women and proposed to free women from their family and child-rearing duties. Feng responds that, if a society does not offer any opportunity for women in terms of childcare and career accommodation, what could women do to further this path toward liberation?

Feng sees two solutions. The conservative one is to reaffirm women's position in the family as housewives. Men would like to see women at home even in a society of social production. The movement in Germany to push women back to the kitchen intended to reaffirm women's position at home. Yet, in a society based on social production, Feng advocates, women can't and shouldn't wholeheartedly accept the position as housewives. The solution is to solve the problem of childcare with reliable professional institutions, which are the key for women to work outside the household with a good conscience. Feng points out that childcare institutions should not set profit as their only goal so that women could leave their children in good hands and concentrate on their work without much financial burden. Only with such a reform could women achieve true equality with men. Women and men could then live together independently. The problem of women could only be solved through sufficient offerings of quality childcare in a society, Feng concludes.[91]

Indeed, Feng is an advocate of women's rights and equality with men in Chinese society. His appeal to understand the Confucian ethics in its historical context can be interpreted as his conservatism in defense of an outdated social order. At the same time, his understanding of Chinese society is congruent with his promotion of Chinese philosophy as an integral part of world philosophy. Feng does not propose to radically abandon the past as the foundation of the present, which again is reminiscent of Dewey's question during Feng's dissertation defense. Feng uses the method of historicization and contextualization to reveal the value and validity of Confucianism in its given historical situation. While being an advocate for women's rights, Feng strongly promotes Confucian ethics as the spiritual strength in China's defense against Japanese invasion and Western imperialism because morality has sustained the existence of Chinese society for thousands of years. He insists that basic human moral values, such as loyalty, trustworthiness, and gratitude, will not change despite historical transformation and cultural difference.

Hence Feng claims that China needs to bond its community with its inherited moral values to debunk the invasion and warfare. Feng mentions that there are two aspects of Chinese spirit: the Confucian and Mohist (*mo jia*, 墨家) seriousness (*yan su*, 严肃); and the Taoist composure and detachment from one's own life and death (*chao tuo*, 超脱).[92] These two aspects form a dialectical pair that requires people to fully commit to their duties and, at the same time, reminds them of the transience of things in this world. Focus and relaxation are not opposed to each other but are blended to enable the best possible form of life. Feng's proposal of social life echoes his philosophical vision of a sage.

When Feng was composing the Six Books during the Sino-Japanese War, he reported that he had heard about many examples of genuine Chinese people (真正底中国人) during the war. One journalist met a soldier who volunteered to organize a guerrilla force in northern China. During their conversation, the soldier showed his confidence in China's final victory. "What would you do after the victory?" asked the journalist. The soldier responded calmly, "I will already have died by then. During this war, almost all soldiers will die." One businessman in Hangzhou lost all his fortune during the war and fled to Shanghai. When asked what he would do next, he said, "It does not matter. I will do it again."[93] Feng comments that they were simple and ordinary people in China, but they showed such a detached composure as well as moral seriousness in times of great duress. Feng believes that only the cultivation over thousands of years could give birth to such a moral strength: society could change, adopt modern sciences and technologies, and develop more legal regulations, but the essence of Chinese moral spirit does not need to be modernized or Westernized. China's past depended on people with such a spirit; China's future also depends on such genuine people, Feng forcefully claims. This morality, however, is not only Chinese. It also belongs to the world. Feng recounts another anecdote: the University of Oxford wrote to the president of the Chinese Nationalist Government, Chiang Kai-shek, that they were once skeptical about the value and meaning of Chinese culture. However, they had no doubt today about the leading force of world culture when they learned about the violence of Japan's narrow-minded nationalism and China's solemn composure in its war of defense.[94] For Feng, this external observation from an international institution of higher learning demonstrates the significance of Chinese philosophy as a meaningful contribution to a world philosophy.

Indeed, Feng's philosophical understanding and discussion almost always concerns itself with the world and is rarely only confined to the national context. Feng reflects that "world" means different things for the ancient Chinese and the ancient Greeks. "China is a continental country. To the ancient Chinese, their land was the world. There are two expressions in the Chinese language which can both be translated as the world. One is 'all beneath the sky' and the other is 'all within the four seas.' To the people of a maritime country such as the Greeks, it would be inconceivable that such expressions could be synonymous. But that is what happens in the Chinese language, and it is not without reasons."[95] While Feng's comment on the cosmopolitan quality of the Chinese language intends to reveal the Chinese openness to the world, the German dramatist Bertolt Brecht finds in ancient Mohism a creative sphere for philosophical translation.

Mi-en-leh taught: Introducing democracy can lead to dictatorship; introducing dictatorship can lead to democracy.

—Antony Tatlow, ed., *Bertolt Brecht's Me-ti: Book of Interventions in the Flow of Things*

BERTOLT BRECHT'S *ME-TI* OR THE AESTHETICS OF TRANSLATION: UNIVERSAL LOVE, MUTUAL BENEFITS, AND TRANSIENCE

Bertolt Brecht's aphorism in *Me-ti: Buch der Wendungen* (*Me-ti: Book of Transformation and Usage*) expresses the dialectic of two seemingly antithetical political systems.[1] Mi-en-leh is meant to be Lenin, whose name Brecht reinvents in a Chinese-like style. Likewise, the book itself is allegedly Brecht's own German "translation" of *Mozi*, a book of ancient Chinese philosophy of Mohism, from an English translation. Yet Brecht's self-stylization as the German translator and the alleged English translation of *Mozi* are both fictive. His creative negotiation with Mohism contains an aesthetics of translation through which he connects ancient Chinese philosophy, Marxism, and sociopolitical situations in the twentieth century in *Me-ti*.

Even though *Me-ti* was first published posthumously in 1965, Brecht had started working on this project beginning in the 1930s.[2] This project accompanied Brecht throughout his exile and his late years in East Germany. Despite its fragmentary status, *Me-ti* maintains an essential position in Brecht's oeuvre. Fredric Jameson reads it as Brecht's "principal work in the dialectic" and as "a set of political commentaries on the leftist politics of the period."[3] Hans-Peter Krüger interprets *Me-ti* as a major intervention in the dialectic of the art, comparable to Hegel's dialectic of thinking and Marx's dialectic of capitalism, because Brecht sees in art its own limits and thus seeks its liberation from its ritualist and cult-like functions.[4] Foregrounding Marxist dialectic, Jameson and Krüger don't mention the role of Chinese Mohism in *Me-ti*, despite the obvious relation between these two. Roland Jost summarizes that Mohism serves as an exotic garment over twentieth-century issues to achieve the V-effect of the materialistic dialectic.[5] Thus the Chinese element merely serves as form and has little to do with the philosophical content of *Me-ti*. More recently, Markus Wessendorf argues that Mohism, along with Confucianism, belongs to "respected counterparts and foils that allowed him to develop and articulate his own materialist-ethical positions. Because of their cultural difference and historical remove from Brecht's own context they provided an echo chamber and testing ground that allowed him to estrange and historicize his own ideas as well as the Marxist discourse of his time, thereby rendering both developable."[6] I propose to take Wessendorf's argument of the general "echo chamber" one step further and inquire what Brecht precisely does on the "testing ground" without falling back onto the same argument that he is merely concerned with Marxism and socialism. Interestingly, Günther Heeg suggests that *Me-ti* is not an amalgamation of Chinese philosophy and Marxism but a creation without context (*Zusammenhanglosigkeit*) because Brecht takes both out of their contexts and rearranges them in a third constellation.[7] Yet Heeg's analysis only remains within the text of *Me-ti* itself. To understand the role of Mohism in *Me-ti*, we need to come back to the question of translation.

Translation, an issue that hasn't been properly addressed in *Me-ti* scholarship, promises to take us to different contexts and yield a deeper understanding of Brecht's textual and contextual practice. Even though Brecht's work is not a translation from one language to another, it is a "translation" of philosophical ideas between ancient Mohism and twentieth-century Marxism. Focusing on Brecht's notion of alienation effects (*Verfremdungseffekt*) and his Chinese poems and plays, such as *The Good Person of Szechwan* (*Der gute Mensch von Sezuan*, 1943), Eric Hayot also observes that it is rather immaterial to question after the authenticity of Brecht's China as it is presented in his literary works. It is more important to recognize the adherence to the spirit or the idea, as it is expressed in Chinese poetry and performance art, in its re-creation and representation in another artistic and historical context in twentieth-century Germany.[8] From this perspective, *Me-ti* is also the result of the interpolation and extrapolation of thought experiments between Mohism and Marxism. Moreover, the narrative style of *Me-ti* also resembles that of the Chinese book *Mozi* in that it collects an eclectic number of anecdotes, aphorisms, statements, and comments. *Me-ti* is thus also a transliteration. If we take seriously Brecht's aesthetic practice of translation, then we need to close-read the related texts and detect the intertextual traces to render Brecht's meticulous art of translation visible and intelligible. *Me-ti* provides a unique opportunity to read Brecht in an intercultural and global context that hasn't been properly explored yet. Instead of reading from the perspective of Marxist dialectic, I venture to read *Me-ti* from some major vantage points of Mohism: universal love, mutual benefit, and the transience of life. I argue that Brecht's vision of socialism, called the Great Order in *Me-ti*, reflects the Mohist ideals of universal love based on the logic of mutual benefit; Brecht's understanding of dialectic, called the Great Method in *Me-ti*, stresses metamorphosis and transience of things in different forms and times. Before the analysis of the Great Order and the Great Method, I will first discuss the historical context of the translations of *Mozi* from Chinese into European languages. I will also show that Brecht's interest in Mohism is not singular because there was a renaissance of Mohism among Chinese intellectuals, which prompted the translation of Mozi into European languages. We thus should take Mohism more seriously than it has been regarded in *Me-ti* scholarship. It is too limiting to merely read *Me-ti* within the Western context. Mohism is not merely an external style of V-effect but also an internally integrated philosophical content that Brecht has integrated with Marxism to articulate his own dialectic.

BRECHT'S "TRANSLATION" AND THE RENAISSANCE OF MOHISM AS A GLOBAL MOMENT

In the foreword to *Me-ti* in the 1965 edition, Brecht claims that he used for his German translation Charles Stephen's English translation of *Mozi* (墨子), which registers the teachings of the philosopher Mo Zi, meaning Master Mo, and his followers in later times.[9] Master Mo, named Mo Di (墨翟), supposedly lived in the fifth or fourth century BCE, during the Warring States Era in Chinese history. Mo was most probably a contemporary of Confucius. While Brecht's claim about the English translation sounds plausible, as many books in Chinese were first translated into English and then from that into other European languages, in reality, the English translator doesn't exist. Brecht, of course, is not the German translator of *Mozi* in the literal sense.

The first comprehensive translation of *Mozi* into a European language is Alfred Forke's, from Chinese into German, in 1922: *Mê Ti, des Sozialethikers und seiner Schüler philosophische Werke* (*Me Ti, Philosophical Works by the Social Thinker and his Students*).[10] Forke's translation is based on the 1895 edition of *Mozi Jiangu* (墨子間詁, *A Concise Commentary of Mozi*) by the Chinese scholar Sun Yirang (孫詒讓, 1848–1908). Sun was an eminent Confucian philologist around 1900, toward the end of the Qing Dynasty (1636–1912).

His critical edition of *Mozi* has been considered the most authoritative modern Chinese edition of the classic to date. *Mozi*'s English translator, Ian Johnston, mentions that there are four partial translations of *Mozi* before Forke's, with the earliest dating back to 1861: two into English, one into German, and one into French.[11] Several other partial translations into English and German occurred after Forke's, until the most complete English translation by Johnston appeared as late as 2010.[12] No translator, however, was named Charles Stephen, as Brecht claimed. In fact, Brecht owned a copy of Forke's translation and used it intensively to study Mohism. He even had it bound in black leather. "Me-ti in leather" was one of the few things that Brecht took with him in his Swedish exile.[13] Obviously, Mohism remained important to Brecht for decades.

Then why did Brecht invent such an English translator—a question few scholars have asked so far? Why did he portray himself as a fictive German translator? He could just simply claim that the stories and aphorisms in his book were inspired by his reading of *Mozi* in Forke's translation. Perhaps the desire to be a translator moves beyond the obvious joy of literary creation and reveals a deeper insight into merging philosophical thinking with literary creation, the present with the past, and the East with the West. It is a nonbinary and nonnormative attempt of Brecht's that welds ancient Chinese Mohism with Marxism and twentieth-century politics to create a new form of thinking characterized by intertextuality. Brecht's *Me-ti* bridges the gap between what he claimed was an ancient Chinese socialist thinking and the twentieth-century international socialist movement. Brecht's self-portrayal as the German translator of a fictive English translation manifests his creative method of "translating" the ancient Mohist philosophy into a twentieth-century model of thinking as well as his awareness that this type of "translation" has gone through layers of interpretations and is further from its original. It is also a transliteration because Brecht transforms phrases in Forke's translation into his own and, at times, makes Master Mo comment on the sociopolitical situations in Germany or the Soviet Union, creating a V-effect and jumping a huge time gap of more than two thousand years. Mohism is visible in both the form and content of *Me-ti*.

Brecht also invents a series of Sinicized names for countries, well-known personalities, and his friends. For example, Germany is Ga or Ge-el; the Soviet Union is Su; Lenin is Mi-en-leh; Karl Marx is Ka-meh; Hegel is Meister Hü-jeh or He-leh; Stalin is Ni-en; Hitler is Hi-jeh, Hu-ih, Hui-jeh, or Ti-hi; Brecht's friend and teacher Karl Korsch is Ko or Ka-osch; his lover and collaborator Ruth Berlau is Lai-tu, and Brecht himself is Kin, Kin-jeh, or Kien-leh. These names are "translations" from the twentieth century to antiquity and from German or Russian to their Chinese-like versions. Toward the end of the foreword, Brecht endeavors to strengthen the readers' impression of the authenticity of his claims by claiming that some chapters in the book, such as those on music and conduct, are really written by Master Mo, while some other chapters are not, even though these too are ancient teachings; the remaining chapters, however, are written more recently but use the old style of the text.[14] Brecht reflects that, from a strictly scientific (*streng wissenschaftlich*) point of view, books like *Me-ti* might not qualify as a serious book. But if the readers do not merely care about the stamp of authenticity (*Echtheitsstempel*) but rather focus on the content, then they may very well gain something valuable through reading this eclectic (*eklektisch*) collection.[15] In conclusion, Brecht hopes, his insertions of modern thoughts and the comparisons between modern history and ancient Chinese philosophy could also amuse his readers. Indeed, the word "eclectic" reveals Brecht's aesthetic method and practice of "translating" Mohist ideas into something that can be used for contemporaneous issues. Brecht's argument about the unnecessity of authenticity also indirectly points out his idea of borrowing and applying philosophical ideas from one context to another.

Brecht also claims that the Chinese classic *Mozi* had suffered from an almost complete repression (*fast völlige Verdrängung*) by Confucianism and thus isn't part of the classics of the Chinese antiquity. Brecht reports that the teachings of Master Mo, however, experienced a renaissance in the nineteenth century because some elements resembled certain Western philosophical trends (*westliche philosophische Strömungen*) and appeared almost modern (*fast modern*). Even though one could doubt the veracity of Brecht's claim after finding out the fictionality of the English translator, the marginalization of Mohism in the Chinese intellectual history, as Brecht ascertains, is confirmed by a consensus among scholars. Johnston considers Mohism "the most serious challenge" to the dominating Confucianism and its neglect a consequence of the firm establishment of Confucianism as the orthodox state philosophy and social value system until the mid-nineteenth century.[16] The lack of interest in Mohism in the West reflects Chinese paucity. Hence Johnston's complete translation of *Mozi* (2010) serves the purpose of reviving the study of Mohism in as late as the twenty-first century. Forke also claims that "the answer to the question after the most important philosophical or religious systems in ancient China has been commonly Confucianism and Taoism until now. Yet there was a third system that is usually completely ignored or merely mentioned in passing: Mohism, the teaching of Mê Ti. He has challenged the status of his rivals of Confucius and Laozi for centuries; then his teaching disappeared, and he was almost forgotten for two millennia."[17]

Forke further comments that Chinese scholars started to pay more attention to Mohism after their intensive and violent encounters with Western powers and China's own social reform, both of which challenged the absolute authority of Confucianism. After Chinese students had studied in the West, they started to observe China's intellectual history from a different perspective. Thus came *Mozi*'s renaissance in the early twentieth century. Forke's view is confirmed by his Chinese contemporary scholar Fang Shouchu (方授楚, 1898–1956). In his well-known study on Mohism, *Moxue Yuanliu* (墨学源流, *The Origin and Trends of Mohism*, 1936), Fang contends that Mozi was the only classical Chinese thinker who was seriously read and discussed among Chinese intellectuals around 1900. Because of the disappointment with the Confucian tradition, which had not succeeded in debunking Western imperialist encroachment, the younger generation in the early twentieth century started to actively study European thinkers and reassess the Chinese tradition. Indeed, with the downfall of the ancient dynastic system in 1912, Confucianism lost its unquestionable authority as political philosophy and cultural value in a country that had been challenged by Western imperialism and industrial modernity. Confucianism was not considered effective in defending China against imperialist invasions. Hence Mo Zi as an anti-Confucianist came into favor. His twin ideas of universal love (兼爱, *jian ai*) and distaste against warfare (非攻, *fei gong*), as well as his attention to the ordinary and the poor people beyond family and national boundaries, impressed Chinese scholars who were looking for new points of orientation for China in the world. Well-known scholars and politicians including Liang Qichao (梁启超), Hu Shi (胡适), Zhang Binglin (章炳林), Qian Mu (钱穆), and Feng Youlan (冯友兰) all published monographs discussing Mohism's use for modern China.[18] Unlike Confucius, who was an impoverished aristocrat, Master Mo was a low-status craftsman. Mo's personal name *Di* (翟) means "dark" or "black" in classical Chinese, referring to his low-status dirty work as an artisan. Fang stresses Mo Zi's low social status as a decisive factor in his thinking, contending that Confucius's perspective aligned with that of the ruling class, while Mozi established his philosophy from the position of the less privileged.[19] Fang argues that Mohism was revolutionary in the turbulent and conflictive period of the Warring States in Chinese history. Fang considers equality the most important element in Mozi's teaching.

Against this backdrop, Brecht's claims about the marginalization and the renaissance of Mohism are not only true but also reflect his own social and intellectual interests, concurring with those of the Chinese intellectuals. Brecht's argument about Mohism's affinity with Western philosophy and modernity is closely connected to the renaissance of Mohism in both China and the West. Forke recounts that many European sinologists, such as Ernst Faber, Cognetti de Martiis, and Alexandra David, considered Master Mo the oldest socialist in East Asia. Chinese and Japanese scholars concurred with this view. Forke argues, however, that Mo Zi is not a socialist in terms of social democracy but rather a social aristocrat, because he does not renounce social classes and monarchism. As the title of Forke's translation already betrays, he sees Mo Zi as a social moral philosopher (*Sozialethiker*). According to Forke, Master Mo and his followers promote an ethical socialism that fosters universal and equal love for everyone, transcending social boundaries that Confucianism strictly observes.[20] Forke comments that Mohism's universal love contains "an essential communist quality because, if one should love those who are loosely related (*Fernstehenden*) as much as those who are closely related to oneself, then all sanguine relations, friendships and patriotism would be dissolved and sublated. A complete equality exists for all."[21] Mohism's universal love is reminiscent of Christianity—Forke mentions that Chinese scholars even call Mo Zi the Chinese Jesus and are proud that socialism, a set of internationally influential ideas, also finds echo in East Asian intellectual antiquity. In addition to the twin ideas of universal love and distaste against warfare, Forke also considers two other principles crucial for Mohism: respect for and promotion of people of ability in state affairs, regardless of their social backgrounds and status, and reduction and elimination of superfluous luxury and the arts, which, Forke comments, echoes with the communist theories of François-Noël Babeuf and Robert Owen.[22]

Given the interest in socialist thinking and Mohism in both Europe and China, it is a global intellectual historical moment to which Brecht refers. Forke's translation not only introduces a more or less complete textual foundation of Mohism into a European language but also opened up a channel for Europeans to understand the recent intellectual movement in China. Without the renaissance of Mohism in China and the recession of Confucianism in the early twentieth century, as Fang informs us, Forke might not have made the effort to translate the complete *Mozi* if it had not been edited and discussed by Chinese intellectuals. Hence Brecht's creative engagement with Mohism further contributes to the global circulation of knowledge and creates a new aesthetics for philosophical "translation" between the East and the West and between antiquity and modernity.

The global intellectual historical context in which Brecht's *Me-ti* is deeply embedded calls our attention to Brecht's aesthetics of translation. It also raises the question about Brecht's practice of translation in creating a meaningful inter-text connecting both Mohism and dialectic materialism. Since *Me-ti* basically remains a fragment, it is a very difficult task to interpret or even to make sense of it. Brecht researcher Werner Mittenzwei confirms that no other manuscript among Brecht's papers is as difficult for the editors of Brecht's works as the *Me-ti* material. Brecht had left behind neither a general plan for publication nor a clear order for all the stand-alone chapters in the manuscript folders. The four different editions of *Me-ti* have different organizations. While the editors of the first two editions of *Me-ti* (published in 1965 and 1967), Uwe Johnson and Klaus Völker, more or less followed the order in which *Me-ti* was found in the Brecht archive, Jan Knopf, the editor of the *Berliner und Frankfurter Ausgabe* (1995), followed the chronological order in which the episodes were written. Mittenzwei, the editor of the third edition (1975), however, divides the materials into five sections based on the themes in Forke's translation because this organization reflects "the inner order and the compositional principle of the entire *Me-ti* materials."[23] Mittenzwei's edition bestows on *Me-ti* a philosophically meaningful structure and situates Brecht's writing within the context of Mohism.

Even though Mittenzwei's edition reflects the essentiality of Mohism in Brecht's fragment, he does not discuss the intertextual connections between Forke's translation and Brecht's *Me-ti*, let alone in relation to the Chinese original of *Mozi*. Instead, he warns not to treat Forke's translation of *Mozi* as the foil or foundation for *Me-ti* and opines that Brecht's dialectic and ethics are better than Mohism. Then he follows a similar track as the other critics to interpret *Me-ti* within the context of Western socialist art movement and Marxism. He argues that *Me-ti* experiments with a new thinking through art and literature and demonstrates a materialist dialectic with V-effect.[24] Mittenzwei contradicts himself in that he first emphasizes and then downplays the importance of Mohism for Brecht. Given the philosophical significance of *Me-ti* and the historical background of Mohism, it is indispensable to trace Brecht's practice of philosophical translation in the intertextuality between the Chinese original, Forke's German translation, and Brecht's *Me-ti*. Among the five sections, *Book of the Great Method* and *Book of the Great Order* are the two sections on which I will focus next because they both reflect Brecht's vision about how to reach the ideal of socialist order with the method of dialectic.[25]

THE GREAT ORDER: SOCIALISM

In the anecdote "Gespräche über Su" ("Conversations about Su"), Kin-jeh (Brecht) tells Ko (Karl Korsch) about a legal case in Su, referring to the Soviet Union. A farmer goes to a city to work in a blacksmith's shop. The farmer lives with a family that has a vacant room in their house. Both parties agree that the farmer will move out when the family's son comes back. Yet, when the son returns, the farmer refuses to move out because it is very difficult to find other lodgings. The house management takes the case to the local court. The judge, however, does not pass any verdict on the case. Instead, the judge commissions the house management to find an apartment for the farmer and promises that he will also look out for an apartment for him. Kin-jeh praises the judge because he understands that moving out of one place means moving into another. Ko, however, does not believe that such a story could happen because it is too good to be true. Ko argues that, in Su, too many things are not done according to the principles required by the masters, who are supposedly Marx, Engels, and Lenin.[26] When Kin-jeh insists that this story indeed happened because he has witnessed it, Ko contends that the judge only faked it because Kin-jeh was present. Kin-jeh answers that, even though the judge does so merely because of his presence, it is still a great achievement of the judge, even to make such a reasonable (*vernünftig*) decision only once. Kin-jeh draws an analogy: If Ko hears that a man can run faster than everyone else but only does so when Ko is present, isn't it still a great achievement of the runner?[27]

Yun-Yeop Song points out that Brecht has generally integrated the Mohist idea of universal love and usefulness (*Nützlichkeit*) into his thinking about the socialist social order.[28] Indeed, the story of the farmer and the apartment is a concrete application of the Mohist principle of universal love and the equal care for the rich and the poor in a socialist society. The equal treatment of both family members and nonfamily members corresponds to the second chapter on Universal Love in *Mozi*. Master Mo asks a question about the causes that harm the state and then responds:

> It arises through lack of mutual love. Nowadays, feudal lords know only to love their own states and not to love the states of others, so they have no qualms about mobilizing their own state to attack another's state. Nowadays, heads of houses know only to love their own house and not to love the houses of others, so they have no qualms about promoting their own house and usurping another's house. Nowadays, individual people know only to love their own person and not to love the persons of others, so they have no qualms about promoting their own person and injuring the persons of others. . . . When the people of the world do not all love each other, then the strong inevitably dominate the weak, the many inevitably plunder the few, the rich inevitably despise the poor, the noble inevitably scorn the lowly, and the cunning inevitably deceive the foolish.[29]

The only cure, Master Mo argues, lies in the "methods of universal mutual love and exchange of mutual benefit." Mo Zi explains that, if people view others as their own, either in terms of political state, household, or individual, then they would attack less, discriminate less, and deceive less. "Within the world, in all cases, there would be nothing to cause calamity, usurpation, resentment and hatred to arise because of the existence of mutual love."[30] Mohist universal love transcends the borders of states, the barriers between families, the hierarchies between nobility and commoners, and the difference between the rich and the poor. Mohist love imagines an absolute equality among all peoples and communities. It radically breaks with social hierarchy and conventional boundaries between groups and individuals. More importantly, this love is immediately bound to the pragmatic realm of benefit. It is thus not merely a theoretical construction or an abstract idea. Rather, it is a concrete suggestion about how to practice universal love and for what purpose. In other words, without mutual benefits, mutual love can't be expressed and demonstrated. Only through the deeds that lead to mutual benefits is the principle of universal love confirmed, visible, and tangible. At the same time, the foundation for mutual benefits should be firmly rooted in universal love, not in any other sentiment or motivation.

Kin-jeh's interpretation of the farmer's story follows the Mohist philosophy of mutual love and benefit. The story challenges the common understanding of family and justice in a twentieth-century bourgeois society. Usually, the family's son is considered closer to the family than the farmer, a stranger. The farmer's room is situated in the family's apartment, which causes a breach in this family-based unity. The agreement to move out acquiescently accepts the convention of familial love and its boundaries. When the farmer refuses to follow this logic, the boundary of love is being challenged, and the bourgeois convention needs to defend its validity. The judge, however, does not support this bourgeois convention in the Soviet Union. Instead, he practices universal love in demonstrating understanding for both the farmer's and the family's situations. His instruction to the house management and his own promise to find housing for the farmer reveal his intention to address the needs of both sides. According to the passage in *Mozi*, since the family only loves their own son and does not care about the farmer, the conflict emerges as a result of the lack of universal love. Justice thus should be achieved on the basis of equality and love, not on the boundaries of love. The judge, however, also does not demand that the family continue to provide housing for the farmer. This solution would not be as useful for the family's son, who also needs housing. The establishment of justice thus needs a pragmatic and forward-looking spirit that seeks to solve problems collectively as a society. The farmer who then becomes a worker in a blacksmith's shop clearly is a member of the industrial proletariat. The family with a spare room probably belongs to a more privileged class. With the Mohist sense of universal love, the judge moves beyond the boundaries of class and family and avoids conflicts caused by bourgeois conventions.

Furthermore, Kin-jeh and Ko's conversation about practicing good deeds only in the presence of others resembles a conversation between Master Mo and his student Wu Ma Zi (巫马子):

> Wu Ma Zi spoke to Master Mo Zi saying: "You, Sir, practice righteousness but I don't see people submitting to you and I don't see ghosts blessing you. Still you practice it. You must be mad!" Master Mo Zi said: "Suppose now there were two officials—one who carried out his duties when he saw you, but not when he did not see you, and one who carried out his duties whether he saw you or not. Which of these two men would you value?" Wu Ma Zi replied: "I would value the one who carried out his duties whether he saw me or not." Master Mo Zi said: "In that case, then, you would also be valuing one who is mad!"[31]

Master Mo praises the honesty of working diligently, no matter whether it is visible to others. It is a kind of honesty that one chooses for oneself and, in Mohist understanding, for the heaven and the spirits. Yet Brecht's story takes a different turn to argue that, even if the event is singular, it is still remarkable. The recognition of both parties' needs and the willingness to help both, even if it only happens once in Kin-jeh's presence, is still a great insight and practice, and it has the potential to develop into more established legal routines in Su. This corresponds to the pragmatic tendency of Mohism in that it does not merely insist on the moral principles of love and honesty as something abstract but also recognizes the meaning and importance of the ideas in the practice itself. Indeed, Kin-jeh's argument about the fastest runner contains the encouragement to do so more often because this man already has the potential to run fast, while many others don't have the ability to do so.

In Forke's translation, we read, "A smaller good deed is the same like the generosity of a great deed. Analogy in: extension. . . . People love their fellow humans not because of praise. Analogy in: caring for the elderly."[32] Obviously, Kin-jeh's argument about the importance of even a one-time good deed echoes the statement about extending the good deed from a smaller to a larger dimension. The analogy between the judge and the runner in Brecht's story also imitates the style in this passage presenting an argument first and then an analogy. Both the content and form of *Mozi* are reflected in Brecht's writing. The Mohist ideas and practice of universal love and mutual benefits correspond to Brecht's vision of socialism, as described in this story.

Brecht's emphases on the individual practice, extension, and encouragement of universal love and mutual benefits can be found in many other episodes in *Me-ti*. In the chapter "Die Grosse Ordnung und die Liebe" (The Great Order and Love), Me-ti defends love as something that inherently belongs to the Great Order because the enemies of the Great Order eliminate love.[33] Similar to Master Mo, Brecht understands universal love as the foundation for a socialist society. In "Die Köchin soll den Staat lenken können" (A Female Cook Should Be Able to Lead the State), Mi-en-leh, referring to Lenin, promotes the idea that the state should be organized and reformed like a kitchen and vice versa. Every female cook has the ability to organize a kitchen as well as a state.[34] This anecdote reveals Brecht's belief in the power of an individual in the realization of a collective plan. The comparison of a female cook with the head of a state also breaks the class boundary and social hierarchy and empowers women. The female cook reminds us of the noble character of Grusche in Brecht's drama *Der kaukasische Kreidekreis* (*The Caucasian Chalk Circle*, 1944). Individual effort induces colossal changes. A commoner with a "low" social status can perform a "high" status job just as well. Here Brecht already expresses his dialectic, the Great Method, that guarantees or leads to the Great Order, the socialism with universal love and mutual benefit.

THE GREAT METHOD: DIALECTIC

In the original typescript of *Me-ti* in the Bertolt Brecht Archive in Berlin, I saw the Chinese character *ming* (名) placed next to a section title *On the Great Method* (*Über die große Methode*).[35] The Chinese character, however, is omitted in all print editions of *Me-ti*. As mentioned in Chapter 5, Feng compares Plato's notion of matter to the Confucian idea of *ming*, meaning the fundamental principles and moral laws in the world. The fact that Brecht put this character next to the title on the great method, which I interpret as the dialectic, reveals his understanding that the dialectic is for him the fundamental moral principles in the world, like that in Mohism or Confucianism.

In *The Principle of Inequality in the Great Method* (*Der Ungleichheitssatz in der großen Methode*), Brecht discusses the dialectic between identity and change or between a linguistic concept and its changing object in reality. The speaker, Me-ti himself, reflects on the philosophy of He-leh, referring to Hegel, and states:

> The sentence "one is not equal to one" points to certain difficulties but is in itself tricky. It ought really to be "one is not only equal to one but is also not equal to one."

It expresses the thought that you can't find one thing that you can induce to be true to itself over a long period of time; nor can you find a concept that proves ready to stick to the point at least for as long as you're speaking if you're saying more than one sentence.[36]

According to Knopf's commentary, the sentence "one is not equal to one" could allude to Hegel's *Science of Logic* (*Wissenschaft der Logik, 1812*), in which Hegel maintains that absolute laws of thinking (*absolute Denkgesetze*) are caught in a constant contradiction between a thesis and an antithesis and their sublation.[37] Brecht's text, however, refers to the temporality of a concept, the fluidity, the ephemerality, and the flexibility between an idea and what it refers to in a constantly changing reality. Even though an indirect reference to Hegel's dialectic of thinking could be contained in Brecht's statement, it also reveals Brecht's negotiation with a Mohist idea.

The Mohist dialectic expresses itself laconically:

Completely applicable: There is only either being at rest or being in motion. . . . A beginning: Time in some cases has duration and in some cases does not. A beginning is a specific instant of time without duration. . . . A transformation: Like a water frog becoming a quail. . . . Stopping: Not stopping when there is no duration corresponds to "ox is not horse" and is like "an arrow passing a pillar." Not stopping when there is duration corresponds to "horse is not a horse" and is like "a man passing a bridge."[38]

The frog and quail are biologically completely different creatures. But, from the perspective of the transformation of life energy, Mohism does not preclude the possibility of metamorphosis through which one form of life could change into another. A horse is not equal to a horse because time changes, despite the duration of a life. Even though the horse still remains the horse, it is no longer the same horse, because the horse could have become older or thinner or slower during the years. Conceptually speaking, a horse is thus not equal to a horse. This point could have inspired Brecht's statement about the change of a thing over time and the instability of a concept (*Begriff*). Temporality plays an important role in the Mohist dialectic. The movement of time, however, is not conceived of as conflict and synthesis, as it is in the Hegelian manner; rather, it is conceived of as a transformation and transition from one form of existence to another. Of course, the Hegelian conflict and its synthesis are themselves a movement within time. Yet the Mohist dialectics stresses the changes that one entity or one form of existence undergoes during time.

Brecht once contemplated to use the title *Buch über den Fluß der Dinge*

(*Book on the Flowing of Things*) for *Me-ti*, which reflects the Mohist dialectic about motion, duration, and transformation. Yet again, Brecht doesn't remain at the abstract level but seeks to put this idea into practice. In "Über den Fluss der Dinge" (On the Flowing of Things), To-tsi, referring to Trotzki, observes that workers in a blacksmith's shop have first organized strikes against the exploitation by the shop owners and demanded better payment. Yet, when the shops are closed for a lack of iron, the workers insist on the continuation of exploitation (*Fortführung der Ausbeutung*).[39] To-tsi comments that life means for the workers to be exploited, and now they are afraid of losing their lives. They are now angry with the shop owners and drive them away because the owners refuse to continue exploiting the workers. While it is satiric to conclude that the workers desire to be continuously exploited because their existence is otherwise in danger, this anecdote reveals the changing historical realities in different scenarios during the proletariat revolution. While exploitation in and for itself should be condemned and prevented in principle, if its elimination induces unemployment and jeopardizes livelihood, then being able to work is considered more practical and more important than the bare theory about exploitation and resistance. Social reality is more complex than ideological thinking based on fixed principles. Ideology needs to be constantly adjusted to the changing social reality. One needs to recognize the most pressing need at the moment and act accordingly. Nothing is cast into stone. Just like a frog could become a quail and a horse doesn't remain a horse, the fact of exploitation is in principle to be condemned but could also be desired and could save lives at times.

Brecht writes in another episode with the same title, "Über den Fluss der Dinge," that nothing is completely dead, not even those that have died. Even dead stones, which can't really die, still breathe and induce changes.[40] Brecht argues that we need to call the things, for example the moon, "dead" for the sake of a concept. If we don't do so, we lose a description, the word "dead," and the possibility to name something that we experience.[41] At the same time, since we notice that the moon is not completely dead, we need to keep both sides in mind and treat it as "something that is both dead and not dead, though actually more dead, in a certain sense deceased, in this sense absolutely and irretrievably deceased, but not in every sense."[42] While Brecht discusses the delicate balance between death and life and argues here about life in death, in a later episode he warns not to focus too much on the transience and disregard the duration of things and its possible harm. In "Gefahren der Idee vom Fluss der Dinge" (Dangers of the Idea about the Flowings of Things), Brecht reflects that one might see something as less severe based on the assumption that it would eventually disappear (*vorübergehen*), but these things can do damage.⁴³ Changes don't happen by themselves. Changes need to be made so that harmful things could be forced to disappear (*zum Vergehen gezwungen*).⁴⁴ A conscious choice in life is still necessary, even though the flow of things is inevitable. This idea echoes a statement in *Mozi*: "Promote benefit and do away with harm; the analogy lies in stopping a leak."⁴⁵ The flow of water is often compared to the flow of time. The dripping of water is change, but it is a change toward the disadvantage of the container, which could symbolize resources in a society. It is dangerous if one merely thinks that all things change and doesn't plug the hole that causes the leak. The stop of the leak is necessary to restore good social order.

The practical application of this idea is echoed in the statement "Frieden und Krieg" (Peace and War) in *Me-ti*. Brecht writes that imperialism must be eradicated by the proletariat revolution because imperialism would not vanish by itself but needs to be forced to disappear:

> We saw that the nation, which lived in peace with other nations, fostered a war between its own classes. But the war against other nations, which was caused by the war between its own classes, brought about a truce among the classes. And yet at the same time it worsened the war of the classes; so the truce collapsed and the war of the classes ended the war between nations.⁴⁶

According to Knopf's commentary, the war of the classes in the first sentence alludes to the class struggles against exploitations in Germany before World War I, while the same phrase in the last sentence refers to the Russian Revolution in 1917 and the German Revolution in 1918. The German political party SPD (*Sozialdemokratische Partei Deutschlands*) directed the internal conflict outward and passed a bill to allow Germany to follow imperialist foreign policies, to which the war with other nations in the quote refers.⁴⁷ Brecht argues here that German imperialism abroad, however, does not pacify the class struggles in the country itself but rather intensifies them. To stop the leak of the warring logic of the German Social-Democratic Party, the international proletariat's revolution is necessary to end the wars on time. It is dangerous to passively wait for time to make changes. The dialectic between peace and war works in favor of the future Great Order of socialism that promises universal love and equality not only in one country, but in an international order. International class solidarity is the cure of the leak of imperialism worldwide.

The reading of the Great Order and the Great Method in *Me-ti* alongside Mozi demonstrates Brecht's aesthetics of "translation" between ancient Mohism and contemporaneous Marxism, between theory and practice, and between art and reality. *Me-ti* evinces an intertextuality inflecting both *Mozi*'s teaching and Brecht's own understanding of universal love, mutual benefit, and the dialectic of transience. Of course, Brecht did not translate *Mozi* from English into German. Rather, he translated the content and the spirit of *Mozi* from its ancient context into the twentieth-century setting of the international communist movement. Hence translation is not merely an action from one language to another but also a trans-situational movement between historical periods, ideological orientations, and civilizations. It is also a political or an ideological translation, an engagement that stresses the practical and ethical function of literature in intellectual debate and political movement. Brecht's self-styling as the German "translator" and his imitation of the aphorismic style of *Mozi* also reveal his translation as transliteration, moving beyond linguistic, historical, ideological, national, cultural, and class boundaries. *Me-ti* represents a form of world literature that is translation and transliteration both in form and content. The perspective of translation uniquely allows us to place *Me-ti* within the swinging realm of dialectic without reducing Mohism to an exotic garment merely for the V-effect or overemphasizing materialist dialectic as the only real content. Translation thus functions as a perfect medium and a time machine for Brecht to negotiate with ancient Mohist philosophy and find his own expressions. He in turn gives Mohism a new life in Europe after more than two thousand years. Without the renaissance of Mohism in China around 1900, however, Forke wouldn't have translated *Mozi* into German and Brecht wouldn't have had the opportunity to write *Me-ti*. Hence *Me-ti* is also a product of a global intellectual history that conceals and reveals more connections and crosscurrents than we could have realized. In his copy of Forke's translation, Brecht underlines in red pencil the sentence "One can find pleasure in the benefit of the world (*Man kann an dem Wohl der Menschheit seine Freude haben*)."[48] Indeed, Brecht articulates a generous love to the world through his *Me-ti* that creatively connects, wittily translates, dialectically infuses aesthetics and politics beyond the inside and the outside.

CODA: CONSERVATISM OR ALTERNATIVE MODERNITY

Each of these European and Chinese thinkers used classical Chinese philosophy to promote various intellectual and political agendas and to imagine a world culture that diverges from Western modernity. Critiquing capitalist rationalism and Western imperialism, these philosophers emphasized the importance of ethics and highlighted the irrational, emotional, spiritual, and intuitive dimensions of life. I delineate these thinkers' intense engagement with Chinese philosophy to unsettle the habit of following European genealogy as the only source for global dissemination and transformation of ideas and concepts. The inextricable entanglements among these philosophers reveal the subversive force of a non-European intellectual tradition in exemplifying a different global intellectual history for the future. This book bears my hope of "redirecting our desire and placing our eyes on ourselves as the double or mirror image" so that we, Westerners and non-Westerners alike, "begin to take each other seriously" and incorporate ideas and feelings from around the world within us.[1] It was the philosophers' vision of a world culture defined by common ethical values and rational governance that would transgress any boundaries defined by nations, languages, ethnicities, or any imaginable identities.

Throughout the book, I mentioned several times that the Chinese thinkers discussed here have been considered a conservative force in modern Chinese intellectual history. In the 1976 study *The Limits of Change: Essays on Conservative Alternatives in Republican China*, some leading scholars of modern Chinese intellectual history at that time define the New Confucianists as cultural conservatives, yet not sociopolitical conservatives.[2] The New Confucianists' promotion of well-worn religio-philosophical values in Confucianism, Buddhism, and Taoism earned them the label of "conservative" in their historical context. Their ideas were considered backward-looking and outdated in contrast to those of the nationalists who ushered in the 1911 Chinese Revolution as well as those of the communists who were part of the international communist movement. The historians, however, also recognize the New Confucian intellectual endeavors as foundational for Chinese modernity. Charlotte Furth perceptively comments:

> When the new Confucianists ask whether some principle validated their moral intuitions, justified their pain, and explained what the universe is fundamentally all about, they asked it as people sharing a universal human condition, transcending the social circumstances of any time or place. To call conservative those who have continued to use Confucian symbols to allude to their meaning is to say that the historical specificity of the religious form is inseparable from the timeless truth being expressed, and that this embodiment of the eternal in the historically conditioned human is seen by the believer as both necessary and right. New Confucianists certainly accepted this view. Furthermore their assertion of Confucian value has taken place within the historical context of a worldwide post-Enlightenment trend toward the secularization of society and thought, to which contemporary restatements of the believer's message, by Chinese and others, have been a conscious response.[3]

Furth's observation elegantly summarizes a New Confucian vision of world culture and potentially points toward global context. Yet she routinely returns to the national framework to situate and interpret New Confucianism—a move that many scholars of Chinese intellectual history have also meaningfully followed in the decades before and after.

My endeavor, however, is to situate the Chinese philosophers in a global intellectual history and highlight their visions of world culture as an alternative modernity. And that yields a slightly different outcome. In the global public sphere, from the perspective of the twenty-first century, the New Confucian thinkers' anti-imperialism, decolonization efforts, insistence on national independence and sovereignty, the intention and action to revive the less industrialized and disadvantaged rural areas, and the philosophical engagement to establish transcultural metaphysics for the entire world, these positions are not conservative but rather progressive today.[4] Their positions also prove beneficial for the contemporary debates about a more equal and just world order, greater world peace as well as warfare, competition, and power politics. No more would they today qualify as "conservatives," but rather as avowedly global citizens. Political labels such as "conservative" or "progressive" thus need historical and geographical contextualization. Their so-called conservatism back in the early twentieth century seems now rather immaterial. Their intellectual programs of world culture bear greater importance for a global future.

Indeed, the German-speaking thinkers, including Brecht, joined force with the Chinese philosophers and repurposed ancient Chinese philosophy for the imagining of a different global modernity. The discussion of the New Confucian "conservatism" could also prove valid for at least certain ideas of Keyserling, Weber, and Eucken. The emphasis on spirituality in the age of capitalist materialism and imperialism, shared by both the German and Chinese philosophers, resonates with the twenty-first century's acute awareness of ecological crisis and global capitalist exploitation as well as the hope for a "dialogic transcendence" as a "moral force" to mediate the rational and the metaphysical and render the conceptual divide between the East and the West meaningless.[5]

Last, but not least, the philosophical discourse of world culture in the early twentieth century is merely a fraction of the interconnected global network of science, philosophy, and creative energy. The inspiration of Confucian and Taoist self-cultivation, which we see in Weber and late Foucault, was profoundly explored and vibrantly imagined in literary modernism. When Weber refers to Taoism as a magic garden (*Zaubergarten*), it is not a random metaphor. The word "magic" appears and reappears in modernist literature, ranging from Hermann Hesse, Thomas Mann, and Franz Kafka to Alfred Döblin. Concomitant with the philosophical discourse, literary modernism was also fascinated with Chinese and Asian religious ideas and practices and explored paths of individual psychic and physical healing and social reform. A future study of European-Asian modernism and spirituality would accompany this philosophical account to further examine the intersections of literary imagination, cognition, and spiritual consciousness and their therapeutic effects in world culture then and now.

ACKNOWLEDGMENTS

This book wouldn't have been possible without the aid and generosity of many others over a prolonged period of time. The University of California at Davis allowed me to take leave time in Germany for research and writing. Alexander von Humboldt Foundation provided very generous financial support to make this book possible. I'd like to thank my hosts Dominic Sachsenmaier (for a long-term research fellowship), East Asian Studies at the University of Göttingen, and Michael Gamper (for a short-term re-invitation fellowship) in Peter Szondi Institute of Comparative Literature, Freie Universität Berlin, for providing institutional platforms in Germany. A fellowship from Käte Hamburger Center for Advanced Study *Heritage in Transformation* at Humboldt Universität Berlin made the final stage of this book possible. I'd like to thank the co-directors of the Center: Sharon Macdonald and Eva Ehninger. Friedrich Schlegel Graduate School of Literary Studies, Dahlem Humanities Center, and the Excellence Cluster *Temporal Communities: Doing Literature in a Global Perspective*, all at Freie Universität Berlin, offered generous institutional affiliations, research support, and opportunities for collaboration before, during, and after the global pandemic. My gratitude goes out to Anita Traninger, Stefan Keppler-Tasaki, and Miltos Pechlivanos.

Over the years, I received valuable encouragement from mentors, colleagues, and friends for the book from its inception to its end. The 2011 NEH summer seminar "Shanghai and Berlin: Cultures of Urban Modernism in Interwar China and Germany" at Stanford University, led by Russell Berman and Ban Wang, sowed the first seeds of this book. It was a legendary intellectual and social experience for me. Furthermore, I am deeply indebted to the years-long mentorship and enduring support from Ban Wang, Veronika Fuechtner, Carl Niekerk, Daniel Purdy, and Glenn Penny. I had numerous opportunities to present part of the book around the world, despite Covid. For their invitations, I thank Kurt Beals, Zongqi Cai, Sarah Colvin, Matthew Erlin, Frank Kelleter, Ervin Malakaj, Carl Niekerk, Jakob Norberg, Stephen Roddy, Lynne Tatlock, Rochelle Tobias,

Wang Hui, Andrew Webber, and Zhang Hui for inviting me to Johns Hopkins University in Baltimore (MD), Peking University in Beijing (China), Tschinghua University in Beijing (China), University of Cambridge in Cambridge (UK), Duke University in Durham (NC), Georg-August-Universität in Göttingen (Germany), and Washington University in St. Louis (MI), as well as online at Freie Universität Berlin (Germany), the University of British Columbia (Canada), and the University of Illinois Urbana-Champaign. For thoughtful consultations and smart conversations, I am grateful to Susan Buck-Morse, Michael Foster, Frieder Günther, Reto Hoffmann, Alessa Johns, Edith Hanke, Sheldon Lu, Flagg Miller, Jakob Norberg, Stefan Keppler-Tasaki, Martin Powers, Mert Bahadir Reisoglu (and his tarot prediction), Chris Reynolds, Ritchie Robertson, Haun Saussy, Jocelyn Sharlet, Michael Subialka, Baki Tezcan, Gabriel Trop, Tobias Warner, Wang Hui, Lora Wildenthal, Shuchen Xiang, and many more. Sebastian Conrad's colloquia on global history at FU Berlin has introduced me to many interesting ideas over years. The students in the two seminal graduate seminars deserve a special thank you for their brain power to help me think through the initial architecture of the book. David Lummus, an award-winning Renaissance scholar in his own right, generously offered editorial expertise in scholarly prose—his help is truly invaluable. A very special thank you goes to Thomas Lay, the acquisition editor at Fordham University Press, Paul North and Jacques Lezra, the series editors of *Idiom: Inventing Writing Theory*, and Pu Wang and Ban Wang, the two reviewers. Your intellectual vision and fine perception transformed my manuscript into a book.

Archivists and librarians played key roles in my research for this book. In particular, Edith Hanke from Max Weber Arbeitsstelle in Munich and Iliane Thiemann from Bertolt Brecht Archive in Berlin impressed me with their expertise, generosity, and patience and made many findings in this book possible. An earlier version of Chapter 1 was published as "Hermann Graf Keyserling and Gu Hongming's Ethics of World Culture: Confucianism, Idealism, and Anti-Colonialism," in *Transnational Framings: The German Literary Field in the Age of Nationalism, 1848–1919*, edited by Lynne Tatlock and Kurt Beals with Camden House, 2023, 208–27. A previous version of the first section in Chapter 2 was previously published as "Max Weber's Confucian Care of the Self," *Critical Inquiry* 48 (Spring 2022): 594–610; © 2022 The University of Chicago, all rights reserved. The second section in Chapter 2 was previously published as "Max Weber and the Re-enchantment of Charisma," in *Journal of the History of Ideas*. Chapter 6 was previously published as "Bertolt Brecht's *Me-ti* and the Aesthetics of Translation: Universal Love, Mutual Benefit, and Transience," in *Germany From the*

Outside: Rethinking German Cultural History in an Age of Displacement, edited by Laurie Johnson with Bloomsbury Publishing, 2022, 303–22.

Jonathan Hess has been in my mind all these years after his sudden passing in 2018. When I encountered a writing blockade or thinking impasse, I would carry out imaginary conversations with him and silently ask Jonathan what I should do. I felt his smart and sharp eyes were always on me, quietly reminding me of writing clearly, revising incessantly, and boiling down conglomerate ideas to direct and meaningful arguments. "Less is more," his famous oxymoron, has become an entrenched motto for me in scholarly writing. I am always your student. And, of course, my friends stood by me with their warm and capable hands whenever I needed to touch base with myself or use a pair of extra eyes to discern life's puzzling turns.

My family has been the bedrock for my adventures. My darling sons, Jiayu and Peilin, have enriched my life in the dearest way. I appreciate beyond words their patience and acceptance of a mother who did not always want to play with them because she wanted to read and write. Thank you for being part of my life. Nothing in the world would replace my experience with the two superheroes for me: Mama and Baba, whom I always look up to in the past, present, and future everywhere in the world. It is an eternal admiration and gratitude that defy changes in time and space. Even though I have been trying really hard throughout my life, I know I will never reach the level of Baba, who embodies creativity, hard work, perseverance, optimism, pragmatism, and authenticity. I also know very well that I will never grow up enough to be Mama, who is an inexhaustible fountain of love, attentiveness, patience, tolerance, wisdom, generosity, and hard work. Without their innate Confucian values, nothing of me would have been possible, let alone this book. In front of them, I am always the impatient and lazy little girl who came into their lives and cried for help. 谁言寸草心, 报得三春晖 I dedicate this book to Mama, Baba, Jiayu, and Peilin.

NOTES

INTRODUCTION: GLOBAL INTELLECTUAL HISTORY, ECOLOGY OF LITTLE BEINGS, AND WORLD CULTURE

1. See Max Weber, *Die Wirtschaftsethik der Weltreligionen: Konfuzianismus und Taoismus*, Studienausgabe der Max Weber-Gesamtausgabe (Tübingen: J. C. B. Mohr [Paul Siebeck], 1991), 134.

2. See John Dewey, "Transforming the Mind of China," *Asia: Journal of the American Asiatic Association* XIX, no. 11 (1919): 1103–8; Bertrand Russell, *The Problem of China* (New York: Century, 1922).

3. See Jessica Ching-Sze Wang, *John Dewey in China: To Teach and to Learn* (Albany: State University of New York Press, 2007); John Dewey, *Lectures in China, 1919–1920* (Honolulu: University Press of Hawaii, 1973).

4. See Daniel A. Bell, *China's New Confucianism: Politics and Everyday Life in a Changing Society* (Princeton and London: Princeton University Press, 2008); Daniel A. Bell, ed., *Confucian Political Ethics* (Princeton and Oxford: Princeton University Press, 2008); Arif Dirlik, "Confucius in the Borderlands: Global Capitalism and the Reinvention of Confucianism," *boundary 2* 22, no. 3 (1995): 229–73.

5. See George Steinmetz, *The Devil's Handwriting: Precoloniality and the German Colonial State in Qingdao, Samoa, and Southwest Africa* (Chicago and London: University of Chicago Press, 2007), 490–507. Yet it is, at least in this case, not necessarily a "German" intention to appear more superior to their British and French colonial rivals, an argument or a political strategy that has been used by the British to portray themselves as better colonizers to compete with the Spanish in the colonization of the Americas in the long eighteenth century. Kris Manjapra argues that Hermann von Keyserling, in his travel diary documenting his journey in India, shows a sense of German superiority to the British so that the Germans could be potentially better colonizers. Yet Keyserling didn't so much identify himself as a German national as see himself as a Prussian Junker, an outdated category stemming from the declining monastic order of Europe. As I argue in Chapter 1, Keyserling was more interested in restoring aristocratic rule in Europe and disliked social democratic movements in the West in general. See Kris Manjapra, *Age of Enlightenment: German and Indian*

Intellectuals across Europe (Cambridge, MA, and London: Harvard University Press, 2014), 56–70.

6. The Nietzsche fever, for example, was not only a phenomenon in the early twentieth century but reemerged in the 1980s after the decade of the Cultural Revolution. Prominently, the Warring States School (*zhanguoce pai*, 战国策派) in the 1940s, basically comprising university professors who all studied in Germany, promoted the Nietzschean ideas of *Übermensch* and dionysianism and advocated authoritarian statism and irrational heroism to secure China's independence. They challenged New Culture Movement's scientism and positivism and propagated state militarism. See Wu Guo, "The "Zhanguoce" School's Effort of Wartime Cultural Reconstruction, 1940–1942," *Journal of Modern Chinese History* 3, no. 1 (2009): 45–69; David A. Kelly, "The Highest Chinadom: Nietzsche and the Chinese Mind, 1907–1989," in *Nietzsche and Asian Thought*, ed. Graham Parkes (Chicago and London: University of Chicago Press, 1991). In addition, modern Chinese literature intensely negotiated with Western literary phenomena such as European Romantic lyricism and Rainer Maria Rilke's sonnets in the poetry of Guo Moruo (郭沫若) and Feng Zhi (冯至). Zong Baihua (宗白华) compares Western and Chinese arts and their histories in his essay collection *An Aesthetics Anthology* (美学散步, 1981). See Hsiao-yen Peng and Isabelle Rabut Peng, eds., *Modern China and the West: Translation and Cultural Mediation* (Leiden and Boston: Brill, 2014); Pu Wang, *The Translatability of Revolution: Guo Muruo and Twentieth-Century Chinese Culture* (Cambridge, MA: Harvard University Asia Center, 2018).

7. See Lydia H. Liu, *Translingual Practice: Literature, National Culture, and Translated Modernity—China 1900–1937* (Stanford, Calif.: Stanford University Press, 1995).

8. See Richard Wilhelm, *Die Seele Chinas* (Berlin: Verlag von Reimar Hobbing, 1926); Dorothea Wippermann, *Richard Wilhelm: Der Sinologe und seine Kulturmission in China und Frankfurt* (Frankfurt am Main: Societäts-Verlag, 2020).

9. See Hui Wang (汪晖), *Xiandai Zhongguo Sixiang de Xingqi* (现代中国思想的兴起) (*Rise of Modern Chinese Thought*) (Beijing: Sanlian, 2015), 2:834.

10. See Wang, *Xiandai Zhongguo Sixiang de Xingqi*, 2:851–81.

11. Liu, *Translingual Practice*, 26.

12. Liu, *Translingual Practice*, 26.

13. Books and articles in this area abound. Yet even if the universal cosmological thinking of New Confucian thinkers is recognized, they were more or less situated in national contexts. More specifically, on New Confucianism, see Charlotte Furth, "Culture and Politics in Modern Chinese Conservatism," in *The Limits of Change: Essays on Conservative Alternatives in Republican China*, ed. Charlotte Furth (Cambridge, MA, and London: Harvard University Press, 1976). Edmund S. K. Fung, *The Intellectual Foundations of Chinese Modernity: Cultural and Political Thought in the Republican Era* (Cambridge: Cambridge University Press, 2010). More generally on Chinese or Asian intellectual history related to this book, in addition to those referenced else-

where in the book, other notable examples are: Viren Murthy, *Pan-Asianism and the Legacy of the Chinese Revolution: An Intellectual History of Pan-Asianist Discourse in the Twentieth Century* (Chicago: University of Chicago Press, 2023); Viren Murthy, *The Politics of Time in China and Japan: Back to the Future* (London: Routledge, 2022); Cemil Aydin, *The Politics of Anti-Westernism in Asia: Visions of World Order in Pan-Islamic and Pan-Asian Thought* (New York: Columbia University Press, 2007); Graham Parkes, ed., *Heidegger and Asian Thought* (Honolulu: University of Hawai'i Press, 1987); David Chai, ed., *Daoist Resonances in Heidegger: Exploring a Forgotten Debt* (New York: Bloomsbury, 2022); Chunling Peng (彭春凌), *Ruxue Zhuanxing Yu Wenhua Xinming: Yi Kang Youwei, Zhang Taiyan Wei Zhongxin (1898–1927)* (儒学转型与文化新命。以康有为、章太炎为中心 (1898–1927) (Beijing: Peking University Press, 2014); Daniel Leonhard Purdy, *Chinese Sympathies: Media, Missionaries, and World Literature from Marco Polo to Goethe* (Ithaca, NY: Cornell University Press, 2021).

14. Haun Saussy, *Translation as Citation: Zhuangzi Inside Out* (Oxford: Oxford University Press, 2017).

15. Samuel Moyn and Andrew Sartori, "Approaches to Global Intellectual History," in *Global Intellectual History*, ed. Samuel Moyn and Andrew Sartori (New York: Columbia University Press, 2013), 6; Joseph R. Levenson, *Confucian China and Its Modern Fate: The Problem of Intellectual Continuity*, vol. 1 (Berkeley and Los Angeles: University of California Press, 1958); Joseph R. Levenson, *Confucian China and Its Modern Fate: The Problem of Monarchical Decay*, vol. 2 (Berkeley and Los Angeles: University of California Press, 1964); Joseph R. Levenson, *Confucian China and Its Modern Fate: The Problem of Historical Significance*, vol. 3 (Berkeley and Los Angeles: University of California Press, 1965).

16. Joseph R. Levenson, *Revolution and Cosmopolitanism: The Western Stage and the Chinese Stages* (Berkeley and Los Angeles: University of California Press, 1971), 5.

17. Levenson, *Revolution and Cosmopolitanism*, 157.

18. Moyn and Sartori, "Approaches to Global Intellectual History," 190.

19. Moyn and Sartori, "Approaches to Global Intellectual History," 198.

20. Moyn and Sartori, "Approaches to Global Intellectual History," 199.

21. Moyn and Sartori, "Approaches to Global Intellectual History," 5.

22. Bruno Latour, *An Inquiry into Modes of Existence: An Anthropology of the Moderns* (Cambridge, MA, and London: Harvard University Press, 2013), 41.

23. Latour, *Inquiry into Modes of Existence*, 41–42.

24. Latour, *Inquiry into Modes of Existence*, 42.

25. See Sebastian Conrad, *What Is Global History?* (Princeton and Oxford: Princeton University Press, 2016), 65.

26. Moyn and Sartori, "Approaches to Global Intellectual History," 6.

27. Scholarly efforts have been made to place non-European perspective on historiography at the center stage. See, for example, Prasenjit Duara, Viren Murthy,

and Andrew Sartori, eds., *A Companion to Global Historical Thought* (Malden, MA: Wiley, 2014).

28. See Dipesh Chakrabarty, *Provincializing Europe: Postcolonial Thought and Historical Difference* (Princeton: Princeton University Press, 2000), 6.

29. Moyn and Sartori, "Approaches to Global Intellectual History," 19.

30. Moyn and Sartori, "Approaches to Global Intellectual History," 24.

31. Andrew Sartori, *Bengal in Global Concept History: Culturalism in the Age of Capital* (Chicago and London: University of Chicago Press, 2008).

32. Sartori, *Bengal in Global Concept History*, 48.

33. Sartori, *Bengal in Global Concept History*, 48.

34. Sartori, *Bengal in Global Concept History*, 60.

35. Sartori, *Bengal in Global Concept History*, 17.

36. Aamir R. Mufti, *Forget English! Orientalisms and World Literatures* (Cambridge, MA: Harvard University Press, 2016), 10.

37. Latour, *Inquiry into Modes of Existence*, 13.

38. Latour, *Inquiry into Modes of Existence*, 13.

39. Latour, *Inquiry into Modes of Existence*, 11.

40. Latour, *Inquiry into Modes of Existence*, 23.

41. Latour, *Inquiry into Modes of Existence*, 23.

42. Latour, *Inquiry into Modes of Existence*, 410.

43. Latour, *Inquiry into Modes of Existence*, 410.

44. Latour, *Inquiry into Modes of Existence*, 410–11.

45. Latour, *Inquiry into Modes of Existence*, 425. Emphases in original text.

46. Latour, *Inquiry into Modes of Existence*, 433. Emphasis in original text.

47. Latour, *Inquiry into Modes of Existence*, 435.

48. Latour, *Inquiry into Modes of Existence*, 10.

49. See David Harvey, *Cosmopolitanism and the Geographies of Freedom* (New York: Columbia University Press, 2009), 83.

50. See Seyla Benhabib, *Another Cosmopolitanism* (Oxford: Oxford University Press, 2006).

51. Following Kant's optimism about the market economy, the philosopher and jurist Jeremy Waldron advocates for a globalization marked by the spread of Coca Cola and the commercialization of ethnic food, costumes, and accessories. See Jeremy Waldron, "What Is Cosmopolitanism?," *Journal of Political Philosophy* 8, no. 2 (1999): 227–43; Jeremy Waldron, "Minority Cultures and the Cosmopolitan Alternative," in *University of Michigan Journal of Law Reform* 25 (1992): 751–92. Martha Nussbaum's concept of a cosmopolitan education illuminates us with her vision of a morality without teleology. Following Kant, Nussbaum argues that innate reason and divinity lead to mutual respect and a greater global justice. See Nussbaum, *Not for Profit: Why Democracy Needs the Humanities* (Princeton: Princeton University Press, 2010). Kwame Anthony Appiah points out the permanence of differences, the unavoidability

of relativism, and truth's partiality. Tolerance and conversation are always indispensable for mutual understanding. See Appiah, *Cosmopolitanism: Ethics in a World of Strangers* (New York and London: Norton, 2006).

52. Bruce Robbins, "Cosmopolitanism: New and Newer," in *boundary 2* 34, no. 3 (2007): 47–60; Bruce Robbins, *Perpetual War: Cosmopolitanism from the Viewpoint of Violence* (Durham, NC, and London: Duke University Press, 2012).

53. Pheng Cheah and Bruce Robbins, eds., *Cosmopolitics: Thinking and Feeling beyond the Nation* (Minneapolitis and London: University of Minnesota Press, 1998); Samuel P. Huntington, "The Clash of Civilizations?," *Foreign Affairs* 72, no. 3 (1993): 22–49.

54. Sebastian Conrad and Dominic Sachsenmaier, eds., *Competing Visions of World Order: Global Moments and Movements, 1880s–1930s* (New York and London: Palgrave Macmillan, 2007), 1–25.

55. Mizoguchi Yūzō, "China as Method," *Inter-Asia Cultural Studies* 17, no. 4 (2007): 516.

56. Mizoguchi, "China as Method," 513.

57. Mizoguchi, "China as Method," 516.

58. Mizoguchi, "China as Method," 516.

59. Mizoguchi, "China as Method," 517.

60. Mizoguchi, "China as Method," 518.

61. Kuan-Hsing Chen, *Asia as Method: Toward Deimperialization* (Durham, NC, and London: Duke University Press, 2010), 212.

62. Ban Wang, ed., *Chinese Visions of World Order: Tianxia, Culture, and World Politics* (Durham, NC, and London: Duke University Press, 2017), 4.

63. See Ban Wang, *China in the World: Culture, Politics, and World Vision* (Durham, NC and London: Duke University Press, 2022), 18.

64. Wang, *Xiandai Zhongguo Sixiang de Xingqi*, 4:1394.

65. Wang, *Xiandai Zhongguo Sixiang de Xingqi*, 4:1314.

66. Wang, *Xiandai Zhongguo Sixiang de Xingqi*, 4:1327.

67. Wang, *Xiandai Zhongguo Sixiang de Xingqi*, 4:1395.

68. See chapters 12, 13, and 14 in Wang, *Xiandai Zhongguo Sixiang de Xingqi*.

1. ENCOUNTER IN BEIJING: HERMANN GRAF KEYSERLING, GU HONGMING, AND CONFUCIAN COSMOPOLITANISM

1. Edward W. Said, *Orientalism* (New York: Vintage, 1979), 21.

2. See, for example, Garrett Wallace Brown and David Held, eds., *The Cosmopolitanism Reader* (Cambridge: Polity, 2010).

3. See Armin Mohler, *Die Konservative Revolution in Deutschland 1918–1932: Ein Handbuch* (Darmstadt: Wissenschaftliche Buchgesellschaft, 1972). See also the sixth edition of Mohler's book, continued by Karlheinz Weissmann: Armin Mohler and Karlheinz Weissmann, *Die Konservative Revolution in Deutschland 1918–1932: Ein*

Handbuch, 6th ed. (Graz: Ares Verlag, 2005), and Sebastian Kaufmann and Andreas Urs Sommer, eds., *Nietzsche und die Konservative Revolution* (Berlin and Boston: Walter de Gruyter, 2018).

4. See Jeffrey Herf, *Reactionary Modernism: Technology, Culture, and Politics in Weimar and the Third Reich* (Cambridge: Cambridge University Press, 1984).

5. Klaus Dethloff, "Hugo von Hofmannstahl und eine konservative Revolution," *Deutsche Vierteljahrsschrift für Literaturwissenschaft und Geistesgeschichte* 92 (2018): especially see 543–45.

6. Benjamin I. Schwartz, "Notes on Conservatism in General and in China in Particular," in *The Limits of Change: Essays on Conservative Alternatives in Republican China*, ed. Charlotte Furth (Cambridge, MA, and London: Harvard University Press, 1976), 18.

7. Ute Gahlings, *Hermann Graf Keyserling: Ein Lebensbild* (Darmstadt: Justus von Liebig Verlag, 1996), 115.

8. Hermann Graf Keyserling, *Das Reisetagebuch eines Philosophen* (Frankfurt am Main: Ullstein Verlag, 1990), 7.

9. As discussed in the Introduction, Wilhelm's translations and commentaries on Chinese classical philosophies have been widely read and have remained influential from the early twentieth century until today. Wilhelm also translated Gu Hongming's *The Story of a Chinese Oxford Movement* from English into German as Hung-ming Ku, *Chinas Verteidigung gegen europäische Ideen*, ed. Alfons Paquet (Jena: Eugen Diederich, 1917).

10. See Keyserling, *Das Reisetagebuch eines Philosophen*, 407.

11. Keyserling, *Das Reisetagebuch eines Philosophen*, 433; Hermann Keyserling, *The Travel Diary of a Philosopher*, trans. J. Holroyd Reece (New York: Harcourt, Brace, 1925), 2:75.

12. Keyserling, *Das Reisetagebuch eines Philosophen*, 434; Keyserling, *Travel Diary of a Philosopher*, 2, 76–77.

13. Keyserling, *Das Reisetagebuch eines Philosophen*, 408, my emphasis; Keyserling, *Travel Diary of a Philosopher*, 2, 51–52.

14. Keyserling, *Das Reisetagebuch eines Philosophen*, 408; Keyserling, *Travel Diary of a Philosopher*, 2, 52.

15. Keyserling, *Das Reisetagebuch eines Philosophen*, 430; Keyserling, *Travel Diary of a Philosopher*, 2, 73.

16. Keyserling, *Das Reisetagebuch eines Philosophen*, 431; Keyserling, *Travel Diary of a Philosopher*, 2, 74.

17. Keyserling, *Das Reisetagebuch eines Philosophen*, 432; Keyserling, *Travel Diary of a Philosopher*, 2, 75.

18. Keyserling, *Das Reisetagebuch eines Philosophen*, 445–46; Keyserling, *Travel Diary of a Philosopher*, 2, 87.

19. Gottfried Wilhelm Leibniz, *Writings on China*, trans. Jr. Daniel J. Cook and Henry Rosemont (Chicago and La Salle, IL: Open Court, 1994), 46.

20. Leibniz, *Writings on China*, 61.

21. Keyserling hoped to use his connections to the British foreign minister, Arthur James Balfour, whom he met before the war; Lord Charles Hardinge, who was the vice king of India from 1910 to 1916 and hosted Keyserling during his visit in India; and Lord Philip Weardale, with whom he has family relations. He sent his essay to the British delegation to the Paris Peace Conference after World War I and was ready to travel to Paris and London to discuss his ideas if there were interest in them. The result, however, was disappointing. The British was not interested in supporting Keyserling's political goals. After Keyserling published the essay in *the Westminster Gazette*, he was criticized by the Estonian diplomatic envoy in London. See Gahlings, *Hermann Graf Keyserling*.

22. Keyserling, *Das Reisetagebuch eines Philosophen*, 438.

23. See Chunjie Zhang, "From Sinophilia to Sinophobia: China, History, and Recognition," *Colloquia Germanica* 41, no. 2 (2008): 97–110.

24. See Harry Liebersohn, *Aristocratic Encounters: European Travelers and North American Indians* (Cambridge: Cambridge University Press, 1998).

25. See Daniel I. O'Neill, *Edmund Burke and the Conservative Logic of Empire* (Oakland: University of California Press, 2016).

26. Chunjie Zhang, "Garden Empire or the Sublime Politics of the Chinese-Gothic Style," *Goethe Yearbook* 25 (2018): 91.

27. See Keyserling, *Das Reisetagebuch eines Philosophen*, 440.

28. Keyserling, *Das Reisetagebuch eines Philosophen*, 430; Keyserling, *Travel Diary of a Philosopher*, 2, 72.

29. See Keyserling, *Das Reisetagebuch eines Philosophen*, 420.

30. Keyserling, *Das Reisetagebuch eines Philosophen*, 490.

31. See Keyserling, *Das Reisetagebuch eines Philosophen*, 445.

32. See Keyserling, *Das Reisetagebuch eines Philosophen*, 498.

33. See Keyserling, *Das Reisetagebuch eines Philosophen*, 446–47.

34. Hermann Graf Keyserling, *Über die innere Beziehung zwischen den Kulturproblemen des Orients und des Okzidents: Eine Botschaft an die Völker des Ostens* (Jena: Verlag bei Eugen Diederich, 1913), 29.

35. Keyserling, *Über die innere Beziehung*, 30.

36. Keyserling, *Über die innere Beziehung*, 15.

37. Keyserling, *Über die innere Beziehung*, 19.

38. Keyserling, *Das Reisetagebuch eines Philosophen*, 466–67; Keyserling, *Travel Diary of a Philosopher*, 2, 106.

39. Keyserling, *Das Reisetagebuch eines Philosophen*, 467; Keyserling, *Travel Diary of a Philosopher*, 2, 106.

40. Hung-Ming Ku, "The Spirit of the Chinese People," *Peking Daily News*, 1915, 117–18.

41. Ku, "Spirit of the Chinese People," 2. "Chinaman" is the original wording in Gu's book, which he wrote in English.

42. See more details about Gu's life in Chunmei Du, *Gu Hongming's Eccentric Chinese Odyssey* (Philadelphia: University of Pennsylvania Press, 2019), 1–9.

43. Yuan-ning Wen, "Ku Hung-Ming," *T'ien Hsia Monthly* IV, no. 4 (1937): 386.

44. See Wen, "Ku Hung-Ming," 386.

45. See Wen, "Ku Hung-Ming," 387.

46. See Homi K. Bhabha, "Of Mimicry and Man: The Ambivalence of Colonial Discourse," in *The Location of Culture* (London: Routledge, 1994), 86. See also Frantz Fanon, *Black Skin, White Masks* (New York: Grove Press, 1967).

47. See Chunmei Du, "Travel Along the Mobius Strip: Somerset Maugham and Gu Hongming East of Suez," *International History Review* 36, no. 1 (2014).

48. Chunmei Du, "Gu Hongming as a Cultural Amphibian: A Confucian Universalist Critique of Modern Western Civilization," *Journal of World History* 22, no. 4 (December 2011): 719.

49. Hung-Ming Ku, *The Story of a Chinese Oxford Movement* (Shanghai: Shanghai Mercury 1910), 6.

50. For more details, see William Ayers, *Chang Chih-Tung and Educational Reform in China* (Cambridge, MA: Harvard University Press, 1971), 65–66.

51. Chih-Tung Chang, *China's Only Hope: An Appeal by Her Greatest Viceroy Chang Chih-Tung with the Sanction of the Present Emperor, Kwang Sü*, trans. Samuel I. Woodbridge (Westport, CT: Hyperion Press, 1900), 100–101.

52. Quoted in Chang, *China's Only Hope*, 15–16.

53. Ku, "Spirit of the Chinese People," ii.

54. Ku, "Spirit of the Chinese People," 4.

55. Ku, *Story of a Chinese Oxford Movement*, 3–4.

56. Ku, *Story of a Chinese Oxford Movement*, 34.

57. Ku, *Story of a Chinese Oxford Movement*, 107.

58. Ku, *Story of a Chinese Oxford Movement*, 107.

59. See Harold Z. Schiffrin, *Sun Yat-sen and the Origins of the Chinese Revolution* (Berkeley: University of California Press, 1970).

60. Lydia H. Liu, *The Clash of Empires: The Invention of China in Modern World Making* (Cambridge, MA, and London: Harvard University Press, 2004), 172–73.

61. Liu, *Clash of Empires*, 180.

62. Ku, *Story of a Chinese Oxford Movement*, 136.

63. Ku, *Story of a Chinese Oxford Movement*, 136.

64. See Derk Bodde, *Tolstoy and China* (Princeton: Princeton University Press, 1950).

65. Ku, *Story of a Chinese Oxford Movement*, 137.

66. Ku, *Story of a Chinese Oxford Movement*, 139.
67. See Du, "Travel Along the Mobius Strip," 2.

2. RE-ENCHANTING CONFUCIANISM: MAX WEBER, CARE OF THE SELF, AND CHARISMA

1. See Wolfgang J. Mommsen, *Max Weber and German Politics 1890–1920*, trans. Michael S. Steinberg (Chicago and London: University of Chicago Press, 1984).

2. Herbert Marcuse, "Industrialization and Capitalism," *New Left Review* 30, no. March/April (1965): 3–17.

3. See Andrew Zimmerman, "Decolonizing Weber," *Postcolonial Studies* 9, no. 1 (2006): 53–79; John M. Hobson, "Decolonizing Weber: The Eurocentrism of Weber's IR and Historical Sociology," in *Max Weber and International Relations*, ed. Richard Ned Lebow (Cambridge: Cambridge University Press, 2017). Zimmerman also enumerates a wide range of Weber defenders, including Talcott Parsons, Günther Roth, Benjamin Nelson, and Reinhardt Bendix, as well as Weber's Nazi critics such as Carl Schmitt and Christoph Steding.

4. See Jürgen Habermas, *Theorie des kommunikativen Handelns*, vol. 1, *Handlungsrationalität und gesellschaftliche Rationalisierung* (Frankfurt am Main: Suhrkamp, 1981), 207–24. Also see Sven Eliaeson, "Max Weber and His Critics: Critical Theory's Reception of Neo-Kantian Methodology," *International Journal of Politics, Culture, and Society* 3, no. 4 (1990): 513–37. Eliaeson argues that Habermas is both a critic and a follower of Weber.

5. See Talcott Parsons, *The Structure of Social Action: A Study in Social Theory with Special Reference to a Group of Recent European Writers* (New York: Free Press, 1949), 539–52; Wolfgang Schluchter, *Religion und Lebensführung: Studien zu Max Webers Religions- und Herrschaftssoziologie*, vol. 2 (Frankfurt am Main: Suhrkamp, 1988); Su-Jen Huang, "Max Weber's *The Religion of China*: An Interpretation," *Journal of the History of the Behavioral Sciences* 30, no. January (1994): 3–18; Hui Wang, "Weber and the Question of Chinese Modernity," in *The Politics of Imagining Asia* (Cambridge, MA: Harvard University Press, 2011), 264–306.

6. See Otto B. van der Sprenkel, "Max Weber on China," *History and Theory* 3, no. 3 (1964): 348–70; Wolfgang Schluchter, ed., *Max Webers Studie über Konfuzianismus und Taoismus: Interpretation und Kritik* (Frankfurt am Main: Suhrkamp, 1983); Wolfgang Schluchter, *Rationalism, Religion, and Domination: A Weberian Perspective*, trans. Neil Solomon (Berkeley and Los Angeles: University of California Press, 1989); Andreas E. Buss, ed., *Max Weber in Asian Studies* (Leiden: Brill, 1985); Andreas Buss, "Introductory Comments on Max Weber's Essays on India and China," *International Sociology* 2, no. 3 (1987): 271–76; Timothy Brook, "Weber's Religion of China," in *Max Weber's Economic Ethic of the World Religions: An Analysis*, ed. Thomas Ertman (Cambridge: Cambridge University Press, 2017); R. Bin Wong, "The Chinese State, Social Order and Economic Change," in *Max Weber's Economic Ethic of the World*

Religions: An Analysis, ed. Thomas Ertman (Cambridge: Cambridge University Press, 2017); Dingxin Zhao, "Max Weber and Patterns of Chinese History," in Ertman, *Max Weber's Economic Ethic of the World Religions*.

7. See Ying-shih Yu (余英时), "Zhongguo jinshi zongjiao lunli yu shangren jingshen (中国近世宗教伦理与商人精神)," in *Rujia lunli yu shangren jingshen (儒家伦理与商人精神)* (Guilin, China: Guangxi Shifan Daxue Chubanshe, 2004).

8. The bibliographic details of Weber's journal publications of world religions are as following: "Die Wirtschaftsethik der Weltreligionen: Religionssoziologische Skizzen; Einleitung. Der Konfuzianismus I. II.," *Archiv für Sozialwissenschaft und Sozialpolitik* 41 (1915): 1–87; "Der Konfuzianismus III. IV: Zwischenbetrachtung," ibid. 41 (1915): 335–421; "Die Wirtschaftsethik der Weltreligionen: Hinduismus und Buddhismus," ibid. 41 (1915): 613–744; "Hinduismus und Buddhismus. (Fortsetzung)," ibid. 42 (1916/1917): 345–461; "Hinduismus und Buddhismus (Schluß)," ibid. 42 (1916/1917): 687–814; "Die Wirtschaftsethik der Weltreligionen: Das antike Judentum," ibid. 44 (1917/1918): 52–160, 349–443, 601–26; "Das antike Judentum," ibid. 46 (1918/1919): 40–113, 311–67, 541–605. When the first treatise *Konfuzianismus* was published as a book, Weber changed the title to *Konfuzianismus und Taoismus*.

9. See Hans-Peter Müller and Steffen Sigmund, eds., *Max Weber-Handbuch: Leben-Werk-Wirkung* (Stuttgart: J. B. Metzler Verlag, 2020), 371–72.

10. See Wolfgang Schluchter, ed., *Max Weber: Wirtschaft und Gesellschaft: Entstehungsgeschichte und Dokumente*, I/25, Max Weber Gesamtausgabe (Tübingen: J. C. B. Mohr (Paul Siebeck), 2009), 1:93–105.

11. See Schluchter, *Max Weber*, 1:109–11.

12. See Max Weber, *The Religion of China: Confucianism and Taoism*, ed. and trans. Hans H. Gerth (New York: Free Press, 1951). Weber's study on Hinduism and Buddhism appeared in English as Max Weber, *The Religion of India: The Sociology of Hinduism and Buddhism*, ed. and trans. Hans Gerth and Don Martindale (Glencoe, IL: Free Press, 1958).

13. The "Introduction" and the "Intermediate Reflection" were translated and published as "The Social Psychology of the World Religions" and "Religious Rejections of the World and Their Directions" in H. H. Gerth and C. Wright Mills, eds., *From Max Weber: Essays in Sociology* (New York: Oxford University Press, 1946). 267–301, 323–62.

14. Max Weber's "Vorbemerkung," in *Gesammelte Aufsätze zur Religionssoziologie* (Tübingen: Verlag von J. C. B. Mohr, 1920), was first translated as Weber, "Author's Introduction," in *The Protestant Ethic and the Spirit of Capitalism*, trans. Talcott Parsons (New York, 1930), 13–31. More recently, it has been translated as "Prefatory Remarks to *Collected Essays in the Sociology of Religion* (1920)," in Max Weber, *The Protestant Ethic and the "Spirit" of Capitalism and Other Writings*, trans. Peter Baehr and Gordon C. Wells (New York and London: Penguin, 2002), 356–72; and in Max Weber, *The Protestant Ethic and the Spirit of Capitalism*, trans. Stephen Kalberg (New

York and Oxford: Oxford University Press, 2011), 233–50. While Talcott Parsons's 1930 translation is based on the 1920 version of Weber's text, Peter Baehr and Gordon Wells decided to base their translation on the 1905 version. They argue that the 1905 version is conceptually and stylistically different from the 1920 version and contains a different research program. The 1905 version is also the foundation for the critical responses that Weber published from 1905 to 1920, which Baehr and Wells also include in their careful translation. See Baehr and Wells's "Introduction," in Weber, *Protestant Ethic and the "Spirit" of Capitalism and Other Writings*, xxxiii–xlii. Stephen Kalberg's translation is also based on the 1920 version. But he points out inadequacies in Parsons's translation to justify his new translation. Because Kalberg aims to reach a broader readership, the language in his translation is less academic than that of Baehr and Wells. While Kalberg's translation also contains materials related to the main text, they are, however, taken from other English translations. Weber's "Vorbemerkung" is translated from a German text published in 1972: see Kalberg's "Introduction to the Translation" and "Introduction to *The Protestant Ethic*," in Weber, *Protestant Ethic and the Spirit of Capitalism*, 3–7, 8–66. Kalberg also groups "Vorbemerkung" with two other short writings about Protestantism and capitalism in one section of his translation and gives it the title "The Protestant Sects in America and the Uniqueness of Western Rationalism," which was not Weber's intention. In so doing, Kalberg somehow reenacts the interventions of Marianne Weber and Melchior Palyi; see Weber, *Protestant Ethic and the Spirit of Capitalism*, 183; Stephen Kalberg, "The *Spirit of Capitalism* Revisited: On the New Translation of Weber's *Protestant Ethic* (1920): 41–58," *Max Weber Studies* 2, no. 1 (2001). Since I consider the 1920 version of *The Protestant Ethic* more relevant to Weber's treatise on Confucianism, I use Kalberg's translation here. However, I use Baehr and Wells's translation of the "Vorbemerkung" elsewhere in the article.

15. Weber, *Protestant Ethic and the "Spirit" of Capitalism and Other Writings*, 366. Strictly speaking, these two essays were both revised and published in 1920. Originally, they were published in 1905 and 1906, respectively. The latter bore a different title: *"Kirchen" und "Sekten" in Nordamerika*.

16. See S. N. Eisenstadt, "This Worldly Transcendentalism and the Structuring of the World: Weber's 'Religion of China' and the Format of Chinese History and Civilization," in *Max Weber in Asian Studies*, ed. Andreas Buss (Leiden: Brill, 1985); Brook, "Weber's Religion of China"; Zhao, "Max Weber and Patterns of Chinese History"; Wong, "Chinese State, Social Order and Economic Change." Among these scholars, Dingxin Zhao differs from others in that he is concerned to defend some of Weber's specific arguments, such as the development of the Chinese city as a political center instead of an economic community and the view of Confucianism as an ethical system. Zhao is also very invested in the question of why capitalism did not arise in China but in Europe. Yet Zhao still assumes that Weber has argued about the uniqueness of the emergence of capitalism in Europe and the US and thus its superiority. Zhao does

not critique Weber's alleged Eurocentrism and argues that Weber is right about China's inability to develop capitalism.

17. Schluchter, *Rationalism, Religion, and Domination*, 115–16.

18. Weber, *Protestant Ethic and the "Spirit" of Capitalism and Other Writings*, 367; Weber, "Vorbemerkung," 13: "Der Sinologe, Indologe, Semitist, Aegyptologe wird in ihnen natürlich nichts ihm sachlich Neues finden. Wünschenswert wäre nur: daß er nichts zur Sache Wesentliches findet, was er als sachlich falsch beurteilen muß."

19. See Weber, "Vorbemerkung," 14.

20. Weber, "Vorbemerkung," 15–16.

21. Adopting "the way of life" as a translation for *Lebensführung* brings us closer to the Chinese context because "way" is often used to translate the Chinese word *dao* (道), and the German word *führen* is etymologically related to the meanings of "drive" and "path."

22. See Weber, "Vorbemerkung," 4.

23. See Weber, "Vorbemerkung," 6–7: "die rational-kapitalistische Organisation von (formell) freier Arbeit."

24. See Weber, "Vorbemerkung," 10: "die Entstehung des bürgerlichen Betriebskapitalismus mit seiner rationalen Organisation der freien Arbeit."

25. See Weber, "Vorbemerkung," 11–12.

26. The social status of merchants in early modern Japan was similar to that in China. They were placed as the lowest of the four major social groups, which included aristocrats, farmers, and craftsmen in a descending order. In China, the order was scholars, farmers, craftsmen, and merchants.

27. Tetsuo Najita, *Visions of Virtue in Tokugawa Japan: The Kaitokudō Merchant Academy of Osaka* (Chicago: University of Chicago Press, 1987), 11.

28. See Najita, *Visions of Virtue*, 16.

29. See Max Weber, *Die protestantische Ethik und der Geist des Kapitalismus*, ed. Dirk Kaesler (Munich: C. H. Beck, 2004), 70.

30. See Weber, *Die protestantische Ethik*, 74.

31. Weber, *Protestant Ethic and the Spirit of Capitalism*, 80; Weber, *Die protestantische Ethik*, 78.

32. Weber, *Protestant Ethic and the Spirit of Capitalism*, 97; Weber, *Die protestantische Ethik*, 95.

33. Schluchter also points out that Weber uses a duality of temporality in his works, applying both a comparative and a developmental history perspective. Wolfgang Schluchter, "Max Weber's Sociology of Religion: A Project in Comparison and Developmental History," trans. Jeremiah Riemer, in Ertman, *Max Weber's Economic Ethic of the World Religions*; Schluchter, *Religion und Lebensführung*, 2:93–102.

34. Weber, *Die protestantische Ethik*, 95.

35. Schluchter, *Religion und Lebensführung*, 2:27–37.

36. See Weber, *Die protestantische Ethik*, 79.

37. See Weber, *Die protestantische Ethik*, 275.

38. Schluchter, *Religion und Lebensführung*, 2:70–71; also see Weber, *Die protestantische Ethik*, 79.

39. Guoxun Su (苏国勋), *Lixinghua Jiqi Xianzhi: Weibo Sixiang Yinlun (Rationalization and Its Limits: An Introduction to Weber's Thinking* (理性化及其限制：韦伯思想引论) (Shanghai: Shanghai Renmin Chubanshe, 1988).

40. See Guoxun Su (苏国勋), "Makesi weibo: Jiyu zhongguo yujing de zai yangjiu (马克斯·韦伯：基于中国语境的再研究) (Max Weber: New Studies on the Basis of the Chinese Context)," *Society* (社会) 5, no. 27 (2007). See also Po-Fang Tsai, "The Introduction and Reception of Max Weber's Sociology in Taiwan and China," *Journal of Sociology* 52, no. 1 (2016).

41. Wei-ming Tu, ed., *The Triad Chord: Confucian Ethics, Industrial East Asia and Max Weber* (Singapore: Institute of East Asian Philosophies, 1991).

42. See Tze-ki Hon and Kristin Stapleton, eds., *Confucianism for the Contemporary World: Global Order, Political Plurality, and Social Action* (Albany: State University of New York Press, 2018), xiv–xvi.

43. Weber, *Die protestantische Ethik*, 96.

44. Weber, *Protestant Ethic and the Spirit of Capitalism*, 104; Weber, *Die protestantische Ethik*, 101.

45. Weber, *Die protestantische Ethik*, 106.

46. Weber, *Die protestantische Ethik*, 181.

47. See Weber, *Die protestantische Ethik*, 154.

48. See Weber, *Die protestantische Ethik*, 184.

49. See Weber, *Die protestantische Ethik*, 194.

50. See Weber, *Die protestantische Ethik*, 105.

51. See Weber, *Die protestantische Ethik*, 145.

52. Weber, *Die protestantische Ethik*, 79.

53. Karl Marx, *Capital: A Critique of Political Economy* (London: Penguin, 1976), 1:171–72. In *Capital*, Karl Marx interprets Crusoe as a human being in the ideal mode of production, which is based on needs, not on profit.

54. Weber, *Die protestantische Ethik*, 150.

55. Weber, *Die protestantische Ethik*, 201. The English expression "iron cage" is introduced by Talcott Parsons in his 1930 translation of Weber's work. The direct meaning of *stahlhartes Gehäuse* is "steel-hard casing."

56. Weber, *Protestant Ethic and the Spirit of Capitalism*, 178; Weber, *Die protestantische Ethik*, 201.

57. See Weber, *Die protestantische Ethik*, 200.

58. See Max Weber, *Wissenschaft als Beruf/Politik als Beruf*, ed. M. Rainer Lepsius Horst Baier et al., Max Weber Gesamtausgabe (Tübingen: J. C. B. Mohr (Paul Siebeck), 1992).

59. See Qichao Liang (梁启超), *Ou You Xin Ying Lu* (欧游心影录) (Beijing: Shang Wu Yin Shu Guan, 2014), 22 and 31.

60. As Buss points out, "In spite of the shortcomings of Weber's analysis of China,

the Weberian perspective, in particular the institutional approach he used in the analysis of Western rationalism, and his typological and comparative method, still offer the best starting point for an analysis of modern Asia." Buss, "Introductory Comments," 275.

61. See Max Weber, *Die Wirtschaftsethik der Weltreligionen: Konfuzianismus und Taoismus*, Studienausgabe der Max Weber-Gesamtausgabe (Tübingen: J. C. B. Mohr [Paul Siebeck], 1991), 112.

62. See Weber, *Die Wirtschaftsethik der Weltreligionen: Konfuzianismus und Taoismus*, 113.

63. See Weber, *Die Wirtschaftsethik der Weltreligionen: Konfuzianismus und Taoismus*, 116.

64. See Weber, *Die Wirtschaftsethik der Weltreligionen: Konfuzianismus und Taoismus*, 125.

65. See Weber, *Die Wirtschaftsethik der Weltreligionen: Konfuzianismus und Taoismus*, 130.

66. See Weber, *Die Wirtschaftsethik der Weltreligionen: Konfuzianismus und Taoismus*, 128.

67. See Weber's comments on the popularity of the Confucian *laissez-faire* theory and practice in Weber, *Die Wirtschaftsethik der Weltreligionen: Konfuzianismus und Taoismus*, 91, 161, 183, 200. Weber was not explicit about his sources for *laissez-faire*. He mentioned Albrecht Tschepe's *Histoire du Royaume de Tsin (1106–452)*, published by the *Mission catholique* in 1910, in the context of the *laissez-faire* discussion, but he was reticent about a direct reference. Weber's point about Confucian economic policy is reminiscent of the French physiocrat François Quesnay's influential Sinophile treatise on Chinese economics *Despotism in China* (*Le despotisme de la Chine*, 1767), in which Quesnay maintains that the Chinese mandarins keep their philosophical composure while overseeing busy agriculture and trade. This is the evidence for government by Natural Law, to which the emperor, mandarins, and all society are subject. Quesnay considers such an enlightened despotism essential in a civilized society underpinned by legislation. Weber's extensive bibliography does not include Quesnay's work. Nor does the bibliography contain Adam Smith's *The Wealth of Nations* (1776) as a popular reference to laissez-faire. In addition to understanding laissez-faire as an economic theory, Weber mentions that laissez-faire is the translation of the Taoist concept *wu wei* (无为). Weber does not show his reference in this case, either. He refers to the Dutch sinologist and Berlin professor Jan Jakob Maria de Groot's *Religion in China* (1912) a bit earlier in the text, but de Groot translates *wu wei* as inactivity, nothingness, emptiness, not as laissez-faire. The questions as to whether Adam Smith took the term of laissez-faire from Quesnay's treatise and whether this term is a translation from Chinese deserve further exploration. Smith may have read Quesnay's book; yet Smith's promotion of foreign trade differs from Quesnay's praise of China as an agriculture-based inland economy. See Lewis A. Maverick, *China: A Model for Eu-*

rope (San Antonio, TX: Paul Anderson, 1946), 131. See a careful comparison between Quesnay's and Smith's work: Gabriel Sabbagh, "Quesnay's Thought and Influence through Two Related Texts, *Droit naturel* and *Despotisme de la Chine*, and Their Editions," *History of European Ideas* 46, no. 2 (2020): 131–56; J. J. M de Groot, *Religion in China. Universism: A Key to the Study of Taoism and Confucianism* (New York and London: G. P. Putnam's Sons, 1912). Weber wrote, "Aber auf die Dauer blieben die Literaten immer wieder siegreich": Weber, *Die Wirtschaftsethik der Weltreligionen: Konfuzianismus und Taoismus*, 133.

68. See Weber, *Die Wirtschaftsethik der Weltreligionen: Konfuzianismus und Taoismus*, 143.

69. See Weber, *Die Wirtschaftsethik der Weltreligionen: Konfuzianismus und Taoismus*, 154.

70. See Weber, *Die Wirtschaftsethik der Weltreligionen: Konfuzianismus und Taoismus*, 134, 45. 134, 145: Die Magie ist machtlos gegen die Tugend.

71. See Weber, *Die Wirtschaftsethik der Weltreligionen: Konfuzianismus und Taoismus*, 151.

72. See Weber, *Die Wirtschaftsethik der Weltreligionen: Konfuzianismus und Taoismus*, 152.

73. See Weber, *Die Wirtschaftsethik der Weltreligionen: Konfuzianismus und Taoismus*, 155.

74. See Weber, *Die Wirtschaftsethik der Weltreligionen: Konfuzianismus und Taoismus*, 171.

75. See Weber, *Die Wirtschaftsethik der Weltreligionen: Konfuzianismus und Taoismus*, 155.

76. Weber, *Die Wirtschaftsethik der Weltreligionen: Konfuzianismus und Taoismus*, 161.

77. See Weber, *Die Wirtschaftsethik der Weltreligionen: Konfuzianismus und Taoismus*, 171.

78. See Weber, *Die Wirtschaftsethik der Weltreligionen: Konfuzianismus und Taoismus*, 173.

79. See Weber, *Die Wirtschaftsethik der Weltreligionen: Konfuzianismus und Taoismus*, 177.

80. The metaphor *Zaubergarten* appears in the German writer Hermann Hesse's novella *Klingsors letzter Sommer*. Weber visited the life reform colony in Monte Verità, Switzerland, in 1913 and 1914 and then intensively dealt with Eastern religions. *Confucianism and Taoism* was first published in 1915. Hesse was a long-term resident at Monte Verità, and his works have extensively discussed Taoism and Buddhism. Weber might be influenced by Hesse's metaphor. Thomas Mann's Zauberberg could also be a possible reference, even though magic is not positively connotated in Mann's work, as it is in Weber and Hesse's works. It is also possible that Weber took the idea of Taoism as a magic garden from the Dutch Sinologist Jan Jakob Maria de Groot. Weber referred

to de Groot's work and his idea of universism of Chinese religion in his book several times.

81. See Weber, *Die Wirtschaftsethik der Weltreligionen: Konfuzianismus und Taoismus*, 193.

82. See Weber, *Die Wirtschaftsethik der Weltreligionen: Konfuzianismus und Taoismus*, 193.

83. See Weber, *Die Wirtschaftsethik der Weltreligionen: Konfuzianismus und Taoismus*, 194.

84. See Weber, *Die Wirtschaftsethik der Weltreligionen: Konfuzianismus und Taoismus*, 207.

85. See Weber, *Die Wirtschaftsethik der Weltreligionen: Konfuzianismus und Taoismus*, 207.

86. See Weber, *Die Wirtschaftsethik der Weltreligionen: Konfuzianismus und Taoismus*, 208.

87. Weber's thesis reminds us of the discussion of the great divergence in recent years. Prominent economic historians such as Roy Bin Wong and Kenneth Pomeranz have endeavored to revisit the rise of the West and make sense of the striking similarities between East Asia and Europe between 1400 and 1800. Pomeranz's well-recognized thesis is that the great divergence between East Asia and the West was conditioned on Europe's colonial possessions all over the world. Not industrialization but the colonial exploitation of resources made the great divergence possible; see Kenneth Pomeranz, *The Great Divergence: China, Europe, and the Making of the Modern World Economy* (Princeton and Oxford: Princeton University Press, 2000). The intellectual historian Jonathan Israel argues that a small group of radical Enlightenment *philosophes*, following Baruch Spinoza's anticlerical atheism, spread the ideas of rationality, democracy, and freedom to enable modernity's arrival in Europe and then all over the world; see Jonathan I. Israel, *Radical Enlightenment: Philosophy and the Making of Modernity 1650–1750* (New York: Oxford University Press, 2001). While Pomeranz pays attention to structural problems and objective resource conditions around 1800, Israel is more interested in the intellectual uniqueness of Europe in the eighteenth century. Weber, however, disputes such structural differences and almost purely emphasizes the difference in spirituality and way of life as the watershed between the Occident and China.

88. See John O'Neill, "The Disciplinary Society: From Weber to Foucault," *British Journal of Sociology* 37, no. 1 (March 1986); Petra Neuenhaus, *Max Weber und Michel Foucault: Über Macht und Herrschaft in der Moderne* (Pfaffenweiler: Centaurus-Verlagsgesellschaft, 1993); Carsten Kaven, *Sozialer Wandel und Macht: Die theoretische Ansätze von Max Weber, Norbert Elias und Michel Foucault im Vergleich* (Marburg: Metropolis-Verlag, 2006); David Owen, *Maturity and Modernity: Nietzsche, Weber, Foucault and the Ambivalence of Reason* (London: Routledge, 1994); Colin Gordon, "Plato in Weimar: Weber Revisited via Foucault; Two Lectures on Legitima-

tion and Vocation," *Economy and Society* 43, no. 3 (August 2014): 494–522; Thomas Lemke, "Max Weber, Norbert Elias und Michel Foucault über Macht und Subjektivierung," *Berliner Journal der Soziologie*, no. 1 (2001): 86.

89. Arpád Szakolczai, *Max Weber and Michel Foucault: Parallel Life-Works* (London: Routledge, 1998).

90. Michel Foucault, "The Ethics of the Concern for Self as a Practice of Freedom," in *Ethics: Subjectivity and Truth*, ed. Paul Rabinow, Essential Works of Foucault 1954–1984 (London: Penguin, 1994), 301.

91. Foucault, "Ethics of the Concern for Self," 282.

92. Foucault, "Ethics of the Concern for Self," 282.

93. Foucault, "Ethics of the Concern for Self," 284.

94. Foucault, "Ethics of the Concern for Self," 286.

95. Foucault, "Ethics of the Concern for Self," 298.

96. Foucault, "Ethics of the Concern for Self," 299.

97. Foucault, "Ethics of the Concern for Self," 300.

98. Foucault, "Ethics of the Concern for Self," 300.

99. Michel Foucault, "Technologies of the Self," in Rabinow, *Ethics*, 224.

100. Foucault, "Technologies of the Self," 226.

101. See Richard Utz, "Charisma," in Müller and Sigmund, *Max Weber-Handbuch*, 54–58.

102. See Joshua Derman, *Max Weber in Politics and Social Thought: From Charisma to Canonization* (Cambridge: Cambridge University Press, 2012), 198–207.

103. See Derman, *Max Weber in Politics and Social Thought*, 202.

104. See Derman, *Max Weber in Politics and Social Thought*, 207–12. See also Utz, "Charisma," 57–58.

105. Derman, *Max Weber in Politics and Social Thought*.

106. Derman, *Max Weber in Politics and Social Thought*, 212.

107. "What Ever Happened to Charisma?," *Time*, October 17, 1969, 40.

108. Ian Kershaw, *Hitler: Profiles in Power* (London and New York: Routledge, 2013), 10.

109. While the English translation of the title *The Profession and Vocation of Politics* reflects the double meaning of the German word *Beruf* with greater precision, as Weber intended it to be, for the sake of concision, I have chosen to use the more common translation *Politics as a Vocation*, which reflects Weber's emphasis on the vocational side of doing politics. See Max Weber, "The Profession and Vocation of Politics," in *Weber: Political Writings*, ed. Peter Lassman and Ronald Speirs (Cambridge: Cambridge University Press, 1994).

110. For example, Friedrich H. Tenbruck maintained that "the theory of charisma suddenly appears without any recognizable forerunners in the 'Economic Ethics of World Religions.'" Tenbruck then cited Weber's posthumously published *Wirtschaft und Gesellschaft* as the only reference to charisma. Tenbruck, "Max Weber and Eduard

Meyer," in *Max Weber and His Contemporaries*, ed. Wolfgang J. Mommsen and Jürgen Osterhammel (London: German Historical Insitutute, 1987), 249.

In the scholarship on Weber's *Confucianism and Taoism*, the discussion of charisma remains at the level of a brief acknowledgment. See Stephen Molloy, "Max Weber and the Religions of China: Any Way out of the Maze?," *British Journal of Sociology* 31, no. 3, special issue: *Aspects of Weberian Scholarship* (1980): 377–400; see chapter 6 in Helle, *China: Promise or Threat?* (Leiden: Brill, 2017); Buss, *Max Weber in Asian Studies*; Brook, "Weber's Religion of China."

111. See, for example, Schluchter, *Religion und Lebensführung*, 2:535–54; Schluchter, Rationalism, Religion, and Domination; Peter Ghosh, *Max Weber and the Protestant Ethic: Twin Histories* (Oxford: Oxford University Press, 2014), 305–17; Derman, *Max Weber in Politics and Social Thought*, 54–58; Utz, "Charisma," 54–58; John Breuilly, "Max Weber, Charisma and Nationalist Leadership," *Nations and Nationalism* 17, no. 3 (2011); Steven Klein, "Between Charisma and Domination: On Max Weber's Critique of Democracy," *Journal of Politics* 79, no. 1 (2016): 179–92; David Norman Smith, "Faith, Reason, and Charisma: Rudolf Sohm, Max Weber, and the Theology of Grace," *Sociological Inquiry* 68, no. 1 (1998): 32–60; Wolfgang J. Mommsen, "Max Weber's Political Sociology and His Philosophy of World History," *International Social Science Journal* 17, no. 1 (1965): 23–45.

Some scholars cite passages in *Konfucianismus und Taoismus* or *Politik als Beruf* in their discussion of charisma; yet they are not explicit about the role of these texts and Confucianism in Weber's conceptualization of charisma. They treat these passages as abstractly as those in *Wirtschaft und Gesellschaft*. See Christopher Adair-Toteff, "Max Weber's Charisma," *Journal of Classical Sociology* 5, no. 2 (2005); Martin Riesebrodt, "Charisma in Max Weber's Sociology of Religion," *Religion* 29 (1999): 1–14.

112. See the chapters on India and ancient Israel in Thomas Ertman, ed., *Max Weber's Economic Ethic of the World Religions: An Analysis* (Cambridge: Cambridge University Press, 2017), 175–348.

113. Hugo Drochon, *Nietzsche's Great Politics* (Princeton and Oxford: Princeton University Press, 2016), 8.

114. See Max Weber, *Wirtschaft und Gesellschaft: Die Wirtschaft und die gesellschaftlichen Ordnungen und Mächte; Nachlaß*, Max Weber Gesamtausgabe (Tübingen: J. C. B. Mohr [Paul Siebeck], 2005), 493. Weber also refers to Eduard Meyer's work *Geschichte des Alterthums* as evidence for charismatic leadership. See also Weber, *Wirtschaft und Gesellschaft*, 500; Tenbruck, "Max Weber and Eduard Meyer"; Smith, "Faith, Reason, and Charisma."

115. Ghosh, *Max Weber and the Protestant Ethic*, 306–7.

116. Smith, "Faith, Reason, and Charisma," 52.

117. See Hans Joas, *The Creativity of Action* (Cambridge: Polity Press, 1996), 44–49. Joas interpreted charisma mainly as creativity and criticized that Weber's action theory fails to discuss creativity in everyday practice.

118. Smith, "Faith, Reason, and Charisma," 41.

119. See Robert Eden, "Weber and Nietzsche: Questioning the Liberation of Social Science from Historicism," in Mommsen and Osterhammel, *Max Weber and His Contemporaries*. Eden argues that Weber inherited from Nietzsche the philosophical critique of historicism and further broke away from Hegelian and Marxian historicism in social science and historiography. See also Mommsen, "Max Weber's Political Sociology and His Philosophy of World History."

120. Mommsen, "Max Weber's Political Sociology and His Philosophy of World History," 45.

121. See Drochon, *Nietzsche's Great Politics*, 115–28.

122. See Tamsin Shaw, *Nietzsche's Political Skepticism* (Princeton: Princeton University Press, 2007), 14.

123. Weber, *Die Wirtschaftsethik der Weltreligionen: Konfuzianismus und Taoismus*, 4. The English translations of this work are all mine.

124. See Guy Oakes, "Weber and the Southwest German School: The Genesis of the Concept of the Historical Individual," in *Max Weber and His Contemporaries*, ed. Wolfgang J. Mommsen and Jürgen Osterhammel (London: German Historical Institute, 1987).

125. See Oakes, "Weber and the Southwest German School"; Gerhard Wagner and Claudius Härpfer, "Neo-Kantianism and the Social Sciences: From Rickert to Weber," in *New Approaches to Neo-Kantianism*, ed. Nicolas de Warren and Andrea Staiti (Cambridge: Cambridge University Press, 2015).

126. Beatrice Centi, "The Validity of Norms in Neo-Kantian Ethics," in de Warren and Staiti, *New Approaches*, 127.

127. Centi, "Validity of Norms in Neo-Kantian Ethics," 135.

128. Mark R. Rutgers and Petra Schreurs, "Weber's Neo-Kantian Roots," *Administrative Theory & Praxis* 26, no. 1 (March 2004): 107.

129. Ghosh, *Max Weber and the Protestant Ethic*, 308.

130. See Weber, *Die Wirtschaftsethik der Weltreligionen: Konfuzianismus und Taoismus*, 1.

131. Weber, *Die Wirtschaftsethik der Weltreligionen: Konfuzianismus und Taoismus*, 22. Italic emphasis is in the original text.

132. See Weber, *Die Wirtschaftsethik der Weltreligionen: Konfuzianismus und Taoismus*, 22.

133. Ghosh, *Max Weber and the Protestant Ethic*, 307.

134. Weber, *Die Wirtschaftsethik der Weltreligionen: Konfuzianismus und Taoismus*, 22.

135. Weber, *Die Wirtschaftsethik der Weltreligionen: Konfuzianismus und Taoismus*, 22.

136. Weber, *Die Wirtschaftsethik der Weltreligionen: Konfuzianismus und Taoismus*, 22.

137. See Weber, *Die Wirtschaftsethik der Weltreligionen: Konfuzianismus und Taoismus*, 23.

138. Ghosh comments that "today's methodologists and sociologists, operating in a partially dehistoricized environment. . . . Their idea of a concept is a static one. But Weber was one of the most sophisticated products of the most historically conscious generation in all European history, and vitally concerned with surmounting the problems posed by historicist relativism." Ghosh, *Max Weber and the Protestant Ethic*, 311.

139. Weber, *Die Wirtschaftsethik der Weltreligionen: Konfuzianismus und Taoismus*, 48–49. *Shen* is the transliteration of the Chinese word 神, meaning spirit or divinity. But Weber is apparently using the meaning of spirit, *Geist* in the German original.

140. Weber, *Die Wirtschaftsethik der Weltreligionen: Konfuzianismus und Taoismus*, 115. Also see page 134, in which Weber claims Confucianism as pacifistic and thus standing against militarism.

141. Weber, *Die Wirtschaftsethik der Weltreligionen: Konfuzianismus und Taoismus*, 51.

142. Weber, *Die Wirtschaftsethik der Weltreligionen: Konfuzianismus und Taoismus*, 55.

143. See Weber, *Die Wirtschaftsethik der Weltreligionen: Konfuzianismus und Taoismus*, 120.

144. See Weber, *Die Wirtschaftsethik der Weltreligionen: Konfuzianismus und Taoismus*, 112.

145. Weber, *Die Wirtschaftsethik der Weltreligionen: Konfuzianismus und Taoismus*, 130.

146. Weber, *Die Wirtschaftsethik der Weltreligionen: Konfuzianismus und Taoismus*, 128–29.

147. Christopher Adair-Toteff also observes that when Weber recognized charisma's "contemporary sociological importance and its future political implications, he discussed its essence and its effects in considerable detail. Although he preferred to discuss 'ideal types,' he also was enough of an historian and realist to see the ramifications of the charismatic leader in religious circles, in social settings, as well as in political groups. Many of his ideas have received the recognition that they deserve and have become part of classical sociology." Adair-Toteff, "Max Weber's Charisma," 199.

148. Weber, "Profession and Vocation of Politics," 312; Max Weber, *Wissenschaft als Beruf 1917/1919*, 1:161.

149. Weber, "Profession and Vocation of Politics," 327–28; Weber, *Wissenschaft als Beruf 1917/1919*, 1:184–85.

150. See Weber, *Wissenschaft als Beruf 1917/1919*, 1:184–85n. Also see Amy Matthewson, "Cui Malo? Cui Bono? Reflections on a Literary Forgery: The Case of The Memoirs of Li Hung Chang," *Partial Answers: Journal of Literature and the History*

of Ideas 19, no. 1 January (2021): 19–34; William Francis Mannix, ed., *Memoirs of Li Hung Chang* (Boston and New York: Houghton Mifflin, 1913).

151. Weber, "Profession and Vocation of Politics," 328; Weber, *Wissenschaft als Beruf 1917/1919*, 1:185–86.

152. See Weber, *Wissenschaft als Beruf 1917/1919*, 1:188.

153. Weber, "Profession and Vocation of Politics," 357; Weber, *Wissenschaft als Beruf 1917/1919*, 1:233.

154. Weber, "Profession and Vocation of Politics," 352; Weber, *Wissenschaft als Beruf 1917/1919*, 1:226–27.

155. Weber, "Profession and Vocation of Politics," 353; Weber, *Wissenschaft als Beruf 1917/1919*, 1:227.

156. Weber, "Profession and Vocation of Politics," 367–68; Weber, *Wissenschaft als Beruf 1917/1919*, 1:250.

157. Weber, "Profession and Vocation of Politics," 368; Weber, *Wissenschaft als Beruf 1917/1919*, 1:251.

158. See Weber, *Wissenschaft als Beruf 1917/1919*, 1:251.

159. See Weber, *Wissenschaft als Beruf 1917/1919*, 1:252.

160. The Protestant ethics, however, demands from its believers that if they are slapped on one cheek to offer the other. Weber pungently calls it a moral teaching of disgrace (*Würdelosigkeit*). See Weber, *Wissenschaft als Beruf 1917/1919*, 1:230.

161. See Weber, "Profession and Vocation of Politics," 360–61; Weber, *Wissenschaft als Beruf 1917/1919*, 1:238–39.

162. See Weber, *Wissenschaft als Beruf 1917/1919*, 1:244.

163. See Weber, "Profession and Vocation of Politics," 366; Weber, *Wissenschaft als Beruf 1917/1919*, 1:247.

164. Fritz Ringer, *Max Weber's Methodology: The Unification of the Cultural and Social Sciences* (Cambridge, MA: Harvard University Press, 1997), 5.

3. ZHANG JUNMAI AS PHILOSOPHER: RUDOLF EUCKEN, LIFE, AND SPIRITUALITY

1. Junmai Zhang, "Wo Cong Shehuikexue Tiaodao Zhexue Zhi Jingguo (我从社会科学跳到哲学之经过)," in *Zhongguo Jindai Sixiangjia Wenku: Zhang Junmai Juan* (中国近代思想家文库: 张君劢卷), ed. Hekai Weng (翁贺凯) (Beijing: Zhongguo Renmin Daxue Chubanshe [中国人民大学出版社], 2014), 365–66. Unless otherwise noted, all translations from Chinese texts are mine.

2. Junmai Zhang, "Xueshu Fangfa Shang Zhi Guanjian (学术方法上之管见)," in *Zhang Junmai Juan* (张君劢卷), ed. Hekai Weng (翁贺凯) (Beijing: Zhongguo Renmin Daxue Chubanshe, 2014), 78.

3. See Zhang, "Wo Cong Shehuikexue Tiaodao Zhexue Zhi Jingguo," 370.

4. Zhang, "Wo Cong Shehuikexue Tiaodao Zhexue Zhi Jingguo," 370.

5. See Brian Tsui, "The Mutations of Pan-Asianism: Zhang Junmai's Cold War,"

Twentieth-Century China 42, no. 2 (May 2017): 176–97; Roger B. Jeans, *Democracy and Socialism in Republican China: The Politics of Zhang Junmai (Carsun Chang), 1906–1941* (Lanham, MD: Rowman & Littlefield, 1997); Edmund S. K. Fung, "Nationalism and Modernity: The Politics of Cultural Conservatism in Republican China," *Modern Asian Studies* 43, no. 3 (2008): 777–813; Soonyi Lee, "In Revolt Against Positivism, the Discovery of Culture: The Liang Qichao Group's Cultural Conservatism in China after the First World War," *Twentieth-Century China* 44, no. 3 (October 2019): 288–304; Eric S. Nelson, *Chinese and Buddhist Philosophy in Early Twentieth-Century German Thought* (London: Bloomsbury Academic, 2017); Zheng Dahua (郑大华), *Zhang Junmai Xueshu Sixiang Pingzhuan* (张君劢学术思想评传) (Beijing: Beijing Tushuguan Chubanshe 北京图书馆出版社, 1999).

6. Carsun Chang, *Third Force in China* (New York: Bookman, 1952), 23.

7. See Zhang, "Wo Cong Shehuikexue Tiaodao Zhexue Zhi Jingguo," 363–64.

8. Zhang, "Wo Cong Shehuikexue Tiaodao Zhexue Zhi Jingguo," 364.

9. Tsui, "Mutations of Pan-Asianism," 184.

10. See Jeans, *Democracy and Socialism in Republican China*, 31–32. Jeans focuses more on the political engagement of Zhang with Germany and only mentions very briefly Eucken and Zhang's engagement with German idealism.

11. Edmund Fung also briefly points out in his book: "The New Confucians proclaimed the universalism of Confucianism as distinct from the autocratic imperial system. They sought an intellectual marketplace for Confucianism around the world, sending the West the very message that Liang [Shuming] had sent in 1921." Fung, *The Intellectual Foundation of Chinese Modernity: Cultural and Political Thought in the Republican Era* (Cambridge: Cambridge University Press, 2010), 93.

12. Junmai Zhang, "A Manifesto for a Re-appraisal of Sinology and Reconstruction of Chinese Culture," in *The Development of Neo-Confucian Thought* (New York: Bookman, 1958), 455.

13. Zhang, "Manifesto," 457.

14. John Makeham, "The Retrospective Creation of New Confucianism," in *New Confucianism: A Critical Examination*, ed. John Makeham (New York: Palgrave Macmillan, 2003), 27–29.

15. See Lauren F. Pfister, "A Modern Chinese Philosophy Built Upon Critically Received Traditions: Feng Youlan's New Principle-Centered Learning and the Question of Its Relationship to Contemporary New Ruist ("Confucian") Philosophies," in Makeham, *New Confucianism*, 169–72; Lauren F. Pfister, "The Different Faces of Contemporary Religious Confucianism: An Account of the Diverse Approaches of some Major Twentieth-Century Chinese Confucian Scholars," *Journal of Chinese Philosophy* 22, no. 2 (1995): 12–18; Arif Dirlik, "Confucius in the Borderlands: Global Capitalism and the Reinvention of Confucianism," *boundary 2* 22, no. 3 (1995): 229–73

16. Zhang, "Manifesto," 461.

17. This perspective on Confucianism's relationship to Christianity resembles Weber's understanding of charisma's development from religion to ethics in China.

18. Zhang, "Manifesto," 461. The authors used the transliteration of "hsin-hsin" in their text.

19. Zhang, "Manifesto," 463.

20. Zhang, "Manifesto," 458.

21. Zhang, "Manifesto," 464.

22. Zhang, "Manifesto," 463.

23. Zhang, "Manifesto," 464.

24. Zhang, "Manifesto," 466.

25. Zhang, "Manifesto," 480–81.

26. Zhang, "Manifesto," 481.

27. Zhang, "Manifesto," 483.

28. See Fung, "Nationalism and Modernity."

29. Zhang, "Zhi Lin Zaipin Xuezhang Hangao Woshi Wutan Ji Deguo Zhexue Xixiang Yaolue 1920 (致林宰平学长函告倭氏晤谈及德国哲学思想要略 1920)," in *Zhang Junmai Juan* (张君劢卷), ed. Hekai Weng (翁贺凯) (Beijing: Zhongguo Renmin Daxue Chubanshe, 2014), 45.

30. Zhang, "Zhi Lin Zaipin Xuezhang Hangao Woshi Wutan Ji Deguo Zhexue Xixiang Yaolue 1920," 47.

31. See Zhang, "Zhi Lin Zaipin Xuezhang Hangao Woshi Wutan Ji Deguo Zhexue Xixiang Yaolue 1920," 46.

32. "Death of Dr. Rudolf Eucken: The Philosophy of Religion," *Times Educational Supplement* (London), September 18, 1926, 388.

33. "Death of Dr. Rudolf Eucken," 388.

34. Rudolf Eucken, *Rudolf Eucken: His Life, Work, and Travels by Himself* (London: T. Fisher Unwin, 1921), 153.

35. See Rudolf Eucken, "Rudolf Eucken on the Tasks of German Idealism," in *New York Times Current History of the European War,* 1916.

36. See Christian Stoll, "Religiöser Universalismus im Zeitalter der Nation: Friedrich von Hügel und die deutsche Geisteswelt (Eucken, Troeltsch, Naumann)," *Journal for the History of Modern Theology / Zeitschrift für Neuere Theologiegeschichte* 28, no. 2 (2021): 266. Eucken, however, noted in his autobiography that he felt isolated among academic philosophers because they did not take his work seriously. "After publishing my works I had a right to expect a little more recognition in the academic world, especially as my lectures at the university were now attended by larger numbers of students. In point of fact, the German academic world ignored my work with complete indifference, and made it quite clear that it regarded my activity as of no value to science. At that time, there were many changes in the universities, but I have never received a call to one of the great universities. It was a very long time before any invitation elsewhere reached me." Eucken, *Rudolf Eucken*, 145–46; Barbara Beßlich,

Wege in den Kulturkrieg: Zivlisationskritik in Deutschland 1890–1914 (Darmstadt: Wissenschaftliche Buchgesellschaft 2014).

37. The officer in the Japanese navy Kazunobu Kanokogi (1884–1949) received his doctorate in philosophy under the supervision of Eucken, studied with Eucken, and advocated Japanese nationalism and pan-Asianism as a philosophy professor; he was interned as a war criminal after 1945. Wasuke Komaki (1884–1932), the diplomat and navy attaché in the Japanese embassy during the 1920s, had close contact with Eucken. The Japanese prince Takamatsu-no-miya (1905–87) in 1930 visited the house of Eucken, which had become a museum after Eucken's death in 1926. Eucken was invited to lecture in Japan in 1913, but the visit was hindered because of the war. He also corresponded with the writer Shigenori Ikeda (1892–1966) and the historian of religion Ken Ishiwara (1882–1976). See *Weimar—Jena—Tokyo: Beziehungen um 1900*, at https://www.uni-jena.de/unijenamedia/universitaet/universitaetsarchiv/leporello-jena-japan-rz-final.pdf, accessed February 23, 2023.

38. Junmai Zhang, "Woyikeng Jingshen Shenghuo Zhexue Dagai (倭伊铿精神生活哲学大概)," in *Zhang Junmai Juan* (张君劢卷), ed. Hekai Weng (翁贺凯) (Beijing: Zhongguo Renmin Daxue Chubanshe, 2014), 53.

39. See Rudolf Eucken, *Lebensanschauungen der großen Denker* (Leipzig: Veit, 1890); Rudolf Eucken, *The Problem of Human Life: As Viewed by the Great Thinkers from Plato to the Present Time*, trans. Williston S. Hough and W. R. Boyce Gibson (New York: Charles Scribner's Sons, 1910).

40. Zhang, "Woyikeng Jingshen Shenghuo Zhexue Dagai," 55.

41. Eucken, *Problem of Human Life*, xvii.

42. Eucken, *Problem of Human Life*, xvii.

43. Eucken, *Problem of Human Life*, 570.

44. Eucken, *Rudolf Eucken*, 123–24.

45. "Death of Dr. Rudolf Eucken," 388.

46. See Zhang, "Zhi Lin Zaipin Xuezhang Hangao Woshi Wutan Ji Deguo Zhexue Xixiang Yaolue 1920," 46.

47. See Zhang, "Woyikeng Jingshen Shenghuo Zhexue Dagai."

48. The *Times* obituary also confirmed that Eucken's philosophy was "centred on ethics and their relation to religion." "Death of Dr. Rudolf Eucken," 388.

49. Eucken, *Rudolf Eucken*, 146–47.

50. Eucken, *Rudolf Eucken*, 147.

51. Zhang, "Zhi Lin Zaipin Xuezhang Hangao Woshi Wutan Ji Deguo Zhexue Xixiang Yaolue 1920," 46.

52. See Zhang, "Woyikeng Jingshen Shenghuo Zhexue Dagai," 58–62.

53. Strangely, there was no Chinese translation of this book until recently. Apparently, Zhang was no longer interested in introducing Eucken to China with this book.

54. Rudolf Eucken and Carsun Chang, *Das Lebensproblem in China und Europa* (Leipzig: Quelle & Meyer, 1922), iii. Translations from this book are all mine.

NOTES TO PAGES 97–104   225

55. Eucken and Chang, *Das Lebensproblem in China und Europa*, iii: "Diesen Männern schien es wichtig, ihr jetzt in starker innerer Bewegung befindliches Leben in engere Beziehung zum deutschen philosophischen Idealismus und zugleich mit meinem Aktivismus zu bringen."

56. All the quotes in this paragraph are from Eucken and Chang, *Das Lebensproblem in China und Europa*, iii–v.

57. Eucken and Chang, *Das Lebensproblem in China und Europa*, v: "Die Grundlagen von Moral und Sitte sind auch in China schwankend geworden. Wie weit kann das Alte beibehalten werden, wie weit muß die europäische Kultur Aufnahme finden? Dies ist die wichtigste Frage für die chinesische Geisteswelt."

58. Eucken and Chang, *Das Lebensproblem in China und Europa*, 36: "Der leitende Gedanke dieses Lebens ist die Pflicht, die freie Unterordnung unter ein selbstgegebenes Gesetz."

59. Eucken and Chang, *Das Lebensproblem*, 38.

60. See Eucken and Chang, *Das Lebensproblem*, 43 and 199.

61. See Eucken and Chang, *Das Lebensproblem*, 56, 69.

62. Eucken and Chang, *Das Lebensproblem*, 65.

63. Eucken and Chang, *Das Lebensproblem*, 87.

64. See Eucken and Chang, *Das Lebensproblem*, 100–101.

65. Eucken and Chang, *Das Lebensproblem*, 106.

66. Eucken and Chang, *Das Lebensproblem*, 105.

67. Eucken and Chang, *Das Lebensproblem*, 113.

68. Eucken and Chang, *Das Lebensproblem*, 117.

69. Eucken and Chang, *Das Lebensproblem*, 117–18.

70. Eucken and Chang, *Das Lebensproblem*, 111.

71. Eucken and Chang, *Das Lebensproblem*, 111.

72. Eucken and Chang, *Das Lebensproblem*, 147.

73. Eucken and Chang, *Das Lebensproblem*, 124–25.

74. Eucken and Chang, *Das Lebensproblem*, 125.

75. Eucken and Chang, *Das Lebensproblem*, 149.

76. See Eucken and Chang, *Das Lebensproblem*, 168.

77. Eucken and Chang, *Das Lebensproblem*, 194–95.

78. See Eucken and Chang, *Das Lebensproblem*, 183.

79. Eucken and Chang, *Das Lebensproblem*, 193.

80. See Eucken, "Rudolf Eucken on the Tasks of German Idealism." Eucken's speech in Berlin's Urania in 1915 was reported in the magazine *The New York Times Current History of the European War* in a condensed version, titled "Rudolf Eucken on the Tasks of German Idealism. " The magazine aimed to present "the most interesting articles of information and comment found in the current periodicals of Germany, Austria, Russia, France, Great Britain, Italy, Holland, the Scandinavian countries, and the United States" (881). In his speech, Eucken contrasted German idealism to Indian

and Greek idealism. He made clear why German idealism was special: "It aspires to create in man a new life of freedom and cordiality as the upper story of an edifice based on the purely material life. This new world of the spirit, of mental labor, of freedom, and of intellectuality, by no means consists in fleeing from the world, but is victorious and heroic enough no longer to fear the opposition of the world. Through this, the world becomes the workshop of the spirit and the consciousness of this gives one the joy of life, as one feels himself to be a part of the great organization of humanity and can co-operate as an active spirit in the work of elevating and shaping the world" (881). For Eucken, this holistic orientation toward all humans in the world despite cultural or national differences was characteristic of German idealism. Eucken proposed that German idealism would help solve difficult issues in the present world. "For instance, in the criticism of our culture. Idealism should insist upon a drastic sifting of our civilization, strip off its historical associations, and test everything upon the base of imperishable qualities" (881). Eucken considered this type of essentialization as German idealism's contribution to the First World War, calling it the "mental attitude" of the German nation. It thus gave the Germans a sense of human dignity so that they could act "in the real interest of world civilization." Eucken was optimistic about the future: "The multiplicity of our tasks need not frighten us. Idealism strengthens men with its higher aims" (882). Doubtless, Eucken used German idealism, which was his own *Lebensphilosophie*, to justify the German involvement in the warfare and elevate the war to an ideological level. Zhang, however, might not have known Eucken's pro-war attitude, at least at the beginning of World War I. Rather, the spirituality in Eucken's *Lebensphilosophie* deeply impressed him.

81. Eucken and Chang, *Das Lebensproblem*, 196.

82. Eucken and Chang, *Das Lebensproblem*, 197.

83. Eucken, *Rudolf Eucken*, 140–41.

84. See Rudolf Eucken, 大思想家の人生観/*Dai shisoka no jinseikan*, trans. Yoshishige Abe (Tokyo: [東亞堂書房] Toado Shobo, 1914).

85. Wing-Tsit Chan translated the title *Renshengguan* as "philosophy of life," which also makes a lot of sense. For the sake of reflecting more precisely the Chinese linguistic meaning of this term, I chose to use "view of life." See W. M. Theodore de Bary and Richard Lufrano, eds., *Sources of Chinese Tradition* (New York: Columbia University Press, 2000), 2:370.

86. See Chunjie Zhang, "Anna Seghers's Ideological Melodrama, Qian Zhongshu's Cosmopolitan Satire, or On Comparison," in *Composing Modernist Connections*, ed. Chunjie Zhang (London: Routledge, 2019).

87. Junmai Zhang et al., *Kexue yu Rensheng Guan* (科学与人生观) (Hefei (合肥): Huangshan Shushe (黄山书社), 2008), 36. My translation.

88. Wenjiang Ding 丁文江, "Xuanxue yu Kexue 玄学与科学," in Junmai Zhang et al., *Kexue yu Rensheng Guan*, 48.

89. Wenjiang Ding, "Xuanxue yu Kexue," 58.

90. Wenjiang Ding, "Xuanxue yu Kexue," 39.

91. Junmai Zhang, "Zailun Rensheng Guan yu Kexue bing Da Ding Zaijun (再论人生观与科学并答丁在君)," in Zhang et al., *Kexue yu Rensheng Guan*, 95.

92. Zhang, "Zailun Rensheng Guan yu Kexue bing Da Ding Zaijun," 108–9.

93. Zhang, "Zailun Rensheng Guan yu Kexue bing Da Ding Zaijun," 109.

94. Zhang, "Zailun Rensheng Guan yu Kexue bing Da Ding Zaijun," 115.

95. Zhang et al., *Kexue yu Rensheng Guan*, 119.

96. Qichao Liang (梁启超), *Ou You Xin Ying Lu* (欧游心影录) (Beijing: Shang Wu Yin Shu Guan, 2014), 15.

97. See the chapter on Liang Shuming and rural reform. The New Confucian thinkers recognized similar problems in China and in the world.

98. Liang, *Ou You Xin Ying Lu*, 16–17.

99. Liang, *Ou You Xin Ying Lu*, 18.

100. Liang, *Ou You Xin Ying Lu*, 22.

101. Liang, *Ou You Xin Ying Lu*, 27.

102. Liang, *Ou You Xin Ying Lu*, 51.

103. Liang, *Ou You Xin Ying Lu*, 49.

104. Liang, *Ou You Xin Ying Lu*, 31.

4. LIANG SHUMING, WORLD CULTURE, AND RURAL MODERNITY

1. Shuming Liang (梁漱溟), *Dong Xi Wenhua Ji Qi Zhexue*, 东西文化及其哲学 (*Eastern and Western Cultures and Their Philosophies*) (Shanghai: Ren Ming Chu Ban She (人民出版社 People's Press), 2015), 12.

2. Liang, *Dong Xi Wenhua Ji Qi Zhexue*, 19.

3. See Donglin Wang (汪东林), *Liang Shuming yu Mao Zedong* (梁漱溟与毛泽东) (Changchun 长春: Jilin Renmin Chubanshe 吉林人民出版社, 1989).

4. See Jean C. Oi and Steven M. Goldstein, eds., *Zouping Revisited: Adaptive Governance in a Chinese County* (Stanford: Stanford University Press, 2018).

5. See Guy S. Alitto, *The Last Confucian: Liang Shu-ming and the Chinese Dilemma of Modernity* (Berkeley: University of California Press, 1979), 6.

6. Alitto, *Last Confucian*, 3.

7. Alitto, *Last Confucian*, 10.

8. See Charlotte Furth, "Intellectual Change: From the Reform Movement to the May Fourth Movement, 1895–1920," in *An Intellectual History of Modern China*, ed. Leo Ou-Fan Lee and Merle Goldman (Cambridge: Cambridge University Press, 2002), 59–62.

9. Alitto, *Last Confucian*, 13.

10. See Dahua Zheng (郑大华), *Liang Shuming Zhuan*, 梁漱溟传 (Beijing: Renmin Chubanshe, 人民出版社, 2001).

11. See Wang, *Liang Shuming Wenda Lu*, 40–42.

12. Keli Fang (方克立) and Jinquan Li (李锦全) Fang, eds., *Xiandai Xin Rujia*

Xue'an (现代新儒家学案) (Beijing: Zhongguo Shehui Kexue Chubanshe 中国社会科学出版社, 1995), 1:6.

13. Yong Ma (马勇), *Liang Shuming Pingzhuan*, 梁漱溟评传 (Hefei: Anhui Renmin Chubanshe 1992), 99–119.

14. Furth, "Intellectual Change," 60.

15. Thierry Meynard, *The Religious Philosophy of Liang Shuming: The Hidden Buddhist* (Leiden and Boston: Brill, 2011).

16. See Shuming Liang (梁漱溟), *Wo Sheng You Ya Yuan Wu Jin: Liang Shuming Zishu Wenlu*, 我生有涯愿无尽：梁漱溟自述文录 (Shanghai: Shanghai Renmin Chubanshe, 2013), 18.

17. Liang, *Dong Xi Wenhua Ji Qi Zhexue*, 2.

18. Liang, *Dong Xi Wenhua Ji Qi Zhexue*, 3.

19. See Meynard, *Religious Philosophy of Liang Shuming*; John J. Hanafin, "The 'Last Buddhist': The Philsophy of Liang Shuming," in *New Confucianism: A Critical Examination* (New York: Palgrave Macmillan, 2003).

20. See Hanafin, "'Last Buddhist.'" Hanafin challenges Guy Alitto's argument about Liang being the last Confucian and brought ample evidence to show the Buddhist affinity in Liang's thinking. Hanafin also informs us about the Buddhist revival in the early twentieth century. The Mahayana tradition of Buddhism was introduced to China by the monk Xuanzang (玄奘) in A.D. 645 after his strenuous journey to India. In Xuanzang's lead, seventy-five of the six hundred and seven Buddhist sutras and treatises that he brought back from India were translated into Chinese. Xuanzang translated the epistemology of Yogāchāra as weishi (唯识) in Chinese. Mahayana Buddhism also became a major teaching in China in the seventh century but underwent political persecutions throughout the next dynasties, resulting in the loss of canonical texts. In the 1880s, some of the lost texts were brought back to China from Japan. Buddhism achieved prominence again among the learned Chinese. Multiple associations dedicated to the study of Buddhism were founded in the early twentieth century.

21. See Liang, *Dong Xi Wenhua Ji Qi Zhexue*, 204–6.

22. Liang, *Dong Xi Wenhua Ji Qi Zhexue*, 57.

23. See Liang, *Dong Xi Wenhua Ji Qi Zhexue*, 61. 文化并非别的，乃是人类生活的样法。

24. See Meynard, *Religious Philosophy of Liang Shuming*, 26.

25. Furth, "Intellectual Change," 60–61.

26. Liang, *Dong Xi Wenhua Ji Qi Zhexue*, 62. Zhang Junmai later followed Liang's suit and compared Europe, China, and India in his booklet *Tomorrow's Chinese Culture* (*Mingri zhi Zhongguo Wenhua*, 明日之中国文化, 1935). Yet Zhang comments that Liang's model is not rooted in historical and objective research and lacks more substantial content. Thus Zhang attempted to do it in a new way. See Junmai Zhang (张君劢), *Mingri zhi Zhongguo Wenhua*, 明日之中国文化 (Changsha, Hunan: Yuelu Shushe 岳麓书社, 2011), 1–2.

27. Liang, *Dong Xi Wenhua Ji Qi Zhexue*, 56.
28. Liang, *Dong Xi Wenhua Ji Qi Zhexue*, 157.
29. Liang, *Dong Xi Wenhua Ji Qi Zhexue*, 71.
30. Liang, *Dong Xi Wenhua Ji Qi Zhexue*, 125.
31. Liang, *Dong Xi Wenhua Ji Qi Zhexue*, 127.
32. Liang, *Dong Xi Wenhua Ji Qi Zhexue*, 127.
33. See Liang, *Dong Xi Wenhua Ji Qi Zhexue*, 77–81.
34. Liang, *Dong Xi Wenhua Ji Qi Zhexue*, 130.
35. Liang, *Dong Xi Wenhua Ji Qi Zhexue*, 131.
36. Liang, *Dong Xi Wenhua Ji Qi Zhexue*, 132.
37. Liang, *Dong Xi Wenhua Ji Qi Zhexue*, 133.
38. Liang, *Dong Xi Wenhua Ji Qi Zhexue*, 132.
39. Liang, *Dong Xi Wenhua Ji Qi Zhexue*, 135.
40. Liang, *Dong Xi Wenhua Ji Qi Zhexue*, 138.
41. Liang, *Dong Xi Wenhua Ji Qi Zhexue*, 140.
42. Liang, *Dong Xi Wenhua Ji Qi Zhexue*, 146.
43. Liang, *Dong Xi Wenhua Ji Qi Zhexue*, 173.
44. Liang, *Dong Xi Wenhua Ji Qi Zhexue*, 173–76.
45. Liang, *Dong Xi Wenhua Ji Qi Zhexue*, 179.
46. Liang, *Dong Xi Wenhua Ji Qi Zhexue*, 210.
47. Liang, *Dong Xi Wenhua Ji Qi Zhexue*, 210: "孔子说"吾未见刚者。"
48. Liang, *Dong Xi Wenhua Ji Qi Zhexue*, 212.
49. Liang, *Dong Xi Wenhua Ji Qi Zhexue*, 194.
50. Liang, *Dong Xi Wenhua Ji Qi Zhexue*, 202.
51. Furth, "Intellectual Change," 61.
52. Liang, *Dong Xi Wenhua Ji Qi Zhexue*, 213.
53. See Wang, *Liang Shuming yu Mao Zedong*, 1–31.
54. Shuming Liang (梁漱溟), "Xiangcun Jianshe Lilun (乡村建设理论)," in *Liang Shuming Quanji* (梁漱溟全集) (Jinan (济南): China Shandong Renmin Chubanshe (山东人民出版社), 1990), 164.
55. See Liang, *Wo Sheng You Ya Yuan Wu Jin*.
56. Liang contends in the foreword to this book that "our old society is destructed in its deepest depth. We must start from the beginning. The society that develops from this foundation is a completely new organization, something unprecedented in the history of humanity." Liang, "Xiangcun Jianshe Lilun (乡村建设理论)," 146–47.
57. Liang, "Xiangcun Jianshe Lilun," 150: 所有的文化,多半是从乡村而来,又为乡村而设,—法制,礼俗,工商业等莫不如是。
58. Liang, "Xiangcun Jianshe Lilun," 154.
59. Liang, "Xiangcun Jianshe Lilun," 158.
60. This situation in China resembles that existing in India under colonial rule. Indian farmers could not sell their own products while they had to buy products

imported from England and the West. Mahatma Gandhi led the movement of independence to counter this economic inequality controlled by the colonial politics of the British in the 1920s. That happened at the same time that Liang was initiating rural reform.

61. Pearl Buck's novel *The Good Earth* describes the close tie of the Chinese farmers to their land and the difficulties that they were facing in the early twentieth century. See Buck, *The Good Earth* (New York: Washington Square Press, 2012).

62. Liang, "Xiangcun Jianshe Lilun," 164.
63. Liang, "Xiangcun Jianshe Lilun," 168.
64. See Liang, "Xiangcun Jianshe Lilun," 168–69.
65. Liang, "Xiangcun Jianshe Lilun," 171.
66. See Tetsuo Najita, *Visions of Virtue in Tokugawa Japan: The Kaitokudō Merchant Academy of Osaka* (Chicago: University of Chicago Press, 1987).
67. Liang, "Xiangcun Jianshe Lilun," 178.
68. Liang, "Xiangcun Jianshe Lilun," 181.
69. Liang, "Xiangcun Jianshe Lilun," 182–83.
70. Liang, "Xiangcun Jianshe Lilun," 267.
71. Liang, "Xiangcun Jianshe Lilun," 278.
72. Liang, "Xiangcun Jianshe Lilun," 282.
73. Liang, "Xiangcun Jianshe Lilun," 194.
74. Liang, "Xiangcun Jianshe Lilun," 308.
75. Liang, "Xiangcun Jianshe Lilun," 316.
76. Liang, "Xiangcun Jianshe Lilun," 318–19.
77. Liang, "Xiangcun Jianshe Lilun," 320.
78. Liang, "Xiangcun Jianshe Lilun," 345, 29.
79. Liang, "Xiangcun Jianshe Lilun," 346.
80. Liang, "Xiangcun Jianshe Lilun," 348, 49.
81. Liang, "Xiangcun Jianshe Lilun," 365.
82. Liang, "Xiangcun Jianshe Lilun," 412.
83. Liang, "Xiangcun Jianshe Lilun," 557.
84. Liang, "Xiangcun Jianshe Lilun," 557.
85. Liang, "Xiangcun Jianshe Lilun," 560.
86. Liang, "Xiangcun Jianshe Lilun," 561.
87. Liang, "Xiangcun Jianshe Lilun," 561.
88. Liang, "Xiangcun Jianshe Lilun," 564.
89. Liang, "Xiangcun Jianshe Lilun," 565.
90. Liang, "Xiangcun Jianshe Lilun," 565.
91. Liang, "Xiangcun Jianshe Lilun," 567.
92. Liang, "Xiangcun Jianshe Lilun," 566.
93. Hanafin, "'Last Buddhist,'" 188.
94. Youlan Feng (冯友兰), *A Short History of Chinese Philosophy* (中国哲学

简史), trans. Zhao Fusan (赵复三) (Beijing: Foreign Language Teaching and Research Press, 2015), 34.

95. Feng, *Short History of Chinese Philosophy*, 35–36.

5. EARLY FENG YOULAN'S NEGATIVE METHOD: METAPHYSICS, WORLD PHILOSOPHY, AND SAGE

1. Wing-Tsit Chan, ed., *A Source Book in Chinese Philosophy* (Princeton: Princeton University Press, 1963), 751.
2. Chan, *Source Book in Chinese Philosophy*, 753.
3. Xiaoqing Diana Lin also argues about Feng's nationalism and pointed out his openness to Western thought: "Philosophy became Confucianism's response to Western cultural encroachments on China. Chinese philosophers such as Feng Youlan, Xiong Shili (熊十力) (1885–1968), He Lin (贺麟) (1902–92), and Liang Shuming would focus on one aspect of Confucian learning and draw on Western or Indian philosophy to develop a modern Chinese version. . . . nationalism was a strong motivation in Feng's quest for philosophy and for the development of Chinese philosophy: to develop a rational framework of thought related to traditional Chinese thinking and open to Western thought." Lin, *Feng Youlan and TwentiethCentury China: An Intellectual Biography* (Leiden and Boston: Brill, 2016), 6–7.
4. Yu-Lan Fung, "Chinese Philosophy and a Future World Philosophy," *Philosophical Review* 57, no. 6 (November 1948): 539.
5. Fung, "Chinese Philosophy and a Future World Philosophy," 539–40.
6. Fung, "Chinese Philosophy and a Future World Philosophy," 539.
7. Fung, "Chinese Philosophy and a Future World Philosophy," 540.
8. See Fung, "Chinese Philosophy and a Future World Philosophy," 540.
9. Youlan Feng (冯友兰), *Xin Zhi Yan* (新知言), Sansong Tang Quanji (三松堂全集), (Zhengzhou 郑州: Henan Remin Chubanshe 河南人民出版社, 1986), 167.
10. Feng, *Xin Zhi Yan*, 168.
11. Youlan Feng (冯友兰), *A Short History of Chinese Philosophy* (中国哲学简史), trans. Zhao Fusan (赵复三) (Beijing: Foreign Language Teaching and Research Press, 2015), 16.
12. See Youlan Feng (冯友兰), *Sansong Tang Zixu* (三松堂自序), vol. 1, *Sansong Tang Quanji* (三松堂全集), (Zhengzhou 郑州: Henan Remin Chubanshe 河南人民出版社, 1985), 190.
13. See Feng, *Sansong Tang Zixu*, 189–190.
14. Feng, *Sansong Tang Zixu*, 190.
15. Feng, *Sansong Tang Zixu*, 197.
16. Feng, *Short History of Chinese Philosophy*, 6.
17. See Youlan Feng (冯友兰), "The Place of Confucius in Chinese History," reprint, *Chinese Social and Political Science Review* xvi, no. 1 April (1932): 4.

18. Feng, "Place of Confucius in Chinese History," 7.

19. Yu-Lan Fung, *The Spirit of Chinese Philosophy*, trans. E. R. Hughes (London: Kegan Paul, Trench, Trubner, 1947), vii.

20. Feng, *Sansong Tang Zixu*, 229.

21. Youlan Feng (冯友兰), *Xin Li Xue* (新理学), Sansong Tang Quanji (三松堂全集), vol. 4 (Zhengzhou 郑州: Henan Remin Chubanshe 河南人民出版社, 1986), 3.

22. See Feng, *Sansong Tang Zixu*, 259.

23. Feng, *Sansong Tang Zixu*, 260.

24. Chan, *Source Book in Chinese Philosophy*, 753.

25. Feng, *Short History of Chinese Philosophy*, 616.

26. See Feng, *Sansong Tang Zixu*, 255.

27. Fung, "Chinese Philosophy and a Future World Philosophy," 540.

28. Fung, "Chinese Philosophy and a Future World Philosophy," 540.

29. Feng, *Xin Zhi Yan*, 173.

30. Fung, "Chinese Philosophy and a Future World Philosophy," 542.

31. See Feng, *Xin Zhi Yan*, 223–32. Hans-Georg Möller also argues that Feng's own philosophical system is indeed a new metaphysics. For Feng, the most philosophical philosophy is metaphysics. It is the area in which he invested most of his creative energy. See Möller, *Die philosophischste Philosophie: Feng Youlans Neue Metaphysik* (Wiesbaden: Harrassowitz Verlag, 2000).

32. Fung, "Chinese Philosophy and a Future World Philosophy," 541.

33. Plato, *The Republic* (London: Penguin Books, 2007), 241.

34. Plato, *Republic*, 245.

35. Plato, *Republic*, 244.

36. Feng, *Xin Zhi Yan*, 187.

37. Fung, "Chinese Philosophy and a Future World Philosophy," 542.

38. Fung, "Chinese Philosophy and a Future World Philosophy," 542–43.

39. Feng recognizes that, while Taoist and Kantian metaphysics in terms of knowledge are quite similar, Kantian ethics resembles that of Confucianism. The metaphysics of morals and its categorical imperative are not Taoist but rather Confucianist.

40. Fung, "Chinese Philosophy and a Future World Philosophy," 543.

41. Fung, "Chinese Philosophy and a Future World Philosophy," 544.

42. Fung, "Chinese Philosophy and a Future World Philosophy," 544. Li Jinglin comments, "Thus the question of how a 'formalist' system of metaphysical concepts can be merged with the mystical content of the inconceivable and inexpressible and how the positive method of logical analysis can be combined with the negative method of mysticism became a major theoretical issue he had to face and solve." Jinglin Li, "The Positive and the Negative Method and the Spheres of Living: Some Thoughts on Feng Youlan's Philosophical Method," *Social Sciences in China* 32, no. 4 (November 2011): 60.

43. Fung, "Chinese Philosophy and a Future World Philosophy," 545.

44. In Feng's definition, "Neo-Confucianism is indeed the continuation of the idealistic wing of ancient Confucianism, and especially of the mystic tendency of Mencius. That is the reason why these men have been known as the *Tao hsüeh chia* and their philosophy as the *Tao hsüeh*, i.e., the Study of the *Tao* or Truth. The term Neo-Confucianism is a newly coined western equivalent for *Tao hsüeh*." Three major sources constitute neo-Confucianism: Confucianism, Buddhism (particularly Zen Buddhism), and Taoism. Feng comments on the importance of Buddhism and Taoism for neo-Confucianism: "To the Neo-Confucianists, Ch'anism and Buddhism are synonymous terms, and . . . in one sense Neo-Confucianism may be said to be the logical development of Ch'anism. Finally, the third is the Taoist religion, of which the cosmological views of the Yin-Yang School formed an important element. The cosmology of the Neo-Confucianists is chiefly connected with this line of thought. These three lines of thought were heterogeneous and even in many respects contradictory. Hence it took time for philosophers to make a unity out of them, especially since this unity was not simply an eclecticism, but a genuine system forming a homogeneous whole. Therefore, although the beginning of Neo-Confucianism may be traced back to Han Yü and Li Ao, its system of thought did not become clearly formed until the eleventh century. This was the time when the Sung dynasty (960–1279), which reunited China after a period of confusion following the collapse of the T'ang, was at the height of its splendor and prosperity. The earliest of the Neo-Confucianists were chiefly interested in cosmology." Feng, *Short History of Chinese Philosophy*, 492.

45. Feng, *Sansong Tang Zixu*, 1:254.

46. Allan Janik, *Wittgenstein's Vienna Revisited* (New Brunswick, NJ: Transaction, 2001), 199.

47. See Feng, *Xin Zhi Yan*, 217.

48. Feng, *Xin Zhi Yan*, 223.

49. Feng, *Xin Zhi Yan*, 253.

50. See Feng, *Xin Zhi Yan*, 254.

51. See Feng, *Xin Zhi Yan*, 255.

52. Feng, *Xin Zhi Yan*, 259.

53. Feng, *Xin Zhi Yan*, 261.

54. Feng, *Xin Zhi Yan*, 263.

55. Janik, *Wittgenstein's Vienna Revisited*, 197.

56. Ludwig Wittgenstein, *Tractatus Logico-Philosophicus*, trans. D. F. Pears and B. F. McGuinness (London: Routledge & Kegan Paul, 1961), 151. Ludwig Wittgenstein, *Tractatus logico-philosophicus* (Frankfurt am Main: Suhrkamp, 2006), 85.

57. Wittgenstein, *Tractatus Logico-Philosophicus*, 151. Wittgenstein, *Tractatus logico-philosophicus*, 85.

58. Feng, *Xin Zhi Yan*, 262.

59. Wittgenstein, *Tractatus Logico-Philosophicus*, 151. Wittgenstein, *Tractatus logico-philosophicus*, 85.

60. Wittgenstein, *Tractatus Logico-Philosophicus*, 151. Wittgenstein, *Tractatus logico-philosophicus*, 85.

61. Wittgenstein, *Tractatus Logico-Philosophicus*, 149. Wittgenstein, *Tractatus logico-philosophicus*, 85.

62. Michael Morris and Julian Dodd, "Mysticism and Nonsense in the *Tractatus*," *European Journal of Philosophy* 17, no. 2 (2009): 266.

63. See Möller, *Die philosophischste Philosophie*, 132–41.

64. Fung, "Chinese Philosophy and a Future World Philosophy," 545.

65. Fung, *Spirit of Chinese Philosophy*, 217. This is the English translation of *Xin Yuan Dao (New Original Path*, 新原道), the fifth of the six books. This book is a concise history of Chinese philosophy in which Feng discussed his philosophy in the last chapter about a new system.

66. Feng, *Short History of Chinese Philosophy*, 15–16.

67. Feng, *Short History of Chinese Philosophy*, 18.

68. Fung, "Chinese Philosophy and a Future World Philosophy," 546.

69. Fung, *Spirit of Chinese Philosophy*, 219.

70. Fung, *Spirit of Chinese Philosophy*, 220.

71. Fung, *Spirit of Chinese Philosophy*, 220.

72. Fung, *Spirit of Chinese Philosophy*, 220.

73. Fung, "Chinese Philosophy and a Future World Philosophy," 547.

74. Fung, "Chinese Philosophy and a Future World Philosophy," 547.

75. Fung, "Chinese Philosophy and a Future World Philosophy," 547.

76. Fung, "Chinese Philosophy and a Future World Philosophy," 548.

77. Fung, "Chinese Philosophy and a Future World Philosophy," 548.

78. Fung, "Chinese Philosophy and a Future World Philosophy," 548–49.

79. Fung, "Chinese Philosophy and a Future World Philosophy," 549.

80. Feng referred to his preface to *The New Rational Philosophy*, stating that, "even though nothing in this book is concerned with practical reality, the solutions of many contemporary problems are deeply connected to the ideas in this book." Youlan Feng (冯友兰), *Xin Shi Lun* (新事论), Sansong Tang Quanji (三松堂全集), (Zhengzhou 郑州: Henan Renmin Chubanshe 河南人民出版社, 1986), 215.

81. Feng, *Xin Shi Lun*, 222.

82. Feng, *Xin Shi Lun*, 304.

83. Feng, *Xin Shi Lun*, 314.

84. See, for example, Emily S. Apter, *Against World Literature: On the Politics of Untranslatability* (London and New York: Verso, 2013).

85. Feng, *Xin Shi Lun*, 331.

86. Feng, *Xin Shi Lun*, 338.

87. Feng, *Xin Shi Lun*, 339.

88. See Feng, *Xin Shi Lun*, 326–27.
89. Feng, *Xin Shi Lun*, 252–63.
90. See Gayatri Chakravorty Spivak, "Can the Subaltern Speak?," in *Marxism and the Interpretation of Culture*, ed. Cary Nelson and Lawrence Grossberg (Urbana: University of Illinois Press, 1988).
91. See Feng, *Xin Shi Lun*, 277–88.
92. Feng, *Xin Shi Lun*, 363.
93. See Feng, *Xin Shi Lun*, 363–64.
94. Feng, *Xin Shi Lun*, 365.
95. Feng, *Short History of Chinese Philosophy*, 30.

6. BERTOLT BRECHT'S *ME-TI* OR THE AESTHETICS OF TRANSLATION: UNIVERSAL LOVE, MUTUAL BENEFITS, AND TRANSIENCE

1. I translate the word *Wendung* as both transformation, in terms of "wenden," and usage, in terms of "Redewendung," because both elements are prominent in *Me-ti*. I believe that Brecht intentionally uses this word to connect the double meaning in the word *Wendung*. The English translator of *Me-ti*, Antony Tatlow, translates the title as *Book of Interventions in the Flow of Things*, which doesn't reflect the aspect of usage or practicality, which is important for Brecht's dialectic. There are also other versions of translation by other scholars. See Antony Tatlow, ed., *Bertolt Brecht's Me-ti: Book of Interventions in the Flow of Things* (London: Bloomsbury, 2015).

2. See Bertolt Brecht, *Prosa 3: Sammlungen und Dialoge*, Bertolt Brecht Werke, Berliner und Frankfurter Ausgabe (Berlin, Weimar, and Frankfurt am Main: Aufbau-Verlag and Suhrkamp Verlag, 1995), 486–87.

3. See Fredric Jameson, *Brecht and Method* (London and New York: Verso, 1998), 140. Theo Stammen views *Me-ti* as Brecht's most comprehensive reflection and discussion about Marxist dialectic among his writing. See Stammen, "'Me-ti'—Große Methode—Große Ordnung," in *Bertolt Brecht—Aspekte seines Werkes, Spuren seiner Wirkung*, ed. Helmut Koopmann and Theo Stammen (Munich: Verlag Ernst Vögel, 1994), 147.

4. See Hans-Peter Krüger, "Brechts Dialektik-Konzept in 'Me-ti'," in *Brecht und Marxismus: Dokumentation* (Berlin: Henschelverlag Kunst und Gesellschaft, 1983), 210.

5. See Jan Knopf, ed., *Brecht Handbuch: Prosa, Filme, Drehbücher* (Stuttgart and Weimar: Verlag J. B. Metzler, 2002), 3:242. Also see Klaus-Detlef Müller, "Brechts *Me-ti* und die Auseinandersetzung mit dem Lehrer Karl Korsch," *Brecht-Jahrbuch* (1977): 9–29. Müller disputes any real connection to China or Chinese philosophy and contends that *Me-ti* is a discussion with Brecht's friend and philosophical interlocutor Karl Korsch; Mei-Ling Luzia Wang, *Chinesische Elemente in Bertolt Brechts "Me-ti: Buch der Wendungen"* (Frankfurt am Main: Peter Lang, 1990). Mei-Ling Luzia Wang confirms that, even though Brecht is inspired by Mohism, his dialectic is still to be understood

in the context of Marxism and the socialist movement in Germany and the Soviet Union because there are major differences between Mohist and Brecht's dialectic.

6. Markus Wessendorf, "Brecht's Materialist Ethics between Confucianism and Mohism," *Philosophy East & West* 66, no. 1 (January 2016): 138.

7. Günther Heeg, "Brechts chinesische Wendungen: *Me-ti* und die Praxis kultureller Flexionen," *Brecht Yearbook* 36 (2011): 141. Even though Heeg highlights *Me-ti* as a transcultural experiment that resides in a realm between one's own and foreign cultures, he still concludes that Master Mo is not the primary philosopher (*Hauptphilosoph*) in Brecht's *Me-ti*, and Chinese philosophies, including Confucianism and Taoism, are not the real teaching well integrated with Marxism: "Aber die chinesische Philosophie geht nicht als Lehre, als philosophische Doktrin in das Buch der Wendungen ein."

8. See the chapter on Brecht in Eric Hayot, *Chinese Dreams: Pound, Brecht, Tel quel* (Ann Arbor: University of Michigan Press, 2003).

9. See Bertolt Brecht, *Me-ti: Buch der Wendungen* (Frankfurt am Main: Suhrkamp Verlag, 1965). In the 1995 edition, this foreword is identified as the last episode that Brecht wrote for this project. See Brecht, *Prosa 3*, 194.

10. MoZi, *Mê Ti, des Sozialethikers und seiner Schüler philosophische Werke*, trans. Alfred Forke (Berlin: Vereinigung wissenschaftlicher Verleger, 1922), http://worldcat.org.

11. Johnston doesn't mention that probably the earliest study of Mohism in a European language was J. Edkin's five-page *Notice of Character and Writings of Meh-tsi*, published in *Journal of the North-China Branch of the Royal Asiatic Society* in Shanghai in 1859. See MoZi, *The Mozi: A Complete Translation*, ed. and trans. Ian Johnston (New York: Columbia University Press, 2010), lxxviii–lxxxii. See Joseph Edkin, "Notice of Character and Writings of Meh Tsï," *Journal of the North-China Branch of the Royal Asiatic Society* 2 (May 1859): 165–69.

12. Mo Zi, *Mozi*, lxxix.

13. Werner Mittenzwei, "Nachwort: Der Dialektiker Brecht oder die Kunst "Me-ti" zu lesen," in *Brecht Prosa IV*, ed. Werner Mittenzwei (Berlin und Weimar: Aufbau Verlag, 1975), 182: "ME-TI in Leder."

14. In fact, there are no chapters on music in Brecht's fragments, but there are chapters on music in *Mozi*. It is also true that *Mozi* is a collection of both Master Mo's works and those of his later followers. Forke also comments on this fact in the introduction to his translation: "Mê-tsi ist nicht ein einheitliches Werk, sondern eine Sammlung mehistischer Schriften," MoZi, *Mê Ti*, 2.

15. All the quotes in this paragraph are from Brecht, *Me-ti*, 8.

16. MoZi, *Mozi*, xvii.

17. MoZi, *Mê Ti*, vii. All translation of this work is mine.

18. See Shouchu Fang (方授楚), *Mo Xue Yuan Liu* 墨學源流 (Beijing: Beijing Library Press (Beijing Tushu Guan Chuban She), 2003), 231–33.

19. Fang, *Mo Xue Yuan Liu*, 74–76.
20. MoZi, *Mê Ti*, 73.
21. MoZi, *Mê Ti*, 73.
22. See MoZi, *Mê Ti*, 74.
23. MoZi, *Mê Ti*, 236. The translation is mine.
24. Mittenzwei, "Nachwort," 192–94.
25. The five sections comprise the following: the first section, Book of the Great Method (*Buch der Großen Methode*) is about dialectic, the second section, Book of Experience (*Buch der Erfahrung*), is about ethics, the third one, Book about Disorder (*Buch über die Unordnung*), is about fascism, the fourth one, Book of Upheaval (*Buch der Umwälzung*), is on socialist revolution, and the fifth one, Book of the Great Order (*Buch der Großen Ordnung*), is about socialism.
26. See the comment on the masters in Brecht, *Prosa 3*, 511.
27. Brecht, *Prosa 3*, 57–58.
28. See Yun-Yeop Song, *Bertolt Brecht und die chinesische Philosophie* (Bonn: Bouvier, 1978), 290–93.
29. MoZi, *Mozi*, 137–39.
30. MoZi, *Mozi*, 139. The universal love (兼相爱) and mutual benefit (交相利) in Forke's translation are "das Mittel der allumfassenden gegenseitigen Liebe und ... [der] Austausch gegenseitiger Vorteile." MoZi, *Mê Ti*, 245.
31. MoZi, *Mozi*, 645–47; MoZi, *Mê Ti*, 540–41.
32. MoZi, *Mê Ti*, 524–26.
33. Brecht, *Prosa 3*, 105.
34. Brecht, *Prosa 3*, 162. Knopf mentions a poem by Majakowski as the source for the metaphorical figure of a female cook in his comment. See Brecht, *Prosa 3*, 553.
35. See Bertolt-Brecht-Archiv, Me-ti—Buch der Wendungen, Bertolt-Brecht 0133/02.
36. Brecht, *Prosa 3*, 98. Tatlow, *Bertolt Brecht's Me-ti*, 84.
37. Brecht, *Prosa 3*, 528–29.
38. MoZi, *Mozi*, 411–17; MoZi, *Mê Ti*, 449–50.
39. Brecht, *Prosa 3*, 73.
40. Brecht, *Prosa 3*, 73.
41. Brecht, *Prosa 3*, 73.
42. Tatlow, *Bertolt Brecht's Me-ti*, 55. Brecht, *Prosa 3*, 74.
43. Brecht, *Prosa 3*, 113.
44. Brecht, *Prosa 3*, 113.
45. MoZi, *Mozi*, 615. MoZi, *Mê Ti*, 525.
46. Tatlow, *Bertolt Brecht's Me-ti*, 91. Brecht, *Prosa 3*, 113.
47. MoZi, *Mê Ti*, 535.
48. MoZi, *Mê Ti*, 511; MoZi, *Mozi*, 593. Johnston's translation is, "The world's benefit is pleasing." Yet I find it in this case better to translate the German version back to English to better reflect what Brecht has read. See MoZi, *Mozi*, 593.

CODA: CONSERVATISM OR ALTERNATIVE MODERNITY

1. Chishen Chang and Kuan-Hsing Chen, "Tracking Tianxia: On Intellectual Self-Positioning," in *Chinese Visions of World Order: Tianxia, Culture, and World Politics*, ed. Ban Wang (Durham, NC, and London: Duke University Press, 2017), 289.

2. See Benjamin I. Schwartz, "Notes on Conservatism in General and in China in Particular," in *The Limits of Change: Essays on Conservative Alternatives in Republican China*, ed. Charlotte Furth (Cambridge, MA, and London: Harvard University Press, 1976), 3–21; Edmund S. K. Fung, "Nationalism and Modernity: The Politics of Cultural Conservatism in Republican China," *Modern Asian Studies* 43, no. 3 (2008): 777–813; Fung, *The Intellectual Foundations of Chinese Modernity: Cultural and Political Thought in the Republican Era* (Cambridge: Cambridge University Press, 2010); Charlotte Furth, "Culture and Politics in Modern Chinese Conservatism," in *The Limits of Change: Essays on Conservative Alternatives in Republican China*, ed. Charlotte Furth (Cambridge, MA, and London: Harvard University Press, 1976), 22–53.

3. Furth, "Culture and Politics in Modern Chinese Conservatism," 50–51.

4. See Rahel Jaeggi, *Fortschritt und Regression* (Berlin: Suhrkamp, 2023).

5. See Prasenjit Duara, *The Crisis of Global Modernity: Asian Traditions and a Sustainable Future* (Cambridge: Cambridge University Press, 2014).

WORKS CITED

Adair-Toteff, Christopher. "Max Weber's Charisma." *Journal of Classical Sociology* 5, no. 2 (2005): 189–204.

Alitto, Guy S. *The Last Confucian: Liang Shu-ming and the Chinese Dilemma of Modernity*. Berkeley: University of California Press, 1979.

Appiah, Kwame Anthony. *Cosmopolitanism: Ethics in a World of Strangers*. New York and London: Norton, 2006.

Apter, Emily S. *Against World Literature: On the Politics of Untranslatability*. London and New York: Verso, 2013.

Aydin, Cemil. *The Politics of Anti-Westernism in Asia: Visions of World Order in Pan-Islamic and Pan-Asian Thought*. New York: Columbia University Press, 2007.

Ayers, William. *Chang Chih-Tung and Educational Reform in China*. Cambridge, MA: Harvard University Press, 1971.

Bell, Daniel A. *China's New Confucianism: Politics and Everyday Life in a Changing Society*. Princeton and London: Princeton University Press, 2008.

———, ed. *Confucian Political Ethics*. Princeton and Oxford: Princeton University Press, 2008.

Benhabib, Seyla. *Another Cosmopolitanism*. Oxford: Oxford University Press, 2006.

Beßlich, Barbara. *Wege in den Kulturkrieg: Zivlisationskritik in Deutschland 1890–1914*. Darmstadt: Wissenschaftliche Buchgesellschaft, 2014.

Bhabha, Homi K. "Of Mimicry and Man: The Ambivalence of Colonial Discourse." In *The Location of Culture*, 85–92. London: Routledge, 1994.

Bodde, Derk. *Tolstoy and China*. Princeton: Princeton University Press, 1950.

Brecht, Bertolt. *Me-ti: Buch der Wendungen*. Frankfurt am Main: Suhrkamp Verlag, 1965.

———. *Prosa 3: Sammlungen und Dialoge*. Bertolt Brecht Werke. Berliner und Frankfurter Ausgabe. Berlin, Weimar, and Frankfurt am Main: Aufbau-Verlag and Suhrkamp Verlag, 1995.

Breuilly, John. "Max Weber, Charisma and Nationalist Leadership." *Nations and Nationalism* 17, no. 3 (2011): 477–99.

Brook, Timothy. "Weber's Religion of China." In *Max Weber's Economic Ethic of the*

World Religions: An Analysis, edited by Thomas Ertman, 87–108. Cambridge: Cambridge University Press, 2017.

Brown, Garrett Wallace, and David Held, eds. *The Cosmopolitanism Reader*. Cambridge: Polity, 2010.

Buck, Pearl S. *The Good Earth*. New York: Washington Square Press, 2012.

Buss, Andreas [E]. "Introductory Comments on Max Weber's Essays on India and China." *International Sociology* 2, no. 3 (1987): 271–76.

———, ed. *Max Weber in Asian Studies*. Leiden: Brill, 1985.

Centi, Beatrice. "The Validity of Norms in Neo-Kantian Ethics." In *New Approaches to Neo-Kantianism*, edited by Nicolas de Warren and Andrea Staiti, 127–46. Cambridge: Cambridge University Press, 2015.

Chai, David, ed. *Daoist Resonances in Heidegger: Exploring a Forgotten Debt*. New York: Bloomsbury, 2022.

Chakrabarty, Dipesh. *Provincializing Europe: Postcolonial Thought and Historical Difference*. Princeton: Princeton University Press, 2000.

Chan, Wing-Tsit, ed. *A Source Book in Chinese Philosophy*. Princeton: Princeton University Press, 1963.

Chang, Carsun. *Third Force in China*. New York: Bookman, 1952.

Chang, Chih-Tung. *China's Only Hope: An Appeal by Her Greatest Viceroy Chang Chih-Tung with the Sanction of the Present Emperor, Kwang Sü*. Translated by Samuel I. Woodbridge. Westport, CT: Hyperion Press, 1900.

Chang, Chishen, and Kuan-Hsing Chen. "Tracking Tianxia: On Intellectual Self-Positioning." In *Chinese Visions of World Order: Tianxia, Culture, and World Politics*, edited by Ban Wang, 267–92. Durham, NC, and London: Duke University Press, 2017.

Chen, Kuan-Hsing. *Asia as Method: Toward Deimperialization*. Durham, NC, and London: Duke University Press, 2010.

Conrad, Sebastian. *What Is Global History?* Princeton and Oxford: Princeton University Press, 2016.

Conrad, Sebastian, and Dominic Sachsenmaier, eds. *Competing Visions of World Order: Global Moments and Movements, 1880s–1930s*. New York and London: Palgrave Macmillan, 2007.

de Bary, W. M. Theodore, and Richard Lufrano, eds. *Sources of Chinese Tradition*. Vol. 2. New York: Columbia University Press, 2000.

"Death of Dr. Rudolf Eucken: the Philosophy of Religion." *Times Educational Supplement* (London), September 18, 1926.

Derman, Joshua. *Max Weber in Politic and Social Thought: From Charisma to Canonization*. Cambridge: Cambridge University Press, 2012.

Dethloff, Klaus. "Hugo von Hofmannsthal und eine konservative Revolution." *Deutsche Vierteljahrsschrift für Literaturwissenschaft und Geistesgeschichte* 92 (2018): 531–55.

Dewey, John. *Lectures in China, 1919–1920*. Honolulu: The University Press of Hawaii, 1973.

———. "Transforming the Mind of China." *Asia: Journal of the American Asiatic Association* 19, no. 11 (1919): 1103–8.

Ding, Wenjiang (丁文江). "Xuanxue yu Kexue (玄学与科学)." In *Kexue yu Rensheng Guan* (科学与人生观), 39–58. Hefei 合肥: Huangshan Shushe (黄山书社).

Dirlik, Arif. "Confucius in the Borderlands: Global Capitalism and the Reinvention of Confucianism." *boundary 2* 22, no. 3 (1995): 229–73.

Drochon, Hugo. *Nietzsche's Great Politics*. Princeton and Oxford: Princeton University Press, 2016.

Du, Chunmei. "Gu Hongming as a Cultural Amphibian: A Confucian Universalist Critique of Modern Western Civilization." *Journal of World History* 22, no. 4 (December 2011): 715–46.

———. *Gu Hongming's Eccentric Chinese Odyssey*. Philadelphia: University of Pennsylvania Press, 2019.

———. "Travel Along the Mobius Strip: Somerset Maugham and Gu Hongming East of Suez." *International History Review* 36, no. 1 (2014): 1–18.

Duara, Prasenjit. *The Crisis of Global Modernity: Asian Traditions and a Sustainable Future*. Cambridge: Cambridge University Press, 2014.

Duara, Prasenjit, Viren Murthy, and Andrew Sartori, eds. *A Companion to Global Historical Thought*. Malden, MA: Wiley, 2014.

Eden, Robert. "Weber and Nietzsche: Questioning the Liberation of Social Science from Historicism." In *Max Weber and His Contemporaries*, edited by Wolfgang J. Mommsen and Jürgen Osterhammel, 405–21. London: German Historical Institute, 1987.

Edkin, Joseph. "Notice of Character and Writings of Meh Tsï." *Journal of the North-China Branch of the Royal Asiatic Society* 2 (May 1859): 165–69.

Eisenstadt, S. N. "This Worldly Transcendentalism and the Structuring of the World: Weber's 'Religion of China' and the Format of Chinese History and Civilization." In *Max Weber in Asian Studies*, edited by Andreas Buss, 46–64. Leiden: Brill, 1985.

Eliaeson, Sven. "Max Weber and His Critics: Critical Theory's Reception of Neo-Kantian Methodology." *International Journal of Politics, Culture, and Society* 3, no. 4 (1990): 513–37.

Ertman, Thomas, ed. *Max Weber's Economic Ethic of the World Religions: An Analysis*. Cambridge: Cambridge University Press, 2017.

Eucken, Rudolf. *Lebensanschauungen der großen Denker*. Leipzig: Veit, 1890.

———. *The Problem of Human Life: As Viewed by the Great Thinkers from Plato to the Present Time*. Translated by Williston S. Hough and W. R. Boyce Gibson. New York: Charles Scribner's Sons, 1910.

———. "Rudolf Eucken on the Tasks of German Idealism." *New York Times Current History of the European War*, 1916, 881–82.

———. *Rudolf Eucken: His Life, Work, and Travels by Himself*. London: T. Fisher Unwin, 1921.

———. 大思想家の人生観/*Dai shisoka no jinseikan*. Translated by Yoshishige Abe. Tokyo: 東亞堂書房 Toado Shobo, 1914.

Eucken, Rudolf, and Carsun Chang. *Das Lebensproblem in China und Europa*. Leipzig: Quelle & Meyer, 1922.

Fang, Keli (方克立), and Li Jinquan (李锦全), eds. *Xiandai Xin Rujia Xue'an* (现代新儒家学案) Vol. 1. Beijing: Zhongguo Shehui Kexue Chubanshe 中国社会科学出版社, 1995.

Fang, Shouchu (方授楚). *Mo Xue Yuan Liu* (墨學源流). Beijing: Beijing Library Press (Beijing Tushu Guan Chuban She), 2003.

Fanon, Frantz. *Black Skin, White Masks*. New York: Grove Press, 1967.

Feng, Youlan (冯友兰). "The Place of Confucius in Chinese History." Reprint. *Chinese Social and Political Science Review* xvi, no. 1 (April 1932): 1–10.

———. *Sansong Tang Zixu* (三松堂自序). Sansong Tang Quanji (三松堂全集). Vol. 1, Zhengzhou 郑州: Henan Remin Chubanshe 河南人民出版社, 1985.

———. *A Short History of Chinese Philosophy* (中国哲学简史). Translated by Zhao Fusan (赵复三). Beijing: Foreign Language Teaching and Research Press, 2015.

———. *Xin Li Xue* (新理学). Sansong Tang Quanji (三松堂全集). Vol. 4. Zhengzhou 郑州: Henan Remin Chubanshe 河南人民出版社, 1986.

———. *Xin Shi Lun* (新事论). Sansong Tang Quanji (三松堂全集). Zhengzhou 郑州: Henan Renmin Chubanshe 河南人民出版社, 1986.

Foucault, Michel. "The Ethics of the Concern for Self as a Practice of Freedom." In *Ethics: Subjectivity and Truth*, edited by Paul Rabinow. Essential Works of Foucault 1954–1984, 281–301. London: Penguin, 1994.

———. "Technologies of the Self." In *Ethics: Subjectivity and Truth*, edited by Paul Rabinow. Essential Works of Foucault 1954–1984, 223–51. London: Penguin, 1994.

Fung, Edmund S. K. *The Intellectual Foundations of Chinese Modernity: Cultural and Political Thought in the Republican Era*. Cambridge: Cambridge University Press, 2010.

———. "Nationalism and Modernity: The Politics of Cultural Conservatism in Republican China." *Modern Asian Studies* 43, no. 3 (2008): 777–813.

Fung, Yu-Lan. "Chinese Philosophy and a Future World Philosophy." *Philosophical Review* 57, no. 6 (November 1948): 539–49.

———. *The Spirit of Chinese Philosophy*. Translated by E. R. Hughes. London: Kegan Paul, Trench, Trubner, 1947.

Furth, Charlotte. "Culture and Politics in Modern Chinese Conservatism." In *The Limits of Change: Essays on Conservative Alternatives in Republican China*, edited by Charlotte Furth, 22–53. Cambridge, MA, and London: Harvard University Press, 1976.

———. "Intellectual Change: From the Reform Movement to the May Fourth Movement, 1895–1920." In *An Intellectual History of Modern China*, edited by Leo Ou-Fan Lee and Merle Goldman, 13–96. Cambridge: Cambridge University Press, 2002.

Gahlings, Ute. *Hermann Graf Keyserling: Ein Lebensbild*. Darmstadt: Justus von Liebig Verlag, 1996.

Gerth, H. H., and C. Wright Mills, eds. *From Max Weber: Essays in Sociology*. New York: Oxford University Press, 1946.

Ghosh, Peter. *Max Weber and the Protestant Ethic: Twin Histories*. Oxford: Oxford University Press, 2014.

Gordon, Colin. "Plato in Weimar: Weber Revisited via Foucault; Two Lectures on Legitimation and Vocation." *Economy and Society* 43, no. 3 (August 2014): 494–522.

Groot, J. J. M de. *Religion in China: Universism; A Key to the Study of Taoism and Confucianism*. New York and London: G. P. Putnam's Sons, 1912.

Guo, Wu. "The "Zhanguoce" School's Effort of Wartime Cultural Reconstruction, 1940–1942." *Journal of Modern Chinese History* 3, no. 1 (2009): 45–69.

Habermas, Jürgen. *Theorie des kommunikativen Handelns*. Vol. 1, *Handlungsrationalität und gesellschaftliche Rationalisierung*. Frankfurt am Main: Suhrkamp, 1981.

Hanafin, John J. "The 'Last Buddhist': The Philosophy of Liang Shuming." In *New Confucianism: A Critical Examination*, edited by John Makeham, 187–218. New York: Palgrave Macmillan, 2003.

Harvey, David. *Cosmopolitanism and the Geographies of Freedom*. New York: Columbia University Press, 2009.

Hayot, Eric. *Chinese Dreams: Pound, Brecht, Tel quel*. Ann Arbor: University of Michigan Press, 2003.

Heeg, Günther. "Brechts chinesische Wendungen: *Me-ti* und die Praxis kultureller Flexionen." *Brecht Yearbook* 36 (2011): 141.

Helle, Horst J. *China: Promise or Threat?* Leiden: Brill, 2017.

Herf, Jeffrey. *Reactionary Modernism: Technology, Culture, and Politics in Weimar and the Third Reich*. Cambridge: Cambridge University Press, 1984.

Hobson, John M. "Decolonizing Weber: The Eurocentrism of Weber's IR and Historical Sociology." In *Max Weber and International Relations*, edited by Richard Ned Lebow, 143–71. Cambridge: Cambridge University Press, 2017.

Huang, Su-Jen. "Max Weber's *The Religion of China*: An Interpretation." *Journal of the History of the Behavioral Sciences* 30, no. January (1994): 3–18.

Huntington, Samuel P. "The Clash of Civilizations?" *Foreign Affairs* 72, no. 3 (1993): 22–49.

Israel, Jonathan I. *Radical Enlightenment: Philosophy and the Making of Modernity 1650–1750*. New York: Oxford University Press, 2001.

Jaeggi, Rahel. *Fortschritt und Regression*. Berlin: Suhrkamp, 2023.
Jameson, Fredric. *Brecht and Method*. London and New York: Verso, 1998.
Janik, Allan. *Wittgenstein's Vienna Revisited*. New Brunswick, NJ: Transaction, 2001.
Jeans, Roger B. *Democracy and Socialism in Republican China: The Politics of Zhang Junmai (Carsun Chang), 1906–1941*. Lanham, MD: Rowman & Littlefield, 1997.
Joas, Hans. *The Creativity of Action*. Cambridge: Polity Press, 1996.
Kalberg, Stephen. "The *Spirit of Capitalism* Revisited: On the New Translation of Weber's *Protestant Ethic* (1920)." *Max Weber Studies* 2, no. 1 (2001): 41–58.
Kaufmann, Sebastian, and Andreas Urs Sommer, eds. *Nietzsche und die Konservative Revolution*. Berlin and Boston: Walter de Gruyter, 2018.
Kaven, Carsten. *Sozialer Wandel und Macht: Die theoretische Ansätze von Max Weber, Norbert Elias und Michel Foucault im Vergleich*. Marburg: Metropolis-Verlag, 2006.
Kelly, David A. "The Highest Chinadom: Nietzsche and the Chinese Mind, 1907–1989." In *Nietzsche and Asian Thought*, edited by Graham Parkes, 151–74. Chicago and London: University of Chicago Press, 1991.
Kershaw, Ian. *Hitler: Profiles in Power*. London and New York: Routledge, 2013.
Keyserling, Hermann Graf. *Das Reisetagebuch eines Philosophen*. Frankfurt am Main: Ullstein Verlag, 1990.
———. *The Travel Diary of a Philosopher*. Translated by J. Holroyd Reece. 2 vols. New York: Harcourt, Brace, 1925.
———. *Über die innere Beziehung zwischen den Kulturproblemen des Orients und des Okzidents: Eine Botschaft an die Völker des Ostens*. Jena: Verlag bei Eugen Diederich, 1913.
Klein, Steven. "Between Charisma and Domination: On Max Weber's Critique of Democracy." *Journal of Politics* 79, no. 1 (2016): 179–92.
Knopf, Jan, ed. *Brecht Handbuch: Prosa, Filme, Drehbücher*. Vol. 3. Stuttgart and Weimar: Verlag J. B. Metzler, 2002.
Krüger, Hans-Peter. "Brechts Dialektik-Konzept in 'Me-ti.'" In *Brecht und Marxismus: Dokumentation*, 203–11. Berlin: Henschelverlag Kunst und Gesellschaft, 1983.
Ku, Hung-Ming. "The Spirit of the Chinese People." *Peking Daily News*, 1915.
———. *The Story of a Chinese Oxford Movement*. Shanghai: Shanghai Mercury 1910.
Latour, Bruno. *An Inquiry into Modes of Existence: An Anthropology of the Moderns*. Cambridge, MA, and London: Harvard University Press, 2013.
Lee, Soonyi. "In Revolt Against Positivism, the Discovery of Culture: The Liang Qichao Group's Cultural Conservatism in China after the First World War." *Twentieth-Century China* 44, no. 3 (October 2019): 288–304.
Leibniz, Gottfried Wilhelm. *Writings on China*. Translated by Daniel J. Cook Jr. and Henry Rosemont. Chicago and La Salle, IL: Open Court, 1994.
Lemke, Thomas. "Max Weber, Norbert Elias und Michel Foucault über Macht und Subjektivierung." *Berliner Journal der Soziologie*, no. 1 (2001): 77–95.

Levenson, Joseph R. *Confucian China and Its Modern Fate: The Problem of Historical Significance*. 3 vols. Berkeley and Los Angeles: University of California Press, 1958–65.

———. *Revolution and Cosmopolitanism: The Western Stage and the Chinese Stages*. Berkeley and Los Angeles: University of California Press, 1971.

Li, Jinglin. "The Positive and the Negative Method and the Spheres of Living: Some Thoughts on Feng Youlan's Philosophical Method." *Social Sciences in China 32*, no. 4 (November 2011): 59–77.

Liang, Qichao (梁启超). *Ou You Xin Ying Lu* (欧游心影录). Beijing: Shang Wu Yin Shu Guan, 2014.

Liang, Shuming (梁漱溟). *Dong Xi Wenhua Ji Qi Zhexue* (东西文化及其哲学) (*Eastern and Western Cultures and Their Philosophies*). Shanghai: Ren Ming Chu Ban She (人民出版社, People's Press), 2015.

———. *Wo Sheng You Ya Yuan Wu Jin: Liang Shuming Zishu Wenlu* (我生有涯愿无尽：梁漱溟自述文录). Shanghai: Shanghai Renmin Chubanshe, 2013.

Liang, Shuming (梁漱溟). "Xiangcun Jianshe Lilun (乡村建设理论)." In *Liang Shuming Quanji* (梁漱溟全集), 141–573. Jinan 济南 Shandong Renmin Chubanshe 山东人民出版社, 1990.

Liebersohn, Harry. *Aristocratic Encounters: European Travelers and North American Indians*. Cambridge: Cambridge University Press, 1998.

Lin, Xiaoqing Diana. *Feng Youlan and Twentieth-Century China: An Intellectual Biography*. Leiden and Boston: Brill, 2016.

Liu, Lydia H. *The Clash of Empires: The Invention of China in Modern World Making*. Cambridge, MA, and London: Harvard University Press, 2004.

———. *Translingual Practice: Literature, National Culture, and Translated Modernity — China 1900–1937*. Stanford, Calif.: Stanford University Press, 1995.

Ma, Yong (马勇). *Liang Shuming Pingzhuan* (梁漱溟评传). Hefei: Anhui Renmin Chubanshe 1992.

Makeham, John. "The Retrospective Creation of New Confucianism." In *New Confucianism: A Critical Examination*, edited by John Makeham, 25–53. New York: Palgrave Macmillan, 2003.

Manjapra, Kris. *Age of Enlightenment: German and Indian Intellectuals across Europe*. Cambridge, MA, and London: Harvard University Press, 2014.

Mannix, William Francis, ed. *Memoirs of Li Hung Chang*. Boston and New York: Houghton Mifflin, 1913.

Marcuse, Herbert. "Industrialization and Capitalism." *New Left Review* 30, no. March/April (1965): 3–17.

Marx, Karl. *Capital: A Critique of Political Economy*. Vol. 1. London: Penguin, 1976.

Matthewson, Amy. "Cui Malo? Cui Bono? Reflections on a Literary Forgery: The Case of The Memoirs of Li Hung Chang." *Partial Answers: Journal of Literature and the History of Ideas* 19, no. 1 January (2021): 19–34.

Maverick, Lewis A. *China: A Model for Europe*. San Antonio, TX: Paul Anderson, 1946.

Meynard, Thierry. *The Religious Philosophy of Liang Shuming: The Hidden Buddhist*. Leiden and Boston: Brill, 2011.

Mittenzwei, Werner. "Nachwort: Der Dialektiker Brecht oder die Kunst "Me-ti" zu lesen." In *Brecht Prosa IV*, edited by Werner Mittenzwei, 182–234. Berlin und Weimar: Aufbau Verlag, 1975.

Mizoguchi, Yūzō,/ Viren Murthy. "China as Method." *Inter-Asia Cultural Studies* 17, no. 4 (2007): 513–18.

Mohler, Armin. *Die Konservative Revolution in Deutschland 1918–1932: Ein Handbuch*. Darmstadt: Wissenschaftliche Buchgesellschaft, 1972.

Mohler, Armin, and Karlheinz Weissmann. *Die Konservative Revolution in Deutschland 1918–1932. Ein Handbuch*. 6th ed. Graz: Ares Verlag, 2005.

Möller, Hans-Georg. *Die philosophischste Philosophie: Feng Youlans Neue Metaphysik*. Wiesbaden: Harrassowitz Verlag, 2000.

Molloy, Stephen. "Max Weber and the Religions of China: Any Way out of the Maze?" *British Journal of Sociology* 31, no. 3, special issue: *Aspects of Weberian Scholarship* (1980): 377–400.

Mommsen, Wolfgang J. *Max Weber and German Politics 1890–1920*. Translated by Michael S. Steinberg. Chicago and London: University of Chicago Press, 1984.

———. "Max Weber's Political Sociology and His Philosophy of World History." *International Social Science Journal* 17, no. 1 (1965): 23–45.

Morris, Michael, and Julian Dodd. "Mysticism and Nonsense in the *Tractatus*." *European Journal of Philosophy* 17, no. 2 (2009): 247–76.

Moyn, Samuel, and Andrew Sartori. "Approaches to Global Intellectual History." In *Global Intellectual History*, edited by Samuel Moyn and Andrew Sartori, 3–30. New York: Columbia University Press, 2013.

MoZi. *Mê Ti, des Sozialethikers und seiner Schüler philosophische Werke*. Translated by Alfred Forke. Berlin: Vereinigung wissenschaftlicher Verleger, 1922, http://worldcat.org.

———. *The Mozi: A Complete Translation*. Edited and Translated by Ian Johnston. New York: Columbia University Press, 2010.

Mufti, Aamir R. *Forget English! Orientalisms and World Literatures*. Cambridge, MA: Harvard University Press, 2016.

Müller, Hans-Peter, and Steffen Sigmund, eds. *Max Weber-Handbuch: Leben-Werk-Wirkung*. Stuttgart: J. B. Metzler Verlag, 2020.

Müller, Klaus-Detlef. "Brechts *M-ti* und die Auseinandersetzung mit dem Lehrer Karl Korsch." *Brecht-Jahrbuch* (1977): 9–29.

Murthy, Viren. *Pan-Asianism and the Legacy of the Chinese Revolution: An Intellectual*

History of Pan-Asianist Discourse in the Twentieth Century. Chicago: University of Chicago Press, 2023.

———. *The Politics of Time in China and Japan: Back to the Future*. London: Routledge, 2022.

Najita, Tetsuo. *Visions of Virtue in Tokugawa Japan: The Kaitokudō Merchant Academy of Osaka*. Chicago: University of Chicago Press, 1987.

Nelson, Eric S. *Chinese and Buddhist Philosophy in Early Twentieth-Century German Thought*. London: Bloomsbury Academic, 2017.

Neuenhaus, Petra. *Max Weber und Michel Foucault: Über Macht und Herrschaft in der Moderne*. Pfaffenweiler: Centaurus-Verlagsgesellschaft, 1993.

Nussbaum, Martha. *Not for Profit: Why Democracy Needs the Humanities*. Princeton: Princeton University Press, 2010.

Oakes, Guy. "Weber and the Southwest German School: The Genesis of the Concept of the Historical Individual." In *Max Weber and His Contemporaries*, edited by Wolfgang J. Mommsen and Jürgen Osterhammel, 434–46. London: German Historical Institute, 1987.

O'Neill, Daniel I. *Edmund Burke and the Conservative Logic of Empire*. Oakland: University of California Press, 2016.

O'Neill, John. "The Disciplinary Society: From Weber to Foucault." *British Journal of Sociology* 37, no. 1 (March 1986): 42–60.

Oi, Jean C., and Steven M. Goldstein, eds. *Zouping Revisited: Adaptive Governance in a Chinese County*. Stanford: Stanford University Press, 2018.

Owen, David. *Maturity and Modernity: Nietzsche, Weber, Foucault and the Ambivalence of Reason*. London: Routledge, 1994.

Parkes, Graham, ed. *Heidegger and Asian Thought*. Honolulu: University of Hawai'i Press, 1987.

Parsons, Talcott. *The Structure of Social Action: A Study in Social Theory with Special Reference to a Group of Recent European Writers*. New York: Free Press, 1949.

Peng, Chunling (彭春凌). *Ruxue Zhuanxing Yu Wenhua Xinming: Yi Kang Youwei, Zhang Taiyan Wei Zhongxin (1898-1927)* (儒学转型与文化新命。以康有为、章太炎为中心 (1898-1927)). Beijing: Peking University Press, 2014.

Peng, Hsiao-yen, and Isabelle Rabut Peng, eds. *Modern China and the West: Translation and Cultural Mediation*. Leiden and Boston: Brill, 2014.

Pfister, Lauren F. "The Different Faces of Contemporary Religious Confucianism: An Account of the Diverse Approaches of some Major Twentieth-Century Chinese Confucian Scholars." *Journal of Chinese Philosophy* 22, no. 2 (1995): 12–18.

———. "A Modern Chinese Philosophy Built Upon Critically Received Traditions: Feng Youlan's New Principle-Centered Learning and the Question of Its Relationship to Contemporary New Ruist ("Confucian") Philosophies." In *New Confucianism:*

A Critical Examination, edited by John Makeham, 165–84. New York: Palgrave Macmillan, 2003.

Plato. *The Republic*. London: Penguin, 2007.

Pomeranz, Kenneth. *The Great Divergence: China, Europe, and the Making of the Modern World Economy*. Princeton and Oxford: Princeton University Press, 2000.

Purdy, Daniel Leonhard. *Chinese Sympathies: Media, Missionaries, and World Literature from Marco Polo to Goethe*. Ithaca, NY: Cornell University Press, 2021.

Riesebrodt, Martin. "Charisma in Max Weber's Sociology of Religion." *Religion* 29 (1999): 1–14.

Ringer, Fritz. *Max Weber's Methodology: The Unification of the Cultural and Social Sciences*. Cambridge, MA: Harvard University Press, 1997.

Robbins, Bruce. "Cosmopolitanism: New and Newer." *boundary 2* 34, no. 3 (2007): 47–60.

———. *Perpetual War: Cosmopolitanism from the Viewpoint of Violence*. Durham, NC, and London: Duke University Press, 2012.

Pheng Cheah, and Bruce Robbins, eds. *Cosmopolitics: Thinking and Feeling beyond the Nation*. Minneapolitis and London: University of Minnesota Press, 1998.

Russell, Bertrand. *The Problem of China*. New York: Century, 1922.

Rutgers, Mark R., and Petra Schreurs. "Weber's Neo-Kantian Roots." *Administrative Theory & Praxis* 26, no. 1 (March 2004): 103–11.

Sabbagh, Gabriel. "Quesnay's Thought and Influence through Two Related Texts, *Droit naturel* and *Despotisme de la Chine*, and Their Editions." *History of European Ideas* 46, no. 2 (2020): 131–56.

Said, Edward W. *Orientalism*. New York: Vintage, 1979.

Sartori, Andrew. *Bengal in Global Concept History: Culturalism in the Age of Capital*. Chicago and London: University of Chicago Press, 2008.

Saussy, Haun. *Translation as Citation: Zhuangzi Inside Out*. Oxford: Oxford University Press, 2017.

Schiffrin, Harold Z. *Sun Yat-sen and the Origins of the Chinese Revolution*. Berkeley: University of California Press, 1970.

Schluchter, Wolfgang, ed. *Max Weber: Wirtschaft und Gesellschaft; Entstehungsgeschichte und Dokumente*. Edited by Horst Baier et al. 25 vols. Max Weber Gesamtausgabe Tübingen: J. C. B. Mohr (Paul Siebeck), 2009.

———. "Max Weber's Sociology of Religion: A Project in Comparison and Developmental History." Translated by Jeremiah Riemer. In *Max Weber's Economic Ethic of the World Religions: An Analysis*, edited by Thomas Ertman, 39–60. Cambridge: Cambridge University Press, 2017.

———, ed. *Max Webers Studie über Konfuzianismus und Taoismus: Interpretation und Kritik*. Frankfurt am Main: Suhrkamp, 1983.

———. *Rationalism, Religion, and Domination: A Weberian Perspective*. Translated by Neil Solomon. Berkeley and Los Angeles: University of California Press, 1989.

———. *Religion und Lebensführung: Studien zu Max Webers Religions- und Herrschaftssoziologie*. Vol. 2. Frankfurt am Main: Suhrkamp, 1988.

Schwartz, Benjamin I. "Notes on Conservatism in General and in China in Particular." In *The Limits of Change: Essays on Conservative Alternatives in Republican China*, edited by Charlotte Furth, 3–21. Cambridge, MA, and London: Harvard University Press, 1976.

Shaw, Tamsin. *Nietzsche's Political Skepticism*. Princeton: Princeton University Press, 2007.

Smith, David Norman. "Faith, Reason, and Charisma: Rudolf Sohm, Max Weber, and the Theology of Grace." *Sociological Inquiry* 68, no. 1 (1998): 32–60.

Song, Yun-Yeop. *Bertolt Brecht und die chinesische Philosophie*. Bonn: Bouvier, 1978.

Spivak, Gayatri Chakravorty. "Can the Subaltern Speak?" In *Marxism and the Interpretation of Culture*, edited by Cary Nelson and Lawrence Grossberg, 271–313. Urbana: University of Illinois Press, 1988.

Sprenkel, Otto B. van der. "Max Weber on China." *History and Theory* 3, no. 3 (1964): 348–70.

Stammen, Theo. "'Me-ti'—Große Methode—Große Ordnung." In *Bertolt Brecht—Aspekte seines Werkes, Spuren seiner Wirkung*, edited by Helmut Koopmann and Theo Stammen, 147–66. Munich: Verlag Ernst Vögel, 1994.

Steinmetz, George. *The Devil's Handwriting: Precoloniality and the German Colonial State in Qingdao, Samoa, and Southwest Africa*. Chicago and London: University of Chicago Press, 2007.

Stoll, Christian. "Religiöser Universalismus im Zeitalter der Nation: Friedrich von Hügel und die deutsche Geisteswelt (Eucken, Troeltsch, Naumann)." *Journal for the History of Modern Theology/Zeitschrift für Neuere Theologiegeschichte* 28, no. 2 (2021): 246–98.

Su, Guoxun (苏国勋). *Lixinghua Jiqi Xianzhi: Weibo Sixiang Yinlun (Rationalization and Its Limits: An Introduction to Weber's Thinking;* 理性化及其限制：韦伯思想引论). Shanghai: Shanghai Renmin Chubanshe, 1988.

———. "Makesi weibo: Jiyu zhongguo yujing de zai yangjiu (马克斯·韦伯：基于中国语境的再研究) (Max Weber: New Studies on the Basis of the Chinese Context)." *Society* (社会) 5, no. 27 (2007): 1–25.

Szakolczai, Arpád. *Max Weber and Michel Foucault: Parallel Life-Works*. London: Routledge, 1998.

Tatlow, Antony, ed. *Bertolt Brecht's Me-ti: Book of Interventions in the Flow of Things*. London: Bloomsbury, 2016.

Tenbruck, Friedrich H. "Max Weber and Eduard Meyer." In *Max Weber and His Contemporaries*, edited by Wolfgang J. Mommsen and Jürgen Osterhammel, 234–67. London: German Historical Insitutute, 1987.

Tsai, Po-Fang. "The Introduction and Reception of Max Weber's Sociology in Taiwan and China." *Journal of Sociology* 52, no. 1 (2016): 118–33.

Tsui, Brian. "The Mutations of Pan-Asianism: Zhang Junmai's Cold War." *Twentieth-Century China* 42, no. 2 (May 2017): 176–97.

Tze-ki Hon, and Kristin Stapleton, eds. *Confucianism for the Contemporary World: Global Order, Political Plurality, and Social Action*. Albany: State University of New York Press, 2018.

Tu, Wei-ming, ed. *The Triad Chord: Confucian Ethics, Industrial East Asia and Max Weber*. Singapore: Institute of East Asian Philosophies, 1991.

Utz, Richard. "Charisma." In *Max Weber-Handbuch: Leben-Werk-Wirkung*, edited by Hans-Peter Müller and Steffen Sigmund, 54–58. Stuttgart: J. B. Metzler Verlag, 2020.

Wagner, Gerhard, and Claudius Härpfer. "Neo-Kantianism and the Social Sciences: From Rickert to Weber." In *New Approaches to Neo-Kantianism*, edited by Nicolas de Warren and Andrea Staiti, 171–85. Cambridge: Cambridge University Press, 2015.

Waldron, Jeremy. "Minority Cultures and the Cosmopolitan Alternative." *University of Michigan Journal of Law Reform* 25 (1992): 751–92.

———. "What Is Cosmopolitanism?" *Journal of Political Philosophy* 8, no. 2 (1999): 227–43.

Wang, Ban. *China in the World: Culture, Politics, and World Vision*. Durham, NC, and London: Duke University Press, 2022.

———, ed. *Chinese Visions of World Order: Tianxia, Culture, and World Politics*. Durham, NC, and London: Duke University Press, 2017.

Wang, Donglin (汪东林). *Liang Shuming yu Mao Zedong* (梁漱溟与毛泽东) Changchun 长春: Jilin Renmin Chubanshe 吉林人民出版社, 1989.

———. *Liang Shuming Wenda Lu* (梁漱溟问答录). Hong Kong: Sanlian Shudian, 1988.

Wang, Hui (汪晖). "Weber and the Question of Chinese Modernity." Translated by Theodore Huters. In *The Politics of Imagining Asia*, 264–306. Cambridge, MA: Harvard University Press, 2011.

———. *Xiandai Zhongguo Sixiang de Xingqi* (现代中国思想的兴起) (*Rise of Modern Chinese Thought*). 4 vols. Beijing: Sanlian, 2015.

Wang, Jessica Ching-Sze. *John Dewey in China: To Teach and To Learn*. Albany: State University of New York Press, 2007.

Wang, Mei-Ling Luzia. *Chinesische Elemente in Bertolt Brechts "Me-ti. Buch der Wendungen."* Frankfurt am Main: Peter Lang, 1990.

Wang, Pu. *The Translatability of Revolution: Guo Muruo and Twentieth-Century Chinese Culture*. Cambridge, MA: Harvard University Asia Center, 2018.

Weber, Max. *Die protestantische Ethik und der Geist des Kapitalismus*. Edited by Dirk Kaesler. Munich: C. H. Beck, 2004.

———. *Die Wirtschaftsethik der Weltreligionen: Konfuzianismus und Taoismus*. Studienausgabe der Max Weber-Gesamtausgabe. Tübingen: J. C. B. Mohr (Paul Siebeck), 1991.

———. "The Profession and Vocation of Politics." In *Weber: Political Writings*, edited by Peter Lassman and Ronald Speirs, 309–69. Cambridge: Cambridge University Press, 1994.

———. *The Protestant Ethic and the "Spirit" of Capitalism and Other Writings*. Translated by Peter Baehr and Gordon C. Wells. New York and London: Penguin, 2002.

———. *The Protestant Ethic and the Spirit of Capitalism*. Translated by Stephen Kalberg. New York and Oxford: Oxford University Press, 2011.

———. *The Religion of China: Confucianism and Taoism*. Edited and Translated by Hans H. Gerth. New York: Free Press, 1951.

———. *The Religion of India: The Sociology of Hinduism and Buddhism*. Edited and Translated by Hans Gerth and Don Martindale. Glencoe, IL: Free Press, 1958.

———. "Vorbemerkung." In *Gesammelte Aufsätze zur Religionssoziologie*, 1–16. Tübingen: Verlag von J. C. B. Mohr, 1920.

———. *Wirtschaft und Gesellschaft: Die Wirtschaft und die gesellschaftlichen Ordnungen und Mächte; Nachlaß*. Max Weber Gesamtausgabe. Tübingen: J. C. B. Mohr (Paul Siebeck), 2005.

———. *Wissenschaft als Beruf/Politik als Beruf*. Edited by M. Rainer Lepsius Horst Baier, Wolfgang J. Mommsen, Wolfgang Schluchter, and Johannes Winckelmann. Max Weber Gesamtausgabe. 17 vols. Tübingen: J. C. B. Mohr (Paul Siebeck), 1992.

Wen, Yuan-Ning. "Ku Hung-Ming." *T'ien Hsia Monthly* IV, no. 4 (1937): 386–90.

Wessendorf, Markus. "Brecht's Materialist Ethics between Confucianism and Mohism." *Philosophy East & West* 66, no. 1 (January 2016): 122–45.

Wilhelm, Richard. *Die Seele Chinas*. Berlin: Verlag von Reimar Hobbing, 1926.

Wippermann, Dorothea. *Richard Wilhelm: Der Sinologe und seine Kulturmission in China und Frankfurt*. Frankfurt am Main: Societäts-Verlag, 2020.

Wittgenstein, Ludwig. *Tractatus Logico-Philosophicus*. Translated by D. F. Pears and B. F. McGuinness. London: Routledge & Kegan Paul, 1961.

———. *Tractatus logico-philosophicus*. Frankfurt am Main: Suhrkamp, 2006.

Wong, R. Bin. "The Chinese State, Social Order and Economic Change." In *Max Weber's Economic Ethic of the World Religions: An Analysis*, edited by Thomas Ertman, 109–36. Cambridge: Cambridge University Press, 2017.

Yu, Ying-shih (余英时). "Zhongguo jinshi zongjiao lunli yu shangren jingshen (中国近世宗教伦理与商人精神)." In *Rujia lunli yu shangren jingshen* (儒家伦理与商人精神), 234–357. Guilin, China: Guangxi Shifan Daxue Chubanshe, 2004.

Zhang, Chunjie. "Anna Seghers's Ideological Melodrama, Qian Zhongshu's Cosmopolitan Satire, or On Comparison." In *Composing Modernist Connections*, edited by Chunjie Zhang, 32–49. London: Routledge, 2019.

———. "From Sinophilia to Sinophobia: China, History, and Recognition." *Colloquia Germanica* 41, no. 2 (2008): 97–110.

———. "Garden Empire or the Sublime Politics of the Chinese-Gothic Style." *Goethe Yearbook* 25 (2018): 77–96.

Zhang, Junmai (张君劢). "A Manifesto for a Re-appraisal of Sinology and Reconstruction of Chinese Culture". In *The Development of Neo-Confucian Thought*, 455–84. New York: Bookman Associates, 1958.

———. "Wo Cong Shehuikexue Tiaodao Zhexue Zhi Jingguo (我从社会科学跳到哲学之经过)." In *Zhongguo Jindai Sixiangjia Wenku: Zhang Junmai Juan (中国近代思想家文库：张君劢卷)*, edited by Hekai Weng (翁贺凯), 363–70. Beijing: Zhongguo Renmin Daxue Chubanshe 中国人民大学出版社, 2014.

———. "Woyikeng Jingshen Shenghuo Zhexue Dagai (倭伊铿精神生活哲学大概)." In *Zhang Junmai Juan (张君劢卷)*, edited by Hekai Weng (翁贺凯), 48–62. Beijing: Zhongguo Renmin Daxue Chubanshe, 2014.

———. "Xueshu Fangfa Shang Zhi Guanjian (学术方法上之管见)." In *Zhang Junmai Juan (张君劢卷)*, edited by Hekai Weng (翁贺凯). Beijing: Zhongguo Renmin Daxue Chubanshe, 2014.

———. "Zailun Rensheng Guan yu Kexue bing Da Ding Zaijun (再论人生观与科学并答丁在君)." In *Kexue yu Rensheng Guan (科学与人生观)*, 59–129. Hefei 合肥: Huangshan Shushe 黄山书社, 2008.

———. "Zhi Lin Zaipin Xuezhang Hangao Woshi Wutan Ji Deguo Zhexue Xixiang Yaolue 1920 (致林宰平学长函告倭氏晤谈及德国哲学思想要略 1920)." In *Zhang Junmai Juan (张君劢卷)*, edited by Hekai Weng (翁贺凯), 45–47. Beijing: Zhongguo Renmin Daxue Chubanshe, 2014.

———. *Mingri zhi Zhongguo Wenhua (明日之中国文化)*. Changsha, Hunan: Yuelu Shushe 岳麓书社, 2011.

Zhang, Junmai et al. *Kexue yu Rensheng Guan (科学与人生观)*. Hefei 合肥: Huangshan Shushe 黄山书社, 2008.

Zhao, Dingxin. "Max Weber and Patterns of Chinese History." In *Max Weber's Economic Ethic of the World Religions: An Analysis*, edited by Thomas Ertman, 137–71. Cambridge: Cambridge University Press, 2017.

Zheng, Dahua (郑大华). *Liang Shuming Zhuan (梁漱溟传)*. Beijing: Renmin Chubanshe 人民出版社, 2001.

———. *Zhang Junmai Xueshu Sixiang Pingzhuan (张君劢学术思想评传)*. Beijing: Beijing Tushuguan Chubanshe 北京图书馆出版社, 1999.

Zimmerman, Andrew. "Decolonizing Weber." *Postcolonial Studies* 9, no. 1 (2006): 53–79.

INDEX

Abe, Yoshishige, 92, 105
Abel, Theodore, 65
Adorno, Theodor W., 12
Alitto, Guy, 115–16
ancient Greece, 11, 22, 62–63, 69, 97, 104, 176
Appiah, Kwame Anthony, 18
Aristotle, 148, 156
Atatürk, Kemal, 65

Babeuf, François-Noël, 183
Bachmann, Ingeborg, 159
Benhabib, Seyla, 17
Bergson, Henri, 4, 29, 82, 93, 95, 108, 109, 128; *élan vital*, 93
Berlau, Ruth, 180
Beruf, 56, 75, 76
Bildung, 7, 61
Bismarck, Otto von, 46, 91, 94
Bodde, Derk, 149, 150, 166,
Brecht, Bertolt, 3, 8, 24, 105, 176, 177–95; and *Begriff*, 189; dialect of transience, 192; *The Good Person of Szechwan (Der gute Mensch von Sezuan)*, 8, 178; *Der kaukasische Kreidekreis (The Caucasian Chalk Circle)*, 188; *Me-ti: Buch der Wendungen (Me-ti:Book of Transformation and Usage)*, 24, 177–92; and Mohism, 179–84; *The Principle of Inequality in the Great Method (Der Ungleichheitssatz in der großen Methode)*, 188
Buber, Martin, 3
Buddha, 160–61, 164, 167
Buddhism, 4, 5, 8, 12, 23, 48, 53, 71, 99–100, 118, 120–22, 125, 127, 144, 148, 154, 157–65, 169, 193, 215n80; idea of emptiness, 162; metaphysics, 161–65; practice of life, 120; sutras, 160, 228n20. *See also* Zen Buddhism

Cai Yuanpei, 114, 118
capitalism, 2, 6, 7, 16, 27, 46–47, 51–59, 61–62, 70, 80, 102, 117, 123, 128, 148, 177; global capitalism, 12–14, 64, 102, 195; industrial capitalism, 22, 46, 51, 52, 56, 58; Western capitalism, 14, 46, 52, 72
care of the self, 7, 22, 46–48, 60, 61–64, 81; Confucian, 48, 52, 64, 81
Carnap, Rudolf, 159
Castro, Fidel, 65
Centi, Beatrice, 70
Chakrabarty, Dipesh, 11–12, 14; *Provincializing Europe*, 11–12
charisma, 1, 22, 46–48, 59, 64–68, 68–74, 150, 217–18n110, 218n111; as vocation 75–81
Chen Duxiu, 4, 118, 119; *Our Final Enlightenment*, 121
Chiang Kai-shek, 119, 130, 175
Chikusui, Kaneko, 121
China Democratic League, 86, 119
Chinese Civil War, 86, 119, 145
Chinese Communist Party, 86
Chinese literati, 1, 33, 52, 59, 64
Chinese Oxford Movement, 38–43
Chinese Revolution, 19, 25, 42, 118, 171–72, 193
Chinese Revolution (1911), 1, 42, 118, 119, 171, 193
Christianity, 33, 36, 41, 55, 68, 88, 89, 110, 183
Cold War, 17, 46, 49, 55
colonialism: British, 11, 26, 35; European, 11, 12, 44, 109; Western, 42
Comte, Auguste, 91
Confucianism, 1–9, 12, 20–24, 25, 33, 35–37, 39–45, 46–52, 58–68, 73, 75, 78, 80–84, 87–90, 96, 98–104, 109, 112–13, 115–30, 134–36, 141–43, 144, 148–52, 154, 156,

253

Confucianism (continued)
  158, 168–69, 174, 178, 181–83, 188, 193, 198, 211n16, 222n11, 233n44; ethics of, 1, 2, 23, 30, 36, 55, 60, 72, 74, 75, 78, 81, 83, 88, 89, 97, 98, 104, 109, 113, 127, 131, 149, 172, 174; idealism of, 114, 120, 123; and metaphysics, 21, 123; as a new cosmopolitanism, 1, 9, 20, 21–24, 25–29, 37, 38, 42–45; philosophy of life, 123, 128–29, 134
Confucian literati, 22, 33, 48, 59, 60, 64, 66, 70, 73, 75–77, 79, 150
Confucian rationalism, 47, 60, 61, 88, 137–38, 158, 163
Confucius, 12, 24, 33, 38, 43–44, 73, 75, 90, 97–100, 106, 112, 120, 123–29, 146, 165, 179–82; as a deity, 90; philosophy of life, 99, 102; as a sage, 146, 170; as a teacher, 147–50
Conrad, Sebastian, 11, 18
conservatism, 27–28, 45, 117, 193–95
Cultural Revolution, 119, 202n6

Darwin, Charles, 4, 91, 107–8; *On the Origin of Species*, 107–8; theory of evolution, 91
David, Alexandra, 183
Defoe, Daniel, *The Life and Adventures of Robinson Crusoe*, 57
Derman, Joshua, 65
Dewey, John, 121, 128, 148–50, 153, 172, 174
Ding Ling, 105
Ding Wenjiang, 23, 84, 107
Döblin, Alfred, 3, 195
Dostoevsky, Fyodor, 80
Drochon, Hugo, 67
Duan Qirui, 85

Eijkman, Peter H., 105; *L'internationalisme scientifique*, 105
élan vital, 93
Enlightenment (European), 7, 15, 18, 20, 27, 54, 55, 102
Eucken, Rudolf, 3, 4, 14, 22–23, 82–85, 91–109, 128, 164, 195; and *Geistesleben*, 93; and Kant, 100; metaphysics, 94, 103; Nobel Prize for literature, 92; *Die Lebensanschauungen der großen Denker*, 93, 105; and *Lebensanschauung*, 105–6; and philosophy of life, 105–9; *The Problem of Human Life*, 93, 98; *The Struggle for a Spiritual Content of Life*, 95
Eurocentrism, 7, 47, 48, 50

Faber, Ernst, 183
Fang Shouchu, 182–83
Feng Youlan (Fung Yu-lan), 3, 20, 23, 115, 143, 144–76, 182; *Chinese Philosophy and a Future World Philosophy*, 153–54, 164; *A Comparative Study of Life Ideals*, 148; conservatism, 171–72, 174; cosmopolitanism, 169; metaphysics, 144–69; negative method, 169; New Rationalism, 23, 115, 147, 150–53, 158, 160, 165, 168–69; *Short History of Chinese Philosophy*, 143, 149, 165; *The Way of Decrease and Increase with Interpretations and Illustrations from the Philosophies of the East and the West*, 148; and world philosophy, 143, 144–46, 157–58, 166, 169, 174–75; *Xin Lixue*, 151, 152; *Xin Shi Lun*, 169; *Xin Yuandao*, 152
Fichte, Johann Gottlieb, 31, 98, 148
Forke, Alfred, 24, 179–84, 187, 192
Foucault, Michel, 22, 48, 52, 62–64, 195; and care of the self, 22, 62
Fourier, Charles, 131
Frankfurt School, 46
Franklin, Benjamin, 53, 55
Frege, Gottlob, 159
French Revolution, 6, 35, 77
Freud, Sigmund, 62
Furth, Charlotte, 122, 129, 194

Galileo Galilei, 107
Garai, Kinzo, 135–36
German imperialism, 191
German Revolution, 191
Gladstone, William Ewart, 91
global intellectual history, 5–9, 9–12, 14, 16, 45, 47, 106, 158, 192–94
Goethe, Johann Wolfgang, 38, 39, 57, 91
Goldsmith, Oliver, *The Citizen of the World*, 8
Gosh, Peter, 68, 70–71
Gu Hongming (Ku Hung-ming), 2–3, 21–45, 118; critique of Western imperialism, 27, 38; *The Spirit of the Chinese People*, 38; *The Story of a Chinese Oxford Movement: An Essay in Political and Social Criticism in China*, 26, 29, 39, 40, 43

Habermas, Jürgen, 17, 47
Hahn, Hans, 159
Han dynasty, 134
Hanafin, John, 121

INDEX 255

Harvey, David, 17
Hayot, Eric, 178
Heeg, Günther, 178
Hegel, Georg Wilhelm Friedrich, 31, 35, 91, 95, 98, 107, 180, 188–89; dialectics, 148–49, 177, 189; historicism, 9, 13; *Science of Logic (Wissenschaft der Logik)*, 189
Heidegger, Martin, 3, 12, 159
Herder, Johann Gottfried, 13, 35
Hesse, Hermann, 3, 29, 195, 215n80
Hitler, Adolf, 65, 66, 180
Hofmannsthal, Hugo von, 28
Horkheimer, Max, *Dialectic of Enlightenment*, 13
Hundred Day's Reform, 41, 42, 84, 139
Hu Shi, 4, 114, 115, 118, 119, 142, 145, 149, 182; *Outline of the History of Chinese Philosophy*, 149
Huxley, Thomas Henry, 4; *Evolution and Ethics*, 4–5

I ching, 4, 122
Industrial Revolution, 110, 123
Irrationalism, 7, 48, 52, 53, 56, 57, 61
Israel, Jonathan 6; *Radical Enlightenment: Philosophy and the Making of Modernity, 1650–1750*, 6

Jameson, Fredric, 177
Jiang Baili, 119
Johnson, Uwe, 184
Johnston, Ian, 180–81
Jost, Roland, 178
Jung, Carl Gustav, 3, 29
Juzhi, 161

Kafka, Franz, 3, 195
Kang Yu-wei, 85
Kant, Immanuel, 5, 17–18, 23, 27, 30, 31, 70, 88, 91, 95, 98, 100–4, 126, 156, 159, 169, 204n51; and cosmopolitanism, 5, 7, 17–18; *Idea for a Universal History with a Cosmopolitan Purpose (Idee zu einer allgemeinen Geschichte in weltbürgerlicher Absicht)*, 17; ideal of Enlightenment, 126, 167; metaphysics, 70, 88, 123, 167; noumenon, 156–57, 161, 165, 168; *Perpetual Peace: A Philosophical Sketch (Zum ewigen Frieden: Ein philosophischer Entwurf, 1796)*, 17; philosophy of life, 98

Kershaw, Ian, 66
Keyserling, Hermann Graf von, 1–3, 7, 20, 21, 25–38, 44–45, 195; and conservatism, 35; *Travel Diary of a Philosopher (Das Reisetagebuch eines Philosophen)* 1, 25, 29, 38
Kleist, Heinrich von, 80; *Michael Kohlhaas*, 80
Knopf, Jan, 184, 189, 191
Knox, George William, 121; *The Spirit of the Orient*, 121
Korsch, Karl, 180, 184
Kraft, Victor, 159
Krüger, Hans-Peter, 177
Kuan-Hsing Chen, 19

Laozi, 75, 99, 106, 149
Lask, Emil, 69
Latour, Bruno, 6, 10–11, 14, 15–17; beings of passionate interest, 14, 15–17; *An Inquiry into Modes of Existence: An Anthropology of the Moderns*, 15
Lebensanschauung, 105–6
Lebensführung, 47, 51, 52, 64, 74
Lebensphilosophie, 29, 91, 226n80
Legge, James, 38
Leibniz, Gottfried Wilhelm, 33, 102
Lenin, 177, 180, 185, 188
Levenson, Joseph, *Confucian China and Its Modern Fate*, 9
Liang Chi-chao, 85
Liang Qichao, 20–21, 58, 82, 84–85, 92, 105, 109–13, 115, 137, 151, 164, 182
Liang Shuming, 20, 23, 113, 114–43; and Buddhism, 120; and conservatism, 116; and cosmopolitanism, 130; *Eastern and Western Cultures*, 119–22, 130, 131, 136; and New Confucianism 120; philosophy of life, 122–23, 128–29; and rural school, 138–40; *Theory of Rural Construction*, 131
Li Dazhao, 4; *The Fundamental Difference between Eastern and Western Civilizations*, 121
Li Hongzhang, 77
Li Hung Chang, 76–77
Lin Zaipin, 91
Liu Boming, 119
Liu, Lydia H., 4, 43
Locke, John, 32, 85; *Two Treatises of Government*, 85
Loewenstein, Karl, 65
Lu Xiangshan, 100

Lu Xun, 2, 6, 105, 115
Lukács, Georg, 14
Luther, Martin, 56, 80

Mach, Ernst, 159
Mann, Thomas, 29, 195
Mao Zedong, 65, 115–17, 119, 121, 130–31
Marcuse, Herbert, 46
Martiis, Cognetti de, 183
Marx, Karl, 4, 12, 13, 54–55, 57, 107, 172, 177, 180, 185; *Capital*, 54; *The Communist Manifesto*, 148; dialectic of capitalism, 177
Marxism, 10, 24, 27, 55, 177–79, 180, 184, 191
May Fourth Movement, 3, 119
Mazu Daoyi, 160, 162
Mencius, 31, 99, 102, 106, 165, 170; as the "Second Sage," 99
Mill, John Stuart, *On Liberty*, 5
Ming dynasty, 99, 151, 152, 154
Mingyan, 156
Mittenzwei, Werner, 184
Mizoguchi, Yūzō, 19–20
Mo Zi (Master Mo), 126, 179–80, 182–83, 185–87
Mohism, 4, 5, 24, 99, 126, 176, 177–84, 187–89, 191–92, 235n5; dialectics of, 189
Möller, Hans-Georg, 165
Mommsen, Wolfgang J., 46, 69
monarchism, 25–28, 31, 35, 37
Montesquieu, *The Spirit of Law*, 5
Mou Zongsan, 4, 86
Moyn, Samuel, 9–12
Mozi, 24, 106, 148, 179, 182, 191–92
Mufti, Aamir R., 14; *Forget English!*, 14
Mussolini, Benito, 65

Najita, Tetsuo, 53–54
Nazi party, 65; ideology, 27
neo-Confucianism, 48, 53, 88, 97, 99–100, 134, 144, 147, 148, 152, 153, 158, 233n44
neo-Kantianism, 66, 67, 68–70, 73, 150
Neurath, Otto, 159
New Confucianism, 4, 21, 84, 86–87, 106, 115, 117, 120–21, 129, 194, 202n13
New Culture Movement, 2, 3, 105–6, 111, 117–21, 129, 131, 134, 202n6
New Rationalism, 160, 165, 168
Nietzsche, Friedrich 4, 62, 66–67, 68–69, 128, 202n6; *Beyond Good and Evil*, 69; *The Birth of Tragedy*, 69; *Confucianism and Taoism*, 69; *On the Genealogy of Morals* in *Confucianism and Taoism*, 69; *Übermensch* (superman), 69; *Will to Power*, 69

Nkrumah, Kwame, 65
Nussbaum, Martha, 18, 204n51

October Revolution, 172
Oppenheimer, Franz, *The State*, 135
Orientalism, 8, 26–27, 28, 65
Owen, Robert, 183

Palyi, Melchior, 49, 211n14
Paris Peace Conference, 3, 22, 81, 82, 91, 106, 110, 207n21
People's Republic of China, 119
Plato, 93, 107, 112, 148, 154–56, 167, 169, 188; metaphysics of truth, 153, 156, 167; *The Republic*, 154–55
Political Information Society, 85
Protestant ethic(s), 2, 6, 47–48, 52, 79, 80
Protestantism, 22, 47–48, 49, 50, 52–53, 56, 58–59, 80, 211n14; and rationalism, 46, 51, 52
Puritanism, 52, 56, 60–61, 63

Qian Mu, 182
Qing dynasty, 1, 2, 21, 25, 40, 42–43, 84–85, 97, 98, 117, 154, 172, 179
Qing Manchu (emperor), 151

ren, 125–27, 134
Rickert, Heinrich, 69, 70
Ringer, Fritz, 81
Robbins, Bruce, 18
Russell, Bertrand, 1, 117, 159
Russian Revolution, 29, 191
Russo-Japanese War, 101

Sachsenmaier, Dominic, 18
Said, Edward, 26–27
Saint-Simon, Henri de, 131
Sartori, Andrew 9, 11–14; *Bengal in Global Concept History: Culturalism in the Age of Capital*, 13
Saussy, Haun, 7
Schelling, F. W. J., 98
Schiller, Friedrich, 91
Schlick, Moritz, 159
Schluchter, Wolfgang, 50, 54, 55
Schopenhauer, Arthur, 4, 106, 142, 148

INDEX 257

scientism, 23, 84, 105, 108, 113
Seghers, Anna, 105
self-cultivation, 22, 62–64, 99, 195
Sermon on the Mount, 80
Shakespeare, 38, 79
Siebeck, Paul, 49
Sino-Japanese War, 23, 41, 77, 119, 147, 150–53, 169, 175
Sinophilia, 3, 102
Smith, Adam, 107; *The Wealth of Nations*, 4, 214n67
Smith, David Norman, 68
Social-Democratic Party (German), 68, 191
Sohm, Rudolf, 66–67, 68–69; and "charismatic organization," 68; *Kirchenrecht (Church Law)*, 68
Song dynasty, 99, 151, 152, 154, 172, 173
Song-Ming Confucianism, 23, 84, 107–9, 152
Spencer, Herbert, *The Study of Sociology*, 4–5
Spinoza, Baruch, 168, 216n87
Spivak, Gayatri, 173
Spengler, Oswald, 57
Stalin, Joseph, 65, 180
Steinmetz, George, 3
Su Guoxun, 55
Sun Yirang, 179
Szakolczai, Arpád, 62

Tagore, Rabindranath, 29, 128
Tang dynasty, 60, 97
Taoism, 2–5, 8, 12, 23, 28, 52, 58–60, 62, 64, 78, 81, 99, 102, 127, 129, 143–44, 148, 154, 156–58, 164, 169, 181, 193, 195, 215n80, 233n44, 236n7; idea of *wu*, 156; idea of *wuwei*, 156
Thoreau, Henry David, *Walden*, 131
Tian Han, 105
Tolstoy, Leo, 43, 80
transience, 24, 175, 177, 179, 190, 192
Tsui, Brian, 86
Tu Wei-ming, 55

Vienna Circle, 154, 158–60, 163, 165
Völker, Klaus, 184

Waismann, Friedrich, 159
Waldron, Jeremy, 18, 204n51
Wang, Ben, 20, 21
Wang Gen, 142
Wang Guowei, 4

Wang Hui, 20–21, 151
Wang Yangming, 100, 142
Weber, Marianne, 1, 49, 67, 211n14
Weber, Max, 1–3, 6, 14, 20, 22, 46–81, 84, 102, 123, 126, 129, 158, 164, 165, 168–69, 195, 214n67, 215n80, 216n87; and capitalism, 123; and care of the self, 60, 61–64; and charisma, 65, 67–68, 70–71, 81, 150; *The Citizen of the World*, 57; and Confucian literati, 76, 79; *Confucianism and Taoism*, 1, 22, 47–50, 58, 66–71, 75, 81; *Economy and Society*, 67; interpretation of Confucianism, 2, 80, 126; philosophy of life, 50–52, 62, 64; *Politics as a Vocation*, 66–67, 75, 79–80; *The Protestant Ethic and the Spirit of Capitalism*, 22, 46–49, 50–51, 53–55, 58, 70–71, 79, 129; *Science as a Vocation*, 57, 84
Wells, H. G., 108
Weltbewegung, 103
Weltbürgertum, 18
Weltprozeß, 103
Weltwesen, 103
Western imperialism, 2, 4, 6, 11, 21–22, 26–29, 35, 37–44, 58, 85, 91, 102, 106, 115, 116, 118, 133, 142, 144–45, 174, 182, 193
Wilhelm, Richard, 4, 29
Wing-Tsit Chan, 144
Wittgenstein, Ludwig, 4, 24, 147, 158–59, 163–65, 169; *Tractatus logico-philosophicus*, 158, 163–65
Wolff, Christian, 102
women's question, 169, 172–74
world as method, 8, 17–20
world culture, 1–9, 14, 17–22, 24, 36, 47–48, 84, 86–87, 90, 97, 107, 110, 112–13, 114–23, 127, 129–31, 136, 142–43, 146–47, 158, 169, 175, 193–95; aesthetic way of life, 47; and Confucianism, 84, 86, 87, 96, 113, 121–23, 142; and Feng, 146, 147, 158, 169, 175; and Hermann Graf von Keyserling, 36; and Liang Shuming, 20, 112, 115, 117, 127, 129, 143; and Max Weber, 22; moral principles, 28, 30, 34–35, 39, 41; and universal rationalism, 48
world philosophy, 20, 24, 104, 143, 144–46, 153, 157, 158, 166, 169, 174–75
World War I, 3, 22, 23, 29, 41, 49, 58, 64, 66, 75, 79, 80–82, 85, 92, 96, 101, 107, 108, 132, 191, 207n21, 226n80
World War II, 65, 86, 92, 119, 159

xin xing, 87–90, 100, 113
Xiong Shili, 4, 144
Xuanxue yu Kexue, 107

Yan Fu, 4
Yogācāra, 121–24, 142
Yu Ying-shih, 48, 53
Yuan Shikai, 85
Yun-Yeop Song, 185

Zen Buddhism, 23, 154, 157–58, 160–62, 169, 233n44
Zhang Binglin, 182
Zhang Donxun, 119
Zhang Junmai (Carsun Chang), 3, 20, 22, 81, 82–120, 164; and Chinese National Socialist Party, 86; Father of the Constitution of the Republic of China, 84; *A Manifesto for a Re-appraisal of Sinology and Reconstruction of Chinese Culture* (1958), 86–91, 106–9, 113; metaphysics, 107–9; *An Outline of Eucken's Philosophy of Spiritual Life* 92, 96
Zhang Zhidong, 2, 39, 40, 43
Zhu Xi, 100, 154
Zhuangzi (Zhuang Zhou), 12, 99

Chunjie Zhang is Associate Professor of German at the University of California, Davis. She is the author of *Transculturality and German Discourse in the Age of European Colonialism* (2017), editor of *Composing Modernist Connections in China and Europe* (2019), and coeditor of *Gender and German Colonialism: Intimacies, Accountabilities, and Intersections* (2023), *Aesthetics and Politics in the Wake of the Enlightenment* (*The Germanic Review* 2020), and *Asian German Studies* (*German Quarterly* 2020). She coedits the book series "Asia, Europe, and Global Connections" (Routledge).

IDIOM: INVENTING WRITING THEORY
Jacques Lezra and Paul North, series editors

Werner Hamacher, *Minima Philologica*. Translated by Catharine Diehl and Jason Groves

Michal Ben-Naftali, *Chronicle of Separation: On Deconstruction's Disillusioned Love*. Translated by Mirjam Hadar. Foreword by Avital Ronell

Daniel Hoffman-Schwartz, Barbara Natalie Nagel, and Lauren Shizuko Stone, eds., *Flirtations: Rhetoric and Aesthetics This Side of Seduction*

Jean-Luc Nancy, *Intoxication*. Translated by Philip Armstrong

Márton Dornbach, *Receptive Spirit: German Idealism and the Dynamics of Cultural Transmission*

Sean Alexander Gurd, *Dissonance: Auditory Aesthetics in Ancient Greece*

Anthony Curtis Adler, *Celebricities: Media Culture and the Phenomenology of Gadget Commodity Life*

Nathan Brown, *The Limits of Fabrication: Materials Science, Materialist Poetics*

Jay Bernstein, Adi Ophir, and Ann Laura Stoler, eds., *Political Concepts: A Critical Lexicon*

Willy Thayer, *Technologies of Critique*. Translated by John Kraniauskas

Julie Beth Napolin, *The Fact of Resonance: Modernist Acoustics and Narrative Form*

Ann Laura Stoler, Stathis Gourgouris, and Jacques Lezra, eds., *Thinking with Balibar: A Lexicon of Conceptual Practice*

Nathan Brown, *Rationalist Empiricism: A Theory of Speculative Critique*

Gerhard Richter, *Thinking with Adorno: The Uncoercive Gaze*

Kevin McLaughlin, *The Philology of Life: Walter Benjamin's Critical Program*

Alenka Zupančič, *Let Them Rot: Antigone's Parallax*

Adi M. Ophir, *In the Beginning Was the State: Divine Violence in the Hebrew Bible*

Ronald Mendoza-de Jesús, *Catastrophic Historicism: Reading Julia de Burgos Dangerously*

Jacques Lezra, *Defective Institutions: A Protocol for the Republic*

www.ingramcontent.com/pod-product-compliance
Lightning Source LLC
Chambersburg PA
CBHW020401080526
44584CB00014B/1121